All Things Austen

All Things

*A*usten

An Encyclopedia of Austen's World

Volume II

M–Z

Kirstin Olsen

Greenwood Press

Westport, Connecticut • London

Library of Congress Cataloging-in-Publication Data

Olsen, Kirstin.
 All things Austen : an encyclopedia of Austen's world / Kirstin Olsen.
 p. cm.
 Includes bibliographical references and index.
 ISBN 0–313–33032–8 (set : alk. paper)—ISBN 0–313–33033–6 (vol. 1 : alk.
paper)—ISBN 0–313–33034–4 (vol. 2 : alk. paper)
 1. Austen, Jane, 1775–1817—Encyclopedias. 2. Novelists, English—19th
century—Biography—Encyclopedias. 3. Women and literature—England—History—
19th century—Encyclopedias. I. Title.
PR4036.A275 2005
823'.7 B—dc22   2004028664

British Library Cataloguing in Publication Data is available.

Library of Congress Catalog Card Number: 2004028664
ISBN: 0–313–33032–8 (set)
     0–313–33033–6 (vol. I)
     0–313–33034–4 (vol. II)

First published in 2005

Greenwood Press, 88 Post Road West, Westport, CT 06881
An imprint of Greenwood Publishing Group, Inc.
www.greenwood.com

Printed in the United States of America

The paper used in this book complies with the
Permanent Paper Standard issued by the National
Information Standards Organization (Z39.48–1984).

10 9 8 7 6 5 4 3 2 1

All line illustrations, except where otherwise noted, credited to Kirstin Olsen.

For Eric

Contents

Acknowledgments

I would like to thank the staff at the Lewis Walpole Library, particularly Sue Walker and Brian Parker, for their invaluable assistance with many of the illustrations for this book. They truly went above and beyond the call of duty, and I am extremely grateful. I am also thankful to the many people who shared their enthusiasm and expertise, including Eunice and Ron Shanahan, who graciously provided photographs of franked and crossed letters and advised me about the history of postmarks; Eliot Jordan, tea buyer for Peet's Coffee and Tea, who helped me track down information about historical tea varieties; David Lisot of Heritagecoin.com, who granted permission for the use of photos from his company's Web site; and Neil Handley of London's College of Optometrists, who patiently explained turnpin-temple spectacles to me. Any errors in these departments are not theirs but my own. I am indebted to my family for their constant support and their patient pretense of interest when I come to the dinner table overflowing with newly acquired information about tea urns, court plaster, or chamber pots.

Introduction

Jane Austen is normally thought of as avoiding richly detailed settings and confining herself almost entirely to the development and interactions of her characters. Certainly, she is a restrained author, eschewing unnecessary details and emphasizing the revelation of character through dialogue, but this is not to say that historical detail does not occur in her works and does not require explanation. If anything, the details she uses require more explanation rather than less, for she chose them with great care and with an expectation that her readers would understand their full significance.

Astute modern readers can grasp the basics of many of her references through context. It becomes evident, for example, that barouches, phaetons, curricles, and post chaises were all carriages of some kind. For Austen's contemporary audience, however, these vehicles were as different from each other in form, purpose, and connotation as sports cars, minivans, and rental cars today. One misses a great deal of what she says about character and fails to appreciate the truly elegant economy of her language without a full comprehension of the objects and ideas to which she refers.

This book, therefore, attempts to provide the background material that makes her work more fully comprehensible. It discusses types of carriages and the associations they elicited, the value and size of certain coins, the difference between a pelisse and a spencer, and hundreds of other areas in which obsolete or unfamiliar terms distance us from Austen's original intentions. The result is a compilation of the available scholarship on everything from the history of food to the composition of Tunbridge ware and takes us through the dawn of tourism, the discovery of chemical elements, the development of the barometer and the thermometer, and the politics of the sugar trade.

There are six principal components of this book, other than the index, to help readers of Austen navigate through her world. One is the alphabetized series of more than 150 articles, ranging from a few sentences to chapter length, depending on the complexity of the subject and its relevance to Austen's work. The second, embedded in the articles, is a system of abbreviations guiding readers to passages in Austen's writings that pertain to the articles' subject matter. These abbreviations refer to the page numbers of the *Oxford Illustrated Jane Austen* (3rd edition), edited by R. W. Chapman, which is the standard text for Austen scholarship. Most scholars, however, have tended to abbreviate all of Austen's Juvenilia and fragmentary novels with the simple notation "MW," for the "Minor Works" volume in the series. I have chosen to be somewhat more specific, and readers will find a prefix such as "*Visit*" or "*L&F*" before citations from the Minor Works volume. (See the List of Works and Abbreviations.) Thus, a parenthetical notation such as (*L&F, MW* 105) means the juvenile fragment *Love and Freindship* [*sic*], Minor Works volume, p. 105. In some cases, including all references to a particular subject (such as instances of the word "servant") would have been unwieldy; therefore, unless otherwise stated, the references are representative and not exhaustive.

The third major source of information is the illustrations, most of them from the Lewis Walpole Library. They are richly informative in their present state, but the Lewis Walpole Library also has an excellent Web site where the pictures can be viewed in color and in greater detail. Each caption has the LWL call number, which can be entered into a search engine on the Web site for easy access to a specific image. In-text references to illustrations that are found in other articles give a short form of the illustration title followed by the article title in parentheses.

The fourth guide for readers is the Guide to Related Topics, which separates the articles in this encyclopedia by broad topic. For example, the category "Business, Work, and Finance" contains the articles on Agriculture, Alehouse, Enclosure, Income, Inns, Lodgings, Money, Servants, Shops, and Taxes. This listing can serve as a study guide for readers interested in a particular aspect of Austen's works. A fifth important resource is the Timeline, which tracks the achievements and movements of the Austen family alongside contemporary events in the realms of politics, culture, religion, science, and medicine. Under the articles "Places," "Bath," and "London," readers will find maps of most of the locations mentioned by Austen (with the exceptions, noted in the text, of a few far-flung places easy to locate without help, such as Russia and America).

Readers will learn the origin of the term "box office" and will investigate the mystery of exactly what sort of spectacles Frank Churchill was fixing at the Bateses'. They will discover why opera girls were so scandalous and why William Price could not get promoted from midshipman to lieutenant without help. They will discover how a servants' bell worked, what a calling card looked like, and how the games of casino, lottery tickets, and loo were played. Crucially, they will learn how terms still used today, such as "public place," "toy shop," "hobbyhorse," and "pocketbook," differ in their usage from the same terms in Austen's day.

List of Articles

Agriculture
Alehouse
Angels
Animals
Architecture
Army

Barometer
Barouche
Bath
Bathing
Bells
Beverages
Bon Mot
Brickbat

Cards
Carriages and Coaches
Carts and Wagons
Chair
Chaise

Chaperones
Charity
Children
Clergy
Clocks and Watches
Clothing
Clubs
Coffee
Collections
Complexion
Compts
Condescension
Cosmetics
Court
Coxcombs and Dandies
Crime

Dance
Death
Debt
Devoirs

Dishes
Doge
Duels

Education
Enclosure
Entertainment
Etiquette

Fan
Fire
Fishing
Food
Franking
French
French Revolution
Furniture

Gambling
Games
Gardens and Landscape

Guide to Related Topics

List of Works and Abbreviations

Minor Works (abbreviation followed by MW)

Amelia	*Amelia Webster*
Beaut Desc	*A Beautiful Description of the Different Effects of Sensibility on Different Minds*
Cass	*The Beautiful Cassandra: A Novel in Twelve Chapters*
Cath	*Catharine or the Bower*
Clifford	*Memoirs of Mr. Clifford*
Col Let	*A Collection of Letters*
Curate	*The Generous Curate*
E&E	*Edgar & Emma*
Evelyn	*Evelyn*
F&E	*Frederic & Elfrida*
First Act	*The First Act of a Comedy*
H&E	*Henry & Eliza*
Harley	*The Adventures of Mr. Harley*
Headache	*On a Headache*
History	*The History of England*
J&A	*Jack & Alice*
L&F	*Love and Freindship*
Lesley	*Lesley Castle*

LS	*Lady Susan*
Mount	*Sir William Mountague*
Mystery	*The Mystery: An Unfinished Comedy*
Ode	*Ode to Pity*
Plan	*Plan of a Novel*
Popham	*On Sir Home Popham's Sentence, April 1807*
Sand	*Sanditon*
Scraps	*Scraps*
3S	*The Three Sisters*
Visit	*The Visit: A Comedy in 2 Acts*
Watsons	*The Watsons*

Novels

E	*Emma*
MP	*Mansfield Park*
NA	*Northanger Abbey*
P	*Persuasion*
P&P	*Pride and Prejudice*
S&S	*Sense and Sensibility*

References to the Kotzebue play *Lovers' Vows*, included by R. W. Chapman in his edition of *Mansfield Park*, are indicated by the abbreviation *MP, LV*.

Maps

The late eighteenth century was a time of improvement and expansion in English cartography. Improved mathematical calculations, the efforts of nautical explorers such as Captain James Cook, the development of the naval chronometer by John Harrison (which enabled accurate measurements of longitude), and the work of numerous surveyors in America and India allowed British maps to rival and eventually surpass those produced on the Continent. Several excellent atlases appeared during Austen's lifetime, as did large-scale maps of individual counties. Wealthy landowners also hired private surveyors to map their land, and this is no doubt the kind of map Mr. Knightley means when he refers his brother to "our maps" (*E* 107) when planning an alteration to a path.

One difference between Mr. Knightley's maps and the maps of previous eras would have been the lack of superfluous ornament. Mapmakers were beginning to eschew the ornate cartouches, sea monsters, ships, and mermaids that had long decorated the more barren parts of maps. John Cary's map of Hertfordshire from his *New and Correct English Atlas* (1787), for example, has a compass rose behind the map title and a key to indicate scale, with no additional decoration. There are no out-of-scale side views of hills and churches, as might have been found on earlier maps. Instead, roads and towns are clearly indicated without clutter.

Cartographers were also producing special types of maps. There were maps of new turnpike routes, for example, and maps with tables of distances between the principal towns. Land use maps, showing patterns of cultivation, were occasionally made, though most people who owned maps and atlases would not have owned these. Nor would they have been likely to own the first geological map of England, printed in 1815, but they might have owned a single- or multiple-sheet map of their own county and an atlas of England or the world. A good atlas might cost anywhere from four to ten pounds, depending on the edition and the binding.

Globes were made by several English manufacturers, including John Cary's brother William. They came in both terrestrial and celestial varieties; sometimes the map representing the heavens was a separate globe, and sometimes it was printed on the inside of a cover for the terrestrial globe. Globe sections, or gores, were printed and then pasted onto a circular foundation, which might be made of wood or of pasteboard coated with plaster. The globe was then usually mounted in a wooden stand with decoratively turned or carved legs. An example of a large standing globe can be seen near the center of the illustration *Messrs. Morgan and Sanders* (Furniture).

Marines

Austen introduces only one marine officer in her works, but he is certainly memorable. He is, of course, Fanny Price's foul-mouthed, hard-drinking, inconsiderate father, "a Lieutenant of Marines, without education, fortune, or connections" (*MP* 3). Incapable, it seems, of rising through the ranks and "disabled for active service, but not the less equal to company and good liquor" (*MP* 4), he is hardly the sort of exemplary character that her naval officers tend to be. This is perhaps because there was a certain degree of interservice rivalry between sailors and marines, the former priding themselves on their superior knowledge of the ship, the latter comforting themselves with their superior discipline.

The rivalry was at least in part encouraged by naval regulations. Marines had a variety of duties, but they existed in large part to discipline and intimidate sailors. They served in peacetime as guards at dockyards and harbors,* and in wartime prevented impressed men from escaping before they could be assigned to ships. In harbors, they guarded against desertion, and aboard ship, they stood by as an emblem of the king's justice when floggings and other punishments were administered. They also served as guards at various points around the ship: at the galley door when food was being prepared, at the captain's door, and at the doors of the rooms where gunpowder and liquor were stored, to name a few. Afloat or ashore, they discouraged mutiny.

In order to prevent them from developing too strong a sympathy with the men they were supposed to control, the marines were forbidden by regulations to berth or mess with the common sailors. It might be assumed that the marine and naval officers got along somewhat better with each other than the privates and sailors, since at least the officers could dine together, and since the marines were there in part to help preserve order aboard the ship. This, however, was not necessarily the case. Naval captains were sometimes jealous of the marines' fancier uniforms and of the terms of their commissions; naval commissions were somewhat threatening in their wording, hinting at dire consequences for failure. Marines, in turn, chafed at being under the command of naval officers and at ranking lower in the command structure than naval officers of nominally equal rank. A marine lieutenant, for example, ranked not only below a naval lieutenant in the command structure, but even below some warrant officers. The danger of disrespect as a result of this situation was so great that the Admiralty had to issue regulations insisting on proper behavior toward marine officers. Their lesser power, the regulations insisted, was merely a reflection of their lesser involvement with the working of the ship, and they were "to be considered and treated in all respects as a commissioned of-

---

*And were replaced in wartime by militia units.

ficer should be." The Admiralty's insistence, however, did not guarantee universal goodwill; sailor Samuel Leech reported that the captain of the *Macedonian* "had a profound hatred of marines."

Marines were better appreciated in their other capacity, as troops for landing parties and boarding parties. Their original function, to provide musket fire during ship-to-ship combat, had become less important over the centuries as cannon became the chief means of crippling an enemy's crew, but a few marines—perhaps a dozen—could still be found in the rigging as sharpshooters during battle. They also helped to man the great guns, the capstan, and the pumps, but their principal role was in amphibious attacks, where they formed the bulk of landing parties.

Officers and Men

Unlike sailors, marines could not be impressed into service. Instead, they were recruited, with a steadily rising bounty as an incentive. The bounty stood at about 8 guineas in 1794, £26 in 1801, and £30 in 1808, with smaller bounties available for soldiers already serving in the army who were willing to transfer to the marines. Recruits signed on for either the duration of the war or a set number of years and had to swear before a magistrate that they were free from rupture, fits, lameness, apprenticeship, and other military obligations. Officers received their commissions from the Admiralty after verification of their family background, education, and height and a brief period of drilling to confirm their physical ability to handle the job. It was not a particularly stringent application process, but it also tended to attract a less genteel and less well connected candidate than the navy, which had glamour on its side, and the army, which had the possibility of buying a better commission when the opportunity offered. Marine promotions were based strictly on seniority, so a marine lieutenant like Mr. Price would have had to wait, and wait, and wait, for those above him to die or retire. In any case, captain was the highest rank that a marine officer could expect to reach by rising through the ranks, as the higher ranks were generally reserved as sinecures for naval officers. Francis Austen received such a sinecure, a marine colonelcy, in 1825.

Training was entirely confined to land-based skills such as musket drill, marching, and formations. In 1811, regular practice with fixed bayonets was added to the foregoing list. The result was that a marine recruited in peacetime could spend several years in his post without learning the first thing about the parts of a ship, so that when he was actually sent to sea he was regarded by the sailors as an idiot. Sailors' slang included the phrases "Tell it to the marines"—in other words, tell it to someone stupid enough to believe you—and "marine officer," which meant an empty bottle. There was also a perception, encouraged by their minimal sailing duties, that the marines were both greedy and lazy.

In 1793, the principal naval dockyards at Chatham, Portsmouth, and

Plymouth each had about forty companies of marines, each of these companies in turn numbering about 120 men. By 1810, the size of a company had risen to 178, and by 1813, after two decades of almost continuous war, Portsmouth and Plymouth each had forty-nine companies of marines, Chatham forty-eight. In Portsmouth, particularly, the facilities were ill equipped to accommodate so many men. The barracks were small, and, consequently, many men stayed in inns. This situation would no doubt have appealed to the convivial Mr. Price, who could have visited his comrades and gotten drunk at the same time.

Pay reflected the different expenses associated with being at home or at sea. On land, the average marine had to pay a substantial sum for his meals and housing, whereas at sea this was provided for him. Admittedly, at sea, he had other expenses, such as payroll deductions for the surgeon and chaplain, the cost of his bedding, and any "slops" (everyday working clothing) he wore on duty, but these totaled less than the cost of his room and board onshore. Accordingly, pay was higher for marines stationed on land—£1.8.0 per month for a private after 1797, as opposed to 19s. 3d. per month at sea. At seven years' seniority he got an increase of 2s. 4d. per month on land, 1s. 9d. at sea. At fourteen years, the seniority bonus was doubled. Sergeants were paid more than privates and artillerymen more than regular marines; for service on shore, a sergeant got £2.11.4 per month, an artillery private £1.15.7, and an artillery sergeant £3.18.2.

At sea, a detachment of marines was supposed to be provided on every ship with ten guns or more. These troops were commanded by a captain on larger ships, a first lieutenant on frigates, and a sergeant on the smallest ships. On larger ships, the marines made up a somewhat smaller percentage of the entire ship's complement, about one-sixth in 1801, about one-fifth in 1808, versus one-seventh and one-sixth, respectively, for smaller ships. Smaller ships, however, had a higher proportion of noncommissioned officers (sergeants and corporals). A first-rate ship, as an example, would have carried about 113 marines in 1795, about 145 in 1801, and about 170 in 1808; a third-rate ship of sixty-four guns would have carried about half those numbers.

Arms and Uniforms

Marines carried a slightly shorter and plainer version of the standard-issue musket; its ¾" shot, tied up in paper with the powder charge, was pushed into the barrel with a ramrod, and a flint ignited the powder. The effective range of such a musket was about 100 yards. Marines also had a bayonet that could be fixed to the musket for fighting in close quarters and might also have pistols or hand grenades. The commissioned officers wore swords.

Uniforms for marines changed in several ways over the course of Austen's lifetime. Initially, they were red or scarlet coats with the long coattails and double-breasted buttoning characteristic of eighteenth-century frock coats. The lapels were wide, faced with white, and generally worn buttoned back to display the facing color, with a small hook near the top that could be used to fasten the folded-back lapels together. Rank was indicated by several additions to the uniform. Ordinary marines, for example, wore a whitened leather baldric (a double sash crossed in the front and joined at the intersection with a marine badge); officers had only a single white band, and sergeants and commissioned officers each wore a red sash around the waist. NCOs wore a silver shoulder knot, a kind of attenuated epaulette, and officers wore full silver epaulettes. A lieutenant wore one, and captains, majors, lieutenant colonels, and colonels wore two, which grew fancier with each increasing rank, acquiring better fringe and a star at the level of major and an additional star for each increase in rank thereafter. Officers were also distinguished from the men by wearing gorgets. (A gorget, the last vestigial remnant of medieval armor, was a moon-shaped metal plate that hung on a chain just below the throat.) Men and officers alike wore white breeches and, where visible, white waistcoats. Variations existed for both especially cold and especially hot weather.

In 1802, when the marines became the "Royal Marines," the facing color changed from white to blue, and sometime after this, the coat was altered from a frock style to a closed jacket with a higher waist and smaller tails. Officers retained a blue center section to imitate the old contrast between the red coat and the blue facings, and their cuffs were blue, as were their standing collars. The designation "royal" also occasioned a change in epaulette color from silver to gold.

Another set of changes was instituted in 1807. The shoulder knots for sergeants and corporals were replaced by chevrons on the right sleeve—three for sergeants and two for corporals. Uniforms continued to evolve, adopting a new set of epaulette decorations in 1810. The one, two, and three stars for the higher ranks were replaced, respectively, by a star, a crown, and a crown and star together. By 1812 the short, closed jacket was standard, and cocked hats, which had been retained longer by officers than by men, had been replaced by round hats (a slightly tapered top hat) pulled up on each side by a pair of tapes that ran from crown to brim. *See also* Army; Navy.

Marriage

Marriage (*Watsons, MW* 351; *Sand, MW* 421; *P&P* 316; *MP* 4, 42, 43, 46; *P* 92) began, in most cases, with a willingness to marry (*MP* 42; *P* 61). In the case of women, the motivation might be love, but it was often a more pragmatic assessment of the fate that awaited an "old maid" (*Watsons, MW* 317; *S&S* 38; *P&P* 22–23, 221; *E* 65, 84, 85). Unless she had money of her own, a woman considered beyond the marriageable age was thought to be of little use to anyone, besides the relatives for whom she might keep house. She was a burden and, in many eyes, an incomplete woman (*P&P* 122–123). The view of bachelors was more forgiving, but not by very much. Men as well as women were expected to settle down, procreate, and be responsible. How was England to conquer the world, if not by breeding more soldiers and sailors and colonial governors? Therefore, bachelors, too, were encouraged to marry. Popular prints portrayed old maids in hell as post-horses ridden by bachelors, but they also portrayed the reverse situation, with the old maids driving the bachelors. There was a tax on bachelors, which Parson James Woodforde, as a life-long bachelor, was compelled to pay; bachelors paid double tax on the servants they employed.

Those disposed to marry put themselves in the way of likely candidates, either by visiting a social resort town such as Bath or Cheltenham or by looking around their own neighborhood. They went to dinners, balls, and evening parties in the hope of finding a suitable candidate. What was "suitable" depended on the seeker, but in the case of men, Austen's character Charles Adams might speak for the majority: "his wife, whoever she must be, must possess, Youth, Beauty, Wit, Merit, & Money" (*J&A*, *MW* 21). The "improbability of . . . ever meeting with such a Lady" caused many men to settle for the first pretty girl with a decent fortune that caught their eyes.

The decent fortune was of crucial importance. For young people to marry, they had to have a sufficient income not only for their own needs but for the children they would very likely have (*Sand*, *MW* 400; *NA* 135; *P* 66, 217). There were few birth-control options available at the time. Condoms existed, but they were thought of chiefly as guards against contracting venereal disease from prostitutes, and few people even considered using them at home. The menstrual cycle and conception itself were poorly understood, and even cyclical periods of abstinence would have been hard to enforce, as a husband had a legal right to sex with his wife whenever he wanted it. Most women who tried to control their fertility did so after the fact, by swallowing poisonous or nauseating substances, injuring themselves in the abdomen, or douching, and these methods appear to have been more common among the desperately poor—chiefly unwed servant girls—than in Jane Austen's social class. Therefore, a woman who married needed to be prepared for numerous pregnancies, and her husband had to be prepared to pay for the upbringing of a horde of children.

In addition, money was necessary to make more money. Cash payments were required to advance in many professions, such as the army, where commissions were purchased outright. Landowners needed cash to acquire additional acres and to improve the ones they already owned. It was frankly in a father's interest, if he wanted his daughter and grandchildren to have the most comfortable life possible, to ensure that comfort by helping the new couple with a sizable cash gift, the dowry (*Amelia, MW* 48; *Evelyn, MW* 183–184; *Watsons, MW* 321, 353; *NA* 68, 251; *S&S* 3, 194, 224, 266–267, 268, 374; *P&P* 108, 153, 183–184, 302, 304, 308; *MP* 3, 31, 40, 42; *E* 66, 135, 169, 181; *P* 218, 248). This money, once the marriage had taken place, was the property of the new husband, who could do with it as he liked. If he were a sensible young man, he would use it to further his career or invest it and use it to augment the family income; an invested dowry made about 4 or 5 percent interest annually, so Mary Crawford's £20,000 (*MP* 42) would have brought her husband about £900 or £1,000 a year in addition to his own income. If the husband were not sensible, he might use the dowry to pay off gambling debts and incur more or spend it on racehorses or smuggled claret. The wife had little recourse against a man who spent her dowry foolishly.

A woman whose dowry was small had few choices. Working-class women could work in order to augment their dowries, and many did so, saving sums they could proudly hand over

The Successful Fortune Hunter, Thomas Rowlandson, 1802. Courtesy of the Lewis Walpole Library, Yale University. 802.0.19.

to their bridegrooms as proof of their worth, but women of Austen's class were debarred from work, and any job they took—except, in some cases, for intellectual or artistic endeavors, which even then had to be disguised as hobbies—automatically reduced them in caste. Austen had good reason to hide her authorship of her novels from the world. While it would have brought her admiration in some quarters, in others it would have made her seem to be a working woman and no longer a full member of the gentry.

A woman of the upper classes who had no fortune to speak of might take a desperate course in order to avoid a marriage that was "beneath" her or the poverty and loneliness of spinsterhood. She could travel to one of Britain's colonies where Englishmen vastly outnumbered Englishwomen. This entailed a long and sometimes dangerous sea voyage, but women who arrived safely in one of the Caribbean sugar islands or in India found themselves in high demand (*Cath, MW* 194, 205). Jane's aunt Philadelphia, her father's half sister, had done precisely this. She had traveled to India, married a surgeon named Tysoe Saul Hancock, and produced a daughter, Eliza, who was pretty and witty enough to marry a French count and, after his death, Jane's brother Henry. This practice was, however, not universally accepted or admired. Many considered it little better than selling oneself into slavery and decried the shipments of women to the East Indies, but no one did anything to stop the bride boats or to alleviate the need for them.

In exchange for the dowry and the advantages it brought, a man agreed in the "marriage articles" (*MP* 162; *P* 208), or contract, to a certain amount of his estate in the event of his death. He might specify that his wife was to inherit property outright, with the right to do with it as she pleased, but he might also set conditions for inheritance, such as a ban on remarriage. A common strategy was to provide a jointure, a regular income derived from a significant percentage of his property (typically one-third), that reverted to the couple's children after the widow's death. This, of course, presumed that he died with income-generating property. A professional man such as a physician would leave nothing of this kind unless he had saved and invested wisely during his lifetime.

For a woman, the choice of a spouse was the most important decision she would make in her entire life, as she was handing nearly complete legal control over to a man. He would control her earnings, her property, and the raising of her children. He could imprison her, beat her, and rape her, and the legal system would not lift a finger to help her unless the beatings were considered excessive by the standards of the day. Even then, it was frequently not the legal system but the community that stepped in, staging public protests meant to shame a violent husband into behaving himself. A husband could separate his wife from their children and refuse to allow her to have any contact with them. She could not enter into a contract in her own right. If he chose to sue for a divorce (*MP* 464) on the grounds of her adultery, she was not permitted to testify in her own defense, nor could she sue for a divorce if he committed adultery.

Given the wretched legal position of a wife, it was crucial that a woman choose a man who would not abuse his power over her. He had to be a man whom she could respect, control, or at least endure. He ought to be acceptable to her family (*3S, MW* 58), older than she was but not ridiculously so (*F&E, MW* 6–7; *J&A, MW* 26; *3S, MW* 58; *NA* 252), and preferably religious but at the very least possessed of good morals. Of course, he needed to have enough money to support their children and to provide his wife with a decent standard of living (*J&A, MW* 26; *NA* 249–250). The anonymous author of *Female Tuition* (1784) warned, "It is generally from disparity of condition that most unhappy matches take place. There is no time of life in which they can with safety be ignorant of this fact, or inattentive to its consequences." Rich men who took a pretty, but relatively poor, wife (*Evelyn, MW* 184–185) were viewed more generously by society than rich women who "married down," unless they were relatively poor men with titles, buying a "my lady" along with a bridegroom (*Watsons, MW* 324; *P* 74). John Gregory gave extensive advice to his daughters in a book that remained popular throughout the eighteenth century. On the subject of choosing a husband, he offered a great deal of counsel, including the following:

> A rake is always a suspicious husband, because he has only known the most worthless of your sex. He likewise entails the worst diseases on his wife and children, if he has the misfortune to have any.
>
> If you have a sense of religion yourselves, do not think of husbands who have none. If they have tolerable understandings, they will be glad that you have religion, for their own sakes, and for the sake of their families; but it will sink you in their esteem, if they are weak men; they will be continually teasing and shocking you about your principles. . . .
>
> As I look on your choice of a husband to be of the greatest consequence to your happiness, I hope you will make it with the utmost circumspection. Do not give way to a sudden sally of passion, and dignify it with the name of love.—Genuine love is not founded in caprice; it is founded in nature, on honorable views, on virtue, on similarity of tastes, and sympathy of souls.

However, while many authors weighed in on the subject of the choice of a husband, the fact was, as Henry Tilney pointed out, that it was only the prospective husband who chose (*NA* 77). The woman merely got to accept or decline (*F&E, MW* 8–9; *J&A, MW* 21–22). Nevertheless, there were plenty of opinions on the right criteria for acceptance (*L&F, MW* 93; *P&P* 99). Women, however, frequently rejected the sensible, religious type in favor of dashing rakes who talked prettily, flattered, danced well, and displayed a fine calf in their stockings. The danger inherent in a bad choice was especially great for heiresses and wealthy widows, who were subject to a higher-than-average degree of flattery and attention for impoverished fortune hunters (*L&F, MW* 86; *Watsons, MW* 321, 325–326).

For both parties, there was an increasing importance placed on the value of love at the outset of a marriage. Propertied families had long arranged the marriages (*J&A, MW* 25) of their children, trusting that affection or at least mutual respect and tolerance would flourish in time, but in the course of the eighteenth century, a higher value came to be placed on individual choice and romantic attachment, even though writers warned young women that, for men at least, sexual conquest usually ended a man's first passion. They warned that a woman should be prepared for her husband's ardor to cool after six weeks and evolve into something else (*MP* 296)—respect and calm affection if she were lucky, contempt and neglect if she were not. Still, novels and plays continued to push romantic love as a prerequisite for marriage. Marriage for purely mercenary reasons (but not for *partially* mercenary reasons—*P&P* 125, 153) came to seem despicable (*LS, MW* 256; *Watsons, MW* 318; *P&P* 376; *MP* 38, 42).

The Wedding

Once a man and woman had agreed to marry each other, they had to get the consent of their parents or guardians (*F&E, MW* 10; *Evelyn, MW* 185;

GRETNA GREEN.

A Lady of Sixty, and a young woman of seventeen, lately presented themselves with their paramours at Gretna Green. "Hold (said the Matrimonial Vulcan to the Virgin) you are young and can wait a little. I see your Grandmother is impatient, let me put on her fetters first.

Gretna Green, 1802. Two couples have arrived at the stereotypical blacksmith's shop to be married. Courtesy of the Lewis Walpole Library, Yale University. 802.12.15.2.

NA 119, 135, 249; *MP* 40). Under a law passed in 1753, people could no longer marry clandestinely (*L&F, MW* 87), and those under the age of twenty-one needed parental permission to marry within England. The parental-consent requirement did not apply in Scotland, however. Therefore, couples who knew or suspected they would meet with parental disapproval hired a coach and eloped (*J&A, MW* 17; *Lesley, MW* 110) with all due speed to the Scottish border (*S&S* 206; *P&P* 273, 274, 282–283; *MP* 442). (Working-class couples who married there tended to live close by and tended to get there by walking.) They usually made for Gretna Green (*P&P* 274), a town on the very southern end of the border, simply because it was easiest to get to, and there they were married.* Under ecclesiastical law, a clergyman was not actually necessary for the proceeding. The couple simply needed witnesses to a verbal contract in which they bound themselves in marriage to each other in the present (not future) tense. Popular prints typically showed Gretna Green couples being married by a blacksmith, because in this case he was forging chains of a different sort.

An elopement was a particularly appealing tactic for impoverished fortune hunters. They could woo a young heiress with talk of love, whisk her away to Scotland, and come back to face a father who would never, under normal circumstances, have allowed such an unequal marriage. On April 16, 1791, Parson Woodforde noted an item in "one of the London Papers":

> A Reward of 100 Pound offered . . . for apprehending one Richard Perry (eldest Son of John Perry that formerly kept Ashford Inn) for running away with a Miss Clarke (about 14 Years of Age) from a boarding School at Bristol. Her fortune great £6000 per Annum.

It sounds very much like the intended elopement of George Wickham and Georgianna Darcy (*P&P* 202).

Those who did not elope could be married in one of two ways, either

*Austen humorously has one of her fictional couples flee to Gretna Green to be married, even though they are already in Scotland (*L&F, MW* 95).

by publishing the banns (*S&S* 296) or by license (*H&E*, *MW* 35; *P&P* 378; *MP* 88). Publishing the banns meant having the local clergyman announce, on three successive Sundays, that the couple in question intended to marry, giving members of the community due notice and a chance to object to the marriage, a typical reason for objection being the prior engagement or secret marriage of one of the parties. Austen, when she lived at Steventon with her clergyman father, twice jokingly entered banns for herself in the parish record book, each time with a different fictional bridegroom. The banns were announced according to a formula that appeared in the Book of Common Prayer:

> I publish the Banns of Marriage between *M.* of ——— and *N.* of ———.
> If any of you know cause, or just impediment, why these two persons should
> not be joined together in holy Matrimony, ye are to declare it. This is the
> first [or second, or third] time of asking.

Emma Woodhouse makes reference to this formula when she says she will call Mr. Knightley "George" only once: "I do not say when, but perhaps you may guess where;—in the building in which N. takes M. for better, for worse" (*E* 463). Not all editions of the Book of Common Prayer used "M" and "N" to stand for the bride's and groom's names; some used "N" for both. Yet it is particularly appropriate that Austen uses these initials rather than N for both, for *Emma* is full of word games, including the puzzle about the two letters that equal perfection being M-A (Emm-a). "M," of course, sounds like the first syllable of Emma's name, and Knightley's name, which begins with a silent K, starts with the sound of the letter N.

Many members of the upper classes found the banns embarrassing and chose instead to be married by license. They took advantage of a loophole in the statutes that kept an incorrect statement of residency from nullifying a marriage and either temporarily resided in a parish other than their own (*P&P* 318), or simply stated their addresses falsely, in order to acquire a license from a different parish and be married there, away from prying eyes. This was an especially common ploy in London (*P&P* 275, 282–283), where the sheer numbers of people made it difficult to check on residency, even if anyone had been motivated to do so, and many couples got married in London who did not actually live there.

The bride's family spent the days before the wedding amassing a new wardrobe for her—the "wedding clothes" so often mentioned in Austen's works (*F&E*, *MW* 7, 11; *S&S* 182, 215; *P&P* 119, 288, 306, 310; *E* 271; *P* 217). This was not merely the bridal gown but a whole set of new clothes whose cost was proportional to the family income. The groom often spent his time shopping for a new carriage (*S&S* 215; *P&P* 310; *MP* 202, 203; *E* 267, 308), if his income permitted it. Just as a person planning to start a family today might trade in the two-seater sports car for a family sedan,

THE WEDDING.

Published 12 May 1794 by LAURIE & WHITTLE, 53, Fleet Street, London

The Wedding, 1794. The wedding, like most of those in Austen's works, is a simple affair. The bride does not wear white, and only the parson, his clerk, the bridal couple, and a few witnesses are on hand. Courtesy of the Lewis Walpole Library, Yale University. 794.5.12.45.

wealthy men of Austen's time celebrated their new status as husbands by providing a suitable vehicle in which their wives could pay morning visits to friends.

On the day of the wedding, the bride and groom wore their best clothes (*MP* 203). The bride frequently wore a veil (*E* 484), and as white was a fashionable color, she often wore white, but there was no requirement to wear white as yet (*E* 484). Any stylish dress would do. She also frequently wore flowers. Grooms usually wore full dress, which for the gentry meant knee breeches, silk stockings, white waistcoat, and a fine frock coat.

The wedding (*F&E, MW* 10; *L&F, MW* 82; *NA* 123; *S&S* 217; *P&P* 145; *E* 6, 182, 267) typically took place in the morning. The wedding party and a few friends and relatives—more or fewer depending on the size of the neighborhood and the means of the bride's family—either walked or rode to church. The bride and groom stood at the altar, where the presiding clergyman (*MP* 89, 203; *E* 483) read the service from the Book of Common Prayer, beginning with the words:

Dearly beloved, we are gathered together here in the sight of God, and in
the face of this congregation, to join together this Man and this Woman in
holy Matrimony; which is an honourable estate, instituted of God in the
time of man's innocency, signifying
unto us the mystical union that is be-
twixt Christ and his Church; which
holy estate Christ adorned and beauti-
fied with his presence, and first miracle
that he wrought, in Cana of Galilee;
and is commended of Saint Paul to be
honourable among all men: and therefore is not by any to be enterprised, nor
taken in hand, unadvisedly, lightly, or
wantonly, to satisfy men's carnal lusts
and appetites, like brute beasts that
have no understanding; but reverently,
discreetly, advisedly, soberly, and in the
fear of God; duly considering the causes
for which Matrimony was ordained.

Six Weeks after Marriage, 1777. The honeymoon has
expired, and the once-ardent groom is now bored with
his wife. Books of advice for women warned that a
man's ardor would cool shortly after marriage; six
weeks was supposedly the average duration of his initial affection. Courtesy of the Lewis Walpole Library,
Yale University. 777.6.0.2.

After some further words about the
purpose of marriage and a call to both
the congregation and the bride and
groom to announce any impediment
to the marriage, the bride and groom
exchanged vows, and the groom
placed a ring (*NA* 122; *P&P* 316) on
the bride's ring finger. There was no
ring at this time for the groom. After
a short prayer, the parson joined the
couple's hands (*E* 13) and pronounced, "Those whom God hath joined
together let no man put asunder." Further prayers—including one for fertility if the woman was still of childbearing age—and a sermon followed.
The new husband paid the clergyman for his services; Parson Woodforde
reported getting sums of 5s., £1 1s., £2 2s., and so on, according to the
ability of the bridegroom to pay. The church bells were rung (*NA* 252;
E 267), and the bride and groom left the church, where they were pelted
with grains of wheat as a symbol of fertility, rice not having been adopted
yet for this purpose.

Gifts were distributed to the wedding guests at some point during the
morning, either before or after the ceremony. These were often rings,
gloves, or knots of ribbons but might be more substantial for those closely
related to the bride (*E* 322–323). The wedding party then went to some-

one's house for a wedding breakfast (*Lesley, MW* 112–114) of meat, bread and butter, toast, eggs, chocolate, wine (*MP* 203), and the wedding cake (*E* 19), which was a doughy confection flavored with dried fruit and covered with two kinds of layered icing. Bits of the cake were passed through the wedding ring by the bride and handed out as good-luck charms to single people who hoped to marry soon. In some places, the bits of cake had to be passed through the ring nine times for the magic to work. A 1799 poem in the *St. James's Chronicle* ascribed to the cake not the power to lure a potential mate but the power to bring him into a spinster's dreams:

> With her own hand she charms each destined slice,
> And thro' the ring repeats the *trebled thrice*.

> The hallow'd ring infusing magick power,
> Bids Hymen's visions wait the midnight hour:
> The mystick treasure, plac'd beneath her head,
> Will tell the fair—if haply she may wed.

Pieces of cake, other food, and liquor might be distributed to the household servants (*P&P* 307) and to the poor.

The bride's garter was removed by the groom's friends, a procedure for which she usually first partially untied the garter and moved it lower, to lessen this invasion of her skirts. The bedding of the bride, in which the guests acted as witnesses, just outside the door, to the bride's loss of virginity, had been toned down somewhat, and some couples went away after the wedding to get acquainted in relative privacy (*MP* 203). *See also* Chaperones; Hymen; Visiting; Widow.

Masquerade

Emerging in the early eighteenth century, masquerades evolved out of Elizabethan and Jacobean masques. Masques were quasi-theatrical performances with a theme, often classical and allegorical, in which participants presented themselves in costume, often masked. They might dance, speak, or merely process through a banqueting hall, and there was always a point to the performance, such as an elaborate compliment to an honored guest or host.

Masquerades, in contrast, had no particular point except pleasure, and they had no unifying theme except disguise. It was novel, in a society with rigid social structures and expectations of conduct, to let loose and play another part. Men dressed as women and women as men, or grown-ups dressed as children or infants. People dressed as animals, druids, bishops, Punch, the Green Man, foreigners of various nations, and allegorical virtues or vices. The essence of the event was secrecy and the license it brought to do and say forbidden things, so the participants not only wore masks (*Lesley*, *MW* 118) but disguised their voices by speaking in "squeaking" tones.

By the mid-eighteenth century, masquerades were held in several types of environments: homes, assembly rooms, theatres, and public gardens. Masquerades in homes were private parties, while the other venues were open to the public for a fee. Of the public sites, the pleasure gardens of London were perhaps the quickest to cash in on the masquerade fervor. Ranelagh, for example, began holding periodic masquerades in 1742. In the second half of the century, the Venetian opera singer Theresa Cornelys (1723–1796) was the queen of London assembly-room masquerades; she sponsored subscription masquerades from 1760 to 1772 in her rooms at Carlisle House in Soho Square. Events were also held at Almack's club from 1765 and at the Pantheon theatre from 1771. The Pantheon was not the only theatre to participate; the King's Theatre, Haymarket, was holding masquerades into the 1780s, with dazzling numbers of oil lamps being lit for the occasion.*

However, by the 1780s, the masquerade was in decline and had not long to live. The frisson of danger provided by its anonymity was both its chief attraction and the source of its downfall. Warning tales circulated about women who were raped at masquerades by men they thought were their husbands or by assailants whose identity could never be known. Less dramatic, but still disturbing, examples could be cited of women whose masks made them act licentiously. Women talked bawdily; they flirted; they spoke with strangers. The order of society seemed in jeopardy, and the masquerade was laid aside. By 1779, a witness could attest, "From the thinness of the Company at Monday night's Masked Ball, it is pretty clear that these kinds of exotic amusements are so much on the decline, as to promise a total and speedy extinction." By 1790 the fashion was dead.

For novelists, this must have been quite a tragedy. Masquerades present all sorts of interesting dramatic possibilities. One of Austen's literary role models, Fanny Burney, made good use of the masquerade in *Cecilia*, for example, and Austen herself uses it to comic effect in her juvenile work *Jack & Alice* (*MW* 12–14). The conclusion of her episode, however, though not intended to be taken seriously, probably reflects fairly accurately the attitude of the majority toward the moral climate of the masquerade:

> The Masks were then all removed & the Company retired to another room, to partake of an elegant & well managed Entertainment, after which the Bottle being pretty briskly pushed about . . . the whole party . . . were carried home, Dead Drunk.

---

*The man who provided lighting for the theatre charged by the hundred for oil lamps for operas, but he charged by the thousand for masquerades. A musicians' benefit concert was lit for a cost of £3, while a masquerade cost anywhere from £27 to £84.

Medicine

In the eighteenth century, the medical profession was, for almost the first time since the classical era, attempting to formulate completely new theories of disease and treatment. The old theories of humors were on the way out, and physicians were searching for something new to replace them. A new commitment to scientific method led physicians to test long-standing ideas about the causes and remedies for disease. For example, they investigated, under laboratory conditions, the effects of immersion in cold water on fever. At the same time, new tools such as the thermometer enabled experiments to be performed with greater accuracy.

Yet the medicine of Jane Austen's time was still pervaded by medieval relics of faith, folk remedy, and quasi-magical practices such as the use of substances as medicines because they bore some sort of symbolic resemblance to the ailment they were meant to treat. Physicians (*Clifford*, *MW* 43; *Sand*, *MW* 386, 422; *P&P* 40; *E* 454) had relatively few remedies at their disposal—at least, few that actually worked—and, in any case, physicians were the uppermost tier of the medical profession, rare and highly paid. They were seldom consulted by anyone except the very rich and the desperately ill. They were therefore called in late enough in the progress of a disease that there was little hope of a cure, and the consequently high death rate of their patients added to the public perception of doctors as expensive and useless (*Sand*, *MW* 394). Physicians had no X-rays, no antibiotics, and no knowledge of vitamins, and though their focus on a patient's diet might imply that they had a working knowledge of nutrition, their prescriptions in this area were often inimical to health. When Jane's eldest brother, James, experienced ill health, for example, he was put on a diet of bread, water, and meat, a regimen that can hardly have hastened recovery. The training of physicians, especially in England, was still weighted more heavily toward classical learning than toward practical medical skills, and even if physicians had been gifted with all the medical knowledge available at the time, they would still have had only the vaguest inkling of the relationship between germs and infection. The most scrupulous might wash surfaces with vinegar to inhibit pests, but few washed their hands routinely.

On the other hand, there was a basic understanding of epidemiology, even if the agents of disease had not been identified. It was clear that some diseases could be spread from person to person and that some places were unhealthy, though it would be 1854 before John Snow would begin to pinpoint *why* certain locales seemed more inclined to disease than others (*E* 22, 103).* Quarantines, usually voluntary and informal, were frequently

---

*In that year, Snow tracked a cholera outbreak to one contaminated well; the organism responsible was discovered later that year and conclusively linked to cholera later in the nineteenth century.

imposed to halt the spread of some diseases, and smallpox (*Cath*, *MW* 234) inoculation was already common. The technique had been observed in Turkey by Mary Wortley Montagu, who saw women scratching small-pox lesions and then using the same instrument to scratch the skins of healthy people. Edward Jenner made the same procedure safer by substi-tuting the less virulent cowpox, a related virus that caused less serious re-actions to inoculation. Members of the royal family volunteered for the procedure, making it widely accepted, and this went a long way toward ending a scourge that had killed many and disfigured more (*Lesley*, *MW* 136). Novelist Fanny Burney had her son Alexander inoculated in 1797. An incision was made in his arm and the viral material inserted. Three days later he

> suddenly drooped, became pale, languid, hot and short breathed. This con-tinued all Day, and towards evening increased into a restlessness that soon became misery—he refused any food—his Eyes became red, dull, and heavy, his breath feverish, and his limbs in almost convulsive tribulation.

She calmed his convulsions by placing his feet in warm water, but he con-tinued to suffer until a week after the inoculation, when "The spots began to appear." They had vanished within another week or so, and his ordeal was over.

Surgery, too, was on the verge of modernization. Surgeons (*Lesley*, *MW* 113; *Sand*, *MW* 365, 366, 372; *P* 111) were among those performing the most promising experiments and developing the most interesting new tech-niques. Yet surgeons enjoyed less prestige than physicians and inhabited only the fringes of gentility (*Watsons*, *MW* 321, 324).* This may have been because their work lacked the dignified pace of the physician's sedate in-quiries. In the absence of anesthesia, their skill was reckoned by their speed. They performed a limited number of procedures, such as trepanning, the removal of kidney stones, and the excision of cancerous tumors—all oper-ations in which the potential benefit outweighed the significant risk of fatal infection. Surgeons often did not wash their hands—or the surgical table—between patients, and their aprons and floor were awash in blood at the end of a busy day. The lack of gentility was also due to some extent with surgeons' long-standing association with mere barbers. Barbers and sur-geons separated their respective professional associations only in 1745, and surgeons did not have a Royal College for training purposes until 1800.

Fanny Burney, during her residence in France in the early nineteenth century, was diagnosed with breast cancer. She was unusually fortunate in having access to a group of the nation's finest doctors, but her surgery was

---

*Austen's paternal grandfather was a surgeon. Even in her later life, Austen would gently point out to a niece with literary ambitions that in reading the niece's manuscript, "I have also scratched out the Introduction between Lord P. & his Brother, & Mr. Griffin. A Country Surgeon . . . would not be introduced to Men of their rank."

so excruciating that two years later she could barely endure the recollection of it. She tried to be brave during the unanesthetized mastectomy,

> Yet—when the dreadful steel was plunged into the breast—cutting through veins—arteries—flesh—nerves—I needed no injunctions not to restrain my cries. I began a scream that lasted unintermittingly during the whole time of the incision—and I almost marvel that it rings not in my Ears still! so excruciating was the agony. When the wound was made, and the instrument was withdrawn, the pain seemed undiminished, for the air that suddenly rushed into those delicate parts felt like a mass of minute but sharp and forked poniards, that were tearing the edges of the wound—but when again I felt the instrument—describing a curve—cutting against the grain, if I may so say, while the flesh resisted in a manner so forcible as to oppose and tire the hand of the operator, who was forced to change from the right to the left—then, indeed, I thought I must have expired. I attempted no more to open my Eyes,—they felt as if hermetically shut, and so firmly closed, that the Eyelids seemed indented into the Cheeks. The instrument this second time withdrawn, I concluded the operation over,—Oh no! presently the terrible cutting was renewed—and worse than ever, to separate the bottom, the foundation of this dreadful gland from the parts to which it adhered—Again all description would be baffled—yet again all was not over,—Dr Larry rested but his own hand, and—Oh Heaven!—I then felt the Knife rackling against the breast bone—scraping it! . . .
>
> To conclude, the evil was so profound, the case so delicate, and the precautions necessary for preventing a return so numerous, that the operation, including the treatment and the dressing, lasted 20 minutes!

Twenty minutes was indeed an extraordinarily long surgery for the time, and Burney explains that it was prolonged by the consulting doctors searching for every "peccant attom" of the cancer.

Below the surgeon on the social and financial scale was the apothecary (*Sand, MW* 386; *P&P* 33, 40, 41; *E* 19), the type of medical professional most often consulted by ordinary people. Apothecaries dispensed medicines, though they were more than mere druggists, as they often hastened to point out. They were also diagnosticians who referred only the most complicated cases to surgeons or physicians. Jane Austen was treated by apothecaries for most of her life when she was sick, as were most of the people she knew. It is a sign of the rarity of consultation with physicians that even in her final, fatal illness, she was treated not by a physician but by a surgeon, Giles King Lyford of Winchester. Yet her letters express no lack of confidence in apothecaries simply because they were not physicians, anymore than most people today would lack confidence in their family doctors simply because the doctors do not happen to be specialists at leading research hospitals. The apothecary was the standard of care, and anything more was provided only out of necessity or extravagance.

There were also medical practitioners on the fringes of professionalism.

Midwives delivered most babies and were licensed but received no formal training. A host of quack doctors hawked everything from patent medicines to electric current for the relief of pain, while expert bonesetters (*J&A*, *MW* 22) were called in as specialists when a bone had been broken or fractured. Bonesetting took skill and a knowledge of anatomy as well as enormous physical strength, but it was rarely a full-time occupation. Dentistry was performed both by full-time dentists and by farriers with a pairs of pliers and a suitable indifference to the patient's screams. For most ailments, there was nursing at home.

Women who chose nursing as a profession often did so because they were unfit to hold a position as servant in a decent private home—or at least this was the public perception. Professional nurses were accused from time to time of theft, immorality, and drunkenness; even Nurse Rooke, a far more sympathetic character than many of the nurses portrayed in Austen's time, is a sly gossip (*P* 154, 155). Nursing for middle-class and upper-class patients, therefore, was performed by trusted household servants or, better yet, by the women of the family (*Sand*, *MW* 370, 371). Women were considered especially qualified for this task by the combined motivations of duty, feminine compassion, emotional attachment to the sufferer, and, apparently, a high tolerance for boredom and drudgery. The importance of home care (*Sand*, *MW* 367, 386; *MP* 189; *E* 22) is reflected in the cookbooks of the day, which often list recipes for remedies in a section after the chapters devoted to food. Sarah Harrison's *House-Keeper's Pocket-book; And Compleat Family Cook* (1748), for example, offers a nauseating alternative to asses' milk for patients with consumption:

> To three Pints of Water put forty Snails, two Ounces of Eringo-root, and two Ounces of *French* Barley; boil it to a Quart, then strain it, and take two Spoonfuls in half a Pint of Milk, twice a Day.

A much more palatable remedy for the same complaint is made of brown sugar candy, raisins, and oil of sweet almonds, beaten to a jamlike consistency. However, though mothers and sisters were expected to stay home, whip up snail soup, and hover anxiously by the bedside, it is clear that not all of them did so. Mary Musgrove's unwillingness to forgo a dinner out at Uppercross is mirrored in real life by the account of Parson James Woodforde, who reported in his diary in January 1790 that the local squire and his wife had joined him for dinner. The couple stayed until 8:00 P.M. "and would have stayed longer but their eldest Daughter was very bad in the Scarlet Fever." Clearly, Mary Musgrove was not the only woman willing to leave a critically ill child in the care of others for a night.

Disease and Treatment

Diseases (*NA* 186; *E* 6, 163) were not necessarily identified by the same names as today, which can make it difficult to determine exactly what disease is being discussed in many cases. A host of illnesses were lumped together under the heading of "nervous complaints" (*Sand, MW* 407, 411, 415, 416; *S&S* 83, 185; *P&P* 113, 288; *MP* 72–74; *E* 92, 103, 316, 363, 389; *P* 129, 134) and might include everything from chronic headaches (*Sand, MW* 387; *MW* 447–449; *S&S* 162; *E* 263, 322, 389; *P* 77) or fatigue to hypothyroid, seizures (*F&E, MW* 11; *E* 387), or simple hypochondria (*Sand, MW* 412–413). Ted Bader, in *Persuasions Online*, has suggested that Mr. Woodhouse's complaint is not hypochondria but hypothyroid, a disease consistent with his sensitivity to cold, nervousness, and possible difficulty swallowing due to an enlargement of the thyroid gland. Thomas Trotter's *View of the Nervous Temperament* (1807) further indicates that nervous patients tend to become dependent on a "gossiping physician" for contact with the outside world, a situation that is certainly in evidence at Hartfield.

Another large category of disease was "fever" (*E&E, MW* 30; *Clifford, MW* 43; *NA* 151; *P&P* 33; *E* 95, 332, 351, 379), which encompassed typhoid, typhus, diphtheria, some kinds of infection, influenza (*E* 102), and almost any other kind of ailment that included fever among its symptoms. As the causative agents of such diseases were not known, fevers were distinguished from each other not by the particular bacterium or virus at work but by how often the fever spiked or dropped ("remitted"), and by whether or not it was considered infectious, serious, or "putrid" (*E* 109); putrid fever, for example, was another name for typhoid. Different diseases with similar fever profiles, therefore, might be treated identically, while the same disease with a slightly different presentation might be treated entirely differently. William Buchan's *Domestic Medicine* divided fevers into remitting, intermitting, and continual varieties, and Mariane Dashwood's near-fatal fever, as John Wiltshire notes, fits the pattern of a remitting fever.

A common disease of the middle and upper classes was gout (*Evelyn, MW* 186; *Cath, MW* 204; *LS, MW* 296, 298; *Watsons, MW* 344; *Sand, MW* 374; *E* 383; *P* 163–164), a form of arthritis brought on by, among other things, high alcohol intake (*NA* 63) and obesity. Since the diet of prosperous Britons was high in alcohol, fatty meat, bread, and the organ meats and shellfish that can aggravate gout, it was a disease of the wealthy and particularly of men. Jane's brother Edward suffered from gout, as did her uncle James Leigh-Perrot.

Gout tended to attack the lower legs, especially the feet and ankles, and many popular prints of the time show men with gouty feet. Treatment usually consisted of trips to spas (*LS, MW* 295–296, 298; *Sand, MW* 374; *P* 163–164) to bathe the affected limb in warm or hot water, which probably temporarily relieved discomfort and had the added advantage of forcing people to bathe their whole bodies. When not in the bath, the foot was dressed in special stockings, elevated, and wrapped in thick layers of flannel. There was at least a partial understanding of the link between gout and diet, and those who could stand to do so sometimes ate less rich food and drank less alcohol in order to mitigate the effects of the disease. Other forms of joint pain were lumped together under the heading of "rheumatism" (*Cath, MW* 233; *Sand, MW* 415; *S&S* 37, 38; *MP* 189; *E* 383; *P* 152) or "rheumatic complaints."

Treatments for disease ranged from the noninvasive to the dramatic. Many practitioners, in the absence of better alternatives, opted to keep patients warm, dry, well and blandly nourished, and well rested, trusting to time and the patient's strength to effect a cure. Others resorted to the time-honored practices of purging (using noxious compounds such as calomel—*MW* 448–449), bleeding with leeches (*Sand, MW* 387, 424), and "cupping," a procedure in which small heated cups were placed on the skin to raise blisters. Sarah Harrison's *House-Keeper's Pocket-book* lists medicines (*Sand, MW* 413, 416; *E* 317) for colic, jaundice, gout, and ague (*MP* 104), most of them simple decoctions or pastes made with ordinary household ingredients. There are similar recipes for dealing with sore throats, eye infections, dropsy, burns, and fever. For rheumatism, the housewife is to rub linseed oil on the affected area in the morning and at night. For an intermitting fever, she should make an alcoholic syrup:

> Take two Ounces of Jesuit's Bark, infuse it in Spring Water, a Pint to half a Pint, and so strain it off; renew the Water again on the Bark, and so boil it again to the like Quantity, and do so for six Times; then let it stand to settle, and take the clear of it, and mix with half a Pint of the best White Wine, and as much Syrup of Clove-Gilliflowers, and let the Patient take nine Spoonfuls every four Hours, or as you have Occasion, after the Fit is off.

Another alcoholic concoction was bitters (*Sand, MW* 411):

> Take a Gallon of the best *French* Brandy, an Ounce of Saffron, two Ounces of Gentian-roots slic'd thin, Six-pennyworth of Cochineal, and a small Quantity of Orange-peel; put them in a Bottle, and let them stand two or three Weeks.

Harrison also expected her readers to be able to handle coughs (*E* 295), wounds, headaches, pains, fits, scurvy, gripes, and mad dog bites. Injuries, according to household texts like Harrison's and according to more learned medical texts, were generally treated with "plasters" (bandages—*P* 127) or with poultices. The court plaster of *E* 338 was a small dressing made of isinglass and silk. For faintness, ammonia-based smelling salts could be applied under the nose; these were derived from shaved deer antlers and were therefore known as "hartshorn" (*S&S* 178). Embrocations (skin lotions—*E* 102) could be applied for a variety of reasons, including colds, sore throats (*E* 114, 124), and chest congestion.

Colds (*LS, MW* 262; *Watsons, MW* 345; *S&S* 170; *P&P* 31, 35; *E* 102,

161, 236, 295; *P* 154) were not life-threatening, but in the absence of most of the palliative medications available to us today, they were especially uncomfortable. They were blamed, as were many other diseases, on cold or damp conditions; wet ground, wet air, and sudden or prolonged exposure to low temperatures were all considered to be very harmful (*L&F*, *MW* 100, 101; *Cath*, *MW* 210, 233–234; *Sand*, *MW* 415; *NA* 18; *P&P* 31; *MP* 190; *E* 209, 217, 251). Thomas Trotter warned women against wetting their feet:

> The lady of weak health, who may wish to display an ancle, should be very guarded how she throws off her warm socks. Many evils befal the sex from cold feet: such as follow on walking abroad with thin shoes on damp roads . . . I have known some serious nervous ailments brought on by a young lady evading the orders of a judicious parents; and after being dressed, retiring privately to put off the additional petticoat and understockings, that she might dance the more lightly.

The anonymous author of *The Mirror of the Graces* (1811) offered similar advice about sudden changes in temperature:

> The person, when over-heated, should always be allowed to cool gradually, and of itself, without any more violent assistant than, perhaps, the gentle undulation of the neighbouring air by a fan. Streams of wind from opened doors and windows, or what is called *a thorough air*, are all bad and highly dangerous applications. These impatient remedies for heat are often resorted to in balls and crowded assemblies; and as frequently as they are used, we hear of sore-throats, coughs, and fevers.

Other supposed causes of disease included overexposure to heat, too much exercise, and too little exercise.

Consumption (*E&E*, *MW* 30; *L&F*, *MW* 102; *Sand*, *MW* 393; *E* 163) was any disease that tended to have a "wasting" effect on the body—that is, that caused the patient to lose weight. Nutrition was therefore of critical importance to such patients. The most famous of the consumptive illnesses was tuberculosis, also sometimes called "galloping consumption." This is the "pulmonary complaint" (*E* 389) that Jane Fairfax is feared to have contracted, a disease that apparently killed her mother and that was associated in the public mind with people of Jane Fairfax's obsessively artistic temperament. A common prescription in such cases was the alteration of the patient's diet (*Watsons*, *MW* 344; *E* 19). Asses' milk was considered especially good because it was easily digestible (*Sand*, *MW* 393, 401, 422), and other widely recommended foods included gruel (*E* 104–105), meat broth, and arrowroot (tapioca pudding—*E* 391, 403).

Sea-bathing (*Sand*, *MW* 369, 374; *E* 101, 102, 104–106; *P* 97), drinking spa water (*NA* 71; *P* 146), and bathing in mineral springs (*E* 175; *P* 152, 154) were all supposed to be of great value for a variety of complaints. Those with rheumatic disorders could benefit from bathing in the hot mineral baths, while those with "bilious" complaints (digestive disorders—see *Sand, MW* 386, 415) could drink sulphurous-smelling water to cleanse the system. Sea-bathing was recommended for all sorts of illnesses, so many indeed that Mr. Parker's long list is hardly an exaggeration of the claims made by the proponents of seawater (*Sand, MW* 373). A change of "air" (*Lesley, MW* 116, 118; *E* 94) was also often recommended, and although the different air in Bristol or Bath or the south of France probably had little effect on health, a change of scenery and routine might have been of use to some patients.

Some of the home remedies of the time sound so absurd that it is tempting to discount them as the fanciful creations of writers whose advice was seldom followed. Such treatments as eating a fried mouse or wearing a spider sealed in a goose quill to cure whooping cough seem too outlandish to be believed. It is easier to think of people taking patent pills (*Sand, MW* 422; *MP* 297), powders, and tonics (*S&S* 191) such as Daffy's Elixir, or proven remedies such as quinine, also called Jesuit's Bark. Yet people were willing to try anything in order to feel better, and in the absence of scientific proof of the cause and nature of disease, there was no knowing what might have a positive effect. Parson Woodforde invested in such household remedies as quinine, camphor, laudanum, magnesia, ointments, and rhubarb (not edible rhubarb, but medicinal rhubarb, a purgative used to treat nausea), but he also tried quasi-magical charms (*MP* 104) as well. For cramps that bothered him at night, he was advised by his brother "to carry a small Piece of the roll Brimstone sewed up in a piece of very thin Linnen, to bed with me" and hold it near the affected part, which Woodforde tried and believed was efficacious. For an inflammation in his right eye in 1791, he was told that it would be cured if rubbed with the tail of a black cat. Ever the optimist, he "made trial of it, and very soon after dinner I found my Eye-lid much abated of the swelling and almost free from Pain. I cannot therefore but conclude it to be of the greatest service." However, he retained some measure of scientific skepticism, warning that "Any other Cats Tail may have the above effect in all probability—but I did my Eye-lid with my own black Tom Cat's Tail." *See also* Teeth.

Mirror

Britons used both small hand mirrors for personal grooming (*P* 128) and large mirrors for display in public rooms, but until the 1770s, most of the better-quality large mirrors had been made in France. The larger mirrors, or "glasses" (*Cath, MW* 214; *P* 127) had been extremely expensive for most of the eighteenth century, but recent technological improvements had allowed British manufacturers to make larger quantities of good plate glass, and this reduced prices. Mirrors were incorporated into all sorts of furniture such as dressing tables (see the illustration *Progress of the Toilet.—*

The Stays [Clothing]) or were handsomely mounted in specially carved wooden frames and displayed on their own. The traditional location for such a mirror was either above or opposite to a fireplace, and it was called a chimney glass or pier glass, respectively. The ability to make large sheets of glass with little distortion encouraged manufacturers to make cheval glasses as well; these were full-length mirrors that could be turned to different angles and that stood on the floor on stands with splayed feet (see the illustrations *Progress of the Toilet.—Dress Completed* (Clothing) and *Messrs. Morgan & Sanders* (Furniture). In some households, a convex mirror was installed. This large round mirror, also known as a girandole, had a candelabra mounted in front of it and reflected a distorted view of the entire room, a phenomenon that fascinated many a ballgoer. Though all these mirrors had been greatly reduced in price, they still remained beyond the means of many middle-class and laboring families. Parson James Woodforde was flabbergasted at a mirror he saw in August 1783:

> The looking glass which was the finest and largest I ever saw, cost at secondhand 150.0.0. The Height of the Plate was seven feet and half, and the breadth of it was five feet and half, one single Plate of glass only. The frame and Ornaments to it, was carved and gidled and very handsome.

A good, large mirror, even one not quite so magnificent as the one above, could cost tens of pounds, a sum that might equal a poorer family's entire yearly income. Mirrors, therefore, especially large mirrors, remained a sign of status and wealth. Rather large wall mirrors may be seen in the illustrations *A Master of the Ceremonies Introducing a Partner* (Dance) and *Harmony before Matrimony* (Music). *See also* Furniture.

Money

England's official monetary system was bimetallic—that is, it was based on the actual market values of gold and silver, with coins being issued in both metals in sizes that reflected their actual worth. In practice, gold was more abundant than silver, and very little silver coinage was produced during Jane Austen's life. In fact, most of this "English" silver was Spanish silver, Spanish dollars countermarked with a bust of George III that began appearing in 1797. Part of the remainder was produced not by the Royal Mint but by the Bank of England, which began striking five-shilling silver pieces in 1804 and two smaller coins, with values of 3s. and 1s. 6d., between 1811 and 1816. These bore a bust of George III on one side, looking very much like coins produced by the mint, and some sort of indication on the reverse that the coin had actually been produced by the bank. In the case of the five-shilling piece, the legend "FIVE SHILLINGS DOLLAR" ran around an oval band, and BANK OF ENGLAND, in somewhat larger letters, ran just outside it. In the case of the 1s. 6d. coin (*Scraps, MW* 174), the words "BANK TOKEN" appeared on the reverse, along with the coin's value and date. Other banks produced silver coins, as did manufacturers and counties; Hampshire and Cornwall, for example, minted silver coins, often labeling them as intended for the furtherance of trade or for the "accommodation" of the local populace. Silver coins produced by the mint under George III were the crown (worth 5s., or a quarter of a pound), half-crown (2s. 6d.*—see *Watsons, MW* 349; *MP* 119, 163), shilling (12d.—see *Lesley, MW* 117; *LS, MW* 296; *Sand, MW* 374, 400; *NA* 28; *S&S* 218; *P&P* 83; *MP* 151; *E* 85, 334), and sixpence (*Watsons, MW* 352; *S&S* 11; *P&P* 305; *E* 22). Special fourpenny and one-penny silver coins were produced for distribution by the king on Maundy Thursday, but these were not in regular circulation. Note that none of the official coins was a "three-shilling piece"; the one mentioned in *Persuasion* must therefore be a privately issued token (170).

Gold coins included the guinea (*Scraps, MW* 174; *Sand, MW* 414, 424; *NA* 19, 46, 47, 76; *S&S* 65, 291, 370; *MP* 53), weighing 129 39/89 grains, and worth 21 shillings†; the pound, worth 20 shillings (*L&F, MW* 107; *Evelyn, MW* 182; *Watsons, MW* 352; *P&P* 300, 304, 308; *MP* 127, 305, 396); the half-

Farthing, 1806, actual size. Obverse: Bust of George III, date, his name in Latin, and "D : G • REX," an abbreviation of "Dei Gratia Rex," meaning "by the grace of God." Many British coins used this formula, following it with a list of names of places ruled by the monarch. On a farthing there simply wasn't room to list George III's full title. Reverse: a seated Britannia. Courtesy of HeritageCoin.com.

Halfpence, 1799, actual size. Obverse: GEORGIUS III DEI GRATIA REX, with a classically wreathed and draped bust of the king. Reverse: seated Britannia and date. Courtesy of HeritageCoin.com.

Penny, 1797, actual size. Pennies were unusually large because they contained their face value's worth of copper. Obverse: GEORGIUS III • D : G • REX. Reverse: seated Britannia and date. Courtesy of HeritageCoin.com.

*The abbreviations for old-style English coins were "g" for guineas, "£" for pounds, "s" for shillings, and "d" for pennies. The £, s, and d abbreviations are descended from medieval coinage weights and denominations; £ for libra or livre ("pound" in Latin and French, respectively), "s" for solidus, "d" for denarius.

†One guinea was the price of a first edition of *Emma*.

Penny, 1806, actual size. The designs of coins changed throughout Austen's lifetime, as this very different penny shows. The monarch's hair, long and curling in the 1797 bust, is now cropped in a "Titus" cut. Obverse: GEORGIUS III • D : G • REX and date. Reverse: seated Britannia. Courtesy of HeritageCoin.com.

Sixpence, 1790, actual size. Obverse: crowned cipher of GR for "Georgius Rex." Reverse: setaed Britannia and date. Courtesy of HeritageCoin.com.

Shilling, 1817, actual size. A shilling was worth twelvepence. Obverse: Bust of the king, date, and GEOR[GIUS] : III D : G: BRITT[ANIA]: REX F : D:. The "F.D." stood for "Fidei Defensor," Defender of the Faith, a title granted to Henry VIII in his pre-Reformation days by the Pope and retained by British monarchs ever since. Reverse: royal arms surrounded by a buckled garter and the motto "HONI SOIT Q[UI] MAL Y PENSE," the motto of the Knights of the Garter, which translates roughly as, "Evil be to he who thinks evil." Courtesy of HeritageCoin.com.

guinea of 10s. 6d.; the third-guinea of 7s. (*S&S* 370); and the half-pound of 10s. In 1817, the guinea was eliminated and replaced by a 20-shilling coin called a sovereign. Most transactions, however, did not take place using gold coins as the currency. A general shortage of silver and eventually gold currency, especially toward the end of the Napoleonic Wars, necessitated other means of making purchases.

One way of accomplishing this was by buying goods on credit—often with astonishingly long intervals between the provision of services and the rendering of payment. Parson Woodforde of Norfolk, for example, recorded paying a clock cleaner £1 6d. "for cleaning Clocks & Watch from October, 1789, to Dec. 1794." He tipped the clock cleaner an additional sixpence, giving him a total of one guinea, but this hardly seems adequate recompense for waiting five years to have a bill settled.

Another expedient to which many businesses and banks resorted was the coining of token coins, worth very little in themselves but redeemable for gold or silver. Usually made of copper, these coins were often stamped with images celebrating local industry or agriculture, the name of the coining agency, and the place(s) at which the coin could be redeemed. The theory behind the coins, however, was that they would *not* be redeemed but would circulate much as token currencies do today, representing the *idea* of value rather than possessing intrinsic value. Thus, they would further trade by providing readily available coinage with which to make small purchases. A surprising number of businesses, especially copper miners, produced such coins, usually pennies (*Scraps*, *MW* 174; *NA* 124; *MP* 394) and halfpennies, and these tokens were very well received by the public.

Eventually, even the government began to warm to the idea of a copper coinage, which had long been resisted in favor of gold and silver. In 1797, Birmingham industrialists Matthew Boulton and James Watt were authorized to produce copper pennies and twopences for the government. Unfortunately, they chose to abandon the idea of a token coinage and issued huge coins whose metal content made them actually worth their face value. The 2d. coin weighed two ounces, and the penny weighed an ounce, making a pocketful of "small" change a weighty burden. They were never popular, but later halfpenny and farthing (a quarter penny—see *P* 200) denominations caught on, and by the time production was ended in 1807, £679,311 of copper coins had been struck.* Boulton's efficiency was much admired at the time; a contemporary poem celebrates his steam-operated coining machine, which could be run by four boys and produce 30,000 gold guineas per hour.

Bank token, 1s. 6d., 1812, actual size. This coin was issued by the Bank of England, not by the government. Obverse: royal bust and GEORGIUS III DEI GRATIA REX. Reverse: Wreathed legend, "BANK TOKEN 1s. 6D." and date. Courtesy of HeritageCoin.com.

Bank token, three shillings, 1812, actual size. Obverse: royal bust and GEORGIUS III DEI GRATIA REX. Reverse: BANK TOKEN 3 SHILL[INGS] and date. Courtesy of HeritageCoin.com.

Half-crown (2s. 6d.), 1817, actual size. Obverse: royal bust, date, and GEORGIUS III DEI GRATIA. Reverse: Gartered royal arms with HONI • SOIT • QUI • MAL • Y • PENSE on the garter and BRITANNIARUM REX FID[EI]: DEF[ENSOR]: around the border. Courtesy of HeritageCoin.com.

A third way of easing the demand for coin proved to be revolutionary. Traveling merchants had long dreaded the idea of entrusting themselves and a bag full of coins to the toll roads and their burgeoning population of high-

---

*A new copper coinage, this time a token currency, would be issued in the 1820s, after Austen's death.

Crown (5s.), 1820, actual size. Obverse: royal bust, date, and GEORGIUS III D: G: BRITANNIARUM REX F: D:. Reverse: St. George slaying the dragon, with a faint buckled garter and the motto of the Knights of the Garter. Courtesy of HeritageCoin.com.

Third-guinea (7s.), 1810, actual size. Obverse: GEORGIVS III DEI GRATIA and bust. Reverse: crown, date, BRITANNIARUM REX FIDEI DEFENSOR (King of the Britons, Defender of the Faith). Courtesy of HeritageCoin.com.

Half-guinea, 1791, actual size. Obverse: royal bust with long hair and laurel wreath; GEORGIVS III DEI GRATIA. Reverse: royal arms, date, and M • B • F • ET • H • REX • F • D • B • ET • L • D • S • R • I • A • T • ET • E (Latin abbreviations for "By the Grace of God, King of Great Britain, France, and Ireland, Defender of the Faith, Duke of Brunswick and Luneburg, High Treasurer and Elector of the Holy Roman Empire). Courtesy of HeritageCoin.com.

waymen. In order to minimize their risk and the weight they carried, a merchant would secure a note from his local bank that could be redeemed for coin once he reached his destination. Banking was a volatile business, with banks sometimes failing in swarms, to be replaced by similar ventures founded on equal parts of optimism and greed. Still, most of these banks issued notes that were accepted with little question in far-flung parts of the nation.

Paper currency had several distinct advantages other than being lightweight. It could, for example, be cut in half, and the halves sent to a destination via different posts, deterring highwaymen. As a token currency, it could be produced without regard to fluctuating metal values. In theory, banks were supposed to have enough cash on hand to redeem all their notes at once, but not all banks adhered scrupulously to this practice; indeed, in the worst war years, even the government drifted off the gold standard for a time and used paper money as its legal tender. It served as a traveling advertisement for the bank; every time it changed hands, the reputation of the bank was improved. It could be issued in variable denominations—guineas or pounds, from £1 to £500, or whatever amount seemed to be re-

quired. Because by its very existence it increased the supply of money available for trade and investment, it had the potential to stimulate the economy, improve consumer confidence, and relieve some of the necessity for long extensions of credit.

Banknotes (*H&E, MW* 34; *L&F, MW* 92, 96; *NA* 19; *MP* 372) were usually larger and more nearly square than British or American paper money today. In fancy print, they announced their value and the name of the banks on which they were drawn. After an act of 1775, they had to be worth at least £1, and all notes were subject to a stamp tax; the latter provision meant that in the 1780s, nine-guinea notes, a rather odd denomination, were suddenly popular, as the stamp tax increased for values

Guinea, 1795, actual size. Obverse: royal bust and GEORGIVS III DEI GRATIA. Reverse: royal arms, date, and the same heavily abbreviated Latin inscription as the half-guinea. Courtesy of HeritageCoin.com.

of ten guineas and above. The average banknote did not circulate very long, usually only about three or four months, indicating perhaps that the public's faith in them was limited. They were money, true, but not nearly as reassuring as a handful of coins, and they still felt more like a receipt for money than the money itself.

As they occupied a kind of middle ground between the modern idea of paper money and a more archaic idea of paper money as a small-value letter of credit, banknotes might be used in the modern sense or the archaic one. Sometimes banknotes were used to make direct payments. One June 26, 1792, for example, Woodforde records receiving his fee for baptizing the local squire's daughter as "a five Guinea Note from Gurney's bank at Norwich." However, he also records instances in which he cashed a banknote and used the change to make a variety of purchases at different shops. In London in September 1789, he went "into Lombard Street and changed two of Gurneys Bank Notes of 10 Pᵈ each for Cash." In June 1793, he "went again to Gurneys banking Office and there changed two ten pound Notes for ready cash—very bluff Folks." One feels, from reading diaries, letters, and literature of the period, that presenting someone with a banknote was rather like handing them a gift certificate today: "Here," seems to be the assumption of both giver and receiver, "here's a little something—go out and get yourself some money with it." There is still the connotation of paper money as something that is exchanged for the real thing.

There was related uncertainty about the banking industry (*LS, MW* 250; *Watsons, MW* 322; *S&S* 225), which was almost completely unregulated and thus often unreliable. Austen's brother Henry, for example, was one of the owners of a failed bank, which collapsed partly due to irresponsible loan policies and partly due to a general wave of bank failures that ruined 206 banks between 1815 and 1830. From 1808 onward, the government tried to enforce the bankers' responsibility to engage in sound business practices and make good on debts. The initial foray into regulation was forcing bankers to sign promissory notes and take out licenses.

However, despite restrictions and risks, England's growing economy stim-

THE BANK.

The Bank, 1792. The rotunda inside the Bank of England was meant to evoke the bank's solidity and success and to inspire confidence in patrons. Country banks, by contrast, might be little more than a small office with a desk. Courtesy of the Lewis Walpole Library, Yale University. 792.1.0.1.

ulated the establishment of new banks. Within London, the Bank of England reigned supreme and unchallenged, but in the provinces an increasing number of small banks emerged, their assets often limited not to gold or silver but to Bank of England notes. The 12 provincial banks of 1750 became 350 by 1790 and 721 by 1810. These banks took deposits, offered loans, issued banknotes, and allowed their customers to write checks in order to move funds from one bank to another. By 1770 the use of checks was common enough that bank clerks began to meet at a London chophouse in order to settle the transactions in one set of calculations and exchange of coins. This "clearing house" concept was so successful that it soon moved to its own location nearby and became an established feature of London's banking business.

The Bank of England remained the principal symbol of banking and a major symbol of the nation's financial health. It enjoyed special privileges and was subject to special regulations (such as a cap of 5 percent on the interest it could charge on loans of the money it printed). Unlike the humbler country banks, its premises were deliberately grand, meant to reinforce its solidity and reliability. The bank's unique position made it a target of political protest (*NA* 113), most notably in 1780, during the anti-Catholic Gordon Riots, when the bank was attacked by mobs and had to be garrisoned with troops. Even after the troops were dismissed weeks later, a military night guard was sustained at the bank for almost 200 years, and a neighboring church was demolished to prevent its tower from being used as a point from which disgruntled citizens could fire on the bank.

People wishing to preserve and increase their money had relatively few options. They could invest in joint-stock companies, but then as now, such ventures were often risky. Contemporary prints satirized both the jobbers and promoters who sold such stocks and the greedy would-be magnates who bought them. A more conservative investment was the "Navy five per cents," a system of annuities introduced in the 1760s to raise money for "certain Navy, Victualling and Transport Bills, and Ordnance Debentures." Austen herself invested almost all the proceeds of her novels in the navy 5 percents, and she assumes an income of 4 (*P&P* 106) or 5 percent on her characters' invested funds.

Music

Music (*L&F, MW* 78; *Lesley, MW* 119–120, 129; *NA* 56; *S&S* 17, 47, 48, 83, 155, 343; *P&P* 24, 39, 101, 172, 173–174; *MP* 19, 288; *E* 28, 85, 150, 168, 181, 191, 227, 232, 276–277, 282, 301; *P* 43, 58) was an important part of the lives of the gentry, both for the women (and the occasional man) who played it and for the family members and friends who listened to it. Learning to play some sort of musical instrument (*S&S* 105; *P&P* 24, 248, 345; *E* 170, 456; *P* 71) was considered an important, if not essential, part of a young woman's education (*Cath, MW* 206), and parents paid significant sums to have a music teacher come to the house and give lessons (*Cath, MW* 198; *NA* 14) or to send their daughters to boarding schools where a good musical education could be acquired (*LS, MW* 253). Austen's parents appear to have hired George William Chard, the assistant organist of Winchester Cathedral, to teach her, and she remained musical to some extent all her life. Young women who had obtained a suitable musical education were then expected to display their talents (*P&P* 100–101; *E* 229, 276), both in the hopes of attracting favorable male attention and for the purpose of entertaining the family at home (*Lesley, MW* 111; *S&S* 35; *MP* 191; *P* 46, 72). The ideal was that the young woman would practice extensively and become proficient, though then as now, motivating the young student to practice was always the hard part (*LS, MW* 271; *P&P* 173, 175, 176; *E* 231). Austen continued to practice all her life when it was possible; at Chawton Cottage, for example, she practiced every morning, but she does not appear to have enjoyed displaying her talents in public, even in the semipublic forum of an impromptu after-dinner dance.

In order to practice sufficiently, a woman needed access to an instrument and to printed sheet music (*S&S* 342; *E* 242; *P* 38). As published music was often expensive (*S&S* 92, 93), women sometimes borrowed music from friends or relatives and then laboriously copied it out by hand (*S&S* 83), a process that required both skill and time. The Austens' collection of music contained both printed and hand-copied pieces bound into books (*Lesley, MW* 130; *P&P* 51), though what survives is not all of what Jane would have played, as much of her music was sold, along with her first pianoforte, when the family moved to Bath in 1801. Her surviving collection includes two pieces by Mozart, several pieces by Handel (including portions of the Water Music, Judas Maccabeus, and *Zadok the Priest*), various sonatas by Johann Schobert, and fourteen sonatinas by Ignaz Pleyel, an initially celebrated composer who fell out of favor for prolific, but uninspired, pastiches of Handel. She also possessed music by Haydn, Gluck, and the popular composers Dibdin, Arne, and Shield. The pieces by Dibdin included *The Soldier's Adieu*, which Jane, with "fine naval fervor" (*P* 167), amended to *The Sailor's Adieu*.

She owned English, French, and Italian songs (*P* 186), all of which were popular at the time; songs (*F&E, MW* 10; *NA* 122–123) gave a woman a chance to display her voice as well as her playing, while symphonies (then called "overtures"), sonatas, and excerpts from operas (*S&S* 342) focused attention on the music. Keyboard duets (*MP* 14, 20) gave friends a chance to play together, and vocal duets (*NA* 28) offered a man and a woman a chance to unite their voices on the way to uniting their hearts. Country dances (*Lesley, MW* 129; *E* 229, 245; *P* 47) need have no words, only a lively and regular tempo to help the dancers along. Glees (*MP* 112, 113) were part-songs for three voices and were sung either in glee clubs or in private homes. One notable glee club, London's Anacreontic Society (founded 1766), opened every meeting with the song "Anacreon in Heaven," which, with very slight alterations, became the accompaniment to Francis Scott Key's "Star-Spangled Banner."

Intriguingly, with all this variety of music available, Austen mentions relatively few specific songs in her works. She makes a humorous reference to "Malbrook" in *Lesley Castle* as "the only song" a notoriously pedestrian character appreciates (*MW* 130). "Malbrook," a corruption of the title of the duke of Marlborough, was a song popular in France at the end of the eighteenth century. Used widely in satirical French songs, it is an extremely undemanding tune and was slightly adapted in the 1830s as "For He's a Jolly Good Fellow." Another song is used in a far more serious context. One of the songs that Jane Fairfax plays on her new pianoforte is "Robin Adair" (*E* 243). The lyrics of this song by Lady Caroline Keppel are worth quoting in their entirety:

> What's this dull town to me?
> Robin's not near;
> What was't I wish'd to see?
> What wish'd to hear?
> Where all the joy and mirth,
> Made this town heav'n on earth,
> Oh! they've all fled wi' thee,
> Robin Adair.
>
> What made th' assembly shine?
> Robin Adair.
> What made the ball so fine?
> Robin was there.
> And when the play was o'er,
> What made my heart so sore?
> Oh! it was parting with,
> Robin Adair.
>
> But now thou'rt cold to me,
> Robin Adair.
> And I no more shall see,

Robin Adair.
Yet he I lov'd so well,
Still in my heart shall dwell,
Oh! I can ne'er forget,
Robin Adair.

Welcome on shore again,
Robin Adair!
Welcome once more again,
Robin Adair!
I feel thy trembling hand;
Tears in thy eyelids stand,
To greet thy native land,
Robin Adair!

Long I ne'er saw thee, love,
Robin Adair;
Still I prayed for thee, love,
Robin Adair;
When thou wert far at sea,
Many made love to me,
But still I thought on thee,
Robin Adair!

Come to my heart again,
Robin Adair;
Never to part again,
Robin Adair;
And if thou still art true,
I will be constant too,
And will wed none but you,
Robin Adair!

This is clearly a very conscious choice on the part of both Jane Fairfax and her creator Jane Austen. Jane Fairfax plays it, in Frank Churchill's hearing, at a time when she is uncertain of his true feelings toward her. The song refers to a "public place" with assemblies and plays, very much like the Weymouth in which Frank and Jane met; it expresses the anxieties of a woman left behind and offers eternal fidelity "if thou still art true." It was included in Moore's *Irish Melodies* as "Eileen Aroon" and was actually originally an Irish song.

Consistent with the vogue for all things Gaelic at the time, Austen owned two collections of Scottish songs (*Lesley, MW* 124; *P&P* 25, 51–52), though if she owned any Irish music, it has not survived. Nonetheless, she mentions the fashion for Irish tunes as well in her works (*P&P* 25; *E* 242). Always acutely aware of the latest fashions, in music as well as in clothing, she recognized that some of the most interesting and challenging music being produced in her day was by J. B. Cramer and had Frank Churchill send some

Cramer compositions to Jane Fairfax (*E* 242), making Cramer the only composer mentioned in any of Austen's novels. The pieces she herself played frequently were usually undemanding, although there were a few that clearly required more talent to play than the rest. She had, for example, a copy of the difficult Grand Concerto by Steibelt, a noisy and complicated work that may have been intended as the "magnificent concerto" that Marianne plays at Lady Middleton's (*S&S* 149). This was a famous work, well known in 1811 when *Sense and Sensibility* was finally published.

Music was also enjoyed in a public setting. Professional musicians could be found in almost any "public place"—at assembly balls (*Watsons, MW* 327, 328; *NA* 57; *E* 255), when strings like violins (*L&F, MW* 100; *Watsons, MW* 327; *S&S* 171; *MP* 117, 275) were the rule; at the Pump Room in Bath; and in public gardens. Songs and musically accompanied dances filled the intervals between plays at the theater (*MP* 124), and the upper classes enjoyed opera—Italian operas at the King's Theatre, Haymarket, and English operas at Drury Lane and Covent Garden. Public concerts (*Lesley, MW* 133; *NA* 25, 26; *P* 180–193) were held in many cities, often by subscription, meaning that subscribers paid a flat fee to acquire a certain number of tickets to a series of scheduled performances, making the subscription the Georgian equivalent of the season ticket. In the provinces, concerts by top performers were rarer events and sold individual tickets rather than season passes. Parson James Woodforde reported occasionally on such concerts in his diary. In September 1788, he noted in his diary that "The Kettle Drums from Westminster Abbey sounded charmingly, beat by a Mr. Ashbridge. Near 100 performers in the Orchestra." Two years later he saw Nancy Storace, the leading female comic opera star of London, along with "Select pieces from the Messiah, Joshua &c.," for a five-shilling ticket price.

Elsewhere, society hostesses arranged "musical evenings," onetime private concerts with hired music rather than (or in addition to) the normal sequence of amateur after-dinner demonstrations (*S&S* 248; *E* 284). The quality of the professional music depended entirely on the host or hostess' pocketbook, as even the best performers in the nation could be secured for private parties at a price. Austen was in London in 1811 for one such party thrown by her brother Henry and his wife, Eliza, which promised "5 professionals, 3 of them Glee singers, besides Amateurs." Later, she reported that there had been some good harp music and a singer "whose voice was said to be very fine indeed." Note that Austen did not say that she herself found the voice "fine." She was notoriously unenthusiastic about singers and was deeply unimpressed with her one recorded visit to the opera.

Musical Instruments

Although women sometimes played unconventional instruments such as the cello or guitar, the two most popular instruments were the keyboard and the harp, both of which were at their heart stringed instruments. The standard keyboard in Austen's child-hood was the harpsichord (*Lesley, MW* 130; *Cath, MW* 201, 229, 232) or the spinet (*NA* 14; *E* 216), both of which had quills that plucked the strings. The harpsichord was a slightly more com-plicated instrument than the spinet, having one keyboard instead of two.

Both instruments were eclipsed in the late eighteenth century by the pi-anoforte (*LS, MW* 271; *Plan, MW* 428; *S&S* 26, 30, 35, 62, 281, 342; *P&P* 39, 51, 58, 173; *MP* 127, 288, 395; *E* 216, 240, 241, 242, 244, 384; *P* 50), which instead of having quills had hammers that struck the strings. The first pianofortes in England were German-made grand pianos and were

Rowlandson Etching, 1790, detail. One woman plays a square pianoforte while another either sings or holds music. Courtesy of the Lewis Walpole Library, Yale University. 790.6.27.1.

popularized by their use in the theatre. The fact that they used hammers rather than quills made them easier to maintain, as quills needed to be re-placed often, while pianofortes needed to be tuned (*S&S* 144) only occa-sionally. The problem for pianoforte makers was how to produce a case that held all the strings in the best manner possible, and several solutions were proposed. The most obvious was the grand pianoforte, in which the strings were arranged horizontally from longest to shortest, left to right from the perspective of the performer. The grand pianoforte had the ad-vantage of allowing the performer's face to be seen, but its disadvantage was the amount of floor space it took up, which made it practical only in the large homes of prosperous families (*E* 215; *P* 40). Another solution was the square pianoforte (*E* 214–215), which also had horizontal strings but was less monumental. It compressed the space required for the strings by running the longest strings diagonally across the shorter strings at a different level within the case. A third solution was the vertical alignment of the string case, so that the pianoforte was extremely tall, as tall as a large bookshelf. The space left vacant by the shorter strings could be recaptured as a shelf for sheet music, but the sheer height of the longer strings forced the instrument to be positioned against a wall and meant that the player kept her back to the audience and sang toward the wall rather than toward the room. An improvement was the movement of the string case down-ward, so that it rested on the floor, which, combined with the diagonal stringing of the square pianoforte, greatly reduced the height of the in-strument. This still resulted in a cabinet that extended much higher than

Matrimonial-Harmonics, James Gillray, 1805. The husband being entertained by a performance on the grand pianoforte, as well as by his baby's crying and the nurse's attempts to distract it with a rattle, does not appear to take much delight in the hard-won musical skills of his wife. Courtesy of the Lewis Walpole Library, Yale University. 805.10.25.1.

the keyboard, but this "cabinet" piano was nonetheless superior to the very tall models that had preceded it, because it allowed more of the performer's face and body to be seen.

The posture of the performer was almost as important as skill from the perspective of courtship. A musical performance was one of the occasions on which a woman could legitimately draw attention to herself, and she was supposed to make the most of it. *The Mirror of the Graces* (1811) noted the uncomfortably rectilinear qualities of the pianoforte and advised young women how to compensate:

> From the shape of the instrument, the performer must sit directly in front of a straight line of keys; and her own posture being correspondingly erect and square, it is hardly possible that it should not appear rather inelegant. But if it attain not the *ne plus ultra* of grace, at least she may prevent an air of stiffness; she may move her hands easily on the keys, and bear her head with that elegance of carriage which cannot fail to impart its own character to the whole of her figure.

However, noted the author, not all young women heeded this advice. In fact, they made things worse, adopting "such actions and grimaces, as would almost incline one to believe that they are suffering under the torture of the tooth-ach or the gout." In an excess of dramatic song, "Their bosoms heave, their shoulders shrug, their heads swing to the right and left, their lips quiver, their eyes roll; they sigh, they pant, they seem ready to expire!"

Improvements in the pianoforte came rapidly. Early mechanisms had lacked power, requiring a firm "touch" (*E* 220) to strike a note, and in some cases the hammer would stay against the string and dampen the sound or rebound and strike the string a second time. A series of patents, some of them filed by John Broadwood (*E* 214–215), addressed these issues. Increasingly complex internal systems kept the hammer exactly where it was supposed to be, resulting in a lighter touch and better sound.

Broadwood, a Scottish carpenter and joiner, had married the daughter of his employer, a prominent harpsichord maker, Burckhardt Tschudi. He filed his first patent in 1773 and by the 1790s was manufacturing 400 square and 100 grand pianofortes a year. He was acknowledged to be one of the best piano manufacturers in England, and English pianos were generally acknowledged at this point to be the best in the world, with a superior tone (*S&S* 144; *E* 2220, 34) to most Continental instruments, due in part to the use of felt under the leather cover of the hammers. His pianofortes were played by some of the world's greatest performers and composers, including Beethoven. A square pianoforte of the kind probably given to Jane Fairfax would have cost about £26 in 1815, exclusive of the delivery charges and the price of the sheet music. That the "other Jane," Jane Austen, took her music seriously is reflected in the fact that in 1808 she proposed spending up to 30 guineas for a pianoforte at Chawton Cottage.

Other improvements to the pianoforte included the expansion of the keyboard. Early models had a very small number of keys by modern standards, but by the turn of the century keyboards with five and half or six octaves had become the norm. This increase in range, combined with improved reliability, completed the conquest of the harpsichord. Sheet music that had once been for "harpsichord" and then for "harpsichord or pianoforte" was now advertised as being for "pianoforte or harpsichord," with the "or harpsichord" in much smaller letters, or simply for the piano alone. Cabinet, square, and occasionally grand pianos sprouted in the drawing rooms of lords, squires, tenant farmers, and well-to-do artisans.

The harp (*Sand, MW* 383, 421; *Plan, MW* 428; *P&P* 48; *MP* 57, 59, 64–65, 206–207, 227; *E* 301; *P* 40, 47, 50), however, remained an instrument for the rich. It was considered especially graceful and feminine, but it was not as versatile an instrument as the pianoforte. It could not, for instance, be enlisted into the service of a country dance. It therefore remained a means by which women could show off their unique charms. Like the pianoforte, the harp experienced revision and renaissance during

Harmony before Marriage, James Gillray, 1805. The harp was considered an especially feminine instrument. *The Mirror of the Graces* (1811) gushed, "The shape of the instrument is calculated, in every respect, to show a fine figure to advantage. The contour of the whole form, the turn and polish of a beautiful hand and arm, the richly slippered and well-made foot on the pedal stops, the gentle motion of a lovely neck, and, above all, the sweetly-tempered expression of an intelligent countenance; these are shown at one glance, when the fair performer is seated unaffectedly, yet gracefully, at the harp." Courtesy of the Lewis Walpole Library, Yale University. 805.10.25.2.

this period. Its principal improver was Sébastien Erard (1752–1831), originally a piano maker, who in 1808 patented a new method of increasing the range of each string. This double action allowed the string to be functionally shortened by pressing a pedal into one of two notches, which activated a *fourchette* (forked disc) that changed the sound of the string without throwing it out of key as earlier mechanisms had done. Erard's design allowed the flat, natural, and sharp notes to be played on each string, vastly widening the harp's range.

Mythology

Austen makes few references to Greek or Roman mythology (*MP* 18–19), probably because she was acutely aware of anything that tended to verge on the cliché. Mythology, as well as classical art and architecture, had been taken up with fervor during the eighteenth century and applied to virtually every form of contemporary visual or literary art. It erupted in neoclassical architecture, in acanthus-leaf decorations, and in pastoral poetry— a pale imitation of ancient Roman pastorals—with its "nymphs" and "swains" (*L&F, MW* 103). Austen refuses to fall in line with this trend and uses mythology only to ridicule her century's fascination with it. A typical reference refers to "Cupid's Thunderbolts" and "the piercing Shafts of Jupiter" (*L&F, MW* 100). Aside from the fact that it appears in the comic ravings of a madwoman, this allusion is intentionally, amusingly wrong. It was Jupiter, king of the Roman gods, who wielded thunderbolts, and Cupid, boy-god of love, who shot arrows. *See also* Philomel; Zephyr.

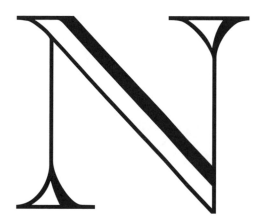

Napoleonic Wars

England was at war with France for most of Jane Austen's life—during the American Revolution (1778–1783), the French Revolutionary War (1793–1802), and, finally, the two Napoleonic Wars (the "Long War," 1803–1814, and the "Hundred Days," 1815). Given that these periods represent over 60 percent of the years of Austen's life, it is remarkable that the wars are barely referred to in her novels. Then again, she was conversant with a variety of subjects that never appear in her works at all, and she probably simply wished to confine herself to those aspects of English life that she knew best. Furthermore, war can be found in her works, if one knows where to look for it.

It is perhaps appropriate to sketch the principal events of the wars. Napoleon Bonaparte came to power in 1799 as "First Consul" of the French Republic. An initial coalition of nations had failed to stop French expansion, and a second coalition disintegrated in 1801 after Napoleon's victory at the Battle of Marengo (1800). Isolated, Britain agreed to the Peace of Amiens, a treaty bitterly opposed by many because it returned captured colonies to the French and left Napoleon's power largely unchallenged. A partial relaxation of military alertness followed, with many military officers being placed on half pay, but tensions between the two nations remained high, and in May 1803 England, threatened by increased militarism on the part of the French, declared war again. This was an extraordinarily risky move, as no Continental power had agreed to form another coalition. Indeed, squabbling and military failures among the allies (chiefly Prussia and Austria) were to plague Britain for most of the Long War.

Napoleon was a brilliant general, but in order to defeat Britain, he knew he would have to master amphibious warfare as well and send a huge number of troops across the English Channel. Accordingly, he made plans to gather a fleet of small boats, protected by an escort of warships, and invade England with 10,000 men. This was no secret in England, and the widely held belief was that an invasion was imminent. Informed opinion—including that of Jane's brother Francis, who was one of those tasked with defending the coastline—was that an invasion would take place somewhere in Kent, where another of Jane's brothers, Edward, possessed large estates. The escort of warships, however, was prevented from joining the troop boats and remained in blockaded ports, unable to stir.

Napoleon tried for nearly two years to free the blockaded ports, and his admirals lured Nelson's fleet as far away as the West Indies and back to the Mediterranean (*MP* 236) in a futile attempt to evade the British. Francis Austen, as captain of the *Leopard*, participated in a blockade of Boulogne

John Bull and His Friends Commemorating the Peace, 1802. The Peace of Amiens was greeted with hopes that high prices would fall and food would once again be plentiful. John Bull celebrates with (roughly left to right) a sirloin, a mug of stout, a loaf of "The Best Wheaten Bread," mutton, hops, a potato, double Gloucester cheese, "Excellent Fresh Butter," rum, port, cognac, and unadulterated flour. Courtesy of the Lewis Walpole Library, Yale University. 802.3.0.1.

and later, as captain of the *Canopus*, engaged in the wild-goose chase to the West Indies. It seemed during this time that the French might escape at any moment. If it did so, an invasion would surely follow. The attempt came in October 1805. Seizing a moment when several ships, including the *Canopus*, had been sent back to Gibraltar to resupply, the French attacked the British off Cape Trafalgar (*Sand*, *MW* 380), with heavy losses on both sides, including Lord Nelson. A joyous British public responded with frenzied glee to the victory and with a despair so deep at Nelson's loss that it was as if the entire nation had known him personally.

In the wake of this savage blow to French naval power, the emphasis shifted to land campaigns. At first Britain merely funded its allies and sent them to fight the battles, but crushing coalition defeats at Ulm (1805), Austerlitz (1805), and Jena-Auerstadt (1806) were the result. In 1808, Bonaparte replaced the Spanish monarch with his brother Joseph, and Britain attempted an invasion of Spain. The first campaign, under Sir John Moore, resulted in a painful retreat to Corunna, where Sir John was killed in 1809 (evoking surprisingly little sympathy from Austen, who infamously wished his heroic death had been more religious). A second push into the Iberian Peninsula under the duke of Wellington was more successful. He made slow progress, and by 1813 almost the entire peninsula was under British control. Meanwhile, the allies had recovered and squelched Napoleon's attempt to invade Russia, forcing him to retreat from Moscow in 1812. It was in 1812 that the *Edinburgh Review*, praising Britain's steadfastness in the fight despite periods of disappointment, hardship, and isolation, noted that most people between the ages of twenty and forty— a group that included Jane Austen—had "passed their whole lives, politically speaking, in a state of universal war; and they only know from history, that there ever was such a thing as peace in the world."

In 1814, the allies defeated Napoleon's army at Leipzig, and in March the British reached Paris. Napoleon abdicated in April, and a celebratory mood gripped most of Europe. Jane's niece Fanny Knight rejoiced at the "glorious news of Buonaparte vanquished and dethroned." By September Napoleon was in exile on the island of Elba, and the gradual demobilization of the military began. Then, to everyone's surprise, Napoleon escaped from his confinement and returned to Paris. Met with enthusiasm by the French, who were already tired of the restored Bourbon monarchs, he attacked Belgium and, despite some early success, was finally trapped and defeated at Waterloo (*Sand*, *MW* 380). His second exile, which lasted until his death, was spent on a far more remote island, St. Helena, located in the South Atlantic.

Since the feared invasion of England never took place, the chief impact of the wars on the English public was economic and psychological. Prices, especially food prices, rose dramatically (*Sand*, *MW* 392–393); in part this was due to a series of poor harvests, and in part it was due to Napoleon's Continental System, a piece of economic warfare designed to close all European ports to British ships. In practice, this policy was only partly successful and in many cases merely raised the price of smuggled goods. It also stimulated English farmers to improve their agricultural methods and place more acres under cultivation, which eventually resulted in higher crop yields.

A more serious economic blow was the system of taxation that supported the funding of foreign allies and the raising and outfitting of British armies and navies. The war was staggeringly expensive; by 1815, the national debt was over £830 million. This was merely the debt; a good deal had already been raised and spent in the effort. All sorts of luxury goods had been taxed, and voluntary tax contributions had been pleaded for with relatively good results. Income tax was introduced in the 1790s, and still it was not enough. From 1813 to 1816, prompted first by bumper crops and then by peace, prices dropped precipitously, which generated a new kind of unease, as farmers and landlords found their profits dropping unexpectedly.

The sense of unease and constant, though distant, jeopardy was one of the most constant effects of the wars. Travel to the Continent, once practically considered the birthright of every robust young man of good fortune, was now impossible. Travel anywhere outside the British Isles was fraught with the danger of capture by a French ship (*MP* 180) or the conquest of the port of destination by French forces. Sugar planters, one of the nation's most prosperous classes, had their trade and income interrupted repeatedly by blockades and short-lived conquests of British colonies by the French. Above all, families worried about male relatives in the army, navy, and marines, some of whom had been "volunteered" largely against their will.

Expectations of women in this time period were somewhat contradictory. On the one hand, discussion of any political matters was considered unladylike; Georgiana, duchess of Devonshire, had been ruthlessly pilloried in the press and portrayed as little better than a whore in satirical prints, merely for taking an active interest in a Westminster election and campaigning on behalf of her preferred candidate. On the other hand, patriotism in general was encouraged. Women were encouraged to support the wars and to use their influence with their menfolk to get them to volunteer for military service. Warren Roberts had argued convincingly that Austen's views gradually shifted over time from genteel feminine reticence on the subject of the war to gentle, but still feminine, boosterism. Her later novels certainly celebrate archetypal Englishmen: the earnest clergyman (Edmund Bertram), the stalwart naval hero (William Price, Frederick Wentworth), and the responsible and sensible farmer (Mr. Knightley). *See also* Army; French Revolution; Navy; Taxes.

Navy

The navy appears repeatedly throughout Austen's works. Its pay, promotions, hazards, reputation, and peculiar rhythms feature prominently in the lives of several of her characters. After the clergy, it is the profession she addresses the most often, and with good reason. The navy grew dramatically during Austen's lifetime. The officer corps, which numbered about 1,400 in 1794, swelled to nearly 4,700 in 1809–1812, when it was at its highest, and her friends and relatives made up some of this glut. Though the Austens could be said to be first and foremost a clerical family, they were almost equally a naval family, with two of the sons and a good many acquaintances serving at sea. Here, as always, Austen sticks to what she knows.

The gaps in what she relates are as revealing as what she chooses to include. For instance, she does not dwell on the role of the merchant marine, which was almost as important to the nation's security as the regular navy. England's vast trading networks were serviced by these civilian sailors. In 1792, perhaps one-eighth of England's 118,000 civilian and naval sailors were engaged in trade with the West Indies, while another significant block of sailors worked on "Indiamen"—the ships of the East India Company—bringing tea, cottons, and coinage home from India (*MP* 381). These sailors necessarily gained a great deal of experience working in all conditions on long voyages, and they were familiar with the very rich colonial regions likely to be contested in wars between European powers.

Therefore, when war broke out, they were encouraged to volunteer for naval service; the government paid a bounty for volunteers, and London merchants added up to £5 per man for able seamen, setting an example that many seaport towns emulated. Different parts of the country were at times required to supply a certain number of able-bodied men for military service, and local officials often provided handsome bounties to avoid an involuntary draft; one advertisement in the *York Chronicle* from 1792 promises that the churchwardens and parish overseers will pay 30 guineas to a volunteer—an enormous windfall to a laborer in those days. When bounties failed to muster enough volunteers, press-gangs found sailors ashore, or even boarded merchant ships and took the men they needed.

Of course, merchants—and the sailors themselves—resented this practice. War meant disruption of trade routes anyway, and a drain on manpower was the last thing the importers and exporters needed. However, the defense of the nation came first and was certainly more prestigious. Upon hearing that Fanny Price has a brother at sea, Mary Crawford remarks, "At sea, has she?—In the King's service of course" (*MP* 60). The "King's service" was more glamorous than ferrying cargoes of wool and timber—at least for the officers, who might grow very rich indeed in the service of the nation. As for the men, who seldom got rich under any circumstances, they tended to prefer the quieter merchant marine if for no other reason than that they could choose to leave a ship at the end of its voyage if they did not like the captain and his style of discipline. Sailor John Nicol served in the merchant marine in peacetime and did not volunteer when war broke out; the press-gangs came anyway and took virtually every able-bodied man aboard his ship, leaving it to be manned, he said, by "ticket-porters and old Greenwich men"—the latter a reference to the Greenwich pensioners, aged and infirm sailors fed and housed by the state. Resentment of such press-gang sweeps ran so strong that merchant captains often hid their sailors, or even deserters. Young Samuel Stokes was pressed into the king's service in 1806 at the age of fourteen; the following year, he escaped from his ship and was fed and helped by a merchant captain.

Press-Gangs

Merchant officers were not the only ones resisting the press-gangs. In a few places, magistrates refused to sign the necessary orders authorizing

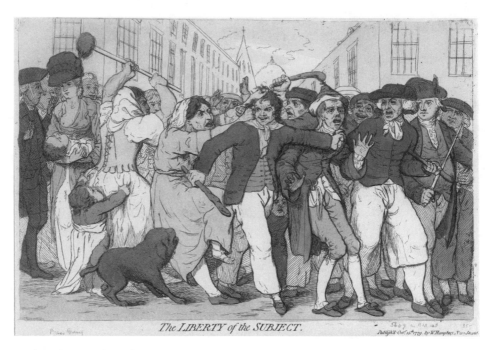

The Liberty of the Subject, 1779. A press-gang seizes a hapless tailor and is attacked by the crowd. Courtesy of the Lewis Walpole Library, Yale University. 779.10.15.1.

press-gangs to act. In others, crowds rioted or colluded to protect men from being taken, but, for the most part, the gangs operated with few limitations, or even with help from informers, who were paid 20 shillings a man for the apprehension of deserters. Magistrates were often eager to foist their local population of vagabonds and criminals into the waiting arms of the press-gang and, in such cases, probably asked few questions about contested seizures. Best of all, from their perspective, the gangs could simply bypass the authorities onshore by raiding homeward-bound merchant ships.

In theory, the press-gangs could seize only seamen, and then only those who lacked a "ticket of liberty" from their home ship and only those who were not otherwise exempt by virtue of their trade specialty. Farm laborers and gentlemen, too, were protected from the gangs. So were sailors on ships bound out of England, captains' apprentices who had served less than two years of their term, Thames watermen (who had a special arrangement to provide a quota of volunteers), foreigners, competent ships' pilots, merchantmen's masters and mates, and boatswains and carpenters serving on ships of more than fifty tons. In practice, the system was more fluid. The burden was on the captured sailor to prove that he had a ticket of liberty or that he belonged to a protected ship or trade. The masters, mates, boatswains, and carpenters mentioned above had to have an affidavit, sworn before a justice of the peace, and they were safe only aboard ship or on ship's business ashore. If such a man decided to make a visit home, for example, he was just as exposed to the gangs as any other sailor. A gentleman who was not dressed as such also risked being mistaken for a member of the vulnerable class. On the other side of the equation, even a man who was fully subject to the gang's roundups could buy his way out of trouble with a substantial bribe—up to £20. Foreign citizenship could also be feigned; false American citizenship papers were forged on both sides of the Atlantic with such frequency that the gangs came to ignore them.*

Once in a while, the sailor got the last laugh. Jack Nastyface (a pseudonym) recorded in his memoirs that he once had a liberty ticket while ashore. He was stopped by soldiers and then pursued by a press-gang. He could simply have shown them his ticket, but for fun he led them on a long chase to waste their time. At an inn, they finally caught up with him, and

one of them grappled me on the starboard, and the other on the larboard side, by the collar of my jacket, demanding the name of the ship I belonged to; when on coolly showing them my liberty ticket, they showered a broadside of curses on me for giving them such a run, and quietly left me to pursue my journey. After this, however, I had to contend with the land sharks, for on my arrival at Alton, I was stopped by a party of soldiers, to whose inspection I had again to exhibit my ticket of leave, and thus for thirty miles from the sea port was a poor seaman hunted by this detestable set, who are constantly watching in the bye lanes and fields, to intercept any seaman who may be passing that way; the inducement held out to each of these men stealers is five pounds for each seaman they may capture; and thus many a poor fellow is hunted by these blood hounds, who chase them with greater eagerness than the hunter pursues the fox.

Nastyface gives the bounty per man as £5, but it was often higher. In 1795, the going rate was £6, and in 1803, when the Peace of Amiens ended and war resumed, the price went up to as much as £20 per sailor.

Pressed men, as well as volunteers, were collected in a holding area of some kind. On shore, this would be some sort of building; afloat, it would be a ship called a tender. (Charles Austen's ship the *Namur* was used as a tender in the last years of the Napoleonic Wars.) In either case, the area would be heavily guarded by armed marines to prevent premature desertions. Jack Nastyface, who first joined the service in 1805 as a volunteer, wrote that he was held on a tender with pressed convicts, locked in the hold with

---

*The boarding of American vessels and seizure of men with American papers were a principal cause of the War of 1812. Many British sailors preferred to serve on American ships, where they found the discipline lighter and the captains more egalitarian.

a guard of Marines placed round the hatchway with their muskets loaded and fixed bayonets, as though we had been culprits of the first degree, or capital convicts. In this place we spent the day and the following night huddled together for there was not room to sit or stand separate. Indeed we were in a pitiable plight, for numbers of them were sea-sick, some retching, others were smoking whilst many were so overcome by the stench that they fainted for want of air. As soon as the officer on deck understood that the men below were overcome with foul air, he ordered the hatches to be taken off, when day light broke in upon us; and a wretched appearance we cut, for scarcely any of us were free from filth and vermin.

Pressed men had few options left to them at this point, but some opted to make the best of a bad situation. Often, left with no alternative, they would sign on as "volunteers," which gave them better options for leaving the service later and also offered a signing bounty. Frequently, they gave false names, as many of them had already deserted the service on at least one occasion.

Few people found the press-gang system satisfactory. Thomas Cochrane, earl of Dundonald (the model for Patrick O'Brian's fictional Jack Aubrey), found it to be necessary only in certain cases: "in the case of unpopular officers, insufficient vessels, or out-of-the-way stations," he wrote, "where the chances of prize-money were few." Captains who had to rely for one of these reasons on pressed men found that what they got was entirely inadequate. "Sorry fellows," "poor ragged souls," "unfit for service and a nuisance to the ship," "ragged and half dead," "landsmen, boys, incurable and cripples," and "more fit for a hospital than the sea" were only a few of the characterizations applied to such levies. In any case, the demand for seamen lessened appreciably after the last Napoleonic conflict ended in 1815, and the system fell out of use after that date. Austen never addresses the press-gang system in her works. Indeed, she never mingles with the common sailors at all. However, she must have been aware of impressment's existence as the background for Britain's naval success.

Ranks and Promotion

At the pinnacle of the navy's hierarchy stood the "first lord" (*MP* 246) of the Admiralty. His immediate underling—but often the more assiduous and important of the two—was the first naval lord; in 1794, the first naval lord was Vice-Admiral Philip Affleck, to whom Austen friends appealed in an attempt to get Francis Austen (*J&A, MW* 12; *Harley, MW* 40) transferred into a frigate. Other naval "lords" constituted the Admiralty Board, which served as the top administrative body in the navy.

However, Jane Austen's interest is less in the bureaucracy of the navy than in its officer ranks—from midshipman up to admiral. At the bottom of this hierarchy were the midshipmen (*J&A, MW* 12; *Harley, MW* 40; *P* 51), who entered on their service when they were no more than boys;

Thomas Cochrane, whose father objected to his joining the navy, finally made it to sea at the extremely advanced age of seventeen and a half. Young as they were, they were officers, entitled to give orders to the most experienced able seamen and entitled to expect absolute obedience from the men. They might command a gun crew; handle sails and ropes; calculate the ship's speed; keep logs; take charge of a watch, pacing the quarterdeck and watching for any sign of trouble; and calculate the ship's position using astronomy, sea charts, wind and current speeds, and chronometers that showed the difference between local time and Greenwich Mean Time. Other duties, such as the command of one of the ship's small boats (*MP* 377) or the running up and reading of the signal flags (*P* 234) that transmitted orders and news, might be assigned at the captain's pleasure. The captain was expected to take a special interest in the education of the midshipmen. They were, in a way, his apprentices. Austen's brother Charles appears to have been particularly adept at this fatherly aspect to the captain's duties, if we are to judge from the recollections of Douglas Jerrold, who came aboard Charles' ship the *Namur* at age ten in December 1813. Charles let the boy keep pigeons and encouraged his interest in natural history and in amateur theatricals. In an earlier instance, Charles had also been kind to the son of the earl of Countess of Leven, who served as a midshipman under him. In 1805, Jane and Mrs. Austen paid a call on the aristocratic couple and apparently heard Charles praised in much the same manner that Mrs. Musgrove praises Captain Wentworth (*P* 52, 66).

However, the midshipmen (*MP* 381) were not thought of kindly by everyone aboard. Grown men, not surprisingly, resented being ordered about by twelve-year-olds. Sailor Samuel Leech, who was fairly young himself when he first went to sea, complained of the midshipmen he knew that

> These little minions of power ordered and drove me round like a dog nor did I and the other boys dare interpose a word. They were *officers* their word was law and woe betide the presumptuous boy that dared refuse explicit obedience.

George Watson, who was a sailor from 1806 to 1814, harbored similar feelings for one midshipman in particular, calling him

> haughty, ambitious, ignorant, vain as a peacock, implacable, revengeful, cowardly, contemptuous and contemptible, hated by all over whom he had any contact. He was one of those creatures that are most useless and offensive in His Majesty's Service, and only calculated to create and nourish sedition and mutiny.

Austen's midshipmen seem unconscious of any animosity from belowdecks, but they do feel keenly their position at the bottom of the officers' ranks. William Price is described as "only a midshipman" (*MP* 233) and a "poor scrubby midshipman" (*MP* 245) unworthy of so fashionable a place as Brighton. Of course, he laments that the "Portsmouth girls turn up their noses at any body who has not a commission. One might as well be nothing as a midshipman" (*MP* 249). Another of Austen's midshipmen, the late Dick Musgrove, really is nothing, partly by virtue of his incompetence (*P* 50–51, 67) and partly by virtue of being dead before the novel begins. She sees midshipmen neither as vile, swaggering officers nor as boys trusted with an extraordinary amount of responsibility but as her brothers must have felt and described themselves—as relative ciphers in the structure of naval command. Thomas Cochrane would probably have echoed their complaints—one of the first things that happened to him aboard ship was that the lieutenant, Jack Larmour, announcing that the new midshipman had brought far too much baggage, sawed open his trunk by way of public punishment.

The way out of the midshipmen's berth and into respectability was by promotion to lieutenant, which in theory was a simple matter of experience and skill. Regulations dictated that a prospective lieutenant had to be twenty years old—an age limit that was lowered to nineteen in 1806—with at least six years' service at sea, at least three of them as a midshipman. When his captain saw fit, the midshipman would be given certificates testifying to his competence, age, years of service, sobriety, and obedience. He would take these documents to a board composed of three captains, who would interrogate him about his logs and his knowledge of seamanship, gunnery, navigation, tides, wind, and a host of other topics. Then, at some point afterward, he would receive a commission to a ship, where he would take a position as the most junior lieutenant (*MP* 368, 384; *Sand*, *MW* 389) aboard. As a lieutenant, he would have similar duties to a midshipman's, but with generally more responsibility: he might lead gun crews or boarding parties, take watches on the quarterdeck, supervise reprovisioning or the taking on of fresh water, navigate and keep logs, and, if an enemy ship was captured, head a small "prize crew" to sail the ship to a friendly port. Lieutenants might be gentlemen's sons, but not always; Admiral Lord Thomas Cochrane, in his autobiography, offered a vivid description of his first superior officer, Lieutenant Jack Larmour, who was

> a specimen of the old British seaman, little calculated to inspire exalted ideas of the gentility of the naval profession, though presenting at a glance a personification of its efficiency. . . . Lucky was the commander who could secure such an officer for his quarter-deck.
>
> On my introduction, Jack was dressed in the garb of a seaman, with marlinspike slung round his neck, and a lump of grease in his hand, and was busily employed in setting up the rigging.

The first lieutenant (*P* 96) served as the captain's administrator and, when the captain was absent or incapacitated, as his surrogate.

In theory, a man rose in an orderly fashion from midshipman to lieutenant and then up through the ranks of lieutenants until he became a first lieutenant. In practice, promotion to lieutenant could be made easier or more difficult by a dazzling variety of circumstances. One was the number of qualified midshipmen versus the number of ships in commission with open lieutenants' positions. In "good" years, when battle and disease between them contrived to carry off a number of lieutenants, a midshipman might get lucky. (The hope of ill-fortune to one's superiors was an uncomfortable, but constant, undercurrent in the service, one that William Price alludes to when "supposing the first lieutenant out of the way" [*MP* 375] in his daydreams of greater glory.) In "bad" years, such as 1812, there might be as many as 2,000 midshipmen who had passed the lieutenant's exam and were waiting impatiently for a commission (*MP* 362). Service in a particularly splendid naval victory was always helpful in getting extra consideration (*MP* 375). Francis (Frank) Austen got his promotion from commander to captain in this way, after his sixteen-gun *Peterel*, with a diminished crew, wrecked two French ships and captured a third in a daring battle. For those who could not manage such a stunning triumph and even for those who could, it was useful to have the influence of powerful "friends."

"Friends," in an eighteenth-century context, were usually not bosom companions but rather people who could be of assistance in one's career (*MP* 109). It was important to have as many of these friends as possible, preferably located in positions of great influence. Naval lords were best; admirals were very nice indeed; and even captains could make themselves useful, either by offering a position as lieutenant or midshipman aboard their own vessels or by entering a friend's or relative's son on the books prematurely. Many a well-connected youth was actually comfortably at home or at school while nominally serving as a sailor aboard an uncle's or a cousin's ship. His name would appear regularly among the ship's company, and in this way he might acquire most or all of his six service years before he ever set foot on the quarterdeck. Thomas Cochrane benefited from connections in both the army and the navy, and reported in his autobiography that his uncle, later an admiral, had acted on his behalf:

> he had entered my name on the books of various vessels under his command; so that, nominally, I had formed part of the complement of the *Vesuvius*, *Carolina*, *La Sophie*, and *Hind*; the object—common in those days—being, to give me a few years' standing in the service. . . .
>
> Having however, a relative in the army, who possessed influence at the Horse Guards, a military commission was also procured for me; so that I had simultaneously the honour of being an officer in his Majesty's 104th Regiment, and a nominal seaman on board my uncle's ship.

The result was that Cochrane became an acting lieutenant within eighteen months of actually joining the navy, and his promotion was made official the following year. Few objected to this practice; commissions in the army were bought and sold, as were the rights to clerical livings. A professional job was in many ways a form of property, and the practitioners of this sort of nepotism argued that it produced, after all, the best naval officers in the world. There was nothing wrong with using one's connections; just look at the result.

It was, however, necessary to have the *right* connections (*P* 26–27). Francis Austen had an apparently powerful patron in Admiral James Gambier, but Gambier's Evangelical tendencies and his public quarrel with the respected Trafalgar veteran Rear Admiral Eliab Harvey made him unpopular in many parts of the service, and Francis' career appears to have suffered as a result. Another patron of Frank's, Lord Moira, accomplished little because he spread his influence too thinly, asking for too many favors on behalf of too many ambitious officers. Charles Austen's principal patron, Thomas Williams (who had married an Austen cousin, Jane Cooper), had little real power to help him until about 1811. Thomas Cochrane, who had enjoyed extensive patronage himself, had difficulties in getting his own favorites promoted, largely because the Admiralty objected to his politics and because he had made an enemy of the influential Lord St. Vincent. Cochrane fumed at the injustice of the system. The Admiralty, he claimed, "would lavishly grant away, in exchange for rotten borough interest, naval commissions which ought to be the reward of those brave officers who had for years devoted their lives at every hazard in the service of their country."

Still, Cochrane and Gambier could do something to help their protégés, whereas, until Admiral Crawford steps in (*MP* 266, 300), William Price has no one to save him from becoming an "oldster"—a grown man bunking year after year with a succession of better-connected boys destined to pass him by (*MP* 249–250). A midshipman could have all the skill in the world, but his commission might go instead to some boy whose father's vote was needed in Parliament to keep the current ministry (and thus the current first lord) in power. A shifting of the political winds could bring disaster to some and relief to others; in 1804, Captain Thomas Fremantle wrote to his wife, "I trust in heaven that these changes in the Administration may bring in some of our friends, there is no getting on without friends in power." One pictures that shifting, fickle wind wafting first to this house, then to that, carrying on its back a steady stream of letters pleading for commissions, ships, better ships, and better stations. In the real world, such letters were a constant annoyance to their recipients, but they were effective: Reverend George Austen's correspondence with the right people got Francis his lieutenancy in 1798 and got Charles transferred into a better ship, a thirty-two-gun frigate. In the fictional world, a flurry of letters traces the chain of influence in the promotion of William Price (*MP* 298–299).

The right combination of luck, competence, and influence could move a lieutenant to the next rank: commander (*MP* 368). A commander was, as the title implies, in command of a ship, but it was such a small ship that it did not qualify for a real captaincy, known as a "post-captaincy" or "post rank." For Francis, this step up came in 1798, when he was given command of the sloop *Peterel* (16). In her, he captured or destroyed more than forty enemy vessels, and his zeal earned him promotion to captain in 1800. The fictional Frederick Wentworth is similarly energetic in his first command, the sloop *Asp*; Jane Austen includes an authentic detail of protocol in his account that might escape many readers. Since the *Asp* is clearly identified as a sloop (*P* 65), we know that Wentworth is only a commander when he travels to the West Indies in her, yet her refers to himself in the third person in his narration of events as "Captain Wentworth" (*P* 66). Most readers think nothing of this, since at the time he is telling the story, he is a full captain. Yet the way he mentions himself makes it clear that he is speaking not of the present but of the time when he commanded the *Asp*. The crucial piece of information is that commanders were accorded the courtesy title of "Captain," although they had not achieved post rank. James Benwick, too, is referred to as "Captain," though he "is only a commander, it is true, made last summer" (*P* 171). The reference to his being "made into the Grappler" means that he has been made a commander and given command of the ship *Grappler* (*P* 108).

Once promoted to post-captain (*F&E, MW* 6*; *Coll Let, MW* 154*; *MP* 60, 236, 394; *P* 50, 66, 75, 96, 169, 248; *Sand, MW* 389), a man had merely to live long enough to rise to admiral; promotion from this point on was a matter of strict seniority; hence, the frantic desire of lower-level officers to be made captains: one had to get on the captains' list as soon as possible in one's career (*MP* 60). Both Charles and Francis Austen saw colleagues promoted ahead of them, simply because they happened to have a slight advantage in seniority. This is not to say, however, that favoritism played no further part in advancement. The influence of "friends" still determined what ship a captain commanded, and it might play some role in whether a captain would receive honors or titles as a reward for particular bravery (*P* 75).

In the Austen brothers' case, their influence was insufficient to get them really good ships. Francis' first command as captain, for example, was the *Neptune* (98), where he served as flag-captain to Rear Admiral Thomas Louis. This would appear to have been an honor; a flag-captain was in charge of the ship on which an admiral sailed and had his floating headquarters. However, as Brian Southam points out, the post was not a desirable one at all. A flag-captain was constantly under an admiral's supervision and never quite the master of his own ship, and any

---

*These are references to captains, but whether to an army captain or a navy captain is not specified.

prize money he earned by capturing enemy ships would have to be shared with the admiral. In any case, Admiral Louis's squadron was engaged in blockade duty, which offered little chance of prize money anyway; few ships would leave port and sail directly into the arms of a superior enemy force. A better appointment would have been to a frigate, cruising alone in the hope of catching one or two prizes at a time and trusting to speedy sailing to escape from any sizable French force. Charles, too, served as a flag-captain, this time to his cousin-in-law Admiral Sir Thomas Williams.

Even admirals (*MP* 43, 60, 232, 266, 400; *P* 20, 68, 169) were subject to the vagaries of politics and nepotism. In December 1810, Francis got a plum assignment as flag-captain to Admiral Gambier aboard the *Caledonia* (120), a magnificent three-decker, but by spring of the next year the unpopular Gambier was moved from the *Caledonia*, and the new admiral turned it into a "family ship," bringing his brother and son-in-law aboard and displacing Francis. Really unfortunate admirals saw flag-worthy commands being given not to admirals but to well-connected captains, according to Thomas Cochrane, who complained of favored captains receiving "large commands of six or seven sail of the line, as many frigates and as many sloops of war," while "there are admirals of ability who have lingered in neglect." His comments lend credence to Mary Crawford's observations about admirals feeling "that they are all passed over, and all very ill used" (*MP* 60).

There was a hierarchy within the ranks of the admirals (*MP* 109, 111). Rear admiral was the most junior rank, followed by vice admiral, and then full admiral. Mary Crawford's ill-considered double entendre turns on the gradations of rank:

> Certainly, my home at my uncle's brought me acquainted with a circle of admirals. Of *Rears*, and *Vices*, I saw enough. Now, do not be suspecting me of a pun, I entreat. (*MP* 60)

Within each rank of admirals, there were three levels. A man began as a rear admiral of the blue, then became a rear admiral of the white (*P* 21), then a rear admiral of the red. The next jump took him to vice admiral of the blue, then of the white, then of the red, and in the same way through the divisions of full admirals. The most senior (full) admiral of the red graduated to the top rank: admiral of the fleet, a rank Francis Austen reached in 1863. When an admiral was sailing aboard a ship, it carried special flags (*MP* 60) to indicate his presence and exact rank. Admirals of the red had a solid red flag flown from the top of one of the masts, admirals of the white a white flag with a red cross, and admirals of the blue a solid blue flag. Rear admirals flew this flag from the mizzen or rear mast, vice admirals from the foremast, and full admirals from the mainmast (*MP* 152). The admiral of the fleet, in place of these, flew a Union Jack from the mainmast. Each admiral also flew a flag from the stern of the ship—solid red, solid blue, or white with a red cross—with one of its upper quadrants filled by the Union Jack.

Set as it were to the side of this hierarchy were two sets of officers who did not rise through the ranks in the same manner. Ships usually had a surgeon (*MP* 380, 384), who might be a man of relatively little medical experience. One of his duties was to revive men who were being flogged, but his job was principally to tend to wounds during battle, a grisly business performed without anaesthetic and in highly unsanitary conditions. Men were brought to him not in order of the seriousness of their injuries but in the order they had been wounded, with exceptions often made for officers, who tended to bypass the queue. It was considered especially noble in an officer to wait his proper turn in line. Surgeons afloat, like surgeons ashore, were on the fringes of gentility. They were not full physicians, with university educations, and their treatment by the other officers depended to a great extent on their affability and manners.

The other quasi officer was the chaplain (*Harley, MW* 40; *Plan, MW* 429; *MP* 111). His presence was not as much a necessity as the surgeon's, as the captain was authorized to act as a chaplain and to read a passage from the Bible to the crew on Sundays. The chaplain was a warrant officer, ranking lower therefore than the commissioned officers such as lieutenants and captains and being approximate in rank to a master gunner, though he might vastly exceed the gunner in education. He received about £12 a year plus fourpence per crewman in salary, a very small rate of pay compared with a good living ashore. Therefore, chaplains tended to be rather desperate men who had been unable to scrape together a living as curates or schoolmasters on land. At one time during Austen's life, there were 282 ships with berths for chaplains and only 39 chaplains in service aboard them. This state of affairs was of little concern to most naval captains, who found talk of religion and brotherhood at variance with the average sailor's earnest desire to kill the enemy. Jane's very religious brother Francis no doubt took a different view from the majority. (Her more practical eldest brother, James, bought a chaplain's berth and the salary that came with it but never bothered to occupy it.)

Given the experience of Austen's brothers, it is hardly surprising that she confines herself to the officers of ships. However, her readers would have known that a typical large naval ship carried a variety of specialists, such as a master gunner (whose wife was often entrusted with the care and feeding of the cabin boys), a cooper (traditionally known as "Bungs"), a carpenter (dubbed "Chips"), the captain's clerk, and the boatswain (*MP* 383) and his mates (who harried, shouted at, and sometimes struck the men to wake them and to keep them at their tasks). Below these were the seamen, divided by skill level and pay into able seamen, ordinary seamen, and landsmen. A fair number of women and boys might also be present.

The women were usually wives of warrant officers, but they were not present merely for companionship. They might cook, nurse the wounded, or, in battle, fetch powder and bring it to the gunners.

Officer Training

There were two principal routes to becoming an officer: the formal training offered by the Royal Naval Academy at Portsmouth (*Curate, MW* 73), and the hands-on training combined with some academic education offered by captains at sea (*P* 52). Both of Austen's brothers chose the former route, or had it chosen for them, but in this they were not typical. Enrollment at the academy was never high during Jane's lifetime; Francis, who entered the academy in April 1786 at a few days shy of twelve years old, was one of a class of twelve; Charles, who matriculated in July 1791, was one of a class of only four. In fact, during the time that Jane would have had an interest in the academy, it was never more than half full. In 1792 to 1794, for example, there were only twenty-eight scholars in all. A typical incoming class numbered only six boys, despite the fact that scholarships were offered to a certain number of officers' sons. In part this was due to a negative impression of the moral climate at the school—not that shipboard life was a much better instructor in that area—and in part it was due to the fact that officers' sons could often find patronage without having to go to a special school.

The typical student at the academy entered at age twelve to fifteen, studied two or three years, and then went to sea. The Austens would have paid £25 per year in fees plus the cost of a uniform; no doubt they gave their boys a little pocket money as well. The curriculum, according to articles drawn up in 1773, was "Writing, Arithmetick, Drawing, Navigation, Gunnery, Fortification, and other useful Parts of the Mathematicks; and also in the French Language, Dancing, Fencing, and the Exercise of the Firelock [musket]." The "other useful Parts of the Mathematicks" included logarithms, geometry, trigonometry, navigational calculation, surveying, mechanics, chronology (the study of the measurement of time, useful for using precise clocks to calculate longitude at sea), and astronomy (which enabled position at sea to be confirmed). French and dancing were useful for diplomatic purposes, while drawing, surveying, and writing were essential for making maps, sketches, and records during one's voyages. It appears that classes were also held in ship construction; Charles Austen, according to the academy's shipwright, learned

> the manner of bringing to and fastening the Main Wales, Lower, Upper, Quarter Deck & Forecastle Clamps, Scarphing the beams etc. of the Swift Sloop—also the use of the Draught, laying off and taking the Bevellings of the Square and Cant Timbers, Crossing and levelling the Floors, getting up and securing the Frame bends and the use of the Bollard Timbers and Nause Pieces.

This was not the full extent of his studies, for the shipwright mentioned several other facets of ship construction that Charles' class had learned, using captured French ships and British ships under construction as models.

Once his training was complete, an academy student could go aboard a ship as a "volunteer." This meant he served without official rank but was treated as an honorary midshipman; some captains resented this system, which was seen as an infringement on their traditional method of educating officers. This was to take several "servants" aboard, four for each 100 men assigned to the ship, each of whom was in training to be an officer. Some of these so-called servants would have been taken on as favors to other officers or patrons; others would buy their way in, thus increasing the captain's salary. These young officers in training, typically twelve or thirteen years old (*S&S* 103), had to bring a uniform (*MP* 390), a sea chest filled with a few belongings (*MP* 305), and an allowance for their food and supplies of perhaps £30 to £40 per year. Thomas Cochrane, in his autobiography, reports being outfitted for sea at a cost of £100, but then he was the son of a peer.

Captains' servants learned exactly what the academy graduates did, once they were finally at sea (*MP* 21, 377; *P* 50). They handled ropes and sails, engaged in gunnery drills, navigated, kept logs, and learned how to manage sailors. Perhaps most important of all, they learned how to cultivate the goodwill of their fellow shipmates. The Reverend George Austen, writing to the newly assigned volunteer Francis Austen, advised friendly, but carefully measured, conduct to all:

> The little world, of which you are going to become an inhabitant, will occasionally have it in their power to contribute no little share to your pleasure or pain; to conciliate therefore their goodwill, by every honourable method, will be the part of a prudent man. Your commander and officers will be most likely to become your friends by a respectful behaviour to themselves, and by an active and ready obedience to orders. Good humour, an inclination to oblige and the carefully avoiding every appearance of selfishness, will infallibly secure you the regards of your own mess and of all your equals. With your inferiors perhaps you will have but little intercourse, but when it does occur there is a sort of kindness they have a claim on you for, and which, you may believe me, will not be thrown away upon them.

"Frank" appears not to have heeded all of this advice; in later years, he became known as a "flogging" captain.

Pay

The base rate of pay in the navy was not especially bad by the standards of the time, but neither was it lavish. An officer's pay was based not on seniority but on the type of ship he commanded; for example, when Francis Austen moved from the fourth-rate *Leopard* (fifty guns) to the third-rate *Canopus* (eighty guns), his salary increased from £182 10s. 0d. to £237 a year, plus miscellaneous payments that approximately doubled his income. Lieutenants, too, were paid on a sliding scale, those on first- or second-rate ships receiving £7 per lunar month, while all others made £5 12s. Captains were "paid off" (*P* 50) at the end of a voyage, when all relevant paperwork, including the ship's log, had been submitted to the Admiralty; this caused Francis some trouble on one occasion, when a fierce storm damaged many of his papers. He had to have all of his logs reconstructed, delaying his payment until nearly two years after his command in the ship had ended. Another difficulty that captains faced was their responsibility for entertaining fellow officers and distinguished guests, which added significantly to expenses, and the larger the ship, the more onerous these expenses became. He had to buy his own provisions, plate and glassware, uniforms, navigational instruments, telescopes, and charts. He also had to pay up to £80 for his own chronometer, a clock that kept to London time and thus, by showing the difference between local noon and London noon, enabled him to establish his longitude.

Captains could, however, supplement their income in various ways. They could, for example, carry freight for the government or for private interests, which was good for the captains but not altogether advantageous for the navy, as hopeful captains might hover near friendly ports in hope of cargo rather than patrolling the waters for the enemy. An extremely profitable type of cargo was "Company Treasure" or "Treasure Money," the proceeds of the East India Company's ventures. In exchange for carrying this currency, a captain would receive a 1 to 2 percent commission; the ultimate authority in distributing such largesse was the governor-general of India, Warren Hastings, who, as it happened, was an Austen family friend. Merchants might also reward diligent captains for protecting their shipping convoys; Francis Austen was, at various times from 1808 to 1809, awarded sums of 200 guineas, 400 guineas, and 500 guineas for convoying East India Company ships. In 1810, he delivered ninety-three chests of company treasure, receiving £1,500 in compensation for his efforts. Cash awards were also sometimes made in cases of valor in battle, as after Trafalgar (*P* 21–22), when Lloyd's Patriotic Fund gave prizes of £25 to £100 to lieutenants and the wounded of the victorious ships. Rewards of this kind were not always directly paid in money. At times, merchants or city governments awarded heroic or conscientious officers with ceremonial swords or gifts of plate. The Trafalgar captains got swords from Lloyd's, and Francis Austen received a gold medal and a vase for his part in the Battle of St. Domingo.

The dread of all officers in peacetime was going on half pay (*Sand, MW* 401); officers still nominally part of the service, but not blessed with active commands, were kept on the books but paid only half their regular salary. Prints, poems, and other printed material often documented the plight of half-pay officers, who had fought for the nation but could seldom make ends meet. The unfortunate Captain Benwick is just such a man, discarded after heroic service, "turned . . . on shore" (*P* 233). On June 8, 1814, the Admiralty announced an attempt to ameliorate the condition of half-pay officers, raising the pay scale somewhat, making the payments twice as frequently, and adjusting pay levels to reflect seniority. It was still a pittance; Charles Austen, on leaving active service in 1816, would have made just £192 a year, an income that any of Austen's heroes or heroines would have considered poverty-level.

Below the officer ranks, pay dropped substantially. An able seaman, who had to be thoroughly adept at his trade, earned only 22s. per month, while an ordinary seaman earned 19s., rates that had not been raised since the mid-seventeenth century. Sea fencibles, a kind of anti-invasion seaside militia, made rather more—a shilling a day in the early nineteenth century—but they were not part of the regular navy.* Seaman Jack Nastyface described the method of paying the crew:

> In the early part of the day, the Commissioners came on board bringing the money which is paid the ship's crew, with the exception of six months pay, which it is the rule of the government to hold back from each man. The mode of paying is, as the names are, by rotation, on the books. Every man when called, is asked for his hat, which is returned to him with his wages in it and the amount chalked on the rim. There is not perhaps one in twenty who actually knows what he is going to receive, nor does the particular amount seem to be of a matter of much concern; for, when paid, they hurry down to their respective berths, redeem their honour with their several ladies and bomb-boat men and then they turn their thoughts to the Jew pedlars, who are ranged round the decks and in the hatchway gratings, in fact the ship is crowded with them.

It was also customary, upon payment of wages, for the men to get extremely drunk. A sailor's pay rarely lasted long.

Prize Money

Officers and common sailors alike dreamed of the ultimate financial bonus, prize money (*MP* 375; *P* 17, 96). This was awarded by the Admiralty for various types of victorious naval encounters. When an enemy ship was captured, the value of its cargo was assessed, and sometimes the ship itself was "purchased into the service," that is, turned into a British naval vessel and rechristened. About 450 ships were so purchased during the French Wars, and a well-equipped thirty-two-gun frigate could be valued at £16,000, a sizable sum. (Here, as elsewhere, political influence could be an important factor. Thomas Cochrane complained of "worthless vessels"

---

*One of Francis Austen's duties in the navy was organizing fencibles from his base in Ramsgate.

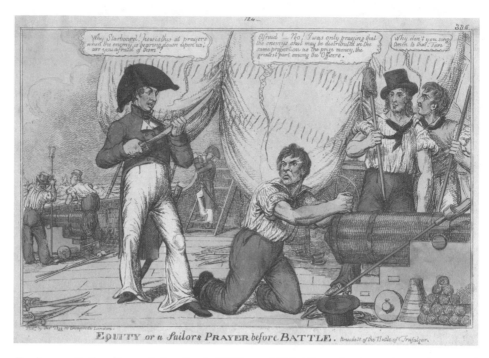

Equity or a Sailors Prayer before Battle, Williams, 1805. The sailor is praying to be spared in the coming battle but "that the enemys shot may be distributed in the same proportion as the prize money, the greatest part among the Officers." Courtesy of the Lewis Walpole Library, Yale University. 805.0.9.

being bought into the service to please captains with politically influential relatives.) The captain and crew received a fixed percentage of the total value—for a merchantman, an average of about £2,500—with rank playing the principal role in the distribution of the spoils.

From 1708 to 1808, the captain received three-eighths of the prize money; any marine or army captains aboard, all the naval lieutenants, the ship's master, and the surgeon split another eighth equally between them; another eighth was split by marine and army lieutenants, the admiral's secretary, the chaplain, the master's mates, and the superior warrant officers; another eighth was shared by inferior warrant officers, midshipmen, marine sergeants, and the mates of the superior warrant officers; and the remaining fourth was shared by the rest of the crew. Amendments in 1808 took away one of the captain's eighths and gave half the prize money to the bottom two categories. By the time the last eighths were distributed among the bulk of the crew, the sums could be quite small. For example, the *Peterel*, in April 1799, captured a boat with a cargo of 9,000 Spanish dollars in foreign currency. The prize money awarded totaled 1,469 Spanish dollars, of which the average petty officer received only 10¼ Spanish dollars and the average foremast man only 2 Spanish dollars.

If the captain were sailing under the direct command of a flag officer, such as a commodore, captain of the fleet, or an admiral, he had to share his loot. Prior to 1808, the flag officer(s) got one of the captain's three-eighths; after 1808, they got one-third of his share. When there was more than one flag officer with a right to claim part of the prize, senior officers got a larger share. However, it was sometimes the case that captains operated under Admiralty orders, with no intervening commander, and in this case they got to keep all their prize money, once it made its way through the slow and expensive "prize courts" that administered awards.

Prize money varied widely. Luck was certainly a factor, but it helped to be clever, to have a fast and powerful ship such as a frigate, and to be stationed close to enemy shipping lanes. Francis Austen, for all his good fortune in convoying valuable cargo, was often stuck on blockade duty, where he paced back and forth waiting for enemy ships to steal out of harbor while having few chances to capture anything. Those manning captured ships were unluckiest of all, for their ships were not officially commissioned by the navy. If a "prize crew" captured another enemy ship on the way back to a friendly port, the new prize and all its goods became the property of the Admiralty.

Prize money certainly added to the zeal of English crews and served as a powerful incentive to enlistment. It also emphasized the intact capture of ships and their cargoes, as ships sunk counted for far less in Admiralty eyes than ships that could be used in the service. Destroyed ships, however, earned a lesser reward: "head and gun" money, calculated according either to the crew size or gun complement of the enemy ship. Admiral Thomas Cochrane complained in his autobiography that the French, hoping to avoid capture, would often run their ships aground once it was clear that a battle was lost, thus depriving the English crews of the chance to salvage the ships and cargoes. Sometimes, a captured ship would be recaptured before it could be brought into a friendly port. At other times, nature intervened; after Trafalgar, most of the seized French ships were so badly damaged that most of those not destroyed in the battle were lost in a subsequent storm; only one ship made it to Gibraltar in usable condition.

Not all prizes, however, were ships. Captured cities could also be a gold mine to a fortunate captain or admiral. All arms, ammunition, and military supplies in captured fortifications belonged to the victor, as did ships captured in port and the goods of conquered (but not voluntarily surrendered) towns.

On occasion, a captured cargo could be more of a burden than a blessing. Cochrane recalled capturing a substantial load of French wine, but similar seizures had glutted the market at Plymouth, and he could not find a good price. However, as a luxury commodity, the wine was subject to a stiff import duty, which he was still required to pay. Unable to pay the duty out of his pocket, he was forced to dump most of the wine overboard.

In most cases, however, prizes were definitely welcome. A skillful and lucky captain could make his fortune (*MP* 60; *P* 17, 27, 247) at sea, and some could make more than one fortune. Frigate captain Josias Rogers made huge sums during the American Revolution, lost half of it when a bank failed, and said, philosophically, "Cheer up, I'll go to sea and get more." In five weeks alone he took nine prizes, which would, had he received their full value, have brought him £10,000. Another captain, Robert Otway, took £50,000 in prizes in only six years. Captain Wentworth's £20,000–25,000 are not without precedent (*P* 75, 248).

Daily Life in the Navy

Life in the navy could be difficult, demanding, and unpredictable. Mail delivery was erratic at best, as a ship could be suddenly ordered away to another station with very little notice (*MP* 377–378, 388). The Austen family letters often reflect this reality. Letters (*P* 51) to and from Charles and Frank might arrive very late or out of order, so the family adopted the practice of many naval families, numbering their letters so that they could be put in order again upon arrival. As she was unsure where her letters might find him, Jane wrote to Francis twice to announce the death of their father in 1805; one letter went to Dungeness, while the other pursued him to Portsmouth. Frank numbered his letters, too. On October 18, 1805, he wrote to his fiancée Mary Gibson that

> your No. 3 has come to hand; it was brought by Brigadier-General Tilson, and was enclosed under cover from Henry. It has been months on the journey. There are still three of yours missing, Nos. 5, 6 and 7, some of which I suppose are gone to seek me in the West Indies.

In typical naval fashion, Frank had been ordered on an arduous journey to the West Indies in pursuit of the French fleet and then back again across the Atlantic to a blockade off Trafalgar.

Naval officers and sailors often missed their families at home (*MP* 232). Parents and spouses died, children were born, finances improved or collapsed, all at a distance and without any knowledge of when a reunion might come. This state of affairs was made even worse during wartime, when the family at home worried constantly about death in battle. At all times, death from disease or accident was a distinct possibility, and the Austens liked to hear frequently from their sailor sons, to be assured of their continuing health. Mr. Austen wrote Frank at the outset of his naval career,

> As you must be convinced it would be the highest satisfaction to us to hear as frequently as possible from you, you will of course neglect no opportunity of giving us that pleasure, and being very minute in what relates to

yourself and your situation. On this account, and because unexpected occasions of writing to us may offer, 'twill be a good way always to have a letter in forwardness. You may depend on hearing from some of us at every opportunity.

Worries about health and welfare extended to any dependents who sailed as well. Jane fretted over the condition of her niece Cassy, Charles' daughter, whom she thought looked thin and unwell due to her life aboard Charles' ship. Cassy had been experiencing another of the discomforts of life at sea: motion sickness.

The pseudonymous sailor Jack Nastyface included, in his memoirs, a vivid description of life aboard a man-of-war. At 4:00 A.M., he wrote, a new watch came on deck and began holystoning the deck:

> Here the men suffer from being obliged to kneel down on the wetted deck and a gravelly sort of sand strewed over it. To perform this work is very injurious. In this manner the watch continues till about four bells or 6 o'-clock; they then begin to wash and scrub the decks till seven bells, and at eight bells the boatswain's mate pipes to breakfast. This meal usually consists of burgoo made of coarse oatmeal and water; others will have scotch coffee which is burnt bread boiled in some water and sweetened with sugar. This is generally cooked in a hook-pot in the galley where there is a range. Nearly all the crew have one of these pots, a spoon and a knife; for these are things indispensable. There are also basons, plates, etc. which are kept in each mess, which generally consists of eight persons who berth in between two of the guns on the lower deck, where there is a board placed which swings with the rolling of the ship and dash all the crockery to pieces; they are then obliged to eat out of wooden or tin utensils, until they come into harbour.

Punishments at 11:00 A.M. were followed by dinner at 12:00,

> and this is the pleasantest part of the day, as at one bell the fifer is called to play "Nancy Dawson" or some other lively tune, a well known signal that the grog is ready to be served out. It is the duty of the cook from each mess to fetch and serve it out to his messmates, of which every man and boy is allowed a pint, that is one gill of rum and three of water, to which is added lemon acid sweetened with sugar. Here I must remark that the cook comes in for the perquisites of office by reserving to himself an extra portion of grog, which is called the over-plus and generally comes to the double of a man's allowance. Thus the cook can take upon himself to be the man of consequence, for he has the opportunity of inviting a friend to partake of a glass, or of paying any little debt he may have contracted.

Cooks who neglected their duties, he reported, were judged by a jury of cooks from different messes; each man took a turn serving as cook for his own group of messmates. Supper, he said, consisted of "half a pint of wine or a pint of grog to each man with biscuit, and cheese, or butter."

Food was always of great concern to the navy, for sailors needed an immense number of calories in order to perform their strenuous duties, and the problem of providing the quantity of food needed for huge numbers of men over long periods of time in limited space was always vexing. Officers filled their own larders. Some brought live animals aboard to be slaughtered as needed, while others brought preserved food of various kinds; Frank Austen once took six hams cured by his mother. On occasion, livestock was bought in port, and the leftover hides might even be tanned aboard ship; Thomas Cochrane reported just such an arrangement aboard the *Barfleur*, which thereby acquired the nickname "the stinking Scotch ship" from the smell of its rotting bullock hides.

There was a limited understanding of scurvy and the role played by fresh provisions in its prevention, though vitamin C, the preventive compound, was a long way from being discovered. Cochrane was in favor of fresh as opposed to salt provisions whenever possible, believing that lime juice alone could not adequately combat scurvy. Salt-preserved food was blamed for everything from general weakness to dysentery, and various types of food were tried as supplements, from sauerkraut to potatoes.

Likewise, there was a good deal of fiddling with the alcoholic beverages consumed by the crew. Grog was the standard drink aboard ship. This was a lightly alcoholic mixture of rum, fruit juice, and water, that was given various names depending on the proportion of rum to water. "Three-water grog," the default recipe, had a ratio of one part rum to three parts water, while "five-water grog"—a mutinously weak drink—had a ratio of 1:5. Experimenters replaced the grog, from time to time, with wine or spruce beer, but these innovations were not popular. Grog and beer were considered the only decent beverages for a sailor, and substitutions were rarely tolerated for long.

The average sailor's diet, however, despite efforts at reform, remained monotonous, copious, and heavily salted. Salt fish, beef, and pork were supplemented with cheese, beer, bread, and "biscuit." The last of these was a hard, round or hexagonal piece of bread, stamped with an iron press to insert holes and to stamp upon it the "broad arrow"—a simple crow's-foot pattern indicating that the biscuit was the property of the navy. Biscuits were to be no more than a fifth of a pound in weight and were stored in barrels.

The officers ate their meals off pewter or silver plates, while the men ate off square wooden plates—hence, "three square meals a day"—with a lip to prevent food from falling off the plates in rough seas. It is possibly a pewter mess kit that William Price seeks from William Turner, a merchant who was recorded as arranging supplies for sailors in Portsmouth in 1811.*

---

*The Austens were acquainted with Turner, who was proposed as an agent for sending a letter to Francis in 1805 and who supplied a rug and corks to Charles in 1808 and 1815, respectively.

In their leisure hours, the men sewed new clothes for themselves, combed lice and fleas from their long hair, and plaited their pigtails and sealed them with tar. Some sang, told stories, or played music. Gambling was rife. Officers might read, keep logs and journals, or lead the men in amateur theatrical presentations.

One activity that was seldom allowed was shore leave. Officers were frequently terrified that their men would desert—a very sensible fear with regard to pressed men—and rarely permitted this greatest of all pleasures. Instead, they let prostitutes come aboard the ship, while peddlers pulled alongside in small boats to offer food, drink, and trinkets for sale. Thomas Cochrane found this state of affairs intolerable, especially as the most senior Admiralty officials lived comfortably on land for long stretches of time. In a parliamentary debate on the subject, he snapped, "With respect to the assertion made by the same gentleman that the health of the men is increased by long cruises at sea, and that of the Commander-in-chief is improved by being on shore, he may reconcile that if he can." Restrictions on shore leave were considerably lighter for the officers than for the men (*MP* 233).

Accommodations, too, were better for the officers, but not by much. They had shared or private cabins, while the men had only fourteen to sixteen inches in which to sling a hammock, but the cabins were usually minuscule, and only the captain enjoyed the remotest approximation of privacy. Thomas Cochrane's first command, the *Speedy*, was a tiny 158-ton sloop packed with eighty-four men and six officers; his cabin

> had not so much as room for a chair, the floor being entirely occupied by a small table surrounded by lockers, answering the double purpose of storechests and seats. The difficulty was to get seated, the ceiling being only five feet high, so that the object could only be accomplished by rolling on the locker. . . . The most singular discomfort, however, was that my only practicable mode of shaving consisted in removing the skylight and putting my head through to make a toilet-table of the quarter-deck.

Still, though life aboard ship was cramped and often uncomfortable, it was not without its conveniences, especially for the officers, who had personal servants to pour their wine, serve their food, and tend to their uniforms (*P* 64). Mrs. Croft found the life quite acceptable, but she was not necessarily typical. Other officers' wives found life aboard ship intolerable, what with seasickness, the fear of death in battle, and the lack of privacy. Betsey Fremantle, who accompanied her husband, Thomas, on a voyage, was disturbed by storms, the noise of the guns, the groans of the wounded, and the brutality of flogging. Partly for the sake of the wives but mostly to avoid distraction, officers' wives were discouraged from accompanying their husbands on their voyages (*P* 31).

Uniforms

Uniforms varied both by rank and by time period. The common sailors wore no particular uniform, dressing in shirts, trousers, jackets, and sometimes waistcoats, all of varying colors. The officers had two types of uniforms—full dress uniforms for formal occasions and undress uniforms for their day-to-day duties. From 1787 to 1795, the undress uniform for midshipmen was a single-breasted navy-blue jacket with a white patch on the collar, relatively unadorned sleeves and pocket flaps, and small buttons with anchors on them. Commanders, captains, and admirals had increasing amounts of gold lace on their cuffs, collars, pockets, and jacket lapels; rank was indicated by the button pattern and the shape of the lace on the lapels. Rank was also reflected to some extent in the type of buttons used. Lieutenants (*MP* 384), commanders, and captains had buttons showing an anchor surrounded by two loops of rope, while admirals had an anchor with a partial border of laurel leaves. Waistcoats (*MP* 381) and breeches were white (and remained so throughout Austen's lifetime). Dress uniforms in this period, the period in which Austen's brothers were just joining the service, were very similar, but had somewhat more gold lace, plus white lapels and cuffs for lieutenants and captains. In both the dress and undress uniforms, officers wore cocked hats (*MP* 381), with commanders and above wearing gold lace on their hats.

From 1795 to 1812, undress uniforms were stripped of almost all their gold lace adornment, and button arrangement no longer identified an officer's rank. Instead, this distinction was made through the use of epaulets. Midshipmen and lieutenants had none; the difference between their uniforms remained the lapels on the lieutenants' uniforms, the white patch on the midshipmen's collars, and differences in buttons and in pocket decoration. Commanders got an epaulet on the left shoulder, captains of fewer than three years in their rank an epaulet on the right, captains of more than three years' seniority epaulets on both shoulders. Admirals, too, had two epaulets, with one star on each for a rear admiral, two each for a vice admiral, and three each for a full admiral. Full dress uniforms, again, were much the same, except for white lapels on the lieutenant's uniform and a general wealth of gold lace around the collars, lapels, pockets, and cuffs.

Uniforms changed once again in 1812 and remained unchanged again until after Austen's death. The admiral of the fleet was given a special undress uniform, while commanders graduated to two unadorned epaulets, and captains of less than and more than three years' seniority got special decorations on theirs: anchors in the former case, anchors and crowns in the latter. Full dress uniforms regained their white lapels for all ranks.

Duties aboard Ship

The duties performed by officers and men have already been detailed to some extent above. It is important to remember that, except in very demanding weather, the actual sailing of the ship took only a fraction of the crew's time. A significant amount of time was spent on maintenance, cleaning, drilling on the massive guns, record keeping, training in the use of small firearms, and navigating. When other ships were encountered, signals would have to be sent back and forth to determine the identity and nationality of the ships, and if both ships were from friendly nations, mail and news might be exchanged. Live animals kept as food sources or as ship's mascots had to be fed and cared for, and food stored in barrels had to be maintained. As the food was used up, the barrels themselves were disassembled to save space and were reassembled as needed when new supplies were gathered. On occasion, officers' family members needed to be ferried from one port to another to be near their loved ones; while captains' wives were discouraged from living aboard ship, the practice was usually overlooked, and it was considered perfectly acceptable for an officer's family to live in the port nearest to his duties (*P* 68–69).

Navigation was accomplished with a variety of tools, including the octant, so-called because it was in the shape of one-eighth of a circle; this was used to measure the altitude of celestial objects. Spyglasses could distinguish landmarks along coastlines, while astronomical charts and an instrument called a "nocturnal" helped calculate position by the stars. The height of the sun at noon determined latitude, on days when the sun could be seen through the clouds, and longitude was calculated by means of lunar observations and comparisons of ship's time with Greenwich time. Depth and the composition of the ocean bottom could be compared to existing charts by throwing out the lead, a length of rope, normally twenty fathoms (120 feet) long, weighted at one end with a lump of lead that usually weighed seven pounds. (A longer line, up to 1,200 feet in length, and with a heavier lead weight, was used in deep water.) The lead was cast overboard and depth recorded; if the bottom of the weight was "armed" with tallow or grease, the silt, shells, or sand on the ocean floor would stick to it, giving some idea of the character of the bottom. Finally, the navigator(s) used charts, knowledge of the ship's direction, and estimates of the ship's speed to plot position. None of these methods alone were accurate by modern standards, but taken together, they enabled the officers to be reasonably sure of their position most of the time.

Calculating a ship's speed had its own set of tools: a twenty-eight-second glass and a log line. The first was a small "hourglass," and the second was a length of rope marked at intervals with knots (hence, "knots" as measurements of naval velocity). One end of the line was hurled overboard, and the rope was unwound as the ship moved. When the twenty-eight-second glass had run its course, the line was stopped and the number of knots counted.

Periodically, the ships had to be resupplied, and this necessitated finding a friendly port and then negotiating with the local authorities. Acquiring freshwater was a huge task in itself; Francis, in 1807, described getting water at Simon's Bay during a convoying voyage to the Cape of Good Hope. At first the crew used hoses and pipes that ran down to the wharf, but that system, ingenious as it sounds, was somewhat unsatisfactory. In the end, he had to fall back on the more traditional method of filling casks in local streams and floating them back to the ship on rafts.

Battle was not a routine occurrence, even in the war years. Many ships did convoy duty, protecting merchant fleets and rarely, if ever, seeing serious combat. Sailor John Nicol called convoy duty "monotonous," and his was one of the kinder characterizations. Others spent long months on blockade duty, tacking back and forth along the same stretch of water, waiting for the emergence of an enemy fleet. Sometimes, at long last, it came out and a battle ensued, as at Trafalgar (which Francis Austen missed, having been sent to resupply at Gibraltar). Many times, however, the enemy ships sat infuriatingly idly in a safe harbor, refusing to offer themselves up as prizes. Blockade duty was frustrating not only for the officers, whose hopes of fortune depended on victory in battle, but also for the men, who were mocked by civilians and by sailors on more active duty. Jack Nastyface explained the situation:

> [W]e soon found we had become *Channel Gropers*, a term given to the Channel fleet in wartime, which is destined to hover about Brest when the wind is fair, for the French fleet to come out, as we were blockading this; and when the wind blows strong into the harbour, so that they could not well get out; in those cases our fleet would sometimes put in at Cows and or Torbay, and might be what sailors call a *fresh beef station*, but it is such as few seamen like, for they say it is neither being abroad nor at home. One reason why they have a dislike of it is that they are open to the ridicule of seamen who may be coming from foreign stations, as well as by the girls and people in the sea-port towns, by cantingly telling them they would never have the scurvy or that they might as well be by their mother's fireside and tied to the apron-strings, as merely running in and out of harbour; and nothing hurts Jack's [i.e., a sailor's] feelings more than being taunted of anything unmanly or inferior.

One argument in favor of blockades, other than the obvious one of keeping the enemy fleet out of action and its merchant vessels idle, was that it kept the English in constant sailing practice, while the French sailors lost their edge in port. This, however, was small consolation to the blockaders.

Even more tedious were administrative duties onshore, which offered little hope of promotion or profit. Francis Austen spent a few years stuck in this sort of post, raising and training a force of "sea fencibles" in Kent. These were mostly armed fishermen, manning tiny boats and hoping to thwart a feared French invasion. Wordsworth celebrated the "men of Kent" in a sonnet, but Francis feared they were underprepared and must have known he was being shelved in an unattractive job. Still, he did his duty, studying the coastline, tides, and weather patterns to determine Napoleon's most probable landing points. By January 1804, he had a force of 250 men and 17 boats. He had also determined that a French invasion would most likely take place at Pegwell Bay, which had favorable tides and an absence of cliffs.*

Though the days of maximum imperial reach were in the future, Britain already had colonial interests throughout the world. Some ships cruised off the East India Station (*P* 22), where both Francis and Charles served for part of their careers; this included not only India but also places such as China and Burma. The North American Station included mostly Canada after the loss of the United States, while the West Indies Station (*MP* 236) included Britain's possessions in the Caribbean; the latter region was a constant battleground, as various European powers sought to snatch poorly guarded, but highly profitable, sugar islands from each other. Charles spent a great deal of time in both areas, some of it after Jane's death. The Home Station defended British waters and offered little excitement but more contact with family and friends; Francis, while serving as a lieutenant in these waters, was part of the squadron that delivered Princess Caroline of Brunswick, future wife of the prince regent (George IV), to England. Gibraltar was the principal base for ships that cruised the Mediterranean (*MP* 236), like the Caribbean a hotbed of activity because so much French-controlled territory fronted the sea. Some ships were less important for their naval function than as troop carriers for land engagements; others, in small groups, guarded as many as 250 to 300 merchant vessels in the Baltic or searched for enemy vessels in the North Sea.

Sailors' Behavior

Sailors were certainly not renowned for pious or mannerly behavior. John Nicol, who served in the navy from 1774 to 1783 and 1794 to 1801 and who served in the merchant marine in peacetime, wrote in his memoirs that he had begun his naval career by engaging in daily prayer and Bible study, but that these habits were gradually abandoned, "and, before long, I was a sailor like the rest." Jack Nastyface noted that the more experienced sailors loved to play tricks on new colleagues, heaping ridicule on them and playing pranks such as mutilating their clothing and stealing their shoes and blankets while their victims slept by using fishhooks and fishing line. Sailors whored, swore, and drank heavily. Samuel Leech, who served in the War of 1812, was repulsed—or at least affected to be repulsed—by the moral climate at sea:

> There are few worse places than a man of war for the favourable development of the moral character in a boy. Profanity in its most revolting aspect;

*Pegwell Bay was only seven miles from Goodnestone, the home of Lady Bridges (mother of Edward Austen's wife); given the family connections, the fear of a French invasion must have been palpable among the Austens.

licentiousness in its most shameful and beastly garbs; vice in the worst Proteus-like shapes, abound there. While scarcely a moral restraint is thrown round the victim, the meshes of temptation are spread about his path in every direction. Bad as things are at sea, they are worse in port. There boatloads of defiled and defiling women are permitted to come alongside; the men looking over the side, select whoever best pleases his lustful fancy and by paying her fare, he is allowed to take and keep her on board as his paramour, until the ship is once more ordered to sea.

Drunkenness, above all, was rampant, especially in the West Indies, where men believed it would protect them from tropical diseases. Leech wrote that

To be drunk is considered by almost every sailor as the acme of sensual bliss, while many fancy that swearing and drinking are necessary accomplishments in a genuine man-of-war's man. Hence it almost universally prevails. In our ship the men would get drunk, in defiance of every restriction. Were it not for the moral and physical ruin which follows its use, one might laugh at the various contrivances adopted to elude the vigilance of officers in their efforts to procure ruin. Some of our men who belonged to boats' crews provided themselves with bladders; if left ashore by their officers a few moments they would slip into the first grocery, fill their bladders and return with the spoil. Once by the ship's side the favourable moment was seized to pass the interdicted bladders into the portholes, to some watchful shipmate, by whom it was carefully secreted to be drunk at the first opportunity.

Another sailor, Samuel Stokes, wrote that when he had prize money, "I think I was not sober one hour while I was awake, while the money lasted."

In part, this decadent behavior was no doubt due to the rare opportunities to relieve a life of hard work and tedium interrupted only by brief periods of mortal danger. In part, it was a symptom of the eighteenth-century way of life, which at times reveled in cruelty, but to a large extent, it was also due to the nature of the shipboard population. The men, especially the pressed men, might be convicts or men who *ought* to have been convicts. Sailor George Watson recalled that there were all sorts aboard a man-of-war but that men of bad habits predominated:

[H]ere are (in disguise) highwaymen, burglars, pickpockets, debauchees, adulterers, gamesters, lampooners, bastard-getters, imposters, panders, parasites, ruffians, hypocrites, [and] thread worn beaux jack-a-dandies.

Behavior among the officer ranks was sometimes only slightly better. Lord Nelson, almost universally lauded as a hero, was widely known to be an adulterer, and he was not the only one; more than one titled officer tried to bring a mistress aboard. Jane Austen's Admiral Crawford may have been intended, says Brian Southam, to represent such a debauched character.

Hazards at Sea: Punishment

The dangers (*MP* 235, 236) and discomforts of life at sea included far more than a tendency to sunburn (*P* 19–20). Sailors might suffer from shortages of food or water, storms, boredom, homesickness (*P* 235), and "ruptures" (hernias). John Nicol, who served on the *Proteus* during the American Revolution, wrote of icy waters in Newfoundland that kept the ship out of harbor and of fog so thick that for three weeks the ship's bow could not be seen from the quarterdeck. At night, if a ship's lights were not properly set, it might be lost to sight and separated from its companions; Thomas Cochrane reported that the loss of convoy ships by morning was the rule rather than the exception. Another difficulty was the state of the ships themselves, which were in some cases old and out of repair (*P* 64–66) and in others slapped together so quickly or provisioned in such haste that lives were risked unnecessarily.

For the men, as opposed to the officers, there was always the fear of corporal punishment. This usually meant flogging (*MP* 440), a punishment attended with much ceremony and observed by the whole crew in the hope of deterring future bad behavior. Flogging could be imposed at the captain's discretion without a court-martial, and three dozen lashes was a typical sentence, although in one instance in 1795, when Francis Austen was a lieutenant, a man aboard his ship was given forty-nine lashes for theft. Flogging could be administered for a wide variety of crimes, including inattention to duty, improper performance of duties, drunkenness, mutinous talk, attempting to strike an officer, or failing to report promptly for one's watch.

Some captains were far more willing than others to order floggings, and these became known throughout the fleet as "flogging captains" or "tartars." They included Charles Paget (one of Charles Austen's superior officers), John Gore, Alexander Frazer (one of Francis' superiors), and, apparently, Francis Austen. Until 1811, reports of floggings were made only after a voyage's end, in the captain's and master's logs. In 1811, the system was altered, and quarterly Returns of Offences and Punishments were required; one of Francis' returns for 1813 reports ninety-eight floggings aboard the *Elephant*, and in a period of eleven months from April 1813 to March 1814, about 25 percent of the ship's crew was flogged— "about three times the average for the service," as Brian Southam notes. The situation was blamed on the persistent drunkenness of the crew, but Charles Austen faced similar difficulties aboard the *Aurora* in 1826 and, from June 1826 to June 1827, ordered only twenty-four floggings of only twenty-three men, or about 9 percent of the crew. Captains like Charles Austen and like Lord Nelson, who did not resort to floggings as a first recourse, were much appreciated by the sailors who served under them. Samuel Leech, who railed against the tyrannical sort of officers, acknowledged that there were many "humane, considerate [officers] . . . who deserve our highest respect."

Men due to be flogged were brought forward by the master-at-arms at about midday—Jack Nastyface gives the proper time as "[a]bout eleven o'clock or six bells"—and lashed to a wooden grating "by the wrists and knees." An announcement of each prisoner's offense was made, and each man had the opportunity to plead his case, but such pleas appear in most cases to have been futile. The punishment was administered with a cat o'-nine tails, a rope whip with nine 2-foot-long, ¼-inch thick strands, each of which had a knot somewhere along its length. The 2-foot-long handle of the cat was also made of rope and might be wrapped with red cloth. George Watson, who was at sea from 1806 to 1814, recalled how much the cat's "tails" hurt:

> I felt them so keenly, being the first and the last time they scratched my back, that I thought I would rather let the rogue that caused what I endured kick me overboard another time, than have those unnatural devil cats at my shoulders.

However, even though the punishment hurt, sailors were expected to be as stoic as possible.

Even worse than an ordinary flogging was "flogging through the fleet." Reserved for serious offenses where an example to all ships present was deemed necessary, such as attempted desertion, this was a circuit of floggings, one at each ship. Unlike a standard flogging, it could be administered only after a court-martial. The prisoner had stockings placed over his wrists to prevent the ropes from cutting into them as he writhed; he was lashed to a capstan bar and, attended by the master-of-arms and the ship's surgeon, was rowed from ship to ship. At each ship, boatswain's mates lashed him a specified number of times—about two dozen, according to Jack Nastyface—and then rolled him in a blanket for his journey to the next ship. If the man fainted, he would be held in the sick bay until he felt better, and then his punishment would resume. Nastyface wrote, "When there are many ships in the fleet at the time of the court martial, this ceremony, if the prisoner can sustain it, will last nearly half the day . . . . his back resembles so much petrified liver." John Nicol recounted the story of a man flogged through the fleet for stealing some treasure from a captured ship. This unfortunate sailor drank a large quantity of rum beforehand to dull his pain, but the stratagem was discovered, and the remainder of his punishment was "delayed until he was sober." His back, according to Nicol, was swollen "like a pillow, black and blue." Vinegar-soaked paper was laid on his wounds, and "his shrieks rent the air."

A common punishment for theft was running the gauntlet. The offender was seated in a tub which was then lashed to a grating and drawn between two rows of men. The boatswain began by giving the offender a dozen lashes, and then the men standing in rows were obliged to strike the prisoner as he passed with a "three yarn nettle," which Jack Nastyface describes as "three rope yarns tightly laid together and knotted." Periodically, the punishment administered by the ship's company was interrupted so that the boatswain's mates could lash him again with the cat o'nine tails. Running the gauntlet could be ordered by the captain without a court-martial.

These were the formal punishments, but there was also a great deal of "starting," an informal beating administered with a rope's end. Men thought to be in dereliction of duty were "started" by a boatswain's mate, who ordered the man to remove his jacket and struck him across the back with the rope's end. Jack Nastyface, always indignant about punishment, provides the best description of the process:

> The boatswain's mate then commences beating him and continues to do so until he is ordered to stop, or unless his arm is tired and then another boatswain's mate is called to go on with the ceremony. Some of these men's backs have often been so bad from the effects of the *starting system* that they have not been able to bear their jackets on for several days. As the punishment is inflicted without tying the man up, he will naturally endeavour to ward off or escape as many blows as possible, and in doing so, frequently gets a serious cut in the face or on the head. This punishment is so common that no mention is made of it even in the log book, and but few men in wartime can escape the above mode of punishment.

This seems to be one of the punishments that Mr. Price recommends for Maria Bertram's adultery (*MP* 440) and indicates that Jane Austen was not ignorant of disciplinary methods aboard ship.

There is also a reference in Austen's works to being "run up the yard-arm" (*P* 108). This could be a reference to the practice of keelhauling, obsolete in Austen's time but well known enough to have become archetypal for severity. In this type of punishment, a rope was slung from one yardarm to another, and the prisoner was raised to one yardarm, dunked in the ocean, and hauled up on the other side, half drowned and much battered by the sharp barnacles on the ship's hull. Austen's reference could equally refer to hangings for mutiny, which were traditionally conducted at the yardarm.

For officers, punishments were very different. A court-martial might issue a reprimand, cashier (dishonorably discharge) the officer involved, or reduce him in rank or seniority. An example of the process can be seen in the March 1807 court-martial of Sir Home Popham, who was accused of disobeying orders by leaving the Cape of Good Hope undefended while he took his squadron on an unauthorized and personally profitable mission to wrest Buenos Aires from the Spanish. Popham was a complex character who had, in 1805, been charged with skimming profits from the repair of his ship; although acquitted, the rumors alone were enough to taint his career. Deeply concerned with the health and safety of his men, he was an expert in combined sea and land maneuvers, the inventor of the sea fencibles, an experimenter with mines and torpedoes, and the creator of an efficient system of signaling that was used at Trafalgar. He was widely distrusted within the navy, however, considered a charlatan, and tarnished by reports of shady business dealings. Austen wrote a poem in his defense (*Popham, MW* 446), perhaps because of her Tory sympathies—Popham was a Tory—and perhaps because of some sort of indirect personal acquaintance, unproven but possible, as Francis Austen and Popham were in the East Indies at the same time, and Henry Austen may have been involved in Popham's attempts to profit from his South American adventure. The evidence in either case is entirely circumstantial. Popham, incidentally, experienced the fate of many reprimanded officers; with a change in government, he was back in favor again.

Hazards at Sea: Battle

A sailor's greatest fear, especially in the heat of the moment, was being killed in battle. Naval battles had once been gentlemanly affairs, in which frigates not taking direct part in a fleet-to-fleet combat were exempt from attack, but in the 1790s this attitude changed, and by the Battle of the Nile in 1798 all ships present were considered fair game. For the officers in particular, who stood to gain substantially both in prize money and in reputation, battle was a thing to be sought; Francis Austen regretted bitterly being temporarily absent from the fleet at the time of Trafalgar. Particularly valuable was "an action with some superior force" (*MP* 375), in which the skill of the officers was made evident, bringing them to the favorable attention of the Admiralty.

For the men, it was a different story. Their share of prize money was small, and their risk was enormous. Battle was confusing and terrifying, as the accounts of ordinary sailors attest. Samuel Leech's job was to run powder cartridges back and forth to his gun. He would dash to the magazine, where boys passed the powder through a hole in a wooden screen, cover a cartridge with his jacket "to prevent the powder taking fire before it reaches the gun," and hurry to the gun so that the crew could fire. He acknowledged being frightened the entire time, but he kept up a brave front because he had no choice, praying all the while to be spared. Though he was fortunate enough to survive the war, he saw his share of death in battle and vividly describes the tearful farewell of one messmate to another, carrying the dead friend's body in the wake of a battle and with his own hands consigning it to the sea. During the battle, gun crews had little information about its progress. They could see only their gun, their little patch of deck, and the view through the gun port; most of their information about the battle came from women and boys carrying gunpowder.

Francis Austen, writing to his wife after the Battle of St. Domingo (*P* 26), noted, "Our people behaved admirably well, and displayed astonishing coolness during the whole time." Other officers, at various times, noted the bravery of their men and their apparent enthusiasm for battle. John Nicol, however, has a different interpretation of this eagerness:

> We rejoiced in a general action; not that we loved fighting; but we all wished to be free to return to our homes, and follow our own pursuits. We knew there was no other way of obtaining this than by defeating the enemy. "The hotter the war the sooner peace," was a saying with us.

Immediately after the battle, he wrote, there was a great deal of tedious and difficult repair work to attend to, and by the time there was leisure to discuss the events of the battle, "we do not choose to revert to a disagreeable subject." Nicol wrote of the heroism of the women on board his ship during the Battle of the Nile, one of whom carried wine to some of the men, some of whom were wounded, and one of whom gave birth during the battle. He also mentioned the bravery of one young man, whose arm was shot off just as he was preparing to light his gun; he seized the lit match from where it had fallen on deck, lit the fuse with his other hand, and then went to the surgeon to have his stump dressed. Nicol also served at Trafalgar and described the preparations before that battle:

> During this time each ship was making the usual preparations such as breaking away the Captain's and officer's cabins, and sending all the lumber below—the doctors, parson, purser and loblolly men, were also busy getting the medicine chests and bandages out, and sails prepared for the wounded to be placed on, that they might be dressed in rotation as they were taken down to the aft-cockpit. In such a bustling and, it may be said, trying as well as serious time, it is curious to notice the different dispositions of the British Sailor. Some would be offering a guinea for a glass of grog, whilst others were making a kind of mutual verbal will, such as: "If one of Johnny Crapeau's shots (a term given to the French) knocks my head off, you will take all my effects, and if you are killed and I am not, why, I will have yours and this is generally agreed to."

After the battle, the bodies of the dead were heaved overboard, and men went around the decks, inquiring after their messmates everywhere they went. Dead sailors were sewn up in their sailcloth hammocks before being buried at sea; the bodies were usually weighted with a cannonball, and the last stitch through the hammock also went through the dead sailor's nose, in case he was faking or merely unconscious.

Small wonder, then, that the average sailor anticipated battle with feelings of dread. He had no way to escape his fate and would be subjected to extraordinary punishment if he tried. He would be oblivious of most of the action and would not know whether his side had won or lost until it was almost too late to do anything about it. He could only hope. For relatives at home, too, there was fear of battle (*P* 252), for actual combat was the condensed version of all their concern for their loved ones.

The goal of a naval engagement was to cripple the enemy without actually sinking her, for a sunken ship meant far less prize money. Accordingly, fire was directed ideally either at the masts, thus taking down the sails by force and rendering the enemy incapable of maneuvering, or at the men on the decks. The latter tactic was particularly important if there was any expectation of having to board the enemy ship. For destroying the masts, cannonballs were used. Rigging and sails could be damaged with chain shot (shaped like two hockey pucks joined by a short, heavy chain) or bar shot (shaped like a dumbbell), while grapeshot and canister shot were effective at killing men. Grapeshot was, according to Leech, a bundle of "seven or eight balls confined to an iron and tied in cloth." Canister shot was "made by filling a powder canister with balls, each as large as two or three musket balls." Both tended to scatter with "direful effect" among the men on deck.

Hazards at Sea: Disease and Injury

For all the terrors of battle, however, the biggest killers at sea were disease and accidental injury. Accounts of the numbers involved vary widely, but it is certain that death from disease and accident were many times more common than deaths in action. Accidents could include falls from masts and rigging, injuries or deaths in fires that spread rapidly aboard wooden ships loaded with gunpowder, and hernias. It is possible that Mr. Price, in Mansfield Park, was injured in battle, but it seems far more likely, according to statistics, that he suffered some sort of accidental injury (*MP* 4).

Illnesses (*P* 66) that afflicted many sailors included scurvy, "yellow jack" (yellow fever), and various sexually transmitted diseases.* Sailor John Nicol described a double outbreak of disease while ferrying troops to Quebec; while on the journey, illness of an unidentified sort was so rife among men and livestock alike that "[w]e threw overboard every morning a soldier or a sheep," and upon arrival, the men "made too free with the river water, and were almost all seized with flux [dysentery]."

Disease flourished in ships, partly because of the lack of fresh food, partly because of the crowded living conditions, and partly because, for all the attention to the ship's cleanliness, there was little understanding of the connection between personal hygiene and health. A great many sailors could not swim and had little occasion to take baths, and the "head"— the ship's toilet—was sometimes smeared with feces as a joke at the expense of the next person to sit down. The ship's surgeon was unlikely to wash his hands between patients, and vermin of all sorts inhabited the ship,

---

*The presence of contagious disease aboard was signaled to other ships by the use of a yellow quarantine flag.

from rats to lice to weevils. The lice were particularly dangerous, as they carried typhus. Casualty rates from disease were especially high in the Caribbean, where the standard complement of military diseases was augmented by a variety of tropical ailments.

The navy itself sometimes contributed to the state of ill health. It took a dim view, for example, of soldiers who contracted venereal diseases, withholding treatment at times "for complaints that might be avoided." Thomas Cochrane was furious at the entire system of naval medicine during the French wars, which was rendered inefficient by bureaucracy and by what Cochrane called "Mistaken economy." Regulations made it difficult for sailors to be admitted to a naval hospital, and, once there, they might be victimized by the unclean conditions that Cochrane described:

> A more barbarous regulation was enforced, viz, that from the expense of *lint* in dressing wounds, *sponge* should be substituted, as it might be used over again! The result was that even slight cases became infected by the application of sponges which had been used on putrescent sores, and this shameful practice cost the lives or limbs of many. . . . Persons so mutilated had no claim on the service for pension or reward.

Invalids, he went on, were forced to work in the harbors, a duty so onerous that many, though unfit, successfully applied to go to sea again as the lesser of two evils.

However, not all commanders and bureaucrats ignored the health of their men. Vice Admiral Sir John Jervis, for example, insisted that the ships for his 1793–1794 Caribbean expedition be equipped with fumigating lamps for ridding each deck of vermin and germs, and the navy agreed and expanded the practice to include the whole fleet. Secretary of State Dundas attempted to improve sailors' diet and to shift the most onerous tasks in the Caribbean to black workers in order to combat disease among British troops.

Desertion and Mutiny

Under the combined weight of press-gangs, crowded living conditions, monotonous food, the fear of death in battle, and the constant threat of disease, it is hardly surprising that some sailors should wish to escape the naval establishment or at least improve their working conditions. Desertions, especially of pressed men, were common. Francis Austen had thirteen men desert his ship at St. Christopher in 1806, shortly before the Battle of St. Domingo. Desertion was especially high in the Caribbean, where the men had a real fear of disease magnified by legend and superstition, and highest of all in Jamaica, which had numerous trade routes and thus more opportunities to sign on to a ship out of the region. From 1793 to 1801 alone, there were 3,000 desertions in the Caribbean. Jack Nastyface claimed that the *Revenge*, a ship on which he served, was "thrice manned"—that is, that casualties and desertions were so numerous that a constant influx of men was required to keep the ship in operation. Even sailors who volunteered sometimes attempted to desert, and many, once legitimately discharged, went to great lengths to avoid being pressed into service again, even dressing as women on occasion to avoid the press-gangs.

Mutinies, unlike desertions, were aimed less at getting away from the service than at improving conditions within it. Men mutinied over the discipline imposed by officers, reductions in grog rations, low pay, and bad food. A significant mutiny erupted at Spithead in 1797, primarily over pay and food; at that time, wages had not been raised since the mid-seventeenth century. Acknowledging the justice of the complaints, the Admiralty granted the men's requests and imposed no punishment on the mutineers. However, a second revolt at the Nore over much the same issues was perceived by the Admiralty as superfluous and disruptive and was harshly suppressed, with several executions of lead mutineers.

Ships

Ships were chiefly categorized by size, rigging, and armament. Austen, as the sister of two naval men, would have been keenly aware of the differences between ships. As her brothers moved from ship to ship, their pay, status, and duties altered, as did their opportunity to take valuable prizes. The number of guns on a ship and the consequent size necessary to sustain that number of guns determined its "rate." First-rate ships were thus the largest, with three gun decks (*MP* 403) and a crew of 900. They carried more than 100 guns until 1810, more than 110 guns after 1810; 120 guns would have been a typical number. Second rates had 84 to 100 guns (90 to 110 after 1810); third rates carried 70 to 84 (80 to 90); fourth rates carried 50 to 70 (60 to 80).

Fifth- and sixth-rate vessels were frigates with only one gun deck. They were less useful for pounding the enemy with monumental broadsides during fleet actions, but they were splendid for sailing quickly across the seas, scooping up prizes. (Francis Austen, like most ambitious captains, longed to command a frigate.) Fifth-rate frigates carried thirty-two to fifty guns (thirty-two to sixty after 1810), and sixth rates, both before and after 1810, had anything up to thirty-two guns, though few of these ships had fewer than twenty guns. A sixth rate, in contrast to a first rate, might have a crew of only 135. A technicality of rank made the same ship either a sixth-rate or unrated, depending on the rank of its captain. A ship of this size with a post-captain was a sixth rate, but the same ship with a commander in charge was merely a sloop (*MP* 299, 372, 384; *P* 65–66). A sloop might also be an even smaller ship of as few as ten guns, seldom able to capture a prize of any value.

Guns were placed symmetrically on both sides of the ship, so that the number of guns was always even; Jane Austen makes a joke about this in a juvenile work, in which she sails her heroes from France to England "in a man of War of 55 Guns" (*H&E, MW* 36). Accounts of ships in the newspapers (*MP* 232; *P* 30, 66), Navy List (*MP* 389; *P* 30, 64), and naval records often indicate the number of guns after the ship's name, for example, *Speedy* (14) or *Neptune* (98). Mr. Price, in praising his son William's new sloop, the *Thrush*, expresses his praise in terms of the number of guns: "anybody in England would take her for an eight-and-twenty" (*MP* 380).

Working the guns was a laborious and dangerous exercise with several steps. Before the gun was prepared for firing, its wheeled carriage was fixed in place by ropes, and its mouth was sealed with a wooden plug called a tompion, which kept out moisture. A typical gun crew first removed and coiled the fastening ropes, then brought the gun's angle parallel to the deck, removed the tompion, stuffed a gunpowder-filled bag called a cartridge down the muzzle of the cannon, followed it with some sort of shot (ball, bar, chain, etc.), "ran out" the gun so that it stuck partly out through the gun port, poured a little gunpowder into a touchhole, aimed the gun, and finally lit the powder in the touchhole with a "match"—not a small stick of cardboard or wood as now, but a long wick or cord that burned fairly slowly. Wooden handspikes, looking rather like tapered chair or table legs, were wedged under the guns at the last minute to make small corrections in aim.

The size of the shot fired, like the number of guns on a ship, was variable. Ships of the line typically carried 12- to 42-pounders, frigates 4- to 6-pounders. (The size of a cannon was indicated by the weight of the ball it could fire; thus, a 12-pounder, such as those on the *Perseverance*, could fire a 12-pound cannonball.) Thomas Cochrane's first command, the *Speedy*, had only fourteen 4-pounders, which he described as "a species of gun little larger than a blunderbuss." His attempts to add a couple of 12-pounders as bow and stern chasers failed because the decks were simply too small and the ship's timbers too fragile to sustain the enormous recoil from these 8-foot-long, 1-ton guns, and even 6-pounders proved to be too big to fit through the *Speedy*'s gun ports. Later, commanding the *Hind*, another sloop with only 4-pound guns, he mocked the meager firepower of his ship by walking "the quarter-deck with a whole broadside of shot in my coat pockets."

A ship's defense and offense, however, depended only in part on the strength of its armament. Another factor was speed and maneuverability, which was largely determined by its sails and rigging. The sails were made of 2-foot-wide panels of heavy flax-and-hemp canvas, stitched by a master sailmaker whose skilled labor earned him much respect, a warrant officer's rank, and freedom from impressment. The outer edge of each sail was sewn to a rope with special twine that was often spun by sailors' widows and was sealed with a compound of beeswax and turpentine. The finished sails were either mounted on the proper yards (horizontal poles attached to the masts) or stored in the hold, marked with a tally, a small flat piece of wood that bore the ship's name, the type of sail, and the amount and weight of canvas in that particular sail.

Other important ship's equipment included rope, tar, additional canvas for making such items as hammocks and clothing, anchors, a lightning rod to minimize the danger of fire, and ballast. Rope was made in special buildings called "ropewalks" that might be as much as a quarter of a mile long. Dried hemp was combed into yarn, which was made into thread and then twisted into strands. The ropemaker walked backwards in the ropewalk with an approximately sixty-five-pound bundle of hemp wrapped around his waist. As he walked, he spun or twisted the rope into various thicknesses. A three-strand rope was "hawser laid"; a pair of two-strand ropes twisted together made a "shroud laid" rope; and three hawser laid ropes spun together were "cable laid." Most ropes were 120 fathoms (720 feet) long, but the ropewalk had to be longer than this, as the strands before they were twisted were longer than 720 feet (just as a braid is shorter than the same hair falling freely).

The rope, tarred for water resistance, was used to hold sails in place and sometimes to keep the ship in place, either by attachment to an anchor or, when in harbor, to a mooring buoy. Jane Austen made a slight mistake in the first edition of *Mansfield Park* when she described the Thrush as under weigh. "Under weigh" implies the weighing of an anchor, which would not have been the case for a ship in harbor, and Austen, perhaps upon advice from one of her brothers, changed it to "slipped her moorings" for the 1816 edition (*MP* 380). When the anchor was dropped, one spoke not of being in harbor but of being at anchorage (*P* 234).

Tar, which was so common on a ship that it gave its name to the slang word for a British sailor, could be made of pitch, pine resin, coal tar, or bitumen. It was used for sealing and waterproofing on sails, hats, coats, planks, and ropes. Sailors used it in their pigtails as a preventive against vermin, and surgeons used it to seal stumps after amputations.

Ballast could be made either of iron or of "shingle," an assortment of seaside stones that was cheap and widely available but more likely to shift and to pummel the inside of the hull. There was plenty of shingle ballast lying on the beaches near Portsmouth, which was fortunate, as the larger warships might have an 8-foot layer of it in their holds, serving to lower the center of gravity and make the ships more stable in the water. Cargo, anchor, cannonballs, and other items could also be embedded in the ballast to keep them from rolling around the hold.

Supplying ships with all this material could take a long time and was one of the principal bottlenecks in getting ships to sea. The process was also, as Cochrane noted, full of corruption and false economy. Bolts were improperly driven to save time. Unsatisfactory clothing was supplied to the sailors at inflated prices. Supplies were damaged, stolen, or resold before their arrival and consequently never even made it to their ships. Fraudulent billing, "hampering" (gifts of wine, ale, etc., to inspectors and clerks), and outright bribery were rampant.

The ships themselves were built of oak in dockyards like the one at Portsmouth or in old ships called "sheer hulks" (*MP* 380), too old for active service and turned instead into floating dockyards. The Portsmouth dockyard was surrounded by a red brick wall and, like most dockyards, housed an enormous supply of timber and other materials; this was an absolute necessity, for a large ship like HMS *Victory*, could require 2,500 large trees—the produce of 60 acres of woodland—to construct. A ship of *Victory*'s size also needed four acres of sails and 30 miles of rope.

Dockyards, because of their scale and activity, were popular tourist attractions. Artists, writers, and ordinary travelers came to marvel at the piles of timber (*MP* 403) and the scurrying shipwrights. At Portsmouth, the dockyard (*MP* 372, 388, 389, 400, 402) covered 82 acres, had forty-five machines (in 1810) producing 130,000 pulley blocks a year, and already had Nelson's *Victory* on display as an added attraction. In the spring and fall* at most dockyards, the anchorsmiths sweltered in the intense heat of their forges, molding immense anchors of up to 3½ tons in weight. Shipwrights planed planks and inserted bolts; Cochrane complained that the *Pallas*, which he commanded in 1805, had been fitted with iron instead of copper bolts, rendering his compass useless. Caulkers pounded oakum (rope fibers mixed with tar) into the gaps between the seams of planks, using a mallet and iron (a wedge with a large striking surface, like an oversized nail head, at the top).

Periodic maintenance was required to keep ships in good condition, and this was sometimes performed at the dockyards and sometimes at sea. The upper portions of the ship were painted, while the portions below the waterline had to be either tarred to prevent infestations of sea worms or brought in occasionally to have the worm-ridden planks replaced. Gaps that developed between planks had to be filled with tar or oakum; the oakum was pounded in, while tar was heated and then ladled into the seams. Drips were sanded away with holystones.

Reputation

Except for a few bleak periods, when consecutive naval defeats accumulated to an embarrassing degree, the navy was highly regarded by the general public (*S&S* 103; *MP* 109; *P* 99, 167). Its officer ranks were considered a perfectly acceptable destination for sons of the gentry and aristocracy (*MP* 91), and the "jolly tars" who made up the crew were fondly regarded by the British citizenry (*P* 18–19). In his derision for the service,

*Summer was too hot for the men, winter too cold for the iron.

Sir Walter Elliot was in a distinct minority, and his prejudice against sailors would automatically have disposed Austen's readers to dislike him (*P* 19–20). The navy was widely referred to as "the wooden walls of England" and considered the best defense against invasion and the protector of British overseas trade. The army and militia fared poorly by comparison, chiefly because the English were deeply suspicious of standing armies as potential instruments of tyranny.

Austen does more than fall in line with the general idea of naval excellence. She specifically notes their "alertness" (*P* 48), "domestic virtues" (*P* 252), and "national importance" (*P* 252). This is a tribute to her sailor brothers and their colleagues, as is her treatment of sailors in general in her works. Her principal naval characters—William Price, Admiral Croft, and Captains Wentworth, Harville, and Benwick—are all virtuous and admirable men, a statement that cannot be made about her clergymen or her soldiers. Even the overly emotional and poetically enthusiastic Benwick, the most likely of all of them to be ridiculous, is handled with gentleness. Dick Musgrove (*P* 67), who appears only indirectly, and some of Admiral Croft's acquaintances, who also never speak, are the only ones referred to in a negative manner. Admiral Crawford is certainly a negative character, but he, too, never appears on center stage and merely influences events from afar.

Austen may have felt a special need to defend the navy, however, at the time she wrote *Persuasion*. Defeats in the War of 1812 had tarnished the reputation of the service. The prince regent was, in Byron's words, "all for the land-service, / Forgetting Duncan, Nelson, Howe, and Jervis," and many Britons agreed with him. In the latter parts of the Napoleonic Wars, attention had shifted away from the early sea victories at the Nile and Trafalgar to the land campaigns in Spain and the final victory at Waterloo. *See also* Army; Marines; Napoleonic Wars; Time.

Neighborhood

When Jane Austen speaks of a "neighborhood" (*L&F*, *MW* 78, 87; *Cath*, *MW* 196; *P&P* 43; *NA* 16, 197–198, 209; *E* 191; *P* 43, 47), she does not mean it in the sense we use today, that is, in the sense of a geographical area. Note, for instance, her use of the phrase "parish and neighborhood" in *Mansfield Park* (93); the parish is a religious, civil, and geographical unit, while the neighborhood is not. She means a social neighborhood, a community of people of approximately the same economic and cultural class (*E* 310) who pay calls on each other (*Lesley*, *MW* 111; *E* 53) and are entertained at each other's houses. In country villages such as Steventon, where Austen grew up, the neighborhood could be quite small, and genteel villagers in similar circumstances often had to walk or ride for miles in order to visit a decent number of people. Neighborhoods could be cozy or claustrophobic in small villages, and good behavior was essential so that everyone could continue to get along—or at least pretend to get along.

An example of the intimacy of neighborhoods may be found in the Lloyd family. There were three daughters, all of whom were friendly with the Austens. The oldest, Martha, lived with the Austen women for years after the death of Mr. Austen and, after Jane's death, became Francis Austen's second wife. Eliza Lloyd married the brother of Tom Fowle, who was Cassandra Austen's fiancé at the time of his death in the West Indies, and Mary Lloyd became the second wife of James Austen, the oldest of the Austen siblings. With few options for guests for tea, let alone for marriage partners, neighborhoods could feel very small indeed.

Newspaper

The newspaper (*Lesley*, *MW* 135; *Cath*, *MW* 215; *NA* 197–198, 203; *S&S* 106, 107, 108; *MP* 110, 118, 389, 439; *E* 206; *P* 43) was born in the early years of the eighteenth century and soon became an essential aspect of urban life. By 1783, London had nine daily papers (*MP* 438) and ten that appeared two or three times a week. In 1790, the numbers had risen to fourteen dailies and nine bi- or triweeklies, and by 1811 the total number of papers had risen again to fifty-two, including several Sunday papers that were technically illegal (due to sabbatarian restrictions) but extremely popular nonetheless. The circulation of these papers differed, but historians of the newspaper industry have theorized that a circulation of about 1,500 to 2,000 was necessary to keep a paper solvent and successful. London's *Daily Gazetteer* had a circulation of about 1,650 in 1790; the *Leeds Mercury* claimed in April 1795 that its circulation was 1,500. The *Morning Post* claimed sales of 5,000 copies per day in 1778, and the *Daily Advertiser* claimed equal circulation in 1779, but both these figures may be inflated. For short periods of time, a newspaper with a popular political perspective might see a jump in its circulation; William Cobbett's *Political Register*, for example, was selling 40,000 to 50,000 copies a week during the political turmoil that followed the Napoleonic Wars, but this dropped to 400 when he was forced to raise prices in the 1820s.

The number of provincial papers also rose dramatically. There had been only ten newspapers outside London in 1710, but this had grown to somewhere between sixty-five and seventy in the 1790s. Sixteen towns had more than one paper. They needed slightly smaller circulation than London papers to survive, but many did much more than survive, and some, in the 1780s and 1790s, were selling as many as 2,500 to 4,000 copies per day. Most borrowed the bulk of their news from London papers, adding items of local interest as necessary and tailoring their choice of copied articles to the reading interests of the local populace. By 1801, provincial papers were selling more total copies than London papers; of the 16 million tax stamps

Bad News, 1791. Four men share a newspaper, probably at an alehouse. Courtesy of the Lewis Walpole Library, Yale University. 791.0.17dr.

sold that year, 7 million applied to London papers and 9 million to papers in the provinces.

Estimating total circulation is somewhat easier because newspapers were subject to a stamp tax. This had been introduced in 1712 and occasionally raised, reaching a peak at the end of the Napoleonic Wars. (Publishers then added a penny or two to cover their costs and generate profit.) Calculating the total number of newspapers produced would seem to be fairly simple: look at the tax records and find the number of papers and readers, but the reality was far more complicated.

In 1775, 12.6 million newspaper stamps were issued, meaning that an average of 34,521 papers were printed each day. Other contemporary estimates put the number higher, with perhaps 41,000 to 45,000 papers being printed each day in London alone. In 1801, 16 million stamps were issued, and in 1816, this had risen to 22 million, but we must assume that the actual number of newspapers was even higher. This was because not all papers paid the tax. Some, like the *Political Register* before the 1820s, operated illegally instead. The tax also, despite being based on the paper's size, does not necessarily show the actual size of a newspaper. Printers evaded the tax by issuing a standard paper and then adding a free supplement that was exempt.

The question of readership is further complicated by the fact that not all newspapers had a single reader or even a single owner. Some newspapers were bought by inns and alehouses and used to entice customers inside. Some were bought by newspaper reading rooms that took in up to eighty different papers and charged readers a fee for access to them all. Others were bought by one man and read aloud to a crowd at an alehouse or on a street corner or lent, when the original owner was finished, to friends (*S&S* 30; *MP* 382, 384). On occasion, although the publishers of newspapers hated this practice and tried unsuccessfully to stamp it out, the vendors (*P* 135) of papers would "rent" a paper for a penny, allowing passersby to read the paper and then return it. Those who bought a paper in the traditional manner would usually take it home, where it would be read by various members of the family. Estimates vary, but each paper produced may actually have been read by as many as ten or twenty people.

The upper classes may have been the biggest consumers of newspapers, as they could afford to pay the high prices necessitated by the increasing stamp tax, but working-class people could share a paper, and some even formed clubs for this purpose. A reported 5,000 such clubs existed between 1746 and 1821, each formed of perhaps half a dozen to a dozen families who shared newspapers. Foreign observers, radicals, and conservatives alike agreed that working-class readership was very high and that the English people as a whole seemed to be remarkably well informed. According to *Lloyd's Evening Post* in 1780, "Without newspapers . . . our Country Villager, the Curate, and the Blacksmith, would lose the self-satisfaction of being as wise [as] our First Minister of State."

Surviving copies show that the standard newspaper for most of the eighteenth century was four pages—one large sheet of paper printed on both sides and then folded crosswise to make four four-column pages. The newspaper of Austen's day, however, was a good deal denser than that of Addison's or Swift's, because smaller type was being used, and articles and advertisements were increasingly warring with each other for space. There were still no illustrations, however. By the end of the Napoleonic Wars, some newspapers, including the *London Times*, had gone to an eight-page format. They were assisted in this expansion by the invention in 1803 of a paper-making machine and the resulting drop in the price of paper. The typical newspaper might be owned jointly by several people, run by a hired editor, and produced by a small staff. The printing was often done by a "jobbing" printer who produced several different newspapers at once.

Newspapers could be picked up at the printer's office or bought from street vendors. They could also be sent through the mail, and from 1792 the Post Office delivered newspapers in this way for free. Some papers were also delivered by newspaper employees to individual houses. In the provinces, successful papers had a widely distributed network of newsmen and agents who sold papers and collected advertisements; the *Sheffield Advertiser*, for example, had agents in nineteen towns in 1790. The printer would deliver copies to the agents and to the newsmen who delivered on foot; in one study of a Derby newspaper, most subscribers got their papers the same day they were printed, and the rest of the customers received theirs by the following morning.

Newspaper Content

Newspapers got their information from all kinds of sources: soldiers serving overseas, diplomats, members of Parliament who wanted to be sure that their speeches were reported accurately, private citizens writing letters, and outright plagiarism from other newspapers. The items were selected and slanted according to the political preferences of the editor, for while many papers claimed to be politically unbiased, many others made no pretense of neutrality. These supported either the government or the opposition by choosing to print articles that favored one side and by printing letters to the editor that espoused only their own viewpoint.

Until late in the eighteenth century, printing speeches made in the House of Commons was illegal, but most papers ignored this stricture. Their reporters sat in the gallery and, forbidden to take notes until the 1780s, remembered as much as they could of what was said and then hurried out to jot it all down. Some reporters had truly prodigious memories and could retain entire speeches, word for word, in their heads. Their job, however, was hampered by the fact that any member could call for the gallery to be cleared at any time and by the fact that the gallery was routinely cleared before a vote, but they were assisted by MPs who wanted their glorious speeches to be printed verbatim. These MPs would slip a reporter a copy of the speech in advance, a tactic that could sometimes prove potentially embarrassing if the speech, for one reason or another, was never made. John Wilkes, for example, once begged for permission to make a particular speech because, he explained, "I have sent a copy to the 'Public Advertiser', and how ridiculous should I appear if it were published without having been delivered."

The government, though it never explicitly limited the freedom of speech of opposition papers, went to some lengths to control the political content. They paid editors to include certain pieces and exclude others and paid "subsidies" to favorite papers. The Post Office, in providing its free delivery, also managed to misdirect opposition papers from time to time. Readers were not oblivious to the slant in coverage and sought the most accurate reporting. Lady Sarah Lennox, for example, writing to her sister in France in December 1778, asked, "Pray, what newspapers do you get? Not the *Morning Post*, I hope, for it's full of lies and no news. The *General Advertiser* has the best intelligence & gives, as I am told, a very correct account of the speeches in the debates, which entertains me vastly." The *Morning Chronicle* and the *Gazetteer* were considered among London's most politically balanced papers.

Politics in one form or another was the staple subject of most newspapers (*NA* 71), but it was far from being the only subject. Spectacular trials and marital scandals (*MP* 439–440) were always popular, as were stories about escaped madwomen, and near-death adventures. Newspapers covered crimes such as robberies by notorious highwaymen, and quite early they began printing shipping news. Arrivals of merchant vessels and of navy ships were noted (*MP* 232), as were the outcomes of naval and land battles (*P* 30). Births (*S&S* 246), deaths (*Evelyn*, *MW* 190), bankruptcies, and marriages (*S&S* 217; *P&P* 336), too, received brief mention, when the parties involved were socially prominent enough to be of interest. Other topics included U.S. and European affairs, fashion, literary and theatrical reviews, economic news such as stock and commodities prices, provincial news, and sports—chiefly horse racing, cockfighting, and cricket.

Dailies tended to be heavier on politics, while weeklies were more like magazines and had a broader and more balanced set of topics.

Newspapers also published advertisements, which took up more room than anything else except political news. There were ads for real estate (*Scraps*, *MW* 177; *MP* 342; *P* 15) and ads for employment (*Sand*, *MW* 366). Clergymen seeking livings or curacies advertised their availability, and those who had the power to bestow clerical livings advertised the value of the living, the likely life span of the current occupant, and the amount for which the living could be bought. Similarly, servants advertised for posts, and employers advertised for servants. Horses (*MP* 342), patent medicines, cream of violet soap, coffee, tea, wine, and cosmetics were all touted in advertisements. Private groups used ads to notify each other of joint-stock company meetings or to lobby for new projects or for the benefit of a particular occupational group. The lottery issued its notices through ads, and people who had lost items advertised for their return. There were political advertisements and announcements of upcoming horse races, pleas to use such-and-such a commercial stable or such-and-such a dentist. Ads, like the newspapers themselves, were taxed, with the person or company placing the advertisement paying a few pennies to the government along with the newspaper's fee.

In July 1780, a reader wrote to the *Reading Mercury, and Oxford Gazette*, signing himself (or herself) "W. C." There is no guarantee that these were his real initials, for letters to the editor were often signed with pseudonyms such as "Britannicus." W. C. may even have been the editor himself, disguising his identity. His observations on the typical Georgian newspaper, however, deserve to be repeated:

> Sir, I have often observed, that there is not so inconsistent, so incoherent, so heterogenious, although so useful and agreeable a thing, as a public newspaper: The very ludicrous contrast in advertisements, the contradictory substance of foreign and domestic paragraphs, the opposite opinions and observations of contending essayists, with premature deaths, spurious marriages, births, bankruptcies, etc. etc. form a fund of entertainment for a world of which it is in itself no bad epitome.

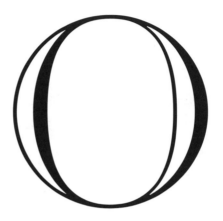

Opera

Going to the opera was in many ways like going to the theater. Like top-quality drama, opera was for most of the year confined to London. The season, like the season at Drury Lane and Covent Garden, was to some extent contiguous with the winter London social season, and operas were not presented over the summer, when most of the city's wealthier residents fled to their country homes or to the seaside. During the summer, however, individual singers might tour the country, performing in provincial towns.

Like drama, as well, opera appeared at a limited number of venues. Drury Lane and Covent Garden had a monopoly on plays and opera in English, explicitly granted by royal patent. There was no such patent for Italian opera, but the price of opera tickets limited the potential audience and thus created a near-monopoly for the King's Theatre, Haymarket. The King's Theatre, which despite its name had no special royal connection or license, remained the dominant presenter of opera throughout Austen's lifetime, though its supremacy was challenged in the 1790s by the more conveniently located Pantheon. Because the King's Theatre held no permanent patent, its management had to secure a license for each season from the lord chamberlain, who vetted the plans to determine whether or not the company seemed likely to remain solvent. As with plays, which had to be approved by his office, the lord chamberlain inspected libretti for subversive or otherwise unacceptable content.

Another similarity between drama and opera was the relative social status of its performers, particularly its women. Female performers of almost all kinds were shunned by polite society, which presumed that most actresses and singers were glorified prostitutes. It must be said, in defense of this attitude, that several high-profile instances of sexual commerce could be named. Perhaps the most famous example was the actress Dorothea Jordan, who had a long-running and much-publicized affair with the duke of Clarence, bearing him ten children. (Jane Austen saw her perform at Covent Garden in 1814.) One satirical cartoon shows her in her bedroom, gazing adoringly at a duchess' coronet, which she hopes someday to wear by marrying her lover. A map on the wall purports to show the route from "Strolling Lane" (i.e., prostitution) through "Old Drury Common" all the way to "Derbyshire Peak." A genealogical chart of the nobility lies on her dressing table, and her bed-hangings are crowned by a Phrygian cap, symbol of the French Revolution. The latter element is intended to ridicule her pretensions to nobility; as a common woman, let alone an *actress*, she should know her place. An even more vicious cartoon satirizes her as a chamberpot—"jordan" was a slang word for this nighttime piss-pot—and shows the duke's maids

[Lilliputian Figures], 1799, detail. An opera dancer adopts an immodest posture. Courtesy of the Lewis Walpole Library, Yale University. 799.7.12.4.

standing around, examining the jordan and criticizing his choice. "Why, it's quite a common thing," says one, and another remarks that it's been "cracked a thousand times."

Some actresses of sterling talent who resisted the temptation to climb to the top of the social scale were exempted from the popular prejudice against performing women. Sarah Siddons, who was generally well respected, is a notable example, but those who seemed to be using their visibility as a means to wealth and comfort were strongly stigmatized. The situation was worse for those without stardom to protect them, and it was worst of all for the "opera girls."

To understand the position of the opera girls (*L&F, MW* 77, 106), it is necessary to understand first what an evening at the opera was like. The audience was composed mostly of the aristocracy, the gentry, and people of means, as the ticket prices were far higher than at the theaters. Boxes, which held four to six people, were reserved, but seats in the orchestra were not, and those in line first got the best seats; wealthier patrons often sent their footmen ahead to hold seats for them. While waiting for the opera to start, people could visit the coffee room, talk with friends, scan the audience for famous faces, or buy a book from the "Fruit Woman" for 1s. 6d. that contained the cast list and the libretto. In theory, once the opera began, all this activity ceased, but in practice, London audiences continued to engage in all this behavior during the performance. If one cause can be assigned for all of the extraneous activity, it is that most operagoers did not understand Italian, and, because of the patents held by Drury Lane and Covent Garden, the King's Theatre could not present its performances in English.

One consequence of the linguistic problem was the lighting of the theater. In a modern theater, or indeed at Drury Lane and Covent Garden, not much light was required in the auditorium itself, but at the King's Theatre, people needed to be able to read the libretto as the opera progressed. Therefore, the auditorium remained brightly lit by oil lamps—2,000 of them by the 1781–1782 season. While the stage was still brighter, with footlights that could be dropped below the stage and chandeliers that could be raised and lowered, the auditorium remained bright enough to allow patrons to observe each other. Frequently, what was going on in the audience was more interesting to its members than what was going on on-stage.

Some people, who went to the opera solely to be fashionable, arrived late, watched a snippet of song or dance, and retired to the coffee room to discuss, in the words of opera critic Antoine Le Texier, "politics and horses." Others remained in the auditorium and simply enjoyed the music. Opera performances were centered not on composers or even on the musicians but on the singers. The *prima donna* and *primo uomo* were highly admired and generously compensated. Usually imported from France or Italy, they could earn as much as £1,000 to £1,500 per season, as compared to lesser singers, who might get only £100; composers and ballet masters, who earned about £300; *figurants*, or chorus dancers, who got about £25 to £70; and house poets, who translated (and in the case of English operas, wrote) libretti, and who earned no more than £150. The star power of singers allowed them the "choice of the book," which was the right to insert any music they liked into the operas they performed. Singers naturally chose arias that flattered their own voices, often to the detriment of the opera as a whole. Songs that were musically and thematically unrelated to the rest of the opera no doubt helped to diminish the audience's intellectual interest in the opera, though the individual songs might be admirable and even thrilling. In some cases, this habit of borrowing from multiple works resulted in "pasticcios," sections of music from many composers fitted awkwardly together into a single work. For much of Austen's life, the pasticcio was a popular way of introducing newly fashionable music into older operas.

General ignorance about the music (*Cath, MW* 197) and of Italian encouraged audiences to focus instead on spectacle. There was great demand for opera with new scenery and costumes; since both of these were expensive, they tended to be recycled as often as the audience would tolerate. Typical backgrounds included palaces, inns, cottage exteriors, city squares, temples, prisons, military camps, bridges, and harbors. Many of the set pieces were quite elaborate. Harbor scenes, for example, often featured movable ships arriving or departing. Storm scenes were popular, as were onstage fireworks, whose use was discontinued after the King's Theatre burned down in 1789.

Novelty always appealed. A typical season might include nine or ten operas, each performed an average of about ten times. Operas and ballets were usually rehearsed over a period of weeks but were sometimes slapped together in as little as twelve days, with predictable prop and set disasters and flaws in memorization. There was high turnover in the cast from season to season, as audiences tired of seeing the same singers or dancers. The constant challenge, particularly when the King's Theatre and the Pantheon were in competition, was to find a new superstar, preferably an Italian singer or a French dancer, to draw in the crowds.

Audiences were fond of ballet, which appeared between the acts of the opera and after its conclusion, and which usually had nothing to do with the opera either in setting or in the tone of the music. Like the opera, which favored the principal singers, it was conceived as a showcase for the best dancers, with few links between one dance and another. Yet it was wildly popular and, in bad years, kept the King's Theatre afloat.

Part of its appeal lay in the variety of settings and costumes, which attracted the very segment of the audience least knowledgeable about music. Part of the appeal lay in the athleticism of the star performers, and part, unquestionably, lay in the revealing attire of the female dancers. Well before the flimsy fashions of the French Revolutionary period, female ballet dancers were wearing diaphanous dresses and comparatively short skirts. In addition, they struck "attitudes," or poses, that enabled men to get a deliciously good look at their feet, ankles, and legs. Even in 1811, when thin muslin gowns had become commonplace among women of fashion, the costumes worn by opera dancers remained scandalous. The conduct book *The Mirror of the Graces* (1811), when discussing footwear, denounces colored or gold "clocks"—ornamental designs running upward from the ankle, tapering to a point at about mid-calf—in terms that explicitly link opera girls and prostitutes:

> But if the clock be a coloured or a gold one, as I have sometimes seen, how glaring is the exhibition! how coarse the association of ideas it produces in the fancy! Instead of a woman of refined manners and polished habits, your imagination reverts to the gross and repelling females of Portsmouth-point, or Plymouth-dock; or at least to the hired opera-dancer, whose business it is to make her foot and ancle the principal object which characterizes her charms.

Contemporary prints, likewise, show opera dancers—at least some opera dancers—as revealing themselves a little too much, and a little too eagerly, to the male gaze. No doubt some of these dancers took advantage of their attractions to better their situation in life, especially since female *figurants* were poorly paid and rarely took pupils in order to increase their income. The opera girl thus united all the superficial spectacle of the opera house to the long-standing prejudices against women who performed. *See also* Theater.

Parish

The parish (*Evelyn, MW* 180; *Cath, MW* 193; *Sand, MW* 365–366, 368; *P&P* 101; *MP* 30, 93; *E* 20, 456; *P* 39, 125) was both a religious and a governmental unit, serving both as a division within the Church of England and as an important center of local administration. It was a legal entity and required an act of Parliament to divide, which was sometimes necessary because certain parishes, especially in the industrializing north, grew so rapidly in population that traditional services were overwhelmed. The number of parishes therefore varied slightly, but for most of the eighteenth century there were about 10,000. There was little consistency as to physical size or population (*E* 456). The parish of Childerley in East Anglia, for example, had a population of only 47 in 1801 and 54 in 1841, while another East Anglian parish, Doddington, had a population of 7,500 in 1830. In theory, one parson was supposed to serve each of these parishes with identical efficiency.

As a religious unit, the parish had a parson (*MP* 248–249), who might or might not have a curate (*S&S* 61) to assist him in his duties. A few of the physically larger parishes had "chapels of ease" so that not everyone had to travel to the main parish church for services. There would also be a parish clerk (*E* 383) who recorded all Anglican baptisms, marriages (*P&P* 318), and funerals and participated in the church services by leading the congregation during responsive readings. Other staff took charge of the graveyard, and a group of leading citizens called churchwardens (*E* 455) made sure the church was kept in good repair. Each parish was part of a deanery, which was part of a larger archdeaconry, which in turn was part of a diocese run by one of England's twenty-six bishops. Again, the number of parishes in each diocese was variable. Rochester had 150 parishes, while Lincoln had ten times that number, and the other dioceses fell somewhere in between.

In its secular capacity, the parish served as the local unit for the collection and distribution of the "poor rates"—local charity dispensed to the poor of that particular parish. Overseers of the poor (*E* 455), who set the rates and dispensed the aid, could be nitpicky about who had the right to charity. Pregnant, itinerant women were sometimes driven away so that their unborn children would not become "chargeable" to the parish, and even unmarried women who were natives of a particular parish were often subjected to pressure from officials to name the fathers of their illegitimate children; if the father could not be made to pay support, at least he might reside in another parish, and the impoverished children would become another region's responsibility.

Overseers of the poor were selected once a year at a meeting of the vestry (*NA* 209), usually at Easter. At this time, the previous year's books were examined and the rates for the new year set. Other parish officers were also installed, such as surveyors of the highways, who were responsible for maintaining the major roads that ran through the parish. Complaints were often made about this system, which tended to fall unfairly on parishes with long stretches of busy roads. Austen does not specify what "parish business" (*E* 221, 425) her characters engage in, but one suspects that some of her gentlemen served the vestry, at one time or another, as churchwardens and possibly as overseers of the poor.

Pen

The pen (*Hist Eng*, *MW* 149; *Cath*, *MW* 192; *LS*, *MW* 283; *NA* 216; *S&S* 180, 203, 287; *MP* 59, 265, 424, 426, 461; *P* 233, 249), toward the end of Austen's life, was on the verge of its first major transformation in centuries, but the pens she used were still more like those used by Shakespeare than those used by Mark Twain or Henry James. Pens were still crafted out of quills, wing feathers collected from a variety of birds, but mainly from geese. Lincolnshire, with its great goose flocks, was a prime producer of quills. Four or five feathers from each wing were gathered during the molting season; according to author Isaac Taylor, writing in 1823, this was near the end of March. The feathers were then "dutched," or baked in hot sand, to remove the outer layer of skin that surrounded the shaft of the feather. Finally, they were cleaned in a solution of alum and tied in bunches to be sold.

The bird's natural wing curvature influenced the shape of the pens; left-wing feathers were said to be more comfortable for right-handed writers, while right-wing quills were better for lefties. The pen's nib, or writing tip, would be formed by using a sharp penknife (*E* 338) to cut an angled slice from the end of the feather; then the remaining thin tip would be slit parallel to the shaft. A new pen, once crafted, had to be tested on a piece of scrap paper to be sure the point would work properly. If it did not, or if it were damaged later and began to spatter, it would have to be mended by having its point cut anew (*P&P* 47). Repeated mendings might eventually whittle a pen away to almost nothing, making it hard to hold. In between uses, it was essential to keep the tip clean and moist, so most inkstands had quill-sized holes around the inkwell in which pens could be safely propped.

Efforts were made to extend the length of pens. In 1809, Joseph Bramah patented a method of cutting one quill into several disposable nibs that could be mounted on a durable holder, but this was a transitional technology. Steel pens, which would come to dominate the nineteenth century, were already on the way. The first known example in England was made in 1780 by a Birmingham manufacturer, Samuel Harrison, for chemist Dr. Joseph Priestley. Such pens were first patented in 1808 and began to be produced by machine in 1822, but the early specimens were awkward to use. Reservoir pens were patented in 1809 but likewise took some time to become widely adopted. *See also* Pencil; Writing.

Pencil

Graphite was a well-known material long before Jane Austen was born; a huge deposit of unusually pure graphite had been discovered in Borrow-dale, Cumberland, in 1564. At first thought to be a type of lead (and named "plumbeus" as a result), graphite was discovered in 1779 to be a carbon compound, and it acquired its modern name, derived from the Greek word "to write," in 1789. As this new name implies, people had rapidly discovered its utility for making marks. Mistakes, it was found, could be scratched out by rubbing bread crumbs on the paper—a laborious process, but much easier than trying to fix an inkblot. Writing with a pencil was also easier than writing with a pen, for a pen required a precise angle, the constant trimming and mending of the nib, dipping in an inkwell, and blotting. Austen, it was noted after her death, abandoned writing in pen when she became too ill to perform all these tasks: "She wrote whilst she could hold a pen, and with a pencil when a pen was become too laborious." Ease of use and ease of correction both contributed to the pencil's success.

Graphite soon became a popular substance for drawing (though not yet for composing letters or other documents). However, when the Borrow-dale deposit was depleted in the seventeenth century, some way had to be found of using less-pure chunks of the material. The most common solution was to grind the graphite into dust and add some sort of adhesive, then roll the resulting mass into a thin stick and place it in a holder. This graphite insert, in a nod to the original name of "plumbeus," was still called a "lead" (*E* 339).

At first the holders were made of metal, later of wood. During the Napoleonic Wars, Nicolas Jacques Conté (1755–1805) developed a process that is still used, with some small changes, to the present day. The graphite dust was mixed with clay and water, shaped in wooden molds, and baked. Austrian Joseph Hardtmuth refined the process by varying the clay content to alter the hardness of the pencil leads.

By Austen's day, therefore, the pencil (*S&S* 41; *MP* 227; *E* 47, 187, 339) was about halfway to its modern form. It was typically a thin, baked, round lead encased in a wooden stick, just as it is today. However, the wooden holders were not equipped with an eraser; though Joseph Priestley, in 1770, had espoused a South American vegetable gum and named it "rubber" for its ability to correct pencil marks, the vulcanization of rubber would not be achieved until 1839, and the affixed pencil eraser would have to wait until the 1850s. Mechanical pencils, also, postdate Austen's life. They would be invented in 1822. *See also* Pen; Writing.

Phaeton

One of the most fashionable vehicles of its day, the phaeton (*Clifford, MW* 43; *NA* 85, 87, 93; *P&P* 158, 168) was a four-wheeled carriage that had many variants. In general, it had four wheels, the back wheels being larger than the front ones. It was most commonly pulled by a pair of horses or ponies (*P&P* 67, 325), harnessed side by side, but one print shows a lady driving a phaeton with four ponies, and one type of phaeton was designed for use with only one horse. Austen's nephew recalled in his *Memoir* that the marchioness of Lansdowne, who lived in Southampton at the same time as Jane Austen, owned a phaeton that she drove out with six or eight ponies, "each pair decreasing in size, and becoming lighter in colour, through all the grades of dark brown, bay and chestnut, as it was placed farther away from the carriage."

A small sleighlike body with room for only two people sat atop very high springs. The body of the carriage might sit very far forward, centered between the pairs of wheels, or even over the back wheels; the "Perch-High" phaeton, for example, had its body directly over the four-foot-high front wheels, with 5'8" rear wheels located far behind, under a platform for servants or baggage. Wherever the body was located, there was generally space underneath it and over the axles for trunks that carried belongings on longer journeys and also lowered the carriage's center of gravity. Some phaetons, but not all, had a folding leather roof that could be lifted in case of rain, but this roof only partially covered the driver and passenger; the phaeton was a fair-weather conveyance.

The tall springs of the phaeton made it unlike any other vehicle on the road and opened it up to ridicule. A 1776 print, *Phaetona or Modern Female Taste*, exaggerates the female phaeton driver's hairstyle and shrinks her horses for comic effect; A 1780 effort, *The Delight of Ply[mouth]*, shows a bulky man climbing a tall ladder to get into his phaeton's seat. However, even realistic depictions show the base of the seat as being above the level of the taller wheels, as indeed it had to be to leave room below for luggage. This height, combined with the overall lightness of the carriage, made the phaeton liable to tipping. Austen therefore uses a phaeton for a fortuitous carriage accident in *Love and Freindship*:

> From this Dilemma I was most fortunately releived by an accident truly apropos; it was the lucky overturning of a Gentleman's Phaeton, on the road which ran murmuring behind us. . . . We instantly quitted our seats & ran to the rescue of those who but a few moments before had been in so ele-

Rowlandson Etching, 1790, detail. A woman driving a four-pony phaeton; a groom follows behind on a horse. Courtesy of the Lewis Walpole Library, Yale University. 790.6.27.1.

vated a situation as a fashionably high Phaeton, but who were now laid low and sprawling in the Dust—. (*MW* 98–99)

The phaeton's dangers, however, only increased its attractiveness to those who were, or wished to appear, daring. It remained popular among fashionable people (*NA* 232) and, along with the curricle, was the sports car of its day. *See also* Carriages and Coaches.

Philomel

Philomela, whose story appears in the works of Sophocles, Ovid, and Apollodorus, was the sister of Procne, who was the wife of the warrior Tereus. Tereus, enchanted with Philomela, raped her, cut out her tongue to prevent her from telling anyone of the crime, and locked her up. Philomela, however, was a skilled weaver, and she managed to depict her story in a piece of cloth, which she arranged to send to Procne. When Procne saw the fabric and interpreted its message, she freed her sister, and together they killed Tereus' son Itys and fed him to Tereus at dinner. They fled, and Tereus pursued them. When he had found them at last and was on the verge of killing them, the gods changed all three into birds: Procne into a nightingale, whose cry reminded the ancient Greeks of the name of her lost son, Itys; Philomela into a swallow, a bird not noted for its voice; and Tereus into a hoopoe, whose song sounds like "where—where—where" in Greek.

Austen uses "Philomel" (*Ode*, *MW* 74) in the conventional manner, as an erudite way of saying "bird." However, the once-fashionable classicism of the earlier eighteenth century was, even before Austen's day, a target for satirists, and she uses this mythological reference with tongue in cheek. It appears in "Ode to Pity," a poem that never addresses the subject of pity and that contains a number of deliberate absurdities and contradictions. Among these is that Austen's "Philomel on airy hawthorn bush / Sings sweet & Melancholy," so that Austen has given the tongueless Philomela, rather than the lovely-voiced Procne, the gift of song. *See also* Mythology.

Phoenix

Ancient Greek historians believed in the existence of this bird, which was said to have only one specimen at a time. The bird lived for an extremely long time—in some versions of the tale 500 or 540 years, most commonly 1,000 years—and returned to its birthplace at the end of its life, where the sun's rays would immolate it. A new phoenix would then be born from the ashes of its parent. By Austen's day, no one believed this was anything but a myth, but the phoenix (*Cass, MW* 44) persisted as a powerful symbol of rebirth and regeneration.

Picturesque

In the 1790s, as Austen began her first mature works of literature, two budding fashions that had been raging for centuries intersected and produced the fashion known as the "picturesque" (*NA* 111, 177; *S&S* 47). One of the new interests was in art. While the ruling class had always had its portraits painted for the sake of posterity (*Sand, MW* 427; *NA* 180–181, 191; *S&S* 215; *P&P* 52–53, 247, 249, 250; *MP* 84–85; *P* 40), the eighteenth century saw a rising interest in the acquisition of "accomplishments" by ladies of leisure (*Cath, MW* 198; *P&P* 39). In theory, accomplishments were supposed to equip them to make their homes decorative, pleasant places for their husbands and children. Art became one of these essential skills, and a well-educated young woman who aspired to gentility was expected to try her hand at sketching or painting in order to see if she had a gift for it (*MP* 18, 19). Artistic performance was less essential to a man's education, but an educated man was expected to be knowledgeable about art (*S&S* 19), and many men drew (*E* 364). Jane's brother Frank, a naval officer, made very competent sketches and maps during his career, for example. Jane's sister Cassandra, too, dabbled in art—it is to her pencil that we owe the only sketch of Jane Austen's face made during her lifetime—and so did many of Austen's characters (*Sand, MW* 421; *S&S* 17, 30, 104, 105, 108, 234–235, 281; *E* 43, 44, 46–47, 85, 150, 455–456). Jane herself, though she received some education in drawing and painting as a child, was never an enthusiastic artist, although she did enjoy visiting galleries of paintings in London.

The other passion that had seized England was the desire to travel, not for business or necessity or religion but merely to see new things. It was the birth of tourism, and much of what we now associate with tourism—standardized expectations of lodgings, professional tour guides, even souvenirs—became widespread during the late eighteenth and early nineteenth centuries. Travel for pleasure was not entirely new; wealthy young men had for decades been taking the Grand Tour, a journey abroad of months or even years as a formal completion of their educations, but tourism by the middle and laboring classes was a new phenomenon, and tourism within England rather than on the Continent was, likewise, quite novel. For the first time, the English were racing around England to *look at things*, and, as anyone would when learning to do something new, they were curious to know how to do it properly.

The third influence in the development of the picturesque was one that had been a continuing interest for generations: landscape gardening. Owners of country estates had long been fiddling with the best way to present their grounds to the eye. During the sixteenth and seventeenth centuries, this had been accomplished by ornate, geometric patterns of paths and plantings, dotted with topiaries and classical statues. Over the eighteenth century, however, an increasing vogue for the natural emerged. Avenues of trees were uprooted, and rigidly regular beds of flowers were razed. In their place, landowners installed lawns and meadows, artificial lakes and streams, and irregular clumps of trees.

These three influences—a shift in the production of art from professionals only to professionals and a large body of amateurs, an itch to travel and look at new things, and a pervasive interest in the shape of individual landscapes—united to produce the fashion for the picturesque. How these different movements shaped each other has been the subject of a great deal of discussion and has produced any number of graduate theses. For our purposes it is sufficient to say that each phenomenon fed off the others. The popularization of the picturesque, however, can be traced largely to the writings of one man, the Reverend William Gilpin (1724–1807), vicar of Boldre in the New Forest.

Gilpin (*Hist Eng*, *MW* 143), like many gentlemen of his time, had been impressed by paintings of the Italian landscape. The masters of this genre, Claude Lorrain, Gaspar Poussin, and Salvator Rosa, created rugged, moody scenes that had captured the imagination of young men who had seen their works while on the Grand Tour. Gilpin, however, did more than admire. He took a series of tours around Britain in the 1770s in which he applied the principles of landscape composition to the scenery he saw. His notes and paintings, circulated privately for a few years and then published, were quite popular and encouraged others to look at the terrain before them as if it were part of a picture—hence the term "picturesque." Gilpin himself defined the term in *Observations on the Western Parts of England*:

> *Picturesque beauty* is a phrase but little understood. We precisely mean by it that kind of beauty which would look well in a picture. Neither ground laid out by art, nor improved by agriculture, are of this kind.

True to his word, Gilpin had nothing but contempt for regularly laid out fields, tidy villages, and objects that were rugged but out of proportion to their environment. In the last category he placed Arthur's Seat, an extinct volcano visible from Edinburgh:

> Arthur's seat is still the principal object, appears still as odd, mishapen, and uncouth as before. It gave us the idea of a cap of maintenance in heraldry; and a view with such a staring feature in it, can no more be picturesque, than a face with a bulbous nose can be beautiful.

Gilpin approved, on the other hand, of water. He liked pictures of rivers that included "shepherds and herdsmen," lakes with "banditti, gypsies, soldiers, or other wild characters," and coastal views of almost all sorts:

> Winding bays—views of the ocean—promontories—rocks of every kind and form—estuaries—mouths of rivers—islands—shooting peninsulas—extensive sand-banks; and all these adorned occasionally with castles—lighthouses—distant towns—towers—harbours—all the furniture of navigation, and other incidental circumstances which belong to sea-coasts, form a rich collection of grand and picturesque materials.

The light, shade, color, and storms all added to the ocean's grandeur, in his opinion. Not every seaside scene, however, met with his approval. Brighton in 1774, then called Brighthelmstone, had nothing to appeal to his critical eye: here the ocean was "adorned with no rocky shore, nor winding coast, nor any other pleasing accompaniment. Nature, contrary to her usual practice, has here laid out the coast by a straight line." Straight lines were abhorrent to the devotees of the picturesque.

Readers ate it up. After all, what more lofty purpose could there be in traveling to new places than to record the landscape in works of art? They gathered their sketchbooks and their watercolors and followed Gilpin's itineraries, standing in the same spots and seeking the same insights about artistic composition. In some cases, they used perspective glasses, devices held up to the eye, in order to limit their view of an expansive scene to what could be contained on a canvas. Following Gilpin's advice, they "improved" the actual landscape by sketching in features that did not occur in nature. Those who chose not to sketch but merely observe the landscape had to imagine the improved scenery even as they gazed at the real thing.

After Gilpin, the most influential proponent of the picturesque was probably Uvedale Price, who brought the circle around completely from landscape to art to travel to landscape again, advising that the lessons gleaned from observation of the land, either directly or in works of art, should be translated into improvements in landscape gardening. In *An Essay on the Picturesque* (1796), he found the vogue for artificial lakes and lawns boring and urged greater "intricacy in landscape," which he defined as *"that disposition of objects which, by a partial and uncertain concealment, excites and nourishes curiosity."* He advocated irregularity in both architecture and landscape design, championing the Gothic style with its "variety of forms, of turrets and pinnacles" and its "appearance of splendid confusion."

The picturesque soon had its own vocabulary of foregrounds (*NA* 111), backgrounds, and middle distances. The ideal view also had to have some sort of boundary at the side—trees, ruins, or mountain slopes—to frame the picture and force the gaze into the middle distance; these objects are the "side-screens" of Henry Tilney's discourse (*NA* 111). From Edmund Burke's 1757 essay *A Philosophical Enquiry into the Origin of Our Ideas of the Sublime and the Beautiful,* the picturesque vocabulary adopted the terms "sublime" and "beautiful" to mean specific kinds of visual appeal. Sublime settings were grand, overpowering, and masculine; beautiful landscapes were soft, sinuous, delicate, and feminine. Gilpin's picturesque was a medium between the two, with a variety of textures, an atmosphere of wildness, and a visual balance of all the elements, even if it meant introducing objects into his pictures that were not present in the original scenery. Later, the term "romantic" came to be applied to similar landscapes, though this term was, like "picturesque," rather vague and greatly overused.

In fact, most elements of the picturesque came to be overused. Its terminology seemed to leach the spontaneity out of tourism, and the paintings that were created under its influence often had laughable inconsistencies, such as Welsh valleys suffused with Mediterranean light, or English lakes threatened by Italian banditti. Crumbling ruins and spectrally dark forests became far more commonplace on canvas than they were in real life. The doyens of the picturesque dictated what was appropriate and attractive, down to the very trees and animals that could be safely depicted; Uvedale Price favored old oaks and elms over beech and ash, Pomeranians and water dogs over sleeker varieties, sheep with ragged fleece over those with even coats, and lions and raptors over domestic animals. Gilpin, in particular, sounds fairly ridiculous even when he praises a scene. His description of the forests near Portsmouth is as enthusiastic as any in his oeuvre, but he cannot resist tinkering with even this setting in his imagination:

> The road, which was every where ample, presented us in one place with an irregular vista; in another it carried us into a lawn interspersed with trees; and often it doubled little shooting promontories composed either of single

trees, or of patches of wood.—The whole is so beautiful a piece of nature that *if it were placed in an improved scene*, it might be made, *with very little art*, to unite happily with the highest style of decoration. (emphasis added)

His highest compliment is that, with a little improvement, the vistas might make part of a picture. The greatest irony of all, however, is that Gilpin's own paintings were bland, insipid failures, so while he encouraged England to view itself with an artist's eye, he was not, himself, much of an artist.

Austen was definitely familiar with this intellectual approach to landscape. Gilpin is mentioned by Henry Austen in the Biographical Notice that accompanied the publication of *Northanger Abbey* and *Persuasion*, and Austen herself makes reference to his "Tour to the Highlands" (*L&F, MW* 105) in which he is so critical of Arthur's Seat. Two of her brothers, James and Henry, followed some of Gilpin's itineraries. In both her letters and her novels, she uses the terminology of the picturesque. Writing from lodgings in Queen's Square, Bath, in 1799, for example, she explains that "the prospect from the drawing-room window, at which I now write, is rather picturesque, as it commands a perspective view of the left side of Brock Street, broken by three Lombardy poplars in the garden of the last house in Queen's Parade." (Three was a pleasant quantity in picturesque theory, whereas four was irritatingly symmetrical, a concept also reflected in Elizabeth Bennet's refusal to walk with Mr. Darcy, Miss Bingley, and Mrs. Hurst, thus making a fourth in their group—*P&P* 53.) Her description of Lyme, furthermore, reads like a section of Gilpin's works, or of the travel writers who imitated him (*P* 95–96).

However, familiarity with the picturesque does not necessarily mean that she agreed with this way of looking at the outdoor world. She seems to have been in the camp of those who thought the picturesque had been taken too far. Among the weary were landscape designer Humphry Repton, who snapped in 1795 that he was not creating the kinds of vistas "well calculated for the residence of banditti," and poet John Aikin, whose 1791 work, "Picturesque; A Fragment," mocks the fashion:

New follies spring, and now we must be taught
To judge of prospects by an artist's rules,
And Picturesque's the word. Whatever scene,
Gay, rich, sublime, stupendous, wide or wild,
Disdains the bounds of canvas, nor supplies
Foreground and background, keeping light and shades
To aid the pencil's power, contracts the brow
And curls the nose of taste's great arbiter,
Too learned far to feel a vulgar joy,
"That station shows too much—the boundless length
Of dazzling distance mars the near effect.
Yon village spire, embosomed in the trees,

Takes from the scene its savage character,
And makes it smack of man."

Aikin preferred to look at mountains, oceans, and vast forests unbounded by the limitations of a picture's compass and unimpeded by notions of what "ought" to be seen:

. . . yet rather far
I'd fill my fancy from those mighty stores
Of vast ideas, graving on my brain
The forms gigantic of those sons of earth,
Than own whatever Claude and Poussin drew.

Austen appears to have agreed. She was certainly not one to dismiss a tidy farm because it appeared too domesticated, and she repeatedly introduces the theory of the picturesque only to reject it. In *Northanger Abbey* she uses the Tilneys' knowledge of the picturesque to establish them as people of education and taste, but she makes it clear that Catherine Morland's less tutored perspective is more genuine and appreciative than theirs (*NA* 110–111).* Marianne Dashwood's appreciation of twisted old trees (*S&S* 92), like the rest of her cultivation of picturesque taste, is extremely well informed, but it is inferior, in Austen's eyes, to Edward Ferrars' broader appreciation of scenery and his unfashionable defense of the prosperous agricultural landscape (*S&S* 88, 97–98).

Places

Austen mentions a large number of specific places in her works, some of them real and some of them fictional. The real ones are listed below; where appropriate, notes about the locations of important fictional places are included in the notes on English counties. Tables indicate on which map(s) locations may be found: Europe and the Mediterranean, England, West Indies, Hampshire, or London area (map abbreviations used in the keys are noted in the map captions). Streets maps of Bath and London may be found accompanying the articles about those cities. Several places have been listed below which do not appear in Austen's works but which have relevance to her life. For the purposes of map clarity, I have chosen to believe that my readers can locate the few regions of the world not contained in maps of Europe, the Mediterranean, and the West Indies. Omitted locations are noted.

Europe, the Mediterranean, and the West Indies

Boundaries between countries are the modern lines, not the Georgian ones.

*The rejection of the view of Bath is a deliberate poke at Uvedale Price, who similarly dismissed this panorama in *On Buildings and Architecture* (1798).

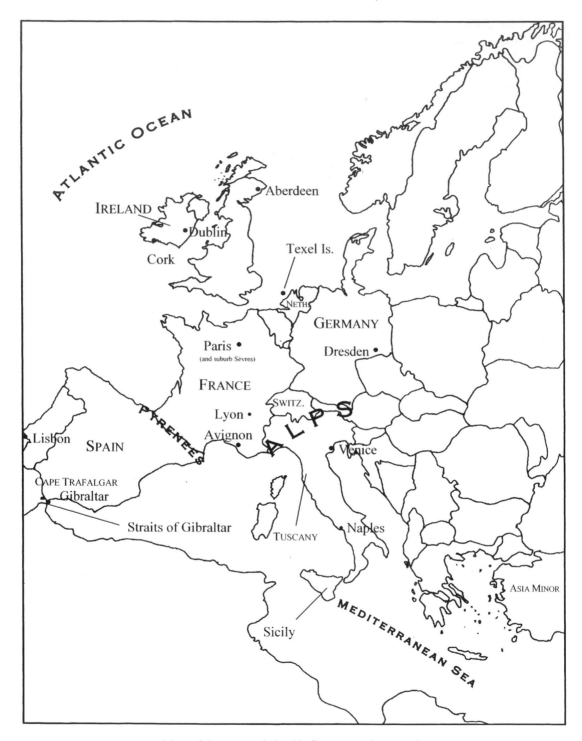

Map of Europe and the Mediterranean (EUROPE).

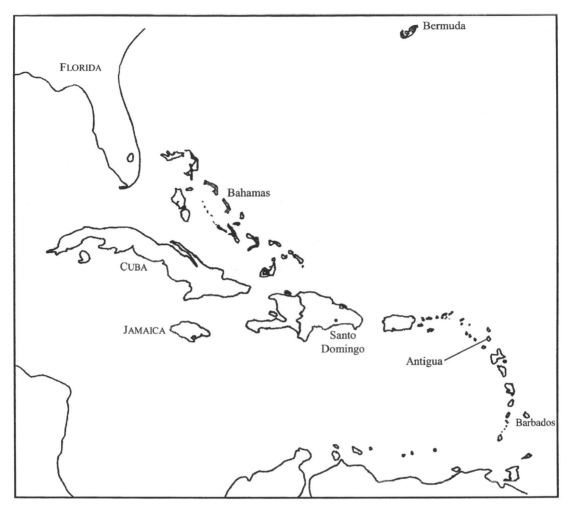

Map of the West Indies (WI).

Location	Map Location	Notes
Aberdeen	EUROPE	*Lesley, MW* 110, 118
Alps	EUROPE	*NA* 200
America	Not shown	*H&E, MW* 38; *MP* 119
		Might refer to any part of North or South America, but in the example from *Mansfield Park*, Tom Bertram is probably referring to the United States.
Antigua	WI	*MP* 30, 107, 177, 251
Asia Minor	EUROPE	*MP* 18
Bahamas	WI	*P* 70
		Mrs. Croft insists that Bermuda and the Bahamas are not part of the West Indies, although the Bahamas at least would be considered so today. Mrs. Croft may be including in her definition of the West Indies only the Greater Antilles (the island group that includes Cuba and Jamaica) and the Lesser Antilles (containing the Windward and Leeward Islands such as Antigua, Martinique, and St. Martin).

(*continued*)

Location	Map Location	Notes
Barbados	WI	*Cath*, *MW* 205
Bermuda	WI	*P* 70

See note to Bahamas.

Charles Austen's first and second wives were daughters of a governor-general of Bermuda.

Location	Map Location	Notes
Cape of Good Hope	Not shown	"The Cape" (*P* 232) is the Cape of Good Hope, at the southern tip of Africa. One of the duties performed by Jane's brother Francis, a naval captain, was convoying merchant ships back and forth to the Cape.
Dresden	EUROPE	*NA* 175
East Indies	Not shown	*Cath*, *MW* 194, 205; *S&S* 51, 206; *MP* 5, 305; *P* 22, 70

"East Indies" was a term used to refer to an extraordinarily wide swath of territory, encompassing everything from parts of Afghanistan to the southeasternmost parts of Indonesia. Sometimes China was included in the term, sometimes not. Bengal (*Cath*, *MW* 205), a region that contains the mouths of the Ganges River and includes Bangladesh and part of northwest India, is the only section of the East Indies named specifically by Austen in her works, though she would have been indirectly familiar with the geography of this part of the world. Both of her naval brothers, Francis and Charles, served in the East Indies and would have reported at length on the sights they had seen, including "nabobs, gold mohrs, and palanquins" (*S&S* 51). Nabobs were rich and powerful men, "mohrs" (actually mohurs) were gold coins of varying size and value, and the palanquin was essentially the Asian version of a litter or sedan chair. Jane also had an aunt who went to the East Indies to find a husband and gave birth to Jane's dashing cousin Eliza de Feuillide. Overall, the region remained for most English people an exotic source of wealth, tea, and textiles, without too much more detail as yet. The English happily dined on curry but were not especially knowledgeable about India's history. *A Compendious Geographical and Historical Grammar* (1795), a text that might be expected to provide historical information about the region, lumps most of Southeast Asia into a page and a quarter of text, most of it concerned with monsoons and paganism.

Location	Map Location	Notes
France	EUROPE	*NA* 83, 200

See also French; French Revolution; Napoleonic Wars.

Location	Map Location	Notes
Avignon	EUROPE	*S&S* 63
Lyon	EUROPE	*Cath*, *MW* 218, 222
Paris	EUROPE	*Lesley*, *MW* 116
Sèvres	EUROPE	*NA* 175
Gibraltar	EUROPE	*MP* 235; *P* 66, 70

Jane's brother Frank's first command, the *Peterel*, was stationed at Gibraltar. Gibraltar was one of the principal ports at which British ships resupplied when cruising in the Mediterranean.

Location	Map Location	Notes
Ireland	EUROPE	
Cork	EUROPE	*P* 70

Cork was the home station of the navy's Irish Squadron.

Location	Map Location	Notes
Dublin	EUROPE	
Italy		*Lesley*, *MW* 116, 138; *NA* 200
Naples	EUROPE	*Lesley*, *MW* 137–138
Sicily	EUROPE	*MP* 254
Tuscany	EUROPE	*NA* 83
Venice	EUROPE	*E* 363
Lisbon	EUROPE	*P* 68, 70
Mediterranean	EUROPE	*MP* 152, 232, 236; *P* 67

Location	Map Location	Notes
New South Wales	Not shown	State in Southeast Australia that includes many major cities, including Sydney. It was the first region of the country to receive transported prisoners from England.
Niagara Falls	Not shown	Huge waterfall on the border between Ontario (Canada) and New York (United States)
Ontario	Not shown	*MW* 443 Province in eastern Canada.
Pyrenees	EUROPE	*NA* 200
Russia	Not shown	*MP* 18; "Kamschatka" is mentioned in *Plan*, *MW* 430.
Santo Domingo	WI	*P* 26
Straits of Gibraltar	EUROPE	*P* 70
Switzerland	EUROPE	*NA* 200; *E* 362, 364, 365
Texel	EUROPE	Island off the coast of the Netherlands
Timbuktu	Not shown	*Sand*, 405–406 Can be found well inland along the Niger River in the Western African nation of Mali.
Trafalgar	EUROPE	The French and British fleets met off this cape in 1805 at the Battle of Trafalgar. *See also* Napoleonic Wars.
"Western Islands"	Not shown	*P* 67 The Azores, located in the north Atlantic Ocean, about 1,300 miles southwest of England.

British Isles

County lines are the old county lines, based primarily on John Cary's 1814 *Cary's Traveller's Companion.*

Before county lines were redrawn, small bits of counties were actually contained entirely within the borders of adjoining counties. These separate areas are omitted on this map for the sake of clarity.

British Isles	Map Location	Notes
Ireland	ENG; EUROPE	*L&F, MW* 90; *Watsons, MW* 326; *E* 159, 161, 168, 285, 298, 343; *P* 149, 188
Scotland	ENG	*L&F, MW* 90, 92; *Lesley, MW* 111; *Hist Eng, MW* 148–149; *S&S* 206; *P&P* 273; *MP* 442

Scotland had, ever since its union with England, been providing its southern neighbor with middle-class and professional men of all sorts. There was initially a resentful backlash against this peaceful invasion (*E* 104), though by the end of the eighteenth century, with the fear of anti-Hanoverian Scottish rebellion laid to rest, there was a vogue for all things Scottish. This interest was deepened by the publication of several popular books about Scotland, including Dr. Johnson's account of his visit there and William Gilpin's guide to the picturesque beauties of the Highlands.

Part of the reason for the Scots' success in such fields as estate management, architecture, medicine, and civil engineering was the Scottish educational system. Scotland had four universities to England's two, and the Scottish curriculum tended to have more relevance to the real world. As the author of *A Compendious Geographical and Historical Grammar* (1795) noted, "Scotland has been for many ages famous for learning. It has produced poets, philosophers, and historians, all excellent in their kind; and its literary reputation continues to be much on the increase."

Aberdeen	EUROPE	*Lesley, MW* 110, 118
Edinburgh	ENG	*L&F, MW* 102, 105; *Lesley, MW* 122
Gretna Green	ENG	*L&F, MW* 95; *P&P* 274, 282–283

Gretna Green was located right on the English–Scottish border and so was a popular destination for couples eloping to take advantage of Scotland's more liberal marriage laws. *See* Marriage.

Perth	ENG	*Lesley, MW* 111, 112
Stirling	ENG	*L&F, MW* 105
Wales	ENG	*J&A, MW* 20; *L&F, MW* 77, 78, 81; *Scraps, MW* 176; *Cath, MW* 203
Holyhead	ENG	*E* 161
Pembrokeshire	ENG	*Scraps, MW* 176–177
Vale of Uske	ENG	*L&F, MW* 77, 81

The Uske River flows north to south through Monmouthshire.

Map of the British Isles (ENG).

England (county/City)	Abbr.	Map Location	Notes
BEDFORDSHIRE	BEDS	ENG	
BERKSHIRE	BERKS	ENG	*J&A, MW* 16 Jane's uncle Leigh-Perrot had an estate here.
Newbury		ENG	*MP* 376
Reading		ENG	*S&S* 304 From 1785 to 1787, Jane and Cassandra attended the Abbey School in Reading. The school was housed in a twelfth-century building that once been home to the third-richest abbey in England.
Windsor		ENG	*E* 388, 394, 442, 454, 459 Eton College (*MP* 21) is located near Windsor.
BUCKINGHAMSHIRE	BUCKS	ENG	*F&E, MW* 10
CAMBRIDGESHIRE	CAMBS	ENG	
Cambridge		ENG	*P&P* 200; *MP* 61
CHESHIRE	CHES	ENG	*P* 4
CORNWALL	CORN	ENG	
CUMBERLAND	CUMB	ENG	*Lesley, MW* 117; *MP* 152 Cumberland, Westmorland, and the upper part of Lancashire contained the Lake District (*LS, MW* 298; *Cath, MW* 199; *P&P* 154, 239, 382), famous for its dramatic scenery.
Carlisle		ENG	*Evelyn, MW* 184–185
DERBYSHIRE	DERBY	ENG	*Col Let, MW* 160–161; *Cath, MW* 200; *P&P* 38, 240, 265, 385 Home of Elizabeth Bennet's aunt Mrs. Gardiner (*P&P* 239) and of Mr. Darcy (*P&P* 10, 239, 240). Featured in William Gilpin's picturesque tour of the Lake District; Derbyshire was the center of the equally picturesque Peak District (*P&P* 240).
Bakewell		ENG	*P&P* 256
Chatsworth		ENG	*P&P* 239
Dovedale		ENG	*P&P* 239 The "dale" or valley of the River Dove runs primarily along the border of Staffordshire and Derbyshire. The sections described by William Gilpin had gray cliffs dotted with trees and a river with small waterfalls.
Matlock		ENG	*Cath, MW* 199, 200; *P&P* 239 Matlock was a warm, sunny, sheltered spa in the Derwent Gorge, very small and rustic. What drew visitors was not the spa but the scenery. It lost some of its charm in the 1790s, when textile mills went up in the surrounding area, and John Byng complained, "Every rural sound is sunk in the clamours of cotton." A boat, with a band to play music on summer nights, took tourists onto the river for 6d.
DEVONSHIRE	DEVON	ENG	*Cath, MW* 215; *S&S* 251 Home of the Dashwoods for most of *S&S* and of Sir John and Lady Middleton (23, 25, 26, 87). Barton is a long day's journey from the fictional Cleveland (*S&S* 280) and 4 miles north of Exeter (*S&S* 25). Location of Allenham, the estate Willoughby is expected to inherit (*S&S* 40). Devon was noted for its seaside resorts, especially Exmouth and Teignmouth; from the 1790s, Sidmouth, Dawlish, and

England (COUNTY/City)	Abbr.	Map Location	Notes
			Torquay were successfully developed as bathing places. A low cost of living made it a popular place of residence for retired East India Company personnel and half-pay officers.
Dawlish		ENG	*S&S* 251, 360, 376

Dawlish was one of Devonshire's principal seaside resorts in the early years of the nineteenth century. The Austens considered taking a holiday there in 1801 but went elsewhere. They finally visited Dawlish the following year. An 1810 guide to bathing places described the town as follows:

"Dawlish is delightfully situate in a valley, on all sides surrounded by high grounds, except towards the east, which opens towards the cerulean expanse; fronting which, on the strand, are some good lodging-houses. Further up the vale a range of neat buildings present themselves; among which are two inns, with tolerable accommodations. Opposite is an overshoot water-mill, which has a very romantic effect; higher up, where the valley contracts, are several genteel lodging-houses, facing the sea, and each possessing a small plat before it, neatly railed in. . . .

The bathing-machines are numerous, and well-conducted. The beach in front of the lodging-houses has a gentle descent to the sea, which is generally pure and clear. The promenade is kept in excellent repair, and extends in a straight line across the strand. It may be lengthened at pleasure by a ramble under the cliffs which are here bold, precipitous and of a tremendous height."

England (COUNTY/City)	Abbr.	Map Location	Notes
Exeter		ENG	*Cath, MW* 240; *S&S* 25, 118, 119, 134, 143, 353, 354, 370
Honiton		ENG	*S&S* 65, 325
Plymouth		ENG	*S&S* 87, 130, 134, 355, 370; *P* 69, 103, 108, 133, 171
Sidmouth		ENG	*P* 105
DORSETSHIRE	DOR	ENG	*S&S* 208; *P* 217

Colonel Brandon's estate, Delaford, is located here (*S&S* 223, 375).

England (COUNTY/City)	Abbr.	Map Location	Notes
Lyme [Regis]		ENG	*P* 94–110, 121, 122, 125, 126, 130, 132, 171, 183

Lyme was a relatively inexpensive haven (*P* 97) for middle-class people. It had a pebbly beach, an assembly room, a card room, and a billiard room in 1810, when a guidebook described the upper part of the town as containing "many respectable looking houses, with pleasant gardens . . . but the streets are steep, rugged and unpleasant. In the lower part the houses are mean, and the streets so intricate, that a stranger . . . will sometimes find himself bewildered. . . . Here the lower order of the inhabitants in general reside, having that position which nature and fortune assigned to them. To be a person of consideration at Lyme, it is necessary to toil up hill, and to fix one's abode where it is in danger of being assailed by every wind that blows." Austen presumably approved of the town more heartily than this author, as she puts a very favorable assessment of it into *Persuasion* (94–95); she had ample opportunity to become acquainted with it, as she and her parents vacationed there in 1803 and 1804.

The Cobb (*P* 95, 108–109) was a jetty in the harbor, originally constructed in the fourteenth century and rebuilt as need-

(*continued*)

England (COUNTY/City)	Abbr.	Map Location	Notes
			ed. It had a platform for walking along the top and steep steps to the beach along its side. The steps from which Louisa Musgrove falls are known as "Granny's Teeth." Some of these steps have risers, but many are simply lumps of stone projecting from the wall like blunt fingertips. Up Lyme and Pinny, both mentioned in *P* 95, were nearby communities. Up Lyme is about a mile inland of Lyme Regis, while Pinhay—which Austen spells "Pinny"—lies west of Lyme along the coast, between Lyme Regis and Seaton. Charmouth (*P* 130) is about a mile and a half east of Lyme.
Weymouth		ENG	*S&S* 114; *MP* 114, 121; *E* 96, 160, 169, 194, 227, 241, 322, 437 One of the most popular of the seaside resorts, Weymouth was visited by George III in 1789. This increased its popularity, and a wave of expansion followed, making it distasteful to Jane, who disliked overbuilt resorts. In 1804, on a holiday in Lyme, she remained at Lyme while Cassandra, her brother Henry, and Henry's wife, Eliza, went on to Weymouth. The town was then in a ferment over the visit of the duke of Gloucester, but Cassandra was apparently more concerned by there being no pastry shop in town where one could buy ice cream. "Weymouth is altogether a shocking place, I perceive," replied Jane, "without recommendation of any kind, and worthy only of being frequented by the inhabitants of Gloucester." The royal family continued to patronize Weymouth, and the city gratefully accepted this attention. When the royal family was in residence, the assembly rooms were divided by a silken cord—one side for those who had been formally presented to the royal family at one time or another, and the other side for those who had not had this privilege and could only gape in awe. Like most large resort towns, Weymouth had a master of ceremonies who enforced certain rules in the public places. Gentlemen were not permitted to wear swords at assemblies, for example, or to dance in colored gloves.
DURHAM	DUR	ENG	
ENGLISH CHANNEL	—	ENG	*MP* 232
ESSEX	ESX	ENG	*Col Let, MW* 160–161
Southend		ENG	*E* 101, 105–106 Charles Austen took his family to Southend for a holiday in 1813.
GLOUCESTERSHIRE	GLOCS	ENG	*NA* 68, 149; *P* 3 Northanger Abbey is located in Gloucestershire (*NA* 139, 140), thirty miles from Bath (*NA* 155). Adlestrop Park, a magnificent Gothic mansion owned by Mrs. Austen's relatives, was located here. The Austen women visited there in 1806 after leaving Bath but before moving to Southampton, staying not at Adlestrop itself but at the rectory, home of Mrs. Austen's cousin, the Reverend Thomas Leigh.
Cheltenham		ENG	*Cath, MW* 203; *MP* 199 Cheltenham was a fashionable resort town, with a pump room, assembly rooms, famously pretty gravel paths sheltered by shady trees, and a theater that attracted London talent. Two of its masters of ceremonies, James King and Richard Tyson, had also served as MCs at Bath. The town attracted a fashionable clientele from the 1780s, though visitor John Byng found it dull,

England (COUNTY/City)	Abbr.	Map Location	Notes
			with poor inns and stables, poor lodgings, and high prices. Improvements were made, and by 1796 the streets had been newly paved and the houses numbered. Its lodging houses were principally brick faced with stucco, and their number gradually increased. A crescent was built in the first decade of the nineteenth century, and one of its units had nine bedrooms. A new theater was built in 1805 at a cost of £8,000, and by the second decade of the nineteenth century, more mineral wells had been dug and more pump rooms built. A period of rapid expansion during the French wars led to improved transportation to and from the town, the founding of a newspaper, and the building of "hotels," a type of dwelling considered more fashionable than a mere inn. Two coffee rooms, one for men and one for women, lent newspapers to their customers, and other shops lent out books and musical instruments. Visitors included King George III in 1788, novelist Fanny Burney in the same year as part of the court, Austen's cousin Eliza de Feuillide in 1797, actress Dorothea Jordan in 1810, and Jane and Cassandra Austen in 1816.
Clifton			See Bristol (SOMERSETSHIRE)
Petty France	ENG		*NA* 156
Tetbury	ENG		*NA* 45
Tintern Abbey	ENG		*MP* 152
HAMPSHIRE	HAMP	ENG	Home of the Misses Parker in *Sanditon* (*MW* 420).
			Hampshire was Jane's home for most of her life. She was born in Steventon and lived there until 1801, when her family moved to Bath. In 1806, she returned to the county to live at Southampton with her brother Frank and his wife; she then moved, in 1809, to Chawton Cottage, owned by her brother Edward. Some of her other brothers occasionally occupied Chawton House, a larger home that Edward also owned in the same neighborhood.
Ashe		HAMP	Home of the Lefroy family from 1783. The Lefroy were friends of the Austens, and the two families visited back and forth.
Basingstoke		HAMP	*Clifford, MW* 44
			When the Austens lived at Steventon, they often attended winter balls in Basingstoke, seven miles away. Their closest doctor was here as well, along with a shop that sold drawing supplies.
Beaulieu Abbey			*Hist Eng, MW* 141–142
Chawton		HAMP	The Austen women and Martha Lloyd lived at Chawton Cottage from 1809. Francis Austen lived at Chawton Great House and in the neighborhood of Alton from 1814 until the end of Jane's life. The cottage was a short walk from the parish church and close enough to Steventon, Ashe, and Deane for occasional visits to old friends and family. It was about a mile from Alton, a market town with a bank, an apothecary, and a few shops. More specialized goods had to be bought from Winchester, Farnham, or Guildford. Chawton was a small town, with a population of only 347 in 1811.
Clarkengreen		HAMP	*Clifford, MW* 44
Deane		HAMP	*Clifford, MW* 43
			Mr. Austen possessed the living of Deane as well as that of Steventon. He rented the parsonage there to the Lloyd family,

(*continued*)

England (COUNTY/City)	Abbr.	Map Location	Notes
			but when his eldest son James married, Mr. Austen made him his curate at Deane, and the Lloyds had to move. The Lloyds then moved to Ibthorpe, about fifteen miles away. Deane was a very small village; when James began his term as curate there in 1792, there were only twenty-four families. Nonetheless, two London coaches stopped there daily. When the Lloyds were living there, the Austens often walked the mile and a half to Deane to visit with Mrs. Lloyd and her three daughters, Eliza, Mary, and Martha.
Ibthorpe	HAMP		In 1792, the Lloyd family, good friends of the Austens, moved to Ibthorpe, over fifteen miles from Steventon. It was a pretty village, considered by William Cobbett "a sight worth going many miles to see."

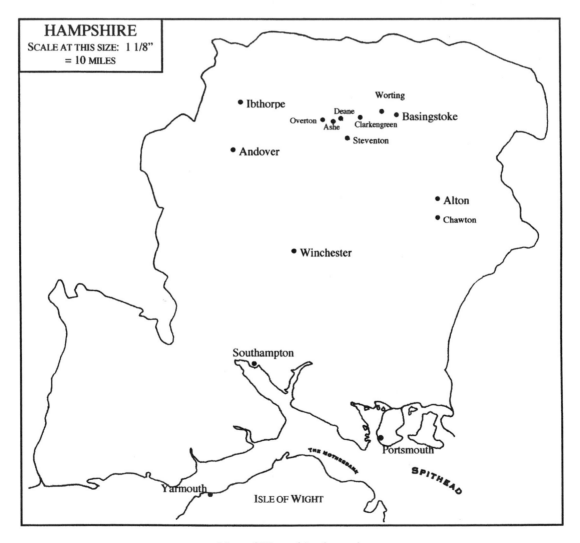

Map of Hampshire (HAMP).

England (COUNTY/City)	Abbr.	Map Location	Notes
Isle of Wight	ENG,HAMP		*Evelyn*, *MW* 184–185; *Sand*, *MW* 387; *MP* 18, 409; *P* 96

The Isle of Wight was a common destination for excursions from Southampton.

Overton	HAMP		*Clifford*, *MW* 43

James Austen's first curacy was at Overton.

Portsmouth	HAMP, PORT		*MP* 249, 368, 371, 373, 392, 401, 416, 443

Site of the Royal Naval Academy (*Gen Cur*, *MW* 73), which Austen's brothers Frank and Charles attended.

Home of the impecunious Price family. Portsmouth was also a major naval port (*MP* 232, 245, 254, 266, 400; *P* 69, 108), and between the natural harbor and the Isle of Wight was a channel called Spithead (*MP* 232, 378, 380, 384, 389, 409). Ships preparing to set sail would head into this channel and await favorable winds (*MP* 388). The far side of Spithead, adjacent to the northeast coast of the Isle of Wight, was known as the Motherbank (*MP* 389).

The town was located on an island and was approached by a road that ran from the north side of the island. The town was, however, in the southwest quadrant of the island, and new construction therefore tended to spread north and east. As an important military base, Portsmouth had a legacy of fortifications—hence the ramparts (*MP* 388, 409) near the water's edge, which by Austen's time had been turned to peaceful uses as a promenade. *The Portsmouth Guide* (1775) described the ramparts as "a beautiful elevated terras walk, of a mile and a quarter round, edged with elm trees, kept in the most regular order. Prom this eminence, the unbounded prospect of the sea, contrasted with the landskip,* which the neighbouring country affords, forms one of the most striking variegated scenes imaginable."

(*continued*)

Section of Thomas Milne's 1791 map of Hampshire, showing Chawton and nearby areas. The cottage that Jane, Cassandra, Mrs. Austen, and Martha Lloyd shared after leaving Portsmouth lay in Chawton, facing the busy main road. The village, as can be seen in Milne's map, is quite a small one, and the ladies had to go north to Alton for many of their supplies. Jane's wealthy brother Edward owned land in this area, including the cottage and the nearby Chawton manor house; the name of his adoptive father, Thomas Knight, appears on the map at the very bottom of this map detail. Courtesy of Jean and Martin Norgate, Old Hampshire Mapped.

*The word "landscape" was pronounced "landskip" and sometimes spelled that way as well.

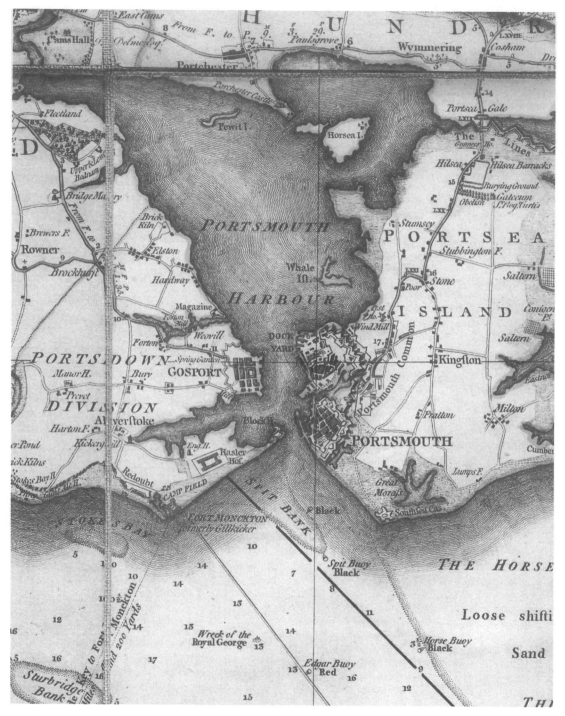

Section of Thomas Milne's 1791 map of Hampshire, showing Portsea Island. The Portsmouth dockyard is in the northern part of the town. The Point is the tip of the north-facing peninsula across the water from the words "Block H." The Promenade was further south, where the High Street ended at the water, and the Garrison Chapel stood nearby, about where the longitude line on the map crosses the southernmost of the buildings it touches. Courtesy of Jean and Martin Norgate, Old Hampshire Mapped.

England (COUNTY/City)	Abbr.	Map Location	Notes

On the landward side, the town was guarded by a moat, drawbridge, and additional fortifications (*MP* 376). A gate called the Landport led into the main part of town whose principal thoroughfare was the High Street (*MP* 376, 401), home of several good shops (*MP* 403), including Turner's at 85 High Street, where William Price shops for supplies before going to sea. The Austens knew Turner's and had had dealings with them on at least two occasions, in 1809 and 1815, and possibly on a third occasion in 1805.

The southern end of the town had a small northward-facing peninsula called the Point; from the end of Broad Street one could stand at this Point and watch ships go in and out of harbor, but once ships passed the Point heading southward out of the large natural harbor, the buildings along Broad Street blocked one's view. A better vantage point was the cannon platform at the base of High Street, which had a less superb view of the initial move out of harbor but a much longer view as the ships passed from the harbor out into the Spithead channel. Austen initially had Mr. Price watching the *Thrush* depart from the Point but changed it in the second edition to the platform instead, perhaps on advice from one of her brothers. A little south and inland of the platform stood the Garrison Chapel, where Fanny Price and her family worship on Sundays (*MP* 408).

(*continued*)

Portsmouth Point, Thomas Rowlandson, 1814. Courtesy of the Lewis Walpole Library, Yale University. 814.0.2.1.

England (COUNTY/City)	Abbr.	Map Location	Notes

Portsmouth had several notable sights, chief among them the dockyard (*MP* 372, 388, 400, 402–403), which was impressive both in its size and in the pace and variety of its activities. The dockyard lay north of the main portion of the town and covered eighty-two acres. It had a massive bakery, a salting-house for the preservation of meat, a rope-making shed a quarter of a mile long, and, just offshore, the huge ships that to William Gilpin resembled "floating castles, and towns."* The dockyard's steam engines and saw mills were regular stops for tourists, who gaped at the forty-five block mills that made 130,000 blocks a year for holding the pulleys that kept ship ropes taut. Designed in the first decade of the nineteenth century by the great engineer Isambard Brunel and built with convict labor, the block mills were an early industrial marvel. Gilpin visited the dockyards in 1774, long before the construction of the block mills, but he still found them impressive. "Every where as we approached Portsmouth," he wrote, "we saw quantities of timber lying near the road, ready to be conveyed to the King's magazines.—This is both a *picturesque* and a *proper* decoration of the avenues to a dockyard."

Southampton — ENG, HAMP — *L&F, MW* 78–79

The first boarding school that Jane and Cassandra attended in Oxford later relocated to Southampton, taking the girls and their cousin Jane Cooper along. While in Southampton, the small population of the school was struck by an epidemic, possibly of diphtheria or typhoid, and both Janes became ill. Jane Austen recovered at school, but Jane Cooper's mother came to claim her and take her home. The little girl regained her health, but not before her mother fell ill, too, and died of the disease.

Jane was not fond of the theater at Southampton. However, other diversions were available. Southampton was a resort town in a small and fading way, and it had the usual assortment of assembly rooms and other amenities associated with "public places." A popular activity was taking boating trips to the Isle of Wight or to the ruined Netley Abbey. Trips on land could be taken to Chiswell and Beaulieu Abbey.

Jane, Cassandra, Mrs. Austen, and Martha Lloyd moved in with Francis Austen and his wife, Mary, partly to save on expenses, and partly to keep Mary company in the long months while Frank was away at sea. They moved into cramped lodgings in 1806 and were happier when they removed to a larger house at No. 2 Castle Square in March 1807. This house had a sizable garden and access to a walkway that had been constructed on the old city walls. The Austen women moved from Southampton to Chawton Cottage in 1809.

An 1810 guide to bathing places praised Southampton for its "clean and dry" streets, its views of the Isle of Wight and the New Forest, its beach, and its elegant buildings. Mary Russell Mitford, writing in 1812, admired the "total absence of the vulgar hurry of business or the chilling apathy of fashion."

Steventon — HAMP — The Austens' home for many years, Steventon was a small village with a small, plain church and an unpaved main street. The

*One of the ships he saw in the harbor was the *Namur*, which would be commanded by Charles Austen beginning in 1811.

England (COUNTY/City)	Abbr.	Map Location	Notes

local manor house was owned by Thomas Knight but rented to the Digweeds, a respectable but not a cultured or scholarly family. When George Austen first became rector there in 1764, there were perhaps only thirty families living in the village; there were no doctor and no shops. The church is much as it was in Austen's day, with the addition of a steeple and a stained-glass window in her honor, but the rectory was torn down in the 1820s.

Winchester — ENG, HAMP — *MW* 451–452

Austen moved here in May 1817 to No. 8 College Street. Desperately ill, she was placed under the care of a surgeon named Giles King Lyford, but though she appears to have experienced a temporary improvement in her condition, she died on July 18 and was buried in Winchester Cathedral.

Winchester had two racecourses, a conventional flat track at Stockbridge Down and a steeplechase course at Worthy Down, the latter track quite old but still quite popular. Austen's last poem, cited above, linked St. Swithin, whose saint's day it happened to be; a long period of rainy weather; and an upcoming horse race advertised in the *Hampshire Chronicle*: a 10-guinea plate to be run for on July 29, a 50-guinea plate on July 30, and a 90-guinea cup on the 31.

(*continued*)

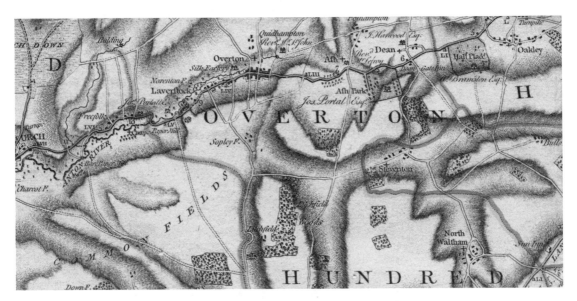

Section of Thomas Milne's 1791 map of Hampshire, showing the area around Steventon. Steventon itself can be found beneath the second "O" in the large word "OVERTON," while nearby towns where friends of the Austens lived can be seen farther north, along the main east-west road that ran to Basingstoke. The Austens' "neighborhood" of social equals included residents of Overton, Ashe, and Deane, towns visible along that road. Looking at this map explains the humorous itinerary of Mr. Clifford in Austen's juvenile work, the *Memoirs of Mr. Clifford*, in which the exhausted hero recuperates for five months in Overton and then takes an entire day to get as far as "Dean Gate, where he remained for a few Days & found himself much benefited by the change of Air" (*Clifford, MW* 43). Courtesy of Jean and Martin Norgate, Old Hampshire Mapped.

England (COUNTY/City)	Abbr.	Map Location	Notes
Worting		HAMP	*Clifford, MW* 44
Yarmouth		ENG, HAMP	*P* 92, 170
			Yarmouth, a minor naval base, had docks, a small theater, and a modest seabathing business aimed mostly at people from nearby villages.
HEREFORDSHIRE	HERE	ENG	
Hereford		ENG	*Scraps, MW* 176; *NA* 224, 239
HERTFORDSHIRE	HERTS	ENG	*P&P* 146, 172, 178–179, 219, 275
			Site of Longbourn, the home of the Bennets, and Meryton, their nearest town (*P&P* 10, 117, 333)
Hatfield		ENG	*P&P* 275
HUNTINGDONSHIRE	HUNTG	ENG	
Huntingdon		ENG	*MP* 3
KENT	KENT	ENG	*LS, MW* 254; *P&P* 172, 178–179
			Rosings Park and Mr. Collins' parsonage are located here (*P&P* 146).
			Jane was familiar with Kent, as her brother Edward's home, Godmersham, was in this county. She and Cassandra often visited Edward, who had been adopted by a wealthy childless couple. His adoptive mother had moved out of Godmersham and given it to Edward, retiring to Goodnestone Farm, where Jane also visited. Jane's wealthy great-uncle, Francis Austen, also lived in Kent, and her first known trip to the county was a visit to his house at Sevenoaks. The Austen women considered tak-

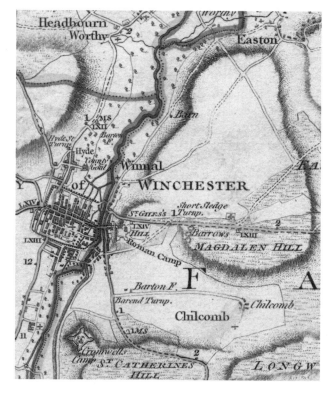

Section of Thomas Milne's 1791 map of Hampshire, showing the city of Winchester. Austen died in this city at 8 College Street and was buried in the cathedral. The cathedral can be seen on this map as a cross near the center of town; College Street lay south of the cathedral and ran roughly east-west parallel to the High Street that cuts through the center of the city. Courtesy of Jean and Martin Norgate, Old Hampshire Mapped.

England (COUNTY/City)	Abbr.	Map Location	Notes
			ing a house in Kent when they left Southampton in 1809 but opted instead for Chawton Cottage in Hampshire.
			Kent, as R. W. Chapman points out, is one of the counties frequently referred to as "the garden of England" (*E* 273).
			Kent had two principal seaside resorts: Ramsgate and Margate.
Bromley	LON		*P&P* 212
Dartford	LON		*S&S* 252
			Jane often traveled through Dartford on her way to visit relatives in Kent. She dined at the Bull and George inn there in October 1798 and at the Bull inn (a different establishment) in 1808. Apparently she also ate at the Bull in 1792, for in a letter about the 1808 visit, she recalled a similar trip "fourteen years ago" and reported, "At Dartford, . . . we went to the Bull, the same inn in which we breakfasted in that said journey, and on the present occasion we had about the same bad butter."
Deal	ENG		*P* 71, 170
Dover	ENG		*H&E, MW* 36; *Mount, MW* 41

(*continued*)

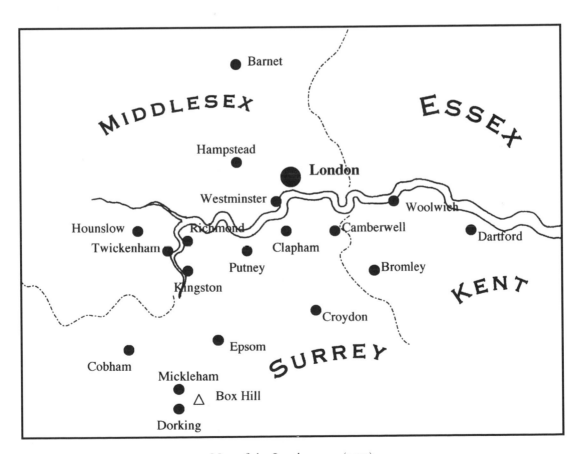

Map of the London area (LON).

England (COUNTY/City)	Abbr.	Map Location	Notes
			Dover was the principal port for travel to and from the Continent. William Gilpin, visiting in 1774, noted the effect that this cross-Channel traffic had on the culture of the town: "The inhabitant of Dover, for instance, is a kind of connecting thread between an Englishman and a Frenchman; partaking in some degree of both. His customs, and manners are half English and half French. His dress also borders on that of his opposite neighbour. In Dover you may eat beef with an Englishman; or ragouts with a Frenchman. The language of both nations are equally understood. The town is full of French; and you may converse either with them, or your own countrymen at pleasure. The very signs are inscribed in both languages."
			One night, unable to sleep because of the noise one party in his inn was making, Gilpin sat up to look at the harbor in the moonlight. "The tide was at its height; and the sea perfectly calm: the moon was full, and perfectly clear. The vessels, which we had seen in the evening, heeling on their sides, each in its station near the quays, were all now in fluctuating motion; the harbour was brim-full, and exhibited a beautiful and varied scene. Many of the ships, preparing to sail, were disentangling themselves from others. Their motions forward and backward, as circumstances occurred, were entertaining: and the *clamor nauticus*, in different tones, from different parts of the harbour, and from ship to ship, had an agreeable effect, through the stillness of the night, when nothing else was heard, but the gentle rippling, and suction of the water among the stones and crannies of the harbour."
Godmersham		ENG	Home of Jane's wealthy brother Edward Austen, who later took the surname Knight in honor of his adoptive parents. Jane and Cassandra were frequent visitors there.
Margate		ENG	A notable seaside resort; Eliza de Feuillide took her chronically ill son Hastings there to bathe for his health in 1791.
Ramsgate		ENG	*P&P* 201; *MP* 51
			A seaside resort where Jane's brother Francis met his future first wife, Mary Gibson.
Tunbridge Wells		ENG	*Lesley, MW* 112; *Sand, MW* 363; *NA* 33; *MP* 199
			A popular spa, though one that had lost its ability to lure an aristocratic clientele, Tunbridge was only a day's journey from London. It had assembly rooms, a circulating library, a theater, and a large number of inns, lodging houses, and stables. Its development stagnated toward the end of the eighteenth century but recovered with the outbreak of war with France in 1793.
Westerham		ENG	*P&P* 62
Woolwich		LON	*MP* 5
			Since 1741, Woolwich had been the site of the Royal Military College, which trained future officers of the artillery and engineer corps. The entrance requirements tended to favor the well-off, sons of gentlemen, and sons of military officers.
LANCASHIRE	LANCS	ENG	
Liverpool		ENG	*P&P* 220; *MP* 178
			A major port for the shipment of sugar, slaves, and cotton; its population rose to 78,000 by 1801, making it the second most populous city in the nation.

England (COUNTY/City)	Abbr.	Map Location	Notes
LEICESTERSHIRE	LEICS	ENG	*NA* 76
Bosworth Field		ENG	*Hist Eng*, *MW* 141 Site of the final battle between the armies of Richard III and the future Henry VII, in which Richard was killed.
Leicester		ENG	Site of Leicester Abbey (*Hist Eng*, *MW* 142).
LINCOLNSHIRE	LINC	ENG	
MIDDLESEX	MDX	ENG	*L&F*, *MW* 82
Barnet		LON	*P&P* 275, 282
Hampstead		LON	*Cass*, *MW* 45
Hounslow		LON	*Scraps*, *MW* 173
London		LON	*See* London.
Twickenham		LON	*MP* 57, 434, 455
Westminster		LON	*S&S* 251; *MP* 61, 212, 469
NORFOLK	NFLK	ENG	Henry Crawford's estate, Everingham, is located in Norfolk (*MP* 40, 114, 193, 393, 411).
Cromer		ENG	*E* 105–106
NORTHAMPTONSHIRE	NHANTS	ENG	Site of Mansfield Park (*MP* 21, 295, 360, 368, 416). Northamptonshire was renowned for the quality of its hunting.
Fotheringhay Castle		ENG	*Hist Eng*, *MW* 145
Northampton		ENG	*MP* 12, 57, 130, 250, 266
Peterborough		ENG	*MP* 255, 282, 288, 354
NORTHUMBERLAND	NTHUMB	ENG	
Newcastle on Tyne		ENG	*P&P* 317, 330
NOTTINGHAMSHIRE	NOTTS	ENG	
OXFORDSHIRE	OXF	ENG	
Banbury		ENG	*MP* 193
Blenheim Palace		ENG	*P&P* 240
Oxford		ENG	*NA* 46, 64, 201, 216; *S&S* 275, 288, 353, 362; *P&P* 240; *MP* 21, 376, 446; *E* 188, 189 One of England's two universities was in Oxford; Jane's father and her brothers James and Henry were all educated there, and Jane went for a short time to a boarding school in the town.
RUTLAND	RUT	ENG	
SHROPSHIRE	SHROP	ENG	*Watsons*, *MW* 321, 350; *P* 134
SOMERSETSHIRE	SOM	ENG	*P* 21, 26 Home of Kellynch Hall and Uppercross (*P* 3, 188). Home of Willoughby (*S&S* 44, 58, 114, 279, 302); site of Cleveland, the home of Mr. and Mrs. Palmer (*S&S* 114, 116, 279, 302).
Bath		ENG	*See* Bath.
Bristol		ENG	*Lesley*, *MW* 114, 118, 119; *NA* 85; *S&S* 280; *E* 183, 272, 359 Bristol lies on the border of Somerset and Gloucestershire and is actually its own county. In Austen's time it was no longer the leading slave-trading port, but it was a busy commercial center with a large shipping industry and a porcelain manufactory. One of its suburbs was the spa village of Clifton (*NA* 85, 87, 89, 97, 105; *E* 307), located on a cliff. Just inside the boundary of Gloucestershire, Clifton had a warm sulphurous spring,

(continued)

England (COUNTY/City)	Abbr.	Map Location	Notes
			assembly rooms, a pump room, and fashionable shops that sold such diverse wares as confectionery and mineral crystals from the Avon Gorge (the "spars" of *NA* 116). The Austens visited Clifton in June 1806. Bath, though near Clifton, was not in direct competition with it, as the towns' seasons did not overlap (*NA* 115).
			Blaise Castle (*NA* 84–85, 86, 101), a Gothic garden structure built in 1766, is located just to the northwest, near Kingsweston Down (*NA* 84; *E* 274). A beautiful mansion called Kingsweston stood two miles from the Severn and commanded extensive views of the surrounding countryside.
Crewkherne		ENG	*P* 121
Keynsham		ENG	*NA* 88
Minehead		ENG	*P* 171
Taunton		ENG	*P* 21, 24, 76
STAFFORDSHIRE	STAFFS	ENG	*LS, MW* 247, 251
			The county was noted for its excellent ceramics (*NA* 175).
			In 1806, the Austen women paid a visit to Stoneleigh Abbey, which Mrs. Austen's cousin Thomas Leigh had just inherited. The abbey bears a marked resemblance to Jane's description of Northanger Abbey. On the same visit to Staffordshire, the women visited Hamstall Ridware, home of Jane's cousin Edward Cooper, an Evangelical parson whose fervor Jane found off-putting.
Burton-on-Trent		ENG	*Sand, MW* 424
Stoke		ENG	*MP* 148, 189
SUFFOLK	SFLK	ENG	*Col Let, MW* 160–161
Newmarket		ENG	*MP* 426
			Famed for its horse racing.
SURREY	SRY	ENG	*H&E, MW* 35; *Mount, MW* 41; *Sand, MW* 387; *E* 273, 274
			The Watson family in *The Watsons* lives in the fictional village of Stanton, supposedly located in Surrey four hours from London (*MW* 321, 356). The "D" and "R" listed as towns nearby are probably Dorking and Reigate (*MW* 317).
			The fictional estates of Hartfield and Donwell Abbey are located in Surrey (*E* 91), as is the town of Highbury, possible modeled on Cobham or Great Bookham. The latter was the home of the Reverend Samuel Cooke, Jane's godfather.
Box Hill		LON	*E* 352, 367
Camberwell		LON	*Sand, MW* 387
Clapham		LON	*P&P* 274, 293, 295
Cobham		LON	*E* 95
Croydon		LON	*Watsons, MW* 319, 348, 350, 353
Dorking		LON	*E* 369
Epsom		LON, ENG	*P&P* 293, 295
Guildford		ENG	*Watsons, MW* 321, 341
Kingston		LON	*E* 32, 244
Mickleham		LON	*E* 369
Putney		LON	*NA* 122, 205
Richmond		LON	*NA* 210; *MP* 435, 455; *E* 317, 333, 383, 387, 393

England (COUNTY/City)	Abbr.	Map Location	Notes
SUSSEX	SSX	ENG	*Lesley*, *MW* 112, 119, 180; *E&E*, *MW* 30; *Scraps*, *MW* 170–171; *Evelyn*, *MW* 185; *LS*, *MW* 254, 271; *Sand*, *MW* 363, 368
			The Dashwoods' original home, Norland, is in Sussex (*S&S* 3, 87).
			Sussex had several notable seaside resorts and gained many more from 1810 to 1820. Hastings had a head start on development, but the prince regent's patronage of Brighton made it the most fashionable of all the seaside resorts of the period. The fictional village of Sanditon is located in Sussex.
Beachy Head		ENG	*MP* 245
Brighton		ENG	Austen did not think much of Brighton (*Lesley*, *MW* 120, 138; *Sand*, *MW* 368; *P&P* 219, 229, 232, 274, 288, 300; *MP* 203, 245), originally named "Brighthelmstone," partly because she disapproved in general of resorts that had become too fashionable and formal and probably also because it was associated with the debaucheries of the prince regent. In January 1799, she wrote in a letter, "I assure you that I dread the idea of going to Brighton as much as you do, but I am not without hopes that something may happen to prevent it."
			The prince's patronage made a huge difference to the fortunes of the town. In 1760 it had about 400 visitors at the peak of its season, but this number rose to over 4,000 in 1794 and to over 7,000 in 1818. By 1801 it was the preeminent resort in Sussex, and its economy had shifted almost entirely from fishing to tourism. It quickly erected dozens of brick-and-stucco lodging houses, two assembly rooms, and two circulating libraries.
			William Gilpin, visiting in 1774, found Brighthelmstone "a disagreeable place" devoid of beauty. He did, however, admire "the sailing of a fleet of mackerel-boats to take their evening station for fishing, which they commonly continue through the night. The sun was just setting when all appeared to be alive. Every boat began to weigh anchor and unmoor. . . . the fleet, the water, and the whole horizon, glowed with one rich harmonious tint from the setting sun."
Chichester		ENG	*Watsons*, *MW* 317, 351; *Sand*, *MW* 407, 409
			William Gilpin, visiting in 1774, noted, "An old cross is one of the most beautiful objects we observed in the town. The cathedral is an ordinary, heavy Saxon pile,—though the cloisters and their appendages are of a more pleasing mode of architecture."
Eastbourne		ENG	*Sand*, *MW* 364, 368, 382, 425; *MW* 444
			A resort for sea-bathing.
Hailsham		ENG	*Sand*, *MW* 367
Hastings		ENG	*Sand*, *MW* 363, 382
			The second-most popular Sussex seaside resort, after Brighton.
Worthing		ENG	*Sand*, *MW* 368
			A smaller and less formal alternative to Brighton, Worthing expanded rapidly from the 1790s on. It had two circulating libraries and a bathhouse in 1798 and erected a theater in 1806 at a cost of £6,992.
WARWICKSHIRE	WARWK	ENG	*Gen Cur*, *MW* 73
Birmingham		ENG	*P&P* 240; *E* 310

(continued)

England (COUNTY/City)	Abbr.	Map Location	Notes
			James Bisset's 1800 poem, *Ramble of the Gods through Birmingham*, described the well-known industrial character of the city. He admired wharves piled with a "thousand tons of coal," the pin factories that could "point and cut twelve thousand pins an hour," the crowds of boats afloat and wagon on shore, the gun works, the buckle works, and the shops where metal buttons were made and gilded and "paper trays japanned."
Kenilworth Castle		ENG	*P&P* 240
Warwick		ENG	*P&P* 240
WESTMORLAND	WESTM	ENG	
WILTSHIRE	WILTS	ENG	Site of the fictional Fullerton, near Salisbury (*NA* 232), where Catherine Morland lives (*NA* 120, 122, 124, 233). Tom Fowle, Cassandra Austen's ill-fated fiancé, had a living at Allington in Wiltshire.
Devizes		ENG	*Clifford*, *MW* 43; *NA* 122
Marlborough		ENG	*S&S* 318
Salisbury		ENG	*NA* 224, 232
WORCESTERSHIRE	WORCS	ENG	*Sand*, *MW* 424 One of the counties typically referred to as "the garden of England" (*E* 273).
YORKSHIRE	YORKS	ENG	*Lesley*, *MW* 117; *Cath*, *MW* 200; *E* 388 Site of Enscombe, Frank Churchill's home, 190 miles from London (*E* 15, 120, 121, 306, 426).
Harrogate		ENG	*MW* 445
Pontefract Castle		ENG	The "Pomfret" of Shakespeare and of *Hist Eng*, *MW* 139.
Scarborough		ENG	*Cath*, *MW* 199, 200; *P&P* 342 Scarborough was northern England's largest resort, with a population of 6,000, forty bathing machines, and thriving fishing and shipbuilding industries.
York		ENG	*Sand*, *MW* 424; *MP* 193

List of English Towns or Physical Features and Their Counties

Barnet	MDX	Charmouth	DOR (Lyme)
Basingstoke	HAMP	Chawton	HAMP
Beachy Head	SSX	Cheltenham	GLOCS
Beaulieu Abbey	HAMP	Chichester	SSX
Birmingham	WARWK	Clapham	SRY
Blaise Castle	SOM (Bristol)	Clarkengreen	HAMP
Blenheim	OXF	Clifton (GLOCS)	SOM (Bristol)
Bosworth Field	LEICS	Cobham	SRY
Box Hill	SRY	Crewkherne	SOM
Brighton	SSX	Cromer	NFLK
Bristol	SOM	Croydon	SRY
Burton-on-Trent	STAFFS	Dartford	KENT
Camberwell	SRY	Dawlish	DEVON
Carlisle	CUMB	Dean Gate	HAMP

Deane	HAMP	Newmarket	SFLK
Devizes	WILTS	Northampton	NHANTS
Dovedale	DERBY	Overton	HAMP
Dover	KENT	Oxford	OXF
Eastbourne	SSX	Peak District	DERBY
Epsom	SRY	Peterborough	NHANTS
Eton	BERKS (Windsor)	Petty France	GLOCS
Exeter	DEVON	Plymouth	DEVON
Fotheringhay Castle	NHANTS	Pontefract Castle	YORKS
Godmersham	KENT	Portsmouth	HAMP
Guildford	SRY	Putney	SRY
Hailsham	SSX	Ramsgate	KENT
Hampstead	MDX	Reading	BERKS
Harrogate	YORKS	Richmond	SRY
Hastings	SSX	Salisbury	WILTS
Hatfield	HERTS	Scarborough	YORKS
Hereford	HERE	Southampton	HANTS
Honiton	DEVON	Southend	ESX
Hounslow	MDX	Taunton	SOM
Ibthorpe	HAMP	Tetbury	GLOCS
Kenilworth Castle	WARWK	Tintern Abbey	GLOCS
Kingston	SRY	Tunbridge Wells	KENT
Kingsweston	SOM (Bristol)	Twickenham	MDX
Lake District	CUMB	Weymouth	DOR
Leicester Abbey	LEICS	Winchester	HAMP
Liverpool	LANCS	Windsor	BERKS
Lyme Regis	DOR	Woolwich	KENT
Margate	KENT	Worting	HAMP
Marlborough	WILTS	Worthing	SSX
Matlock	DERBY	Yarmouth	HAMP
Newcastle	NTHUMB		

See also Bath; London.

Pocketbooks and Reticules

A pocket case or letter case was a folding enclosure that usually folded twice (like a business letter today) and had a clasp or ties of some kind to keep it closed. There were several types; some were made of leather, while others were made of linen or silk and ornately embroidered. Carried by men and women alike, they could hold money, small scissors, letters (*S&S* 329), receipts, newspaper clippings (*Sand, MW* 366), and other small, relatively flat items (*S&S* 60, 329). Some could also be used as covers for pocketbooks.

The pocketbook was precisely what its name implies—a small book (*Sand, MW* 306; *NA* 18–19; *E* 339) that could fit in a pocket, often taking the form of a diary or datebook specific to a certain year. Some contained riddles, a calendar, pages for keeping track of expenses of keeping a diary, recipes, puzzles, or song lyrics. Parson Woodforde mentions buying a lady's pocketbook in 1796 for two shillings; in 1788 he writes of a woman receiving from a suitor the gift of "a very handsome red Morocco Almanack and Pocket Book, gilt with a silver clasp to the same—quite new fashioned." This red leather pocketbook would have had the datebook, then, and possibly a compartment to hold papers and money also. Many pocketbooks, as this one probably did, had a place to keep paper and pencil.

Purses (*Sand, MW* 392; *NA* 116, 229) generally held money and were small bags, usually closed by means of a drawstring, and decorated in some way. The best purses came from France and featured designs made of tiny glass beads, up to 1,000 of them per square inch. Other purses and reticules were embroidered or beaded at home. Some were knitted, with a bead added at every stitch; others were sewn. Some were closed with drawstrings, while others had elaborate metal clasps. Netting was a popular way of making purses; many of these netted purses resembled stockings and were carried loosely in the hand, in the case of women, or in the pockets, in the case of men. They opened in the middle, with a pouch for coins on either side, and often featured stripes of different-colored thread and tassels around the edges. They were a common gift from ladies to gentlemen.

From the 1790s, women began carrying all their different belongings in a larger bag called a reticule (see the illustration *A Fashionable Belle* [Clothing]). Initially called a ridicule (*E* 453) (the name by which it went in France), then an "indispensable," and finally a reticule, this handbag solved a common problem of the late eighteenth century, when more streamlined women's dresses came into vogue. The old way of carrying money, letters, bottles of scent, handkerchiefs, purses, fans, and similar items had been to strap a cloth pocket (*Cass, MW* 46; *NA* 203; *E* 339) around one's waist. Items went into the pocket and were accessed through a slit in the skirt. When the voluminous skirts and projecting bustles that concealed the pockets were discarded, women had to have a way of carrying their belongings, and reticules supplied this need. Because, unlike the pockets, they were designed to be visible, their decoration was a large part of their appeal. They might be round, hexagonal, or lozenge-shaped; decorated with beading, embroidery, or even painting; and either soft or hard. *See also* Clothing; Money.

Politics and Government

Government at the local level depended on the size and history of each community. Some boroughs were run by town corporations, many of them established in the Middle Ages, and these had their own rules and privileges. They typically set taxes and levied tolls, regulated local markets, and performed various other governmental functions. Historically, they had also been able to grant the "freedom" of the city to distinguished persons, conferring citizenship on them.* The chief executive of the borough was the mayor (*P&P* 18), referred to as a "lord mayor" only if that honor had been granted by royal charter. Other local officials included aldermen, who helped to govern London and acted as magistrates; burgesses, who collectively governed the city of Westminster; high sheriffs (*P* 4), who kept the peace in each county and ran elections; and churchwardens.

National government (*NA* 112) was run mainly by Parliament (*S&S* 16; *MP* 20, 161, 214, 425; *P* 4), which consisted of the House of Lords and the House of Commons. Austen does not concern herself very much with the House of Lords, which consisted of the peers (lords temporal) and bishops (lords spiritual) and was led by the lord chancellor (*Cath, MW* 224). However, she often mentions the House of Commons (*Col Let, MW* 169; *Cath, MW* 197, 200, 212; *P* 8), which was composed of 558 members elected by their various counties and boroughs. This sounds more representative than it is, for while substantial landowners and clergymen could vote, women, Catholics, excise officers, and customs officials could not, nor could the vast majority of adult males. County MPs—two from each county—were elected by all male Protestant landowners whose property was worth at least £2 a year, which was enough of an impediment in itself. Though the figure of £2 sounds low, the trick was that it had to come from the ownership, not the rental, of land, and most farmers were renters. Borough MPs, one from each borough (*Wat, MW* 330; *MP* 161), were elected by the electorate of the borough, which in so-called freeman boroughs could be quite sizable. A freeman borough was one that granted the franchise to all who bore the freedom, or citizenship, of the borough, but in other boroughs, there were only a handful of voters. Sometimes the franchise was limited to members of the ruling corporation.

The existence of boroughs with numbers of electors in the single or double digits led to all sorts of abuses. There were "family boroughs,"

---

*The term "freedom" could also refer to the right to practice a trade within a certain town or region, usually obtained by paying a sum of money. The example cited is an interesting confusion of these two meanings. Frank Churchill clearly does not intend to carry on a trade in Highbury and, given his general air of confidence and entitlement, probably means it in the sense of honorary citizenship. Yet he feels he must pay his fine in order to possess it, giving it the sense of a business transaction and therefore implying the second meaning. Either Austen does not mean us to inquire too closely into this little jest, or she meant it as yet another example of his double meanings and misdirections.

where the influence of one local landowning family was so enormous that the electors were forced to vote for any candidate named by the family in power. There were "rotten boroughs," where the size of the electorate was so small that it was embarrassing even to those who manipulated the system. These boroughs went to the highest bidder, and electors had a grand time squeezing the candidates for more money. Admiral Lord Thomas Cochrane, who stood for Parliament in Honiton, reported that during his campaign an "independent elector" informed him, "You need not ask me, my lord, who I votes for, I always votes for Mister Most."

Cochrane took an interesting approach to the question of parliamentary bribery. Though he was the son of an earl, he was impecunious and could not afford to spread large sums around. "To the intense disgust of the majority of the electors," he recalled many years later, "I refused to bribe at all, announcing my determination to 'stand on patriotic principles,' which, in the electioneering parlance of those days, meant 'no bribery.'" He lost the election but afterward paid a small sum to each man who had voted for him anyway. At the next election, many of the other electors, hoping to receive a similar reward, returned him as the member for Honiton, but this time he refused to pay anyone, stating flatly that he had never promised bribes and that those who were disgruntled had only themselves to blame for voting out of greed.

This was an unusually high-minded approach. Most candidates were not afraid of bribes or of pulling strings to get parliamentary friends to do favors for electors, or electors' sons, or electors' great-nephews' cousins' friends, if that would do the trick. Meanwhile, they campaigned (*S&S* 113), holding dinners and picnics and evening parties for whoever they thought could help them and opening their houses in the process to all sorts of people whom they would normally never have permitted out of the kitchen. They invented slogans; "Heathcote and Chute for ever" was one from a Hampshire election in Austen's lifetime. Their followers wore ribbon cockades in their hats in colors that signified their allegiance. Parson James Woodforde described the scene at a fairly typical county election for Norfolk in 1784:

> I mounted my Mare and went of[f to] Norwich and Will: went with me for to be at the County Election for Members of Parliament. We got to Norwich a little after 8 o'clock. . . . About 10 o'clock the Market Place and Streets in Norwich were lined with People and almost all with Wodehouse's Cockades in their Hats. After breakfast I went to Mrs. Brewsters and got 6 Cockades all for Wodehouse—3 of them of blue and Pink with Wodehouse wrote in Silver on the blue, the other 3 plain blue and Pink for my Servants at home. About 11 o'clock Sr. John Wodehouse preceded with a great many flaggs and a band of Musick, made his public Entry on horseback, attended with between two and three Thousand Men on Horseback, They came thro'

St. Giles's, then thro' the Market Place, then marched on to the Shire House on the Castle Hill and there Sr. John Wodehouse with Sr. Edward Astley were unanimously chosen Members for the County. After that they had dressed themselves handsomely and were chaired first round the Castle-Hill and then three times round the Market Place amidst an innumerable Number of Spectators and the loudest acclamations of Wodehouse for ever. Sr. Edwd. Astley met with little Applause, having joined Coke before. I never saw such universal Joy all over the City as was shown in behalf of Sr. John Wodehouse.

Three years later, he did not attend the elections himself but sent his servant Briton for news instead. Briton "returned home from Norwich with a Hobart Favour in his Hat, and highly pleased" to report that his candidate had won by a small margin. Briton, as a servant, could not vote, but even people without the franchise took a deep interest in politics, following news of parliamentary debates in the newspapers, debating public policy, and occasionally taking to the streets when government policies angered them. There was talk, particularly toward the end of the century, of extending the franchise to people like Briton, but the turmoil of the French Revolution and the Napoleonic Wars squelched the idea, and parliamentary reform would not be enacted until the 1830s.

The political system (*Cath*, *MW* 201; *NA* 111; *S&S* 233) was simultaneously a one-party and a two-party system. At the time of the Hanoverian succession in 1714, the Tory Party had thrown its support to the exiled Catholic Stuarts, and in retaliation, George I had given his support to the Whig Party. Tories were ousted from the party and Whigs installed in their places. Whigs were the courtiers, and Whigs ran Parliament. This situation lasted for decades, with the Tories becoming country gentry and looking askance at what it perceived as Whig decadence, but such a state of affairs could not last forever. The Whig Party frequently cracked along internal fault lines, and the American Revolution proved to be a fatal tremor. In a series of political and ideological struggles too complex and long-running to be summarized here, the party broke into two principal factions, one of which (the more radical wing of the two, which favored toleration for Dissent and had been supportive of the American Revolution) endured as the Whig Party, the other of which evolved into the Tory Party of the nineteenth and early twentieth centuries, referred to from the mid-twentieth century as the Conservative Party. For most of Austen's life, Britain was governed by leaders who would later be claimed as Tories, but they did not tend to use this term for themselves as it was still associated in many minds with rebellion and treason. Politicians (*P* 241) were in theory all Whigs, either of the establishment or the opposition. Some went so far as to call themselves "Independent Country Gentlemen," but the name Tory would not be used again for the party until 1818 and not by the party in self-description until 1827.

Yet, while the Tory name was in eclipse, the Tory outlook was still alive and well among the rural gentry, who cast their votes in elections for candidates with conservative views. The Tories, in general, favored the established order of things. They were strong supporters of the monarchy and of the navy, strong opponents of standing armies and Catholicism; in the 1807 election they took up the slogan, "No Popery!" They resisted changes to the established church and were deeply suspicious of the morals of Whig peers and courtiers. Caroline Austen, the author's niece, described her aunt as a Tory, though this should be taken as an indication of Jane's general outlook and political stance rather than as an indication that would have considered her as belonging to the Tory Party. Thomas Pennant, a travel writer of the 1770s, defined the mind-set in a way that Austen might have approved. He described himself as a "moderate Tory," by which he meant that he favored "a well-poised balance between the crown and people." *See also* Court; Parish.

Post

The General Post Office, established in 1660 by act of Parliament, was headed by the Postmasters General and headquartered in London—from 1678 to 1829, at 10 Lombard Street. Initially, the charge for a one-sheet letter carried up to 80 miles was twopence, but prices rose in 1711, 1765, 1784, 1797, 1801, 1805, and 1812, and vagaries in postal regulations could make delivery to one house substantially more expensive than delivery to the house next door. In general, postage varied by the number of sheets sent and the distance traveled. A new rate scheme effective January 5, 1797, set prices based on distances ranging from 15 miles or fewer to more than 150 miles:

single letter	double letter	treble letter	ounce
3–8d.	6–16d.	9–24d.	12–32d.

The 1801 rate hikes introduced new distance categories. Now postage rate benchmarks were set at 15, 30, 50, 80, 120, 170, 230, 300, 400, 500, 600, and 700 miles. The new price ranges, based on these distances, were

single	double	treble	ounce
3–15d.	6–30d.	9–45d.	12–60d.

In 1805, rates were raised across the board by 1d. for single sheets, 2d. for double, 3d. for treble, and 4d. for an ounce; certain twopenny post letters were also raised to 3d. As of July 9, 1812, rates went up yet again:

single	double	treble	ounce
4–17d.	8–34d.	12–51d.	16–68d.

However, these basic charges might be augmented by special local fees, such as those paid in outlying villages to extend post service (*Col Let*, *MW* 155; *LS*, *MW* 262; *Sand*, *MW* 408; *NA* 19; *S&S* 23, 167, 282; *P&P* 294; *MP* 16, 299, 442; *E* 433, 442–443) from a larger town. Villagers who had their letters delivered by a letter carrier, rather than picking up their own letters at the local post office, had to pay an extra penny for this service as well. (After 1774 post towns got free home delivery.) Wealthy Londoners could also pay for early delivery before general delivery began at 9:00 A.M.; this service cost 5s. per quarter or £1 a year. Newspapers, after about 1792, were delivered free of charge, but Post Office service could be a bane to opposition papers, which sometimes found their issues mysteriously detained or misdirected.

The recipient paid for letters but had the option of refusing mail, in which case it would be sent back, free of charge, to the sender; this system was believed to provide the Post Office with a monetary motivation for safeguarding the mail. The chief exception to this policy was London's Penny Post, which required prepayment of postage. Less common exceptions involved letters sent overseas to areas with which Britain had no relevant treaties.

The Penny Post, as its name implies, charged one penny to send a single-sheet letter within specified London boundaries. Delivery to a wider, more metropolitan area cost 2d. Hours and numbers of collections and deliveries were regionally variable until a sweeping set of reforms in 1794 standardized the system. Thereafter, speed and efficiency improved; hours were made more uniform in the receiving houses that accepted letters; the number of collections and deliveries per week was made consistent from one part of the city to another; the number of letter carriers was more than doubled; and prepayment of postage for letters was made optional. Penny Post charges were raised to 2d. in town and 3d. in the suburbs in 1801 as Pitt tried to raise more funds to prosecute Britain's war with France, and the service became known as the Twopenny Post; Austen's direct reference to it is evidence that she revised *Sense and Sensibility* during or after 1801 (*S&S* 161, 277).

Overseas mail was highly variable in price, because of the informal and even illegal way in which such mail was often carried. In theory, all foreign mail had to go to London first, then out to its destination aboard "packets," or ships designated to carry mail. A ship letter office was opened in 1799 to superintend such mail at a cost of 4d. per letter. However, people continued to follow an old practice—depositing their letters at communal mailbags hung up in various public places such as coffeehouses. When a ship departed for the intended destination, it took the mailbag, and the captain received 2d. for each letter carried. The government could not compete with these prices, though it tried repeatedly, albeit halfheartedly, to monopolize the foreign mails. An 1814 Ship Letter Act was no more successful than the 1799 attempt, and in 1815 the government tried again. The new act set postage at 3s. 6d. per letter on packets, 1s. 2d. on outbound private ships, and 8d. on inbound private ships. The higher price for packets reflected the fact that they tended to be faster.

The Post Office had three departments: the Inland Office, the Foreign Office, and the Penny Post Office. The Inland service, the largest of the three sections, carried most letters delivered within Britain and the colonies and also received letters for foreign and London delivery, transferring them to the Foreign and Penny Post departments (the latter headquartered in Throgmorton Street). Within the Inland Office, there were six smaller departments, divided according to the direction that mail traveled when it left London (along the Western, Bristol, Chester, North, Yarmouth, and Kent Roads). Initially, all mail came to London and then traveled outward again, but eventually cross-posts were set up to ferry mail directly from one provincial urban area to another without an intervening stop in London.

At the General Post Office in Lombard Street, Londoners picked up and mailed letters with the help of three men who ran the service windows. The staff, who lived on the premises, might, if related to high-ranking officials, be apprenticed into the Post Office at age fourteen. Other appli-

The Post Office, Pugin, 1809. London's main post office. Library of Congress.

cants had to be between eighteen and thirty, Anglican, able to write, able to post a £200 bond, and willing to take a series of oaths, including the oath of allegiance, the oath of supremacy, the oath of abjuration, and an oath against opening or detaining mail without orders. Inland Office clerks began their service with six weeks' intensive training in postage routes and rate calculation.

It was, by and large, a good job. There were several weeks' vacation in the summer, holidays on Good Friday and Christmas Day, twice-yearly venison feasts at the king's expense, and a yearly feast on the king's birthday. Dismissal was rare and took place only in cases of dishonesty, debt, or drunkenness, and most employees stayed with the Post Office (*E* 296–297) until retirement. There was no consistent retirement plan, though a few employees received government pensions, and some arranged to transfer their jobs to other men in exchange for annuities, a stratagem known as "quartering" that was technically legal, though outright sale of a post was not.

London was also home to numerous letter carriers. They delivered mail directly to houses, charging an extra penny for the service until this practice was abolished. Thereafter, mail delivery was free in certain "post towns," the boundaries of which were set by the postmaster general.

Post Office employees outside London varied widely in their duties and their methods of compensation. Local postmasters, in addition to levying postal rates, held a monopoly on the rental of post-horses until 1780. Postmasters tended to be innkeepers, partly because inns were conveniently located for pickup and drop-off of mail, and partly because inns had plenty of room for the horses and coaches that made long-distance mail delivery possible. There were about 500 of these postal deputies at the end of the eighteenth century, and of these, about 100 were women, many of them widows of former postmasters. Like the General Post Office staff, they had to take oaths and post bonds. Their salaries were not especially high; the lucrative Manchester office was worth only £200 annually, but there were other benefits, such as increased business from travelers and from locals picking up mail, exemption from the land tax, and exemption from quartering troops when regiments were stationed in town.

The Post Office also employed a number of captains and sailors to deliver foreign and colonial mail. The captains might own their own ships or might operate only a ship that was owned in shares by the local port and by London officials. The captains paid the crew and made repairs; in exchange, they received fees from carrying passengers and goods as well as their hire for carrying the mail. This could be a lucrative post; the highest-paid captains made as much as £1,000 a year. However, though they held Admiralty commissions, they lacked some of the privileges of full naval officers, such as exemption from prosecution for smuggling. In the late eighteenth century, these mail "packets," as the ships were called, employed about 850 men.

The methods of collecting and delivering mail were almost as varied as the staff who carried it (*MP* 398, 442). In London, after the 1794 reforms, residents received up to three separate mail deliveries per day, from the Penny/Twopenny Post, the Inland Post, and the Foreign Post, but foreign mail came in less regularly and was home-delivered only in certain areas. By the 1830s, all three deliveries would merge into one. A letter to be sent could be handed to the carrier (and prepaid, in the case of the Penny Post) or taken to one of the receiving houses, which closed at 7:00 P.M. for the General Post and 8:00 P.M. for the Penny Post.*

In the provincial towns and in the countryside, delivery was not necessarily this orderly or easy. Some towns had Penny Posts modeled on London's, and there was home delivery. Others had no post of their own and simply had an office where people could come to send and receive their mail. Those living in the country were almost always required to travel to the nearest town to collect and send mail (*S&S* 30, 84; *MP* 36; *E* 293–296); Parson Woodforde often records sending his servant Briton into Norfolk to collect his mail, while the Austens picked up theirs at the Wheatsheaf Inn south of Steventon. *Emma*'s "stray letter boy" on his "obstinate mule" (*E* 233) is probably on his way to the post for his employer or parents. Sometimes people bypassed the entire formal mail service, enlisting relatives, acquaintances, or servants to deliver letters and parcels as they traveled (*LS, MW* 283; *Wat, MW* 341; *NA* 125). For deliveries within the same town or part of town, servants were frequently employed to carry letters or messages (*S&S* 165). At other times, chiefly in emergencies, people sent a special messenger, known as an "express" (*P&P* 273, 274, 301, 324; *MP* 426, 450).

One problem with provincial mail service in Austen's childhood was its manner of conveyance. Mail was carried on horseback by post-boys (who were not "boys" at all, but men—and, in at least one case in North Wales, a woman) or in slow-moving coaches. The coaches frequently broke down, while the post-boys were exposed both to the elements and to attack by highwaymen. The post-boys were supposed to travel at a blistering speed of six miles per hour, but they so regularly fell short of this target, despite the threat of hard labor for loitering, that in 1782 it still took a letter 38 hours to wend its way from Bath to London. Robberies were so frequent that the Post Office advised customers to cut banknotes in half and send the halves by different posts. Customers, frustrated, were turning to private coaching companies to carry their letters and parcels, depriving the Royal Mail of income (*LS, MW* 311). The system was in desperate need

---

*Two exceptions were the office at Charing Cross and the General Post Office, which stayed open until 8:30 and 9:00, respectively.

of reform, and the reformer who addressed the problem was John Palmer, a brewer, maltster, and founder of Bath's first licensed theater, the Orchard Street Theatre.*

Palmer had some experience in rapid transit. In addition to his involvement with Bath's theater, he owned a theater in Bristol, and he had set up a system of post chaises to carry actors as swiftly as possible between the two venues. In 1784, he tested a new system, which differed from the old stagecoaches in several respects. First, the coach itself was robust, especially after the later adoption of the Besant patent coach. Second, horses were to be changed frequently (the participating innkeepers were paid 3d. a mile for the use of their animals). Third, the number of passengers was strictly limited to four, with no "outsides," the name given to passengers who paid a lower fee to ride on the roof of the coach or in its luggage basket. Fourth, there were to be two employees on the coach: the coachman, who stuck strictly to driving and to repairs of the coach; and the guard, who was responsible for maintaining the schedule and who protected the locked box of mail from highwaymen with his standard armament of a blunderbuss and two pistols. Fifth, unlike the post-boys, the Palmer mail coaches traveled both night and day (explaining why Edmund Bertram can arrive "early by the mail"—*MP* 443). Sixth, mail coaches, like post-boys, were exempt from tolls, so they could travel faster than stagecoaches on toll roads. The guard would sound a horn as the coach approached the toll gate, and the keeper would have to rush out and open the gate before the coach arrived.† The result was a solid success for the new mail-coach system; on the trial run, a coach ran from Bristol to London in sixteen hours, about half the old time. Postmasters were irritated that they had to get up in the middle of the night to receive and hand over their mail, but their objections were drowned out by customers clamoring for both the faster mail service and for seats on the remarkably swift new coaches.

Palmer received permission to expand the service, and it revolutionized mail service. It was not, however, without its problems. The guards were arrogant, some said; others found the schedules confusing; the coaches themselves began to suffer from overuse; and Palmer neared bankruptcy. In 1786, he was given a formal government job and a salary, but he was pushed out of this post in 1792 after a former friend revealed some of

---

*Later the Theatre Royal; this was the theatre the Austens would have patronized in Bath.
†Not all of these innovations were in place in 1784, when Palmer started the service; exemption from tolls, for example, began in 1785. This was always a controversial provision, because local highway districts complained, with good cause, that the mail coaches used the roads frequently yet paid nothing for their upkeep. The improved mail service was more alluring to those at the end of the road than to those whose parishes included sections of the most heavily used roads. Scotland ended the toll exemption in 1813, incurring higher delivery costs as a result, but the toll exemption remained in effect in England to the end of Austen's life.

Palmer's less discreet letters, which, among other things, criticized the postmasters general to a degree that could not be ignored. However, though he himself was superseded, his system flourished. By 1792, sixteen mail coaches arrived in London every day, and sixteen left the city as well, beginning their journeys at 8:00 P.M. at the General Post Office. Not one had been robbed since the inception of the service in 1784.* By 1794 the Royal Mail coaches were carrying so much mail that the drivers complained it was unbalancing their vehicles and causing overturns. Rates of travel reached the "tremendous speed," according to one London-to-Edinburgh mail coach passenger, of seven miles per hour. By 1811, there were more than 220 government mail coaches in service, traveling 11,000 to 12,000 total miles per day. *See also* Carriages and Coaches; Franking; Writing.

Pregnancy and Childbirth

Women who were "breeding" (*H&E, MW* 38) worried a great deal, and with good cause. While most pregnancies (*P&P* 364; *E* 352) were uneventful, the most dangerous years of a woman's life, once she had passed her early childhood, were the years of childbearing. When life-threatening conditions developed during a pregnancy or delivery, few treatments were available, and medical practitioners often made things worse with poor hygiene. Dirty hands and instruments led to puerperal fever, also called childbed fever, an infection that could kill any woman, even one who had already survived multiple births. Even women who had escaped the dangers of awkward fetal position, exhausting labors of fatal duration, and blood loss could succumb to childbed fever, dying days after an otherwise successful delivery. Novelist and political philosopher Mary Wollstonecraft died in childbirth, as did Charles Austen's first wife, Fanny, and Edward Austen's wife Elizabeth (who perished after giving birth to her eleventh child). Small wonder, then, that the process of having a child was taken extremely seriously and that the safety of the mother afterward (*S&S* 246; *E* 452, 461) was a matter of grave concern to all her friends and relatives.

Childbirth (*Lesley, MW* 118; *S&S* 287) was assisted to some extent by the expectant mother's female relatives and female servants, but all these were subordinate to the midwife or obstetrician, who was not usually consulted during the pregnancy for any sort of prenatal care but was instead summoned once labor had begun. Until well into the eighteenth century, female midwives took charge of almost all deliveries; they had little formal training but plenty of hands-on experience and licenses from the state. Midwives appear to have been reasonably competent. Many were ignorant, some were dirty, a few were too inclined to drink heavily during their work,

*Though, between 1796 and 1801, there would be fifteen robberies of mail coaches.

but they seem, from available evidence, to have been at least as skilled as other medical personnel at the time.

There were fears, however, that midwives were too superstitious and unreliable, and, in an era that yearned to put everything on a scientific footing, this arena like all others came under public scrutiny. What was needed, it was thought, were regulation, standardized training, and officially sanctioned medical expertise. Since officially sanctioned medical expertise was available only to men, this occasioned the rise of the "man-midwife," or obstetrician. The man-midwives had no better notion of hygiene than their female counterparts, and their formal medical education, riddled as it was with errors, could at times be more of a handicap than an advantage, but many of them did have a respect for the scientific method, and they were willing to try new techniques and tools. They investigated puerperal fever, trying ventilated rooms and clean linen to see if these would solve the problem and amassing statistics about the frequency of the problem. One prominent obstetrician created a life-size model to enable students to practice deliveries.

The male midwives' experiments, like their scientific attitude, could be a double-edged sword. They relied heavily on forceps to extract fetuses, which no doubt saved some babies' lives but probably injured others—especially considering the wicked-looking shapes of some of the standard instruments—and certainly helped to introduce germs into women's bodies. Their theories, however, were influential, because the full weight of the medical establishment lent an atmosphere of validity to their techniques. This influence was out of proportion to their numbers. Man-midwives remained a minority, mostly because they charged far higher rates than female midwives and were thus a luxury that most people could not afford.

The typical pregnancy was accompanied by a general concern for the woman's welfare, an avoidance of unnecessary travel (*S&S* 107), and an insistence that the expectant mother be allowed to eat whatever she liked. There were old superstitions that blamed all sorts of calamities, including birth defects, on women being deprived of foods they craved. Toward the end of the pregnancy, if she could afford to do so, a woman entered her confinement (*S&S* 108), a period of varying duration in which she refused social engagements out of the house and stayed mostly indoors with family and close friends. When labor, or "lying-in" (*NA* 15; *MP* 5) began, the midwife or doctor was summoned, and the woman was housed in a warm room with all its windows closed. The stale, sweaty air was supposed to be more healthful than fresh air or drafts. The laboring woman was fed liquor or caudle (a weak alcoholic porridge) to keep up her strength.

Most deliveries proceeded smoothly, but if the baby was badly positioned and needed to be extracted, heroic measures were employed. If the midwife could not rotate the baby in the womb, she would attempt a breech delivery, reaching into the uterus, grasping the baby's feet, and pulling it out, a task that required strength and dexterity. Cesarean section was almost always fatal to the mother and was typically used only in cases where the mother was sure to die or already dead, and there was some hope of saving the child. The first successful use of the procedure in the British Isles had been in 1739; the next instance in which the mother actually survived occurred in 1793. More common was the use of the cranioclast; if it became apparent that the child's head would not fit through the cervix, an emergency abortion was performed by breaking the skull and extracting the fetus.

After the delivery, the new mother would be fed broth, caudle, and other warm, bland foods. Novelist Fanny Burney, during her recovery, reported living on "Porter and raw Eggs—incessantly poured down," plus "Bark" (quinine) for an infection in her breast. Infant mortality was high, and even a child born alive (*P* 3) might die in the first days or months. New mothers fretted over every symptom, as a baby, or even a child under the age of five, was at enormously high risk of death from contagious illnesses, infections, diseases of poor hygiene, and even suffocation, if an inattentive wet-nurse should happen to fall asleep on top of it. Medicines for children contained alcohol, opium, and other ingredients that could, in overdose, cause death or illness. Teething was considered an especially dangerous time, and infant deaths were routinely attributed to teething. In short, mothers who seem, in retrospect, to have been overprotective were actually probably fairly reasonable (*S&S* 257).

Prison

For most of the eighteenth century, prisons were considered mere holding facilities for people awaiting trial, rather than as a form of punishment in themselves. Since prisons were viewed neither as fostering rehabilitation nor as housing inmates for long periods of time, there was very little interest in improving conditions within them until just about the time of Jane Austen's life. Until that time, prisons were run as miniature fiefdoms by private contractors, who were paid a set fee per inmate and then allowed to extract the maximum profit in almost any way they saw fit. Inspections were nonexistent or laughably lax, and both the jailers and the other prisoners were permitted to extort all sorts of fees and fines from newcomers. Diseases such as typhus, which was so prevalent that it acquired the nickname "gaol fever," killed a large percentage of the prisoners. Men and women were technically housed separately, meaning that they usually slept apart, but during they daytime they were allowed unlimited access to each other, with the predictable result that prostitution, rape, pregnancy, and sexually transmitted diseases flourished. No beds were provided; some jails offered straw, but it was full of lice and filth and went unchanged for months at a time.

Conditions for wealthy prisoners were significantly better than for the poor. They could pay for superior accommodations in private quarters, or even in the jailer's own house. In exchange for this consideration, they were often expected to pay higher fees than common criminals, and these fees could add up quickly. They included payments for arrival in the prison (called "garnish"), for food beyond the daily allowance of a pennyworth of bread, for the removal of chains, for beer, and for the right to entertain guests from the outside. By the time the assizes* were held, a prisoner might have been waiting for months in jail, and even if acquitted might leave the prison with his health and his finances ruined.

A typical prison did not segregate hardened criminals from those arrested for lesser crimes, and a single prison yard might hold murderers, debtors, children arrested for minor thefts, lunatics, and family members who had accompanied debtors into confinement. A different sort of scene met the eye in the bridewells, named after the original Bridewell prison. These bridewells were workhouses for those whose crimes were attributed to vice, such as vagrants, prostitutes, and women who bore children out of wedlock. The theory behind such places was that hard work, like pounding flax or picking rags, would cure the prisoners of their moral faults.

London had eighteen jails in 1800, many of which were quite famous, or notorious, depending on one's perspective. King's Bench Prison (*Col Let*, *MW* 158) housed both criminals and debtors, the latter of whom were allowed to leave the jail during the daytime to carry on their trades. The Fleet, a debtors' prison, was especially dirty and had a history of particularly corrupt administration. Newgate (*H&E*, *MW* 36; *L&F*, *MW* 97, 89) was the most famous of all London's prisons. It held the worst criminals, and excursions to "Tyburn tree," the famous site of London hangings, left from its gates. After the hanging processions were banned, execution took place in Newgate itself. It had been recently rebuilt and was an imposing structure, carved with ominous statues that seemed to warn potential offenders about the stringency of British justice.

Near the end of the eighteenth century, two changes occurred in the public attitude toward prisons. The first was an increase in humanitarian interest in prison conditions, largely as a result of the work of reformer John Howard (1726–1790), whose books cast the whole system in a truly appalling light. The second was the growing belief that prisons could replace whipping, hanging, transportation, and the like. Reformers hoped that incarceration would prove more humane than corporal and capital punishment, and several model prisons were constructed with the inten-

---

*The assizes (*Sand*, *MW* 424; *P* 71) were countywide circuit courts, held at intervals throughout the year to adjudicate capital criminal cases. These were run by a group of justices of the peace, local magistrates who, when not serving at the assizes, could single-handedly license fairs and alehouses, regulate apprenticeships, punish runaways, and rule on bastardy cases and minor criminal offenses.

tion of rehabilitating offenders through labor, conscientious supervision, and wholesome surroundings. Cleanliness was improved, and sightseers like novelist Fanny Burney were invited in to observe the condition of the prisoners. Jane Austen herself made such a prison visit, to Canterbury's jail, in November 1813. *See also* Crime; Law.

Public Places

Today, a "public place" is simply anywhere outside the home or any place where strangers can observe our behavior. In Austen's time, a public place had similar meanings, but the definition of the phrase was a little more specific. A public place was, indeed, a setting in which one's behavior could be observed by strangers, but it was also a place of amusement—a place in which relative strangers could become acquaintances through shared activities. It was a place in which those who could afford a little idleness, whether for a month or for an afternoon, engaged in a wide variety of diversions specifically planned for their pleasure.

The term "public place" thus carried connotations with which we are not familiar today. The careful person was expected to be not only properly behaved in a "public place" but extremely cautious. For women in particular, a public place, with all its perilous intimacy, could lead to moral lapses and to public disgrace (*Lesley, MW* 120). The anonymous author of *Female Tuition; or, an Address to Mothers, on the Education of Daughters* (1784) is typical of most moralists in his condemnation of "Places of public resort":

> Here all are reciprocally spectacles and spectators; the gay, the great, the effigy of pride, the puppet of envy, and the paragon of fashion, mingle into one circle of thoughtless insipidity and parade; and, as they pass, with insidious civility exchange their places, their glances, and their sarcasms.

It is partly the idleness and hypocrisy that bothered him, but it was also the way in which such places brought young women into public view, as if the male gaze alone could taint female virtue. Even if one did not succumb to the blandishments of some handsome rake, to be observed in doubtful company was a fault in itself:

> Is it even reputable to be often seen in those splendid throngs, which, though chiefly composed of the most brilliant company, have been long branded as haunts of lewdness, where beauty, youth, and innocence, are constantly bought, betrayed, and ruined.

Critics of public places are fond of this theme: that young women brought into social gatherings in which the company cannot be selected are inherently in danger.

Public places (*Lesley, MW* 128, 133; *NA* 104) fell into several broad categories. Among these were "watering places," which could include both sea-bathing resorts and spas where invalids went to drink and bathe in the water of mineral springs. These sorts of places attracted long-term visitors, who made a special journey to relax, recuperate, and enjoy various forms of entertainment over a period of weeks or even months. Then there were pleasure gardens, which attracted visitors for only a few hours. Other places could be considered "public places," but Austen mentions primarily watering places and gardens.

Of the watering places (*Sand*, *MW* 389; *P&P* 237; *E* 146), the spas were longer established than the seaside resorts. The latter were just becoming popular, and they tended to imitate the amenities of the spas. Both types of towns typically had one or more assembly halls (*H&E*, *MW* 35) where balls could be held; visitors to a well-organized town would pay a fee* that entitled them to admittance to these balls and would be greeted soon after their arrival by a master of ceremonies, who would ascertain that they were not irreparably vulgar in origins or demeanor. In practice, few visitors who could pay the steep fees were barred from doing so; the proprietors of the assembly rooms were perfectly happy to take almost everybody's money. However, the master of ceremonies was entitled to issue hints or commands regarding dress code and behavior, and this went a long way toward enforcing a code of conduct.

Watering places also usually had at least one circulating library (*Sand*, *MW* 389), which charged its own fees for book borrowing. There might also be a tearoom, a card room, concerts, lotteries, and raffles, as well as private parties among acquaintances. A theatre was always desirable; some towns, such as Brighton and Weymouth, invested heavily in new, lavishly decorated theatres in the late eighteenth and early nineteenth centuries and worked hard to lure London talent to their stages. Each of these venues might have its own set of fees, and then, of course, there were fees for the ostensible purpose in visiting such a place—taking the waters, whether by drinking or immersion.

Shops of all kinds catered to the wealthy clientele in watering places, selling everything from hats to rock crystals to inlaid wooden boxes. Public works legislation in the more prominent towns improved the lighting, paving, and sanitation; Bath and Clifton, for example, raised their pavements to protect pedestrians from the filthy drainage in the streets. Many towns imitated the example of Bath, building townhouses in imposingly huge rows, terraces, and crescents, the entire swath of houses unified into a single façade, appearing from the street to be one gigantic neoclassical mansion. New construction presented this impressive face to the wide street front, while smaller, less monumental buildings on side streets housed servants, horses, and less prosperous renters.

*In 1799, these could be up to 10s. 6d. for the assembly room and 5s. for the circulating library.

In these settings, people made acquaintances and hoped to guard against impostors and hypocrites. As they might be rubbing shoulders with almost anyone, precautions had to be taken to ensure that any new acquaintances were trustworthy; in part, this function was performed by the master of ceremonies, who vetted candidates for admission to public gatherings and who could therefore introduce suitable strangers to each other. In part, new friendships were formed when people were introduced by mutual acquaintances, but to approach a stranger and strike up a conversation without some sort of formal introduction was unforgivably rude, and if a young woman were one of the parties to such a conversation, the sin was graver still. Even in the best of circumstances, it was possible to end up, unwillingly or unintentionally, being acquainted with a person of annoying habits or dubious reputation. Catherine Morland's association with John Thorpe reflects the common fear of having to "know" someone distasteful because of mutual acquaintances, and *Emma* returns repeatedly to the theme of the superficiality of "an acquaintance formed only in a public place" (372), without the benefit of seeing one's companions in their own environment or of hearing about their faults and virtues from those who have known them all their lives (*E* 169, 428).

At the public gardens, less care could be taken to weed out those deemed undesirable. This was primarily because the fees for entrance into the public gardens were much lower than the subscription fees at spas. London's principal public gardens were Vauxhall (*Lesley, MW* 128), Ranelagh, Marylebone, and Kensington Gardens; Bath, where Austen lived from 1801 to 1806, had Sydney Gardens; and some of the other large towns had similar establishments. Each offered somewhat different terrain and services, but there was a great deal of overlap. The standard public pleasure garden had "serpentine" (winding) paths for strolling, elaborate landscaping designed in fashionable style, refreshments, and both regularly scheduled and special entertainments such as concerts, water shows, and fireworks. Most of the gardens suffered periodically from the public perception that they encouraged vice—all those shady, unchaperoned pathways!—and allowed rabble such as servants and minor tradesmen to sup, walk, and gaze at statuary uncomfortably close to peers and gentlemen.

Vauxhall was the most popular of the great pleasure gardens and the longest-lived; it had its origins in Elizabethan times and survived until 1859. In the mid-eighteenth century it acquired Chinese pavilions, faux ruins, a waterfall, a fifty-piece orchestra, and a 300-guinea statue of Handel. By Austen's lifetime, opinions about it varied; at least one visitor in 1780 found it "a most disagreeable place," while others found it a perfectly acceptable place for young women. The food served included cold meat, sliced thinly in order to extract maximum profit (*Lesley, MW* 128); patrons, irritated at spending a shilling for a parsimonious helping of cold ham, joked that a single ham thus sliced could cover the entire acreage of the gardens.

Vaux-Hall, Thomas Rowlandson, J. Jukes, and R. Pollard, 1785. A crowd enjoys music while parties in boxes eat refreshments. Courtesy of the Lewis Walpole Library, Yale University. 785.6.28.1+.

Ranelagh (*Cath*, *MW* 204), located on the north side of the Thames, was famed for its huge rotunda: 150 feet across inside, it had supper boxes and room for grand balls. Founded in 1742, it had an organ in the rotunda that was played by Mozart in 1764, a lake, a Chinese pavilion, and extremely high entrance fees—2s. 6d., 5s. on nights with fireworks. Vauxhall was less than half as expensive, and Marylebone cost only sixpence, or a fifth as much as Ranelagh. Evelina, in Fanny Burney's novel of the same name, found it "a charming place," brilliantly lit and almost magical in its effect. However, it was to succumb to the eventual fate of most of the great pleasure gardens; it went out of business in 1805.

Marylebone, founded in 1650 and expanded in the first half of the eighteenth century, was lauded for the quality of its food, music, and fireworks. It does not feature at all in Austen's works, however, despite these virtues, for it closed in 1778, when she was not yet three years old. Neither does she mention Sydney Gardens in her published works, though it features in her letters. Established in 1795, Sydney Gardens was, in 1801, a sixteen-acre plot across the river from the core of Bath. It hosted concerts, lavish public breakfasts, and four or five gala nights, complete with thousands of lamps and extensive fireworks, every season. Austen attended one of these, a postponed celebration of the king's birthday, and thought the fireworks "were really beautiful, & surpassing my expectation." A typical gala cost two shillings. The 1801 *Bath Guide* described the gardens in fulsome language, praising its "small, delightful groves," "charming lawns," and "serpentine walks,"

> which at every turn meet with sweet, shady bowers, furnished with handsome seats, some canopied by nature, others by art. It is also decorated with waterfalls, stone, and thatched pavillions, alcoves; the Kennet and Avon canal running through, with two elegant cast-iron bridges thrown over it, after the manner of the Chinese; a sham castle planted with several pieces of cannon; bowling-greens, swings, a labyrinth formed by enclosed path-ways, the principal one of which, after many intricate windings, leads to a fine Merlin Swing, and a Grotto of antique appearance: on this way, four thatched umbrellas are intended to serve as a shelter from sudden rains or storms. All these beauties united, has an effect that commands admiration, and gratifies curiosity. A pleasant and spacious Ride encircles the whole. From the pavillions and bridges, an enlightened observer may fascinate his senses with the most enchanting view of hills, vales, dales and magnificent structures that surround this elysian field.

The Austens' first lodgings in Bath were near Sydney Gardens, and we may assume that Jane often availed herself of its walks, though she was seldom impressed with more formal entertainments such as concerts.

She does make some use of Kensington Gardens, sending Elinor Dashwood there to encounter Anne Steele (*S&S* 271, 274, 276). This public garden began as the seventeen acres of landscaping around William III and Mary II's palace at Kensington. Expanded by Queen Anne in the early eighteenth century and often renovated thereafter, it contained, at various times, wide paths, ponds, a Paddock for exotic animals, and a ha-ha. Initially, the gardens were opened to the public only on weekends when the royal family was not in residence, but by George III's time, the gardens were opening daily to members of the public who appeared well dressed and well behaved. Though the gardens had been a popular gathering place for the aristocracy at one time, by Austen's time they were more of a middle-class promenade. *See also* Bath; Bathing; London; Places; Reading.

Quiz

"Quiz" was a word of great flexibility. Then, as now, it could be either a noun or a verb, but its meaning had to do with ridicule rather than with a test of knowledge. When used as a noun, a quiz was a person or a thing that was notably odd or laughable, like Mrs. Thorpe's "quiz of a hat" (*NA* 49). When used as a verb, it means to tease, to ridicule, or to stare at someone haughtily and pointedly in order to embarrass him. It is unclear in which sense John Thorpe means it when he complains, "when they see you standing up with somebody else, they will quiz me famously" (*NA* 76). He may be claiming that he will be verbally teased afterward, or that he will simply be gazed at archly from across the room. In Tom Bertram's case, however, it is clear that the "quizzing" is verbal (*MP* 49).

The word appears almost exclusively in *Northanger Abbey*, and like most fashionable expressions, appears exclusively in the mouths of vulgar or frivolous people. It is John Thorpe who remarks on his mother's hat; it is also Thorpe who refers to "the four greatest quizzers in the room; my two younger sisters and their partners" (*NA* 59). (R.W. Chapman wonders whether this should be "quizzes," since it appears from context that the sisters are the ones being ridiculed, not the ones doing the quizzing. Perhaps, though, Thorpe is merely coining his own sillier form of the word.) Other than John Thorpe and Tom Bertram, the only other character who quizzes is John's sister Isabella, who can "point out a quiz through the thickness of a crowd" (*NA* 33) and whose skill in this endeavor impresses the naïve Catherine Morland.

Quiz-zing a Filly, James Gillray, 1795. The gentleman inspects his prey through his quizzing glass. Courtesy of the Lewis Walpole Library, Yale University. 795.5.26.1.

R

Reading

Reading (*Lesley, MW* 111; *Cath, MW* 197, 198, 220; *LS, MW* 273; *Watsons, MW* 361; *NA* 60; *S&S* 343; *P&P* 37, 60, 71; *MP* 22, 71; *E* 37, 85, 312; *P* 132, 219) was a common form of entertainment in Austen's time and growing increasingly common as literacy rates steadily rose, facts that should have afforded great satisfaction to intellectuals but did not. Despite the existence of numerous volumes of perfectly acceptable nonfiction, people—especially women—seemed to resist reading these works. Critics claimed that women avoided the nutritious fare of histories (*Lesley, MW* 129; *Cath, MW* 198; *NA* 37), sermons, travel journals (*NA* 108), and religious and moral tracts (*P* 101) in favor of lighter literary junk food. They left "all the Essays, Letters, Tours & Criticisms of the day" (*Sand, MW* 404) on the shelves of the local circulating library but swept the shelves bare of mindless claptrap.

This claim could not have been made about Austen herself, who raided her father's 500-volume library and that of the Austens' neighbor Mrs. Lefroy and who, throughout her life, read a wide variety of material. She was not, for example, among those who, like Catherine Morland, found all histories tedious (*NA* 108–109). The fictional Catherine enjoys books "provided that nothing like useful knowledge" can be derived from them (*NA* 15), but Austen read many histories and accounts of current events, including Oliver Goldsmith's *History of England* (*MP* 419), of which her own *History of England* is a parody; Charles William Pasley's *Essay on the Military Policy and Institutions of the British Empire* (1810), a book whose excellence made her, she joked, "much in love with the Author"; Thomas Clarkson's *History of the Abolition of the Slave Trade* (1808); Robert Henry's *History of England*, unusual in being divided by topic rather than by historical period; and another *History of England* by philosopher David Hume (*NA* 109).

She also read travels, essays, and religious works. Travel writings (*E* 365) were especially popular in an age of exploration, conquest, and discovery, and many people enjoyed reading about the strange customs, flora, and fauna of faraway lands. She refers to accounts of George, Lord Macartney's embassy to China (*MP* 156), a trip that captured the popular imagination and spawned works in various media. She also read Sir John's Carr's *Descriptive Travels in the Southern and Eastern Parts of Spain* (1811), a work that was particularly relevant given Britain's ongoing military forays in Spain against Napoleon and that caused her to revise a detail in *Mansfield Park*.* Austen's reading probably included at least some works

*She changed "Government House" to "Commissioner's" when referring to an event in Gibraltar (*MP* 235).

on art, architecture, or landscape design, as the picturesque and its connection to landscape were topics much discussed in her day. As a child, she was exposed to didactic collections of stories, dialogues, and plays designed to develop her sense of morality. Although these sorts of anthologies were not nearly as entertaining or engaging as later children's literature would be, the very concept of special literature for children was relatively novel.

Her interest in religion and moral philosophy continued, however, throughout adulthood. Though she was not fond of the strident tone of some Evangelicals, including the popular author Hannah More, she consumed some of their works if only to stay apprised of the state of the theological debate. Her sister Cassandra urged her to read More's *Coelebs in Search of a Wife* (1809—*Cath, MW* 232),* a suggestion that Jane resisted and met with ridicule at the awkward name of the hero. She was kinder to Thomas Gisborne's *Enquiry into the Duties of the Female Sex*, another Evangelically authored work that she was initially reluctant to open. This is an extended essay whose description of the female sphere of influence would come to seem all too familiar by the end of the Victorian period, as it was echoed and expanded by hundreds of authors and clergymen, but in 1805 it no doubt seemed fresh and sensible. Several collections of sermons came her way, not only because she came from a family well stocked with clergymen, but also because such books were commonly read by ordinary people for edification and meditation. Her works demonstrate that she was familiar with the *Sermons* of Hugh Blair (*Cath, MW* 232; *MP* 92), as well as his *Lectures on Rhetoric, and Belles Lettres* (*NA* 108). She also refers to James Fordyce's *Sermons to Young Women* (1766—*P&P* 68), another in the long line of works instructing women about their religious and moral duties. Her letters reveal that she was fond of Thomas Sherlock's sermons as well, and this tells us something about her theology, as he was a middle-of-the-road thinker, balancing carefully between Deism and Evangelism, offering reason with one hand and faith with the other. Her Evangelical cousin Edward Cooper did not meet with the same level of approval. He published collections of sermons in 1809 and 1816, and of the latter she wrote to Cassandra, "We do not much like Mr. Cooper's new Sermons;—they are fuller of Regeneration and Conversion than ever—with the addition of his zeal in the cause of the Bible Society." (The Bible Society, or, to give it its full name, the British and Foreign Bible Society, was a pet Evangelical cause that distributed religious texts as a missionary service.) Religious texts themselves are mentioned or quoted in her novels—hardly a surprise given that she was a regular churchgoer and that the words of the Bible and Prayer Book (*MP* 340, 387) must have

---

*A later substitution for her original choice, Archbishop Thomas Secker's (1693–1768) *Lectures on the Catechism of the Church of England* (1769).

been, like those of Shakespeare, in the very air she breathed. Miss Bates, for example, quotes (or, rather, misquotes) Psalm 16 when she says "that 'our lot is cast in a goodly heritage'" (*E* 174).*

Austen's other nonfiction reading included the picturesque tours of William Gilpin, who made several journeys around England and Scotland (*L&F*, *MW* 105) in the 1770s and later published his reflections on the suitability of various sites as the possible subjects of paintings. Elizabeth Bennet's northern tour, which ends at Pemberley, follows the route of Gilpin's *Lakes* tour. We are told that she particularly liked the works of Samuel Johnson, and his words crop up now and again in allusions within her own works. There is a reference to Boswell's *Life of Johnson*, for example, in one of her poems (*MW* 442), and Fanny Price's musings echo a famous sentence from *Rasselas*: "Marriage has many pains, but celibacy has no pleasures" (*MP* 392). His dictionary is alluded to in *Northanger Abbey* (108), and his periodical, *The Idler* (1758–1760—*MP* 156), also shows up on the table of Fanny Price, whose reading habits are clearly meant to be exemplary. R. W. Chapman also argues that the passage in *Love and Freindship* (*MW* 97) that begins, "we left Macdonald Hall" is reminiscent of Johnson's *Journey to the Western Islands* (1775).

Austen mentions other assorted works that would have been found in a literate household, such as pamphlets (*NA* 187) about political affairs (*P* 215) or agricultural improvements, collections of letters (*P* 101), memoirs (*P* 101) and biographies, and accounts of titles and heraldry such as Debrett's *Baronetage of England* (*P* 3–4, 249) and Sir William Dugdale's *Antient Usage in Bearing of Such Ensigns of Honour as Are Commonly Call'd Arms* (*P* 4). Occasionally we see references to works associated with certain professions, such as the "Agricultural Reports" (*E* 29, which R. W. Chapman suggests may be the *General Review of the Agriculture of the County of Surrey*) and the Navy List (*MP* 389; *P* 64). There is a reference to Madame de Genlis' sentimental volume on education, *Adelaide and Theodore* (1783), which embraces the trend toward finding a more natural and holistic method of education (*E* 461); works on education, whether fictionalized or not, were widely read in intellectual circles.

Periodicals mentioned include newspapers and that increasingly popular format, the magazine. Magazines had begun in the early eighteenth century as collections of essays and satires such as the *Spectator* (*NA* 37, 38) and the *Tatler*. Samuel Johnson, one of Austen's favorite authors, contributed to this format with his *Rambler* (*NA* 30) and *Idler*. By the turn of the nineteenth century, there were fashion magazines such as *Ackermann's Repository*, literary magazines such Henry Mackenzie's *The Mirror* (whose issue of March 6, 1779, contains the story "Consequence to Little Folks of Intimacy with Great Ones, in a Letter from John Home-

---

*The actual passage is, "The lot is fallen unto me in a fair ground: yea, I have a goodly heritage."

spun"—see *NA* 241), and magazines with general content such as news, fashion, articles on hunting, society tidbits, and puzzles and games. Some took a political stance, as did the *Quarterly Review* (*MP* 104) and the *Edinburgh Review*. The *Edinburgh Review* supported Whigs and reform, while the *Quarterly Review*, founded in 1809 by publisher John Murray, supported Tory policies and the maintenance of the status quo.

Poetry

Yet, though Austen read such a wide variety of what her contemporaries would have called "serious" books, she was no Mr. Collins, lecturing young women on the importance of reading "books of a serious stamp, . . . written solely for their benefit" (*P&P* 69). As with so many things, including hunting, music, fashion, and food, she urges moderation. The overly studious Mary Bennet (*P&P* 7, 60) is treated no more kindly than the hypocritically superficial reader Caroline Bingley. Nor is she given any particular credit for reading and copying passages from serious texts, for Austen, like most people of her time, thoroughly enjoyed reading poetry, plays, and novels, and endorsed the same enjoyment in others—in *moderation*.

Moderation is, again, the watchword. Austen was an enthusiastic consumer of poetry (*NA* 16; *P&P* 44–45; *P* 215), especially that of William Cowper (*S&S* 18, 47, 92) and Sir Walter Scott (*S&S* 47, 92; *P* 107, 167). Cowper was supposedly her favorite poet, and indeed his name and words appear frequently in her works. Mr. Parker, in *Sanditon* (*MW* 370), quotes Cowper poem "Truth," which sets up a contrast between the French philosopher Voltaire and a simple, but religious, peasant woman:

> Yon cottager, who weaves at her own door
> Pillow and bobbins all her little store;
> Content though mean, and cheerful if not gay,
> Shuffling her threads about the live-long day,
> Just earns a scanty pittance, and at night
> Lies down secure, her heart and pocket light;
> She, for her humble sphere by nature fit,
> Has little understanding, and no wit,
> Receives no praise; but though her lot be such
> (Toilsome and indigent), she renders much;
> Just knows, and knows no more, her Bible true—
> A truth the brilliant Frenchman never knew;
> And in that charter reads with sparkling eyes,
> Her title to a treasure in the skies.
> Oh, happy peasant! Oh, unhappy bard!
> His the mere tinsel, hers the rich reward;
> He praised perhaps for ages yet to come,
> She never heard of half a mile from home:
> He, lost in errors, his vain heart prefers,
> She, safe in the simplicity of hers.

Fanny Price also reads Cowper and thinks of his *Tirocinium* when she feels homesick (*MP* 431); the passage she contemplates can be found in the "Education" entry earlier in this book. One of his best-known poems, *The Task* (1785), is quoted by Fanny when she regrets the felling of the grand avenues of trees at country estates (*MP* 56):

Ye fallen avenues! once more I mourn
Your fate unmerited, once more rejoice
That yet a remnant of your race survives.
How airy and how light the graceful arch,
Yet awful as the consecrated roof
Re-echoing pious anthems! while beneath,
The chequered earth seems restless as a flood
Brushed by the wind. So sportive is the light
Shot through the boughs, it dances as they dance,
Shadow and sunshine intermingling quick.

The Task is quoted again in *Emma* (344), and Austen famously alluded to it yet again in one of her letters, when she announced she intended to plant laburnum and syringa in her Southampton garden because they had been mentioned by Cowper.

Austen refers obliquely to Robert Burns (*Sand, MW* 397) and his imitators in the "Scotch poems" of *Lesley Castle* (*MW* 124), though her sensible character Charlotte Heywood found that Burns' notorious drinking and womanizing spoiled some of her enjoyment of his poems (*Sand, MW* 398). Another of the famous Scottish poets of the time was Sir Walter Scott (1771–1832), whom Jane enjoyed without any such reservations about his private character. She mentions *Marmion* and *The Lady of the Lake* in her works (*Sand, MW* 397; *P* 100) and quotes from *The Lay of the Last Minstrel* in *Mansfield Park* (86). Once again, it is Fanny Price who recalls from memory, "Full many a scutcheon and banner riven / Shook to the cold night-wind of heaven," and the Scottish king buried below a marble stone, though she fails to recall the exact wording (*MP* 86).

Other poets mentioned include James Montgomery (1771–1854), whose works included abolitionist and religious poems (*Sand, MW* 397); William Wordsworth (1770–1850), one of the principal Romantic poets whose verse often described the scenery of his native Lake District (*Sand, MW* 397); and Thomas Campbell (1777–1844), who addressed various subjects in his works, from the beauties of nature to the deeds of famous men. Sir Edward Denham mentions his *Pleasures of Hope* (1799—*Sand, MW* 397) and quotes a line from it. Oliver Goldsmith, whose *History* Austen also read, earns a nod for his poetry as well when Austen summarizes his two-verse poem, *When Lovely Woman Stoops to Folly* (*E* 387)—the "folly," in Goldsmith's poem, being sexual looseness and presumably nothing to do with Mrs. Churchill's character or cause of death.

Matthew Prior (1664–1721) is mentioned (*NA* 37) but not quoted, though his poem *Henry and Emma* is alluded to in the context of Anne Elliot's desire to serve as Louisa Musgrove's nurse. In *Henry and Emma*, Henry tests his lover's constancy by falsely claiming to have been banished. She volunteers to go with him into exile, answering all his objections with promises to endure hardship gladly by his side. Henry then coldly rejects her, stating that if she would go with him, she would go with any man, and therefore she is not worth having. In response, Emma insists upon accompanying him, even as a servant to the woman he chooses to marry instead:

> Yet let me go with Thee; and going prove,
> From what I will endure, how much I love.
> This potent Beauty, this Triumphant Fair,
> This happy Object of our diff'rent Care,
> Her let me follow; Her let me attend,
> A Servant: (She may scorn the Name of Friend.)
> What She demands, incessant I'll prepare:
> I'll weave Her Garlands; and I'll pleat Her Hair:
> My busie Diligence shall deck Her Board;
> (For there, at least, I may approach my Lord.)
> And when Her Henry's softer Hours advise
> His Servant's Absence; with dejected Eyes
> Far I'll recede, and Sighs forbid to rise.
> Yet when encreasing Grief brings slow Disease;
> And ebbing Life, on Terms severe as these,
> Will have its little Lamp no longer fed;
> When Henry's Mistress shows him Emma dead;
> Rescue my poor Remains from vile Neglect:
> With Virgin Honors let my Herse be deckt.

Anne acknowledges that her feelings are not quite as self-sacrificing as Emma's (*P* 116), but she might have taken comfort from the fact that, in answer to this touching tribute, the fictional Henry relents and marries his Emma.

The Beggar's Petition, a work by a much less well remembered poet, Thomas Moss, is one of the pieces that the young Catherine Morland is required to memorize (*NA* 14). It was a conventional and uninspired poem about the pangs of starvation amid wealth:

> My faithful wife, with ever-straining eyes,
> Hangs on my bosom her dejected head;
> My helpless infants raise their feeble cries,
> And from their father claim their daily bread.

Its tired language may be one of the reasons that Catherine has such difficulty committing it to memory.

There is a possible reference to Alexander Pope's *Rape of the Lock* in the phrase "eleven with its silver sounds" in *Persuasion* (144); a watch in that poem makes a "silver sound." A more explicit reference to Pope (*NA* 37; *S&S* 47) can be found in *Northanger Abbey* (15), where Catherine Morland reads his *Elegy to the Memory of an Unfortunate Lady*, with its dead heroine whose friends will not even

> Grieve for an hour, perhaps, then mourn a year,
> And bear about the mockery of woe
> To midnight dances, and the public show.

Mrs. Elton also quotes Pope's *L'Allegro* (*E* 308), and Mr. Elliot alludes to his *Essay on Criticism* (1711) with its famous line, "A little learning is a dang'rous thing" (*P* 150).

George Crabbe's *Tales* (1812), a series of stories told in rhyming couplets, are briefly mentioned as being among Fanny Price's books (*MP* 156). This is a typical Austenian aside. Many of her readers would have been familiar with Crabbe's other works, including the *Parish Register*, which features a young woman named Fanny Price who resists marrying a wealthy man.

John Gay's *Fables* are mentioned in two novels; Catherine Morland learns the fable of *The Hare and Many Friends* (*NA* 14), and Mrs. Elton quotes from the same fable in speaking to Jane Fairfax (*E* 454). The choice of fable is interesting, as the short poem depicts the plight of a hare pursued by hounds. Desperate for assistance, she asks one animal after another to carry her on their backs so that she may fool the dogs, but all of her supposed "friends" refuse for one reason or another to come to her aid. Jane Fairfax has been, for most of the novel, in a similar situation. She, too, is in urgent need of help, but all those who should be of assistance to her—her aunt, Frank Churchill, Mrs. Elton, and Emma—do her harm instead through, respectively, incompetence, deception, officiousness, and jealousy.

This poetic contribution of Mrs. Elton is an example of the fact that it is not only Austen's admirable characters who read and recall poetry. Henry Crawford quotes Milton (*NA* 37) in his reference to "a wife" as "Heaven's *last* best gift" (*MP* 43); the relevant lines are from *Paradise Lost*, Chapter 5, where Adam discovers the newly created, sleeping Eve:

> Her hand soft touching, whispered thus, "Awake!
> My fairest, my espoused, my latest found,
> Heaven's last, best gift, my ever-new delight . . ."

Of course, he subverts Milton's intent by implying that taking a wife is the last thing he personally would wish to do. His sister likewise tampers with a poet's lines. She parodies Isaac Hawkins Browne (1705–1760), who wrote poems on the subject of tobacco in the style of other authors—not only Pope, as in the sample quoted by Mary Crawford (*MP* 161), but also

Jonathan Swift and James Thomson (1700–1748—*NA* 15; *S&S* 92), best remembered for *A Poem Sacred to the Memory of Sir Isaac Newton* and the lyrics to *Rule, Britannia*. Mrs. Elton, too, is well read, for she only slightly misquotes two lines from Thomas Gray's *Elegy Written in a Country Churchyard* (1751—*E* 282)—the last two lines of the following stanza:

> Full many a gem of purest ray serene
>> The dark unfathom'd caves of ocean bear:
>
> Full many a flower is born to blush unseen,
>> And waste its sweetness on the desert air.

It is unclear whether the reader is meant to interpret her misquotation of the passage as a jab at the character's literary pretensions. In *Northanger Abbey*, Austen quotes the same two lines in exactly the same way, using "fragrance" instead of "sweetness" (*NA* 15).

George Gordon, Lord Byron (1788–1824—see *P* 107, 109, 167), is referred to occasionally. His *Bride of Abydos* (1813—*P* 100) is typical Byronic fare, full of exotic settings and savage emotion:

> Where the citron and olive are fairest of fruit,
> And the voice of the nightingale never is mute;
> Where the tints of the earth, and the hues of the sky,
> In colour though varied, in beauty may vie,
> And the purple of Ocean is deepest in dye;
> Where the virgins are soft as the roses they twine,
> And all, save the spirit of man, is divine?
> 'Tis the clime of the East; 'tis the land of the Sun.

The Corsair (1814) was similar in tone; the reference to the "dark blue sea" in *P* 109 may equally come from *The Corsair* or from *Childe Harold* (1812). Byron's *Giaour* (1813—*P* 100) purported to be a "Turkish fragment" of a sweeping tale of lust, revenge, and warfare. It, too, featured foreign locations and plenty of lurid violence, as in this excerpt:

> With sabre shivered to the hilt,
> Yet dripping with the blood he spilt;
> Yet strained within the severed hand
> Which quivers round that faithless brand;
> His turban far behind him rolled,
> And cleft in twain its firmest fold;
> His flowing robe by falchion torn,
> And crimson as those clouds of morn
> That, streaked with dusky red, portend
> The day shall have a stormy end.

Small wonder that Anne Elliot is so concerned that Captain Benwick's reading material is restricted to such verses.

Though she often refers to poets and quotes them, she faults Captain Benwick for his overindulgence in poetry (*P* 100–101), feeling perhaps that the richness of the language and sentiment are making him more, rather than less, morose. In the case of Marianne Dashwood, too, a passion for poetry foreshadows more dangerous passions and a tendency to self-destructive melancholy. It would appear that the character of Sir Edward Denham in *Sanditon* was also meant to be an example of the dangers of greedily consuming too much of the "wrong" kinds of literature, for he is an uncritical and undisciplined reader who is considerably better at gushing than at comprehending (*MW* 397). The goal is to enjoy the language without being dominated by it, as Anne Elliot is capable of doing (*P* 84).

Austen no doubt read all the poems she cites and many more, for she owned several anthologies of poetry. William Whitehead's *The Je ne scai Quoi* (quoted in *MP* 292) appears in an anthology of poems collected by Robert Dodsley, a copy of which Jane Austen owned. A similar anthology, the *Elegant Extracts* (*E* 29), compiled by Vicesimus Knox in 1789, is mentioned incorrectly in *Emma* as the source of the riddle "Kitty, a fair but frozen maid" (*E* 70, 79); R. W. Chapman points out that it first appeared in *The New Foundling Hospital for Wit* (1771) and was thereafter reprinted in numerous subsequent anthologies. Austen owned a copy of *Elegant Extracts*, which she gave to her niece Anna upon moving to Bath in 1801, so perhaps by the time of the composition of Emma she had forgotten where she originally read "Kitty."

Plays

Austen was fond of the theater and went to plays (*NA* 108; *E* 74) whenever she got the chance, but she also read plays at home. Shakespeare (*S&S* 85; *MP* 338) appears to have been a perennial favorite. There are references to *Henry VIII* (*MP* 336–337), *A Midsummer Night's Dream* (*E* 75), *Henry IV, Part II* (*Hist Eng*, *MW* 139), *Hamlet* (*S&S* 85; *MP* 131), *Julius Caesar* (*MP* 126), *Macbeth* (*MP* 131), *Measure for Measure* (*NA* 16), *The Merchant of Venice* (*MP* 123), *Othello* (*NA* 16; *MP* 131), *Richard III* (*MP* 126), *Romeo and Juliet* (*E* 400), and *Twelfth Night* (*NA* 16). She mentions more contemporary plays as well, which are discussed at more length in the "Theater" article. Her novels and Juvenilia contain references to John Home's *Douglas* (*MP* 126, 131), Edward Moore's *The Gamester* (*MP* 131), Hannah Cowley's *Which Is the Man?* (*3S*, *MW* 65), Nicholas Rowe's *Jane Shore* (*Hist Eng*, *MW* 141), and, famously, *Lovers' Vows* (*MP* 122, 168, 191) by Kotzebue, adapted by Elizabeth Inchbald. Three of Richard Brinsley Sheridan's plays are mentioned—*The Rivals* (*MP* 131), *School for Scandal* (*MP* 131), and *The Critic* (*Hist Eng*, *MW* 147), making him her most-mentioned playwright after Shakespeare.

Novels

Her greatest enthusiasm and her most devastating parodies, however, are reserved for the novel, a genre with which she was intimately familiar even before she began to write. Her family did not harbor the prejudice against novel-reading that was a fashionable intellectual stance at the time (*Sand, MW* 403; *NA* 48; *S&S* 43; *P&P* 68). Novels (*Cath, MW* 198–199; *Sand, MW* 389, 391; *NA* 37–38) were widely regarded as being a cause of moral decay among the young and a source of foolish ideas about romantic love that ruined people, especially women, for the realities of marriage. The most criticized novels fell into two classes: romances, which taught readers to expect obstacles to true love such as parental opposition (*L&F, MW* 81) or mismatched wealth, and which, it was thought, encouraged elopements and seductions; and Gothics, which were filled with superstition, exotic scenery, ominous villains (*NA* 181), perjured priests, ghosts, and dark family secrets.

Austen gently parodied both forms. *Sense and Sensibility* pokes fun at novels of sentiment and romance, such as Johann Wolfgang von Goethe's *The Sorrows of Young Werther* (1774—see *L&F, MW* 93), which actually led some young men to commit suicide for love, holding copies of Goethe's book as they died. Such books encouraged readers to fancy themselves supremely sensitive, emotional people brimming with potential suffering and ready to sacrifice all for the sake of love. They celebrated impulse and feeling and often derided conventional mores. Austen demonstrates, through the character of Marianne Dashwood, how difficult and dangerous it can be to live one's life according to such ideals. *Northanger Abbey* subverts the Gothic novel by demonstrating how far removed its dark plots were from everyday Regency life. In the course of demonstrating the shortcomings of the Gothic, Austen names many of the most popular examples of the genre, including Eliza Parsons' *Castle of Wolfenbach* (1793—*NA* 40) and *The Mysterious Warning* (1796—*NA* 40), Francis Latham's *The Midnight Bell* (1798—*NA* 40), Regina Maria Roche's *The Children of the Abbey* (1798—*E* 29) and *Clermont* (1798), Peter Teuthold's *The Necromancer; or the Tale of the Black Forest* (1794—

The First Interview of Werter and Charlotte, 1782. A soft and sentimental illustration of a sentimental story; other artists' versions of episodes from the book sometimes verged on the hysterical. Courtesy of the Lewis Walpole Library, Yale University. 782.10.16.1+.

NA 40), Eleanor Sleath's *Orphan of the Rhine* (1798—*NA* 40), Peter Will's *Horrid Mysteries* (1796—*NA* 40), and Matthew Lewis' notorious *The Monk* (1796—*NA* 48). Charlotte Smith's *Emmeline or the Orphan of the Castle* (1788—*Cath, MW* 199) concerns, in part, the unsuccessful attempts of the hero Frederick Delamere to win Emmeline's love (*Hist Eng, MW* 146). Smith (1749–1806) also wrote *Ethelinde* (1789—*Cath, MW* 199), a novel that, like Emmeline, features copious description of picturesque landscapes.

Ann Radcliffe (*NA* 49, 106, 110), queen of the Gothic, receives the most attention from Austen. There are direct references to her works *The Mysteries of Udolpho* (1794—*NA* 39, 41–42, 49, 83, 86, 106–108, 187) and *The Italian* (1797—*NA* 40) and indirect references to plot points from her novels that readers of Austen's time would have recognized immediately, such as the black veil and "Laurentina's skeleton" from *Udolpho* (*NA* 39, 40) and the roll of paper from *The Romance of the Forest* (1791—*E* 29, 32). At other times, she merely imitates the tone of the Gothic in order to contrast it with the reality of a simple visit to an English country house (*NA* 88, 167, 190–191). Austen also wrings a little humor out of Eleanor Tilney's misunderstanding of Catherine's description of a forthcoming Gothic novel, with "murder and every thing of the kind" (*NA* 112), as a prediction of a London riot.

Austen's minor works took potshots at additional literary conventions, from the epistolary form (*L&F*) to the extended narrative-within-a-narrative (*Plan*) that so often intruded into the clumsier examples of the genre. Both the *Plan of a Novel* and *Northanger Abbey* subvert the tradition of making the heroine an exemplary creature, though the latter work accomplishes the task by making the heroine deliberately ordinary, while the former does it by making her absolutely without a flaw, or even a hint of a flaw.

Austen herself preferred more realistic fiction. She enjoyed Henry Fielding's *Tom Jones* (*NA* 48), a rollicking tale that parodies the vogue for the classical at the same time that it tells the story of an amorous young bastard and his quest for love and fortune. She was also fond of the novels of Samuel Richardson, though she acknowledged that his constant return to the theme of sexual and romantic conquest bordered on the prurient (*Sand, MW* 404). (The "Lovelace" on which Sir Edward Denham patterns himself is the heartless seducer of Richardson's *Clarissa Harlowe*.) Her favorite among his works was *Sir Charles Grandison* (*J&A, MW* 15; *Evelyn, MW* 186; *NA* 41–42), which she tried at one point to turn into a play. Fanny Burney D'Arblay's novels *Evelina, Cecilia* (1782—*NA* 38; *P* 189), and *Camilla* (1796—*Sand, MW* 390; *NA* 38, 49, 111) were also works she admired. (Her father, knowing she appreciated Burney, gave her a subscription to the first edition of *Camilla* as a present, and her name can be found on the list of subscribers.) Burney's plots generally turned on the introduction of a young woman into society and her consequent education in its ways, ending with her marriage to a decent and handsome young man, a series of events that bears a striking resemblance to the pattern of Austen's mature works.

Other novels mentioned include Maria Edgeworth's *Belinda* (1801—*NA* 38), Oliver Goldsmith's *The Vicar of Wakefield* (*E* 29), and Richard Graves' *Columella* (1779—*S&S* 103), in which the hero apprentices his son "to a very celebrated man . . . who had united in his own person the several professions of apothecary, surgeon, man-midwife, bone-setter, tooth-drawer, hop-dealer, and brandy-merchant." There is an allusion to Laurence Sterne's *Sentimental Journey* (1768—*NA* 37) in *Mansfield Park* (99) and to Samuel Johnson's *Rasselas* later in the same book (392).

Naturally, she read a great many novels that are not alluded to in her published works. Maria Edgeworth was a particular favorite, and Austen read many of her works, including *Castle Rackrent* and *Patronage*. She also read novels that are forgotten today, such as Robert Bage's *Hermsprong* (1796) and Sarah Burney's *Clarentine* (1798). She found the latter novel "foolish. . . . [F]ull of unnatural conduct & forced difficulties, without striking merit of any kind." If there was anything that Austen found annoying in literature, it was "unnatural conduct & forced difficulties." She did, however, enjoy the parodies of other authors who, like herself, could not resist calling attention to literary clichés. Among these other authors were Charlotte Lennox, who wrote the romance parody *The Female Quixote* (1752), and James and Horatio Smith, who wrote verse parodies.

Collections of short stories would not become popular until the Victorian age and the dominance of the magazines that printed such stories. However, Austen makes two references to the *Arabian Nights*, a collection of Middle Eastern tales first translated into English in the early eighteenth century. She mentions Scheherazade, the purported narrator of the exciting tales, who told them in order to enchant the sultan and keep him from executing her, in *Persuasion* (229). The tale of Aladdin is mentioned in *Emma* (322) and in a deleted passage in *The Three Sisters* (*MW* 65), in which Mary Stanhope requests as many jewels from her new husband as were possessed by Princess Badroulbadour, Aladdin's beloved.

Buying and Reading Books

A typical novel consisted of a dedication to some illustrious person, who had either given specific permission for this particular work to be dedicated or blanket permission for the dedication of some future work by the author. The dedication served two purposes: for the author, it was a kind of brand name or seal of approval—if the duchess of Whateverington likes my work, so will you—and for the recipient of the dedication it was an irresistible form of public flattery. Most dedications were fawning affairs of one or two paragraphs, attesting to the patron's unfailing commitment to the author's work, the author's unworthiness to receive such tributes, and the author's hope of the patron's satisfaction with this latest humble offering. Austen, who even in childhood studied all forms of writing and grasped what made them recognizable, even in condensed form, could not resist parodying the bloated dedication. Her youthful works are dedicated to all sorts of supposedly illustrious citizens, including her cousin Jane Cooper (*H&E, MW* 33; *Col Let, MW* 149); her brothers Francis (*J&A, MW* 12), Edward (*3S, MW* 57), Henry (*Lesley, MW* 109), James (*Visit, MW* 49), and Charles (*Mount, MW* 40; *Clifford, MW* 42); her mother (*Amelia, MW* 47); her father (*Mystery, MW* 55); her niece Fanny, Edward's daughter (*Scraps, MW* 170); her sister-in-law Mary, James' wife (*Evelyn, MW* 179) and her sister Cassandra, who was fortunate enough to have four works dedicated to her: *The Beautifull Cassandra, Ode to Pity* (*MW* 74), the *History of England* (*MW* 138), and *Catharine or the Bower*. The dedication to *The Beautifull Cassandra* (*MW* 44) is a dead-on imitation of the tone, if not the wording, of most dedications:

> dedicated by permission to Miss Austen.
> Dedication.
>
> Madam
> You are a Phoenix. Your taste is refined, your Sentiments are noble, & your Virtues innumerable. Your Person is lovely, your Figure, elegant, & your Form, majestic. Your Manners are polished, your Conversation is rational & your appearance singular. If therefore the following Tale will afford one moment's amusement to you, every wish will be gratified of
> Your most obedient
> humble servant
> The Author

The dedication to Catharine has a tongue-in-cheek manner yet touchingly betrays the young author's ambition:

> To Miss Austen.
>
> Madam
> Encouraged by your warm patronage of The beautiful Cassandra, and The History of England, which through your generous support, have obtained a place in every library in the Kingdom, and run through threescore Editions, I take the liberty of begging the same Exertions in favour of the following Novel.

One wishes for a time machine, simply to travel back and tell her how far beyond "threescore" her editions would run. One of the dedications is actually to a noblewoman, but the noblewoman in question, "Madame La Comtesse De Feuillide" (*L&F, MW* 76), was in fact Jane's first cousin Eliza, who had married a French count. The only dedication of one of Austen's novels to an illustrious personage in the traditional sense was the dedication of *Emma*, by royal hint (which essentially equaled a royal command), to the prince regent.

Nonfiction works were also often dedicated to a patron or friend whose name had some degree of public recognition. These works would also often have an index, though items in the index might be simply grouped by first letter rather than fully alphabetized. Books of all sorts might have a frontispiece (an engraved illustration facing the title page) and a table of contents that could offer rather more detail about chapter contents than we are accustomed to today. A guide word (the first word or partial word from the following page) appeared at the bottom right-hand corner of each page, both as a help to the bookbinder in assembling the pages in the right order and as a link from one page to the next for those reading aloud (*NA* 107; *S&S* 48; *P&P* 68; *MP* 336–337, 338, 340; *E* 46–47). The paper was made of shredded cotton rags and was far more durable than most paper used in books today. The size of the paper was determined by how many times the large printed sheet was folded. One fold yielded four pages, a folio; two folds yielded eight pages, making a quarto; three folds produced the sixteen pages of an octavo, and four folds the thirty-two pages of a duodecimo (*NA* 113). The pages were printed, folded, and sewn together, and then the folded edges that faced the outer edges of the book were cut with a sharp knife.

Books (*LS, MW* 273; *Sand, MW* 383; *NA* 204; *S&S* 20, 26, 30, 41, 47, 83, 93, 155, 304, 307; *P&P* 12, 54–55, 93, 172, 180, 223, 289; *MP* 151, 200; *E* 34; *P* 38, 82, 97, 100, 131, 234), once printed and collated, were bound (*NA* 107; *MP* 191) either by the printer or by the customer, who could take them to a specialist bookbinder (*Col Let, MW* 158). Binding in "boards"—essentially a thick cardboard front and back with a flexible connection to the spine—was cheaper than binding in leather, and some types of leather were more expensive than others. A print of 1808 shows a Dublin bookbinder's shop, complete with its window, and even the glass panes of the door, full of books propped open with rails behind them to keep them standing up straight. The man behind the counter suggests to his customer that he have his book bound in "Russia," meaning a durable type of leather treated with birchbark oil, and the customer, a bumpkin, replies, "Russia is such a plaguy way off . . . so if it makes no difference to you—I'll have it bound here in *Dublin*." Books were also sold at such shops, by peddlers, and by immense bookshops (*S&S* 92) such as Lackington's in London, which would seem small by today's standards but for the time offered an enormous selection. Booksellers, who often combined their business with printers' shops and circulating libraries, proliferated during Austen's lifetime. By the 1790s, there were almost 1,000 booksellers in the provinces, plus many more in London.

Publishers might agree to pay a royalty of sorts, but more commonly they tried to purchase the copyright to a work. This strategy was risky, but

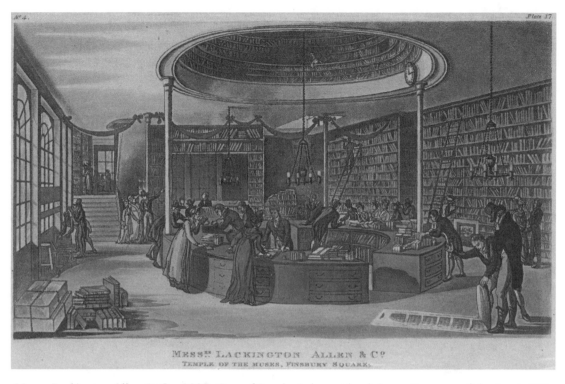

Messrs. Lackington Allen & Co., 1809. One of London's largest bookshops. Courtesy of the Lewis Walpole Library, Yale University. 809.4.1.1.

if the book were successful, the publisher stood to make an enormous profit. In some cases, wary authors sold only the copyright for one edition and held out in the hope of a second or third edition and further income. Other books were printed by subscription, meaning that people agreed to purchase the book in advance, trusting in the author's reputation. They paid a sum and received a copy of the book when it appeared.

Circulating Libraries

Book prices ranged from perhaps nine shillings for a cheap three-volume novel to a guinea per volume for a large, handsomely bound book. Even the cheap novel represented about half a month's wages for an ordinary servant, so it was only the well-off who could afford to amass large personal libraries (*S&S* 343; *P&P* 37, 38, 55, 71, 349; *MP* 27; *P* 99) like the 500 volumes owned by Austen's father. People who did not wish to invest heavily in books, or who simply wanted to read a wider variety than was available to them at home, borrowed books from friends, joined book clubs and societies that jointly acquired volumes, or subscribed to circulating libraries.

Circulating libraries (*Sand, MW* 374, 384, 391, 398–99, 403; *P&P* 30,

THE CIRCULATING LIBRARY.

The Circulating Library, 1804. The shelves marked "Novels," "Romances," and "Tales" are nearly empty, as these books were in high demand. Not too many histories or sermons have been checked out, however. Courtesy of the Lewis Walpole Library, Yale University. 804.10.1.1.

68; *MP* 389; *P* 130) were a feature of most sizable towns. Often run by people who ran a side-business such as bookbinding or trinket-selling (*Sand*, *MW* 389; *P&P* 238), they served not only as libraries but also as social centers. Advertisements for lodgings to rent or servants for hire were sometimes placed there, and the list of subscribers (*Sand*, *MW* 389) offered, at a glance, a sense of the sort of middle- and upper-class society present in town.

Subscription libraries had been established in Scotland in the seventeenth century, gradually spreading south throughout the eighteenth century. Around the turn of the century, working-class libraries began to be founded on the same lines, but with lower subscription rates. A share in a more genteel library might cost anywhere from one to five guineas, with an annual subscription costing perhaps six to ten shillings. The stock of books might be anywhere from a few hundred to a few thousand; one of the largest was a library in Liverpool with 8,000 books in 1801. Book selection was by ballot among the subscribers, and the librarian had little control over the inventory, being merely a paid functionary in many cases. Some librarians owned their libraries, having started them as entrepreneurial ventures, and these were almost certainly people who owned a second business such as a print shop. Bookselling was a natural combination with library lending, as booksellers could lend extra stock to customers for a small fee.

Library hours were quite limited at first. In the 1780s, for example, the Birmingham library was open six days a week, but only from 2:00 to 5:00 P.M. By the turn of the century this library was open for more hours, from 11:00 A.M. to 1:00 P.M., from 3:00 to 6:00, and from 7:00 to 8:00, and the librarian's salary was raised to 40 guineas a year to reflect the additional workload. Fines for late return of books often depended on the size of the book—for example, 1d. per day for pamphlets, 2d. for octavos and duodecimos, 3d. for quartos, and 4d. for folios, as in Leeds in the 1760s. The borrowing period was usually two or three weeks.

When a new library was founded, its proprietor did whatever she could to acquire new business. This might mean advertising in the local paper, as did two partners in Brimingham in March 1787:

> M. and S. Olds respectfully inform their Friends and the Public that they have opened a Circulating Library, No. 13, Suffolk-street, Birmingham, consisting of a variety of Books, in History, Voyages, Novels, Romances, Adventures, Poetry, Plays, etc., which will be lent to read on the following Terms:—Twelve Shillings per Year; Seven Shillings the Half Year; Four shillings per Quarter; Six-pence per Week; or at Two-pence per Volume; and should their Endeavours meet the Support and Patronage of the Ladies and Gentlemen in or near Birmingham, they will annually make Additions to their Collection, so as to make it a general Repository of useful and entertaining Literature.
>   N.B. Stationery and Perfumery of all Sorts.

It might also mean making contact with the local gentry and their families as well as the more prosperous tradesmen. Austen reported in 1798 that she had been approached by a Mrs. Martin, "requesting my name as a Subscriber to her Library which opens the 14th of January, & my name, or rather Yours, is accordingly given." Austen also noted, with some irritation, that the pitch had included a sly attack on novels:

> As an inducement to subscribe Mrs Martin tells us that her Collection is not to consist only of Novels, but of every kind of Literature &c &c—She might have spared this pretension to *our* family, who are great Novel-readers & not ashamed of being so;—but it was necessary I suppose to the self-consequence of half her Subscribers.

Circulating libraries could be found in increasing numbers in resort towns such as Bath, where a subscription cost 15s. a year or 5s. a quarter from 1789. *See also* Gothic; Newspaper; Theater.

Religion

The Georgian age served as a religious lull between the tumultuous sectarian strife of the seventeenth century and the activist enthusiasm of the Victorian era. Religion was, for the most part, a rational, sedate affair, taken as one of the foundations of civilized life, but taken, nonetheless, in moderation. Only toward the end of Austen's life did the Evangelical movement begin to flourish and give hints that it would influence religious discourse for decades. Meanwhile, there were steps toward tolerance for Dissenters and Catholics—steps that were taken tentatively and then usually quickly retracted.

The Place of Religion in Daily Life

The late eighteenth century appeared to be a time of religious malaise. Church attendance seemed to many people to be lagging, and the number of people taking communion was on the decline. In 1789, John Butler, bishop of Hereford, compared the number of communicants with the number in 1747 and concluded that in 1747 there were "many more, so many more, than those reported in the year 1789, that I am unwilling to recite the numbers." Communion, which in theory was supposed to be offered on a monthly basis, was being offered only three or four times a year in most places, not due to the laziness of the clergy but to the lack of demand from parishioners. Servants in particular enjoyed dodging church services and sneaking off to the local alehouse, but workers and sometimes even the presiding gentry failed to show up.

Even the same people who offered unqualified support for the church and who assumed that England's strength was derived at least in part from its religion continued to exhibit a cheerful lack of interest in theological debate or even in the meaning of the liturgy. They enjoyed instead the ritual, the repetition, the pleasure of putting on their best clothes, the display made by the leading citizens in *their* best clothes, and, where it was available, the church music. Parson James Woodforde noted an especially large turnout at a service that featured "Mattishall Singers . . . , attended with a bass-Viol and an Hautboy." Austen wrote a short, humorous poem about a "lab'rer in his Sunday clothes," who

> Likes best the prayers whose meaning least he knows,
> Lists to the sermon in a softening doze,
> And rouses joyous at the welcome close. (*MW* 445–446)

No doubt she knew plenty of people who, like her laborer and *Persuasion*'s Mary Musgrove, went to church primarily out of habit or for social reasons (*P* 130). Others were simply too busy to attend, lived in towns without adequate church seating, found the services too long and dull (*MP* 88), or preferred Dissenting sects.

Yet most people believed in a "Higher Power" (*LS, MW* 267). The gentry and other prominent citizens were expected to attend church and set a good example, and it was noticed by all when they absented themselves. Though weekday church services had all but lapsed except in large towns, attendance at least once every Sunday, at either the morning or evening service, was the assumed norm. Most of Austen's characters attend church so regularly that the question is not whether to go but where to attend and what will happen afterward (*NA* 34; *S&S* 273; *P&P* 157; *MP* 408; *E* 22; *P* 93). The only hero or heroine who skips church is Emma, and she does so only because the weather is too bad to allow travel (*E* 138). A disinclination to attend services is a sure sign of moral decay, as it is in Mary Crawford's case (*MP* 86).

At home, even among families who did not regularly attend church, daily prayers might be read aloud to the assembled family and servants (*MP* 87), using either the Bible or the Book of Common Prayer (*MP* 387). Prayers, for example, were read in the chapel (*MP* 86) every morning at Stoneleigh, one of the ancestral homes of Mrs. Austen's relatives. In the 1780s, morning and evening prayers were read at Sir Robert Gunning's, and prayers were read to the children and servants at noon in Lady Dartrey's house. People read the Bible, either aloud or silently, and many readers enjoyed books of sermons or theology.

Christian principles were assumed by most people to be the basis of civilized modern society (*NA* 197), if not the basis of civilization itself. If we are to believe the biographical notice to *Northanger Abbey* and *Persuasion* and the hints in her works and letters, Austen herself was a serious and well-read Christian, interested in religious study and entirely orthodox in her principles. In this she fulfilled the dream of many an author on such topics, who urged all Britons, but especially women, to maintain their faith in a time of increasing empiricism. Novelist Fanny Burney, confronted in 1780 with a young woman of either Deistic or atheistic tendencies, wrote pityingly of her attitudes:

> Poor Girl! I am really sorry for her,—she has strong and lively parts, but I think her in the high road of lasting destruction! She waits but to *Love* in order to be infamous, and she thinks about *Religion* only to persuade herself there is none!—I recommended to her all the good Books I could think of,—and scrupled not to express warmly and most seriously my surprise and horror at her way of thinking. It was easy to me to see that she attended to my opinions with curiosity, and yet easier to discover that had she not respected me as Author of a Book she happened to be fond of, she would have rallied them unmercifully.

One of the "good books" she might have recommended was the extremely popular *Father's Legacy to His Daughters*, written by John Gregory decades before but much reprinted. An exhortation to his daughters to be generally well behaved, Gregory's book offered advice on marriage, the choice of friends, and, of course, religion:

> Avoid all books, and all conversation, that tend to shake your faith on those great points of religion which should serve to regulate your conduct, and on which your hopes of future and eternal happiness depend.
>
> Never indulge yourselves in ridicule on religious subjects; nor give countenance to it in others, by seeming diverted with what they say. This, to people of good breeding, will be a sufficient check.
>
> I wish you to go no further than the Scriptures for your religious opinions. Embrace those you find clearly revealed. Never perplex yourselves about such as you do not understand; but treat them with silent and becoming reverence.

Later books on female conduct offered similar advice, urging women not to be tempted into a secular perspective, lest they lose their native modesty and become repulsive to men. The anonymous author of *Female Tuition; or, an Address to Mothers, on the Education of Daughters* (1784) submitted a typical reminder: "Forget not that religion is the glory of the sex, and adds to every other feminine excellence superior lustre and grace."

Some people, male and female alike, had genuine spiritual yearnings that they channeled into participation in religious organizations. The Society for the Promotion of Christian Knowledge (SPCK), already a venerable institution by Austen's day, distributed cheap tracts, pamphlets, catechisms, and books. A similar organization, the Religious Tract Society, was founded in 1799. Sunday schools began springing up from the 1780s onward, teaching reading, writing, and Bible stories to working-class children on the one day a week they had off; by 1797, the Sunday Schools Society represented 1,086 schools teaching 69,000 children. The Proclamation Society and Vice Society worked to enforce Sabbath observance and censor books they considered blasphemous. Both of these societies worked to close alehouses on Sundays, meeting with varying success.

Missionary societies, which were viewed with disfavor initially, gained credibility in the first years of the new century. The British and Foreign Bible Society (1804), as its name implied, published religious texts in several languages for use domestically and abroad. The London Society for Promoting Christianity among the Jews (1809), a notably unsuccessful group, worked to proselytize at home, as did the National Society (1811), which worked with poor children. The Particular Baptists founded a foreign missionary society in 1792, and other efforts followed. The Society for Missions to Africa and the East (established by Anglicans in 1799), better known as the Church Missionary Society or CMS, raised funds to convert the inhabitants of Africa and India, while the LMS, an interdenominational equivalent, founded missions in the British Isles as well as overseas. A prospective applicant wrote to the CMS in 1812, if you are in wants of young men to go abroad on the all important Errand of Proclaiming the unsearchable Riches of Christ to the Poor Perishing Heathen, & if after suitable inquiry, and Examination I am approved of, I will thro divine grace with diffidence, Sincerity and Pleasure give up myself to God & to you for the Great, Arduous and Awfully Responsible yet delightful & Honourable work of a Missionary.

Such adoration of missionary work would have been hard to find in previous generations, but the CMS had been hard at work countering the popular perception that its work was imperialism in disguise, and publishing accounts of despicable "heathen" customs that needed to be eliminated. Petition drives in the first decade of the nineteenth century to send missionaries to rescue "the natives of India, both Mohammedan and Hindoo," resulted in limited numbers of missionaries being admitted to British territories in the East Indies. Toward the end of Austen's life, the CMS began publishing popular magazines, such as the *Missionary Register* (1813) and *Quarterly Papers* (1816), the latter a cheap illustrated publication aimed at children and workers, who could have a copy if they pledged to raise a penny a week for the society. The more work that was invested in converting pagans, it seemed, the more interest there was in improving the quality of Christianity in Britain.

Yet it was considered important to avoid the appearance of "enthusiasm." Religious zealotry had led England into a century and a half of turmoil in the sixteenth and seventeenth centuries, and no one was anxious to see such events repeated. Furthermore, enthusiastic movements such as Methodism seemed perfectly designed to make workers discontented with their lot and thus cause poor work habits, disrespectful behavior, and even riots. Overly dogmatic, emotional, or sectarian approaches to religion were therefore greeted with profound suspicion. James Gambier, Francis Austen's naval patron, was despised in the navy for his Evangelical tendencies and dubbed "Preaching Jemmy," "Dismal Jimmie," and "the Bible Admiral."

Thus, Mary Crawford, stung by Edmund Bertram's faith, accuses him of wanting to reform and convert everyone (*MP* 394, 458), energetic activities associated more with Methodists and Evangelicals than with conventional adherents of the church. Many critics have interpreted *Mansfield Park* as a pro-Evangelical work because Edmund and Fanny's more serious religious views are clearly supported by the narrator, but as others have pointed out, the novel is not that clear-cut. It is the silly, idle, stupid Lady Bertram, for example, who, "after hearing an affecting sermon" (453), cries herself to sleep. There is no evidence that the reader is supposed to adopt a newly respectful attitude toward Lady Bertram because she can feel a religious discourse deeply; she has only found another way to indulge herself.

The goal, for Austen as for many others, seems to have been to find a middle ground. Attending Sunday services, avoiding "Sunday-travelling" (*P* 161), taking the Scriptures and the Prayer Book seriously were each important, but morality, not mysticism or passion, was the point of religious study. On the other hand, Deism, increasingly popular since the publication of Thomas Paine's *Age of Reason* in 1795, was to be shunned. One of Austen's favorite theological writers, Thomas Sherlock, stuck firmly to this middle ground. Irene Collins summarizes his balance between Deism and Evangelicalism and his description of redemption and resurrection as "rational and well-founded acts of faith," a phrase that, like a good political speech, offered something for everybody. Like Austen, Collins notes, Sherlock was suspicious of sudden conversions and alterations of character. He would probably have agreed with the judgment of John Bennett, in 1789, that Anglican piety "has a rational, sedate, composed air, and is uniformly grave and decent without pretending to the flights, the fervours and the visions of some, *modern* fanaticks." For Austen, as for these men, religion seems to have been a good habit, a course of study, rather than a profound emotional experience. It was mostly a set of morals and behaviors, yet it was something more than mere morality. In other words, she successfully inhabited the middle ground.

The Established Church

The Anglican Church was the established church, which meant that it had legal ties to the government, and its adherents received preferential treatment. Only Anglicans could matriculate at Oxford or receive degrees from Cambridge. All marriages and baptisms had to take place in an Anglican church, and burial in the parish churchyard could take place only if an Anglican clergyman read the Anglican burial service. All citizens, whether they belonged to the Church of England or not, had to pay taxes for the upkeep of the parish church, and non-Anglicans were barred from many government and military posts. In exchange for these benefits, the church was subject to government oversight, nominally through the king, but in practice through Parliament, which could legislate regarding clerical residence, pluralism, church services, the number of bishoprics and cathedral posts, and financial aid to found new churches or improve clergymen's livings.

Some people—and not only those disenfranchised by this system—found the idea of an established church slightly unfair. Yet every time it seemed that the public, or at least some subset of the public, was willing to offer tolerance to other faiths, there was a major backlash. A bill naturalizing a very small number of foreign-born Jews in the mid-eighteenth century was met with public outrage; a gesture of conciliation toward Catholics led to the terrifying Gordon Riots in London. Whatever doubts the public at large might have had about the necessity of an established church were laid to rest for the time being by the French Revolution and its aftermath, which seemed to serve as a perfect example of what happened when the people set aside their long-cherished traditions and their God-given morality. If the navy was "the wooden walls of England," the church was now perceived as a different sort of national defense, and talk of toleration, in some quarters, was seen as little better than talk of treason.

The church, however, was not a monolith. It had differing strains of thought and internal conflicts, just as it always had. There were several different factions in the church, but, as Austen rarely discussed any of them, even in her letters, a very brief description of most of them will suffice. One of the principal divisions was between "High Church" and "Low Church." Exact definitions of these two camps vary. The High Church philosophy was variously described as a commitment to the apostolic nature of the church, as a proestablishment viewpoint with a high regard for the state's involvement in religious affairs, as a party allied with the court and courtiers, and as a regard for Scripture, the Prayer Book, the catechism, the creeds, the sacraments, and personal sacrifice. Samuel Horsley, in 1790, called it an attachment to the church's doctrine, divine authority, and spiritual independence, while Archdeacon Daubeny defined it in 1798 as "a decided and principled attachment to the Apostolic government of the Church." A few years after Austen's death, J.W. Middelton defined a High Churchman, in terms to reduce nontheologians to tears of confusion, as one who "upheld the Trinity against Arians; the Atonement against the Socinian; and the depravity of our common nature against the Pelagian."

High Churchmen preferred the term "Orthodox" for themselves by the late eighteenth century (though the terms were not perfectly synonymous), while their opponents preferred to label them as greedy, intolerant, Jacobitic crypto-Catholics. High Churchmen tended to favor the Test and Corporation Acts, which kept Dissenters out of the top government posts, and a literal adherence to the 39 Articles,* the points of faith to which clergymen were obliged to swear faith and allegiance. High Churchmen were in general anti-Puritanical and anti-Evangelical, and their spiritual center was the university at Oxford. Associated in the minds of many with the now practically vanished Tory Party, they stoutly defended the historical rights and privileges of the church, the king, and especially bish-

---

*The 39 Articles proved to be one of the most contentious doctrinal issues of the age. Clergymen had to swear to them if they wanted to be ordained, and many clergymen could not in good conscience subscribe to the literal wording of some of the articles, particularly those that dealt with the Trinity and with predestination. Some made peace with their consciences, agreed privately with themselves to interpret the doctrines loosely or figuratively, and swore they believed. Others gave up their careers in order to avoid swearing falsely. Brief rebellions against the articles went nowhere. The most famous instance of opposition, a petition signed by numerous clerics at the Feathers Tavern in 1770, was so soundly rejected by Parliament that it all but killed conscientious objection.

ops. They were out of favor for much of the eighteenth century, but around 1800, their reputation started to improve, particularly after the French Revolution solidified British support for the monarchy.

Low Churchmen tended to be associated with the Whigs and with Cambridge University, and their views were similar, but not identical, to the viewpoint later described as Latitudinarianism. Latitudinarianism was the "middle ground" discussed above—a tolerant, rational, low-key faith, not too loud about itself, and not too powerful. In this philosophy, the Bible was all-important, and later texts such as the Book of Common Prayer were entirely human constructs that could be adapted or altered as needed. The morality and good sense of Christianity were stressed; what could be more sensible, they argued, than practical codes of conduct sealed with a divine stamp of approval?

Low Church adherents were accused by High Churchmen of being little better than Dissenters in disguise, and indeed some Latitudinarians dreamed of winning back the Dissenters through a second Reformation of the church. They were attacked as heterodox Calvinists who would probably have helped to execute Charles I and were undoubtedly remaining in the Church of England purely for their own gain; at heart, it was said, they were all Dissenters.

Then there were the Evangelicals, initially opposed by High and Low Church alike. They were that most dreaded of all things, enthusiastic, insisting on a need for conscious conversion and absorption of the Holy Spirit. Evangelicals differed from the dignified, priestly High Churchmen and the low-key, affable Low Churchmen, arguing for a more passionate faith, a different road to salvation, and an activist interest in the reformation of church and society. Evangelicals favored doctrine over secular morality, the cause of abolition, daily family prayers, and strict Sabbath observance (including a ban on newspapers, concerts, and travel on Sundays). They opposed gambling, even of the moderate social kind; prostitution; masquerades; swearing; card games in general; the wording of the baptismal and funeral services; pluralist clergy; and, in some cases, theater and magazines. They arose from the Low Church sanctuary of Cambridge, but they were distinct from the undemanding Latitudinarians. Disdaining too much reason in religion, they stressed revelation and blind faith instead. The standard complaint about the Evangelicals was that they were subversive troublemakers who did not want anyone to have any fun. John Randolph, in *A Charge Delivered to the Clergy of the Diocese of Oxford* (1802), complained that Evangelicals wanted to "encourage in Religion the very principle, which in Politics has proved so fatal to the peace and good government of states; being no other than giving the reins to private opinion, in opposition to public authority." In other words, he fell back on the ploy of indirectly linking an unpopular religious sect to the "troubles" in France.

Initially only a handful of clergymen and laymen, the Evangelicals slowly gained ground. By 1795, they had about 500 representatives among the clergy, and they were gaining adherents at court; in 1815, they got their first bishop.

Elizabeth Bennet's sister Mary, with her cold approval of moderate "intervals of recreation and amusement" (*P&P* 87), her "extracts," and her "thread-bare morality" (*P&P* 60), seems like a proto-Evangelical, and Austen does not deal kindly with her. Neither was she enthusiastic about her cousin Edward Cooper, a notoriously preachy member of that faction. Critics have debated to what degree Austen disliked the Evangelicals and to what degree she relented as she aged; quotations can be summoned from her letters to support many arguments, and her letters, even if they were complete, would form only a partial representation of her views. There is ample evidence that she was put off by the sanctimonious Evangelical tone, but there is some evidence as well that she approved of at least some of their goals.

Dissenters

Another faction within the Anglican Church that eventually became a denomination of its own was Methodism. Founded by John Wesley in the eighteenth century, Methodism had broad working-class appeal thanks to its emphasis on field preaching. People liked a good sermon, and many found they enjoyed Wesley's dire warnings about the consequences of sin. Others, naturally, preferred quite reminders to be charitable and kind. The duchess of Buckingham, explaining her hatred of Methodists, complained, "it is monstrous to be told that you have a heart as sinful as the common wretches. . . . This is highly offensive and insulting and at variance with high rank and good breeding." Not all aristocrats felt as she did, but Methodism remained a predominantly working-class movement. Its ability to rouse the rabble was one of the reasons that the governor-general of Bermuda (father-in-law of Charles Austen) banned it on his island. Conservative Anglicans also found "Methodist" (*MP* 458) a handy term to fling at anyone who seemed too religiously fundamentalist or enthusiastic. Francis Austen's Evangelical patron Admiral Gambier made himself hated within the navy after successfully calling for a court-martial on a popular fellow officer who had publicly accused him of Methodism.

Besides Methodism, several strains of Nonconformist worship had been around for much longer—in some cases, since the first heady decades of the Reformation. The followers of "Old Dissent" included Presbyterians, Baptists, Quakers, Unitarians, and Independents. As with the Methodists and the Anglican factions, there was a certain amount of name-calling and stereotyping of these denominations. The Unitarians, it was said, were not really Christians at all; the Independents were overly puritanical and proper; the Baptists and Quakers were seldom stereotyped but considered relatively low in social class compared to other Dissenters. Presbyterians were the butt of everyone's jokes, including those of other Dissenters.

Resentment against Dissenters had cooled since the seventeenth century, in part because the Anglicans had found a solution that worked for them: barring Dissenters from full political equality. They were quite tolerant of Dissenters, especially socially, unless this convenient solution was threatened, as it was when, late in the eighteenth century, a campaign to repeal the Test and Corporation Acts was initiated. These acts, relics of the Restoration of the Stuart monarchy, together specified that Catholics could not sit in Parliament and that all civil administrators and military officers take Anglican communion and an oath of loyalty to the crown. The loyalty oath usually presented no problem, but the requirement to have taken Anglican communion within the past year was a stumbling block for all Catholics and Dissenters of conscience. They had to forgo worldly power or rationalize participating in a religious ritual at variance with their beliefs. Countering these acts to some extent were an old Toleration Act, granting some rights to Old Dissent, and annual Indemnity Acts, which could be passed to allow Dissenters to hold some political posts, for example, in city government.

A proposal to repeal the Test and Corporation Acts in the 1780s sparked an outcry from Anglicans; though actual violence against Catholics and Dissenters was rare, propaganda was common. A broadside from the period claimed, in a voice that pretended to be a Dissenter's, that the repeal of the Test and Corporation Acts was just the first intended breach in the Church of England's walls:

> When once the hop'd-for breach is made,
> We'll do whate'er we chuse;
> The Church's-doors shall open stand,
> To papists, Turks, and Jews—

A period of enormous tension ended with the failure of the repeal in 1790, and an atmosphere of tolerance—at least on the surface—was restored. The Anglicans resumed their feeling of comfortable superiority, and the Dissenters waited for a more propitious time to secure their rights. (The more propitious time turned out to be 1828, when the Corporation Act was repealed and the Test Act ceased to be enforced.) In the meantime, Dissenters and Anglicans managed to cooperate on a number of interdenominational religious societies and Sunday schools.

Dissent, which had been somewhat sluggish of late, was reinvigorated by Methodism and would see its aggregate membership increase dramatically in the first four decades of the nineteenth century. In Austen's day, however, numbers were still fairly low. There were an estimated 77,000 Methodists in 1796 and 87,010 in 1801. In 1800, there were perhaps 35,000 Congregationalists, 24,000 Particular Baptists, and only 20,000

Quakers. The Presbyterians were all but defeated; many of their number gave up altogether and became Unitarians or Independents.

Catholicism

Though the attitude toward Dissenters was one of surface toleration, the attitude toward Catholics (*Hist Eng, MW* 145, 147) was still one of barely concealed, implacable hatred. The rare convert from Anglicanism to Catholicism (*Lesley, MW* 137–138) was reviled and grieved for as if dead; when Samuel Johnson's friend Hester Thrale married an Italian, he begged her not to abandon her faith and wrote to ask her to reconsider, if the dreadful deed were not already done. John Bennett's *Letters to a Young Lady* (1789) considered Catholicism nothing but a scam:

> This religion, which has subsisted for such a length of time, and covered so considerable a part of the world, is little else but a system of *political tyranny*, established by the clergy, over the *conscience* . . . , merely to enrich and aggrandize *themselves*.

The consensus was that Catholics were idolatrous, superstitious, foreign, treacherous enemies of freedom. In the public imagination, every Catholic was a slave or a tyrant, and possibly a Frenchman into the bargain. It was the specter of rights for Catholics that sparked the deadly Gordon Riots of 1780, and it would be many years before the questions would be considered again. Even Dissenters agreed that Catholics were the enemy and never seem seriously to have considered joining forces with their fellow second-class citizens to seek religious rights for all. Yet even Catholics benefited from the general mellowing of religious opinion in the Hanoverian age. They were permitted to worship as long as they were discreet, and judges were demonstrating less eagerness to enforce existing statutes against them. *See also* Clergy.

S

Samphire

Samphire (*Sand* 396) is a succulent, plant in the carrot family, similar to Queen Anne's Lace, but with yellow flowers. It grew abundantly on England's southern and eastern coasts, where it was gathered and the stalks and leaves pickled. Because the plant naturally grows very close to the ocean, where it is moistened by the salt spray, it is symbolic of coastal regions. Thus, Austen mentions it, along with gulls, fathoms, and mariners, to evoke the seaside context of Sanditon.

Science

Austen appears not to have taken a great interest in science, although she was not necessarily in the majority. The eighteenth century was a time of intense interest in all branches of science, and scientific method was just beginning to overtake guesswork as the dominant form of discovery. Well-educated people were supposed to know something about geography, "natural philosophy"—that is, physics—botany, biology, chemistry, and astronomy, even if they only a knew a very *little* something about each. Part of what made science exciting was that so many fascinating discoveries were being made, and part of it was that even enthusiastic amateurs could contribute a great deal to the communal store of knowledge. Travelers to newly explored parts of the globe could collect and name new species of plants and animals; tinkerers could experiment with new machines and compounds; rock hounds could find bizarre, fossilized skeletons of beasts that clearly no longer existed.

Austen confines herself, except for one reference to chemistry, to the field of astronomy. The exception is a reference to "the Metals, [and] Semi-Metals" (*MP* 19); evidently the Bertram girls were required to memorize the metallic and quasi-metallic elements, the latter group including, for example, antimony. The periodic table of the elements was in its infancy during Austen's lifetime. Scientists had only recently come to the conclusion that all substances that could not be reduced or separated were elements, rejecting the ancient and medieval notion that all objects were compounds of earth, water, fire, and air, but how the elements were to be isolated and named was a matter of great controversy, especially in the case of oxygen.

Why things burned had long been a mystery. Some scientists at the time of Austen's birth thought that flammable substances contained a quantity of a material called phlogiston, which escaped into the air during combustion and caused the surrounding atmosphere to become "phlogisticated." When the air was fully saturated with phlogiston, the substance stopped burning. After much debate and experimentation, the French chemist Antoine Lavoisier was able to convince most scientists that the phlogiston theory was bunk and that substances burned when in the presence of oxygen. His campaign, however, took many years, and well into Austen's lifetime there were respected scientists, such as Joseph Priestley, who still accepted the phlogiston theory. By the time of her death, thanks in large part to Priestley and Lavoisier, several elements and simple compounds had been isolated and named, including oxygen, carbon dioxide (known as "fixed air"), hydrogen (called "inflammable air"), nitrous oxide, carbon monoxide, hydrogen chloride, nitrogen (called "mofette" or "azote"), chlorine, sulphur, phosphorus, carbon, antimony, arsenic, bismuth, cobalt, copper, gold, iron, lead, manganese, mercury, nickel, platinum, tin, silver, tungsten, and zinc. Lavoisier, writing in 1789, concluded that there were thirty-three elements, some of which, including magnesia and silica, were later proven to be compounds. Scientists were aware of the difference between organic and inorganic substances, of the three states of matter (gas, liquid, and solid), and of the compound nature of water. They did not, however, agree on the exact nature of water and whether or not it contained phlogiston; Lavoisier got it right when he theorized that it was a compound of hydrogen and oxygen.

Austen, however, gives us only a schoolgirl's view of these marvelous discoveries. Elements were, after all, just another list to be memorized, like the list of the continents or the list of England's rulers. She reserves her most frequent comments and her sense of wonder for astronomy. Why she should choose to focus on astronomy is unclear. Perhaps she simply liked the stars (*MP* 71). Perhaps she was simply focusing on something she knew; an essential part of geography in her day was the use not only of terrestrial but celestial globes, and an educated person would have been expected to know something about the placement of stars, constellations (*MP* 113), and planets (*MP* 19). Some families even owned orreries—models of the solar system, articulated so that they could move and demonstrate the orbits of planets, moons, and the sun.

Or perhaps she, like many others, was excited about the variety of new discoveries being made in the night sky. Scientists were exploring new, more complex theories involving gravitation, such as the so-called three-body problem. The three-body problem concerned the interactions of three substantial objects on each other in space and related specifically to calculating the relative movements of the earth, the sun, and the moon. Not all astronomy was this theoretical and mathematical, however. There were also important observational discoveries being made, such as the discovery, in 1801, of the first known asteroid.

Astronomy, like most scientific disciplines, was having its assumptions revised and augmented with startling rapidity. Observatories multiplied, advances in mathematics were made, and observational instruments were improved. The last development was in some ways the most significant, for it caused even the experts to rethink their most cherished theories. Astronomer, musician, and telescope (*Cass, MW* 49; *Sand, MW* 422) manufacturer William Herschel thought he had finished cataloguing all the stars in the night sky when an improved telescope of his own design demonstrated that he had emphatically *not* found them all. He began cataloguing all over again, knowing that a better telescope would probably reveal yet more stars to be counted and charted. Herschel and his sister Caroline were at the center of many of the chief astronomical discoveries of the day. Caroline, who revised Astronomer Royal John Flamsteed's old star catalogue, was also a prolific discoverer of comets, and William discovered the sixth moon of Saturn, Enceladus, as well as the planet Uranus.* Herschel also established, with the help of his superior telescopes, that some nebulae were clouds of gas but that many apparent nebulae were actually clusters of stars. He further calculated that star clusters tended to be found in the same plane as the Milky Way, leading later scientists to a better understanding of the shape of the galaxy. He also studied binary stars, which orbit around each other in pairs, and established that they were moving in a way that could not be attributed to observational error or to the movements of the earth.

Servants

In the early years of the industrial age, when electricity had yet to be harnessed; when laundry was done by hand over a tub heated by fire; when the fire was lit not with matches but with flint, steel, and tinder; and when the water had to be pumped laboriously or carried, still more laboriously, bucket by bucket from a well; the labor of servants (*Clifford, MW* 43; *L&F, MW* 107; *Lesley, MW* 119; *Col Let, MW* 159; *Evelyn, MW* 181, 189; *Cath, MW* 194; *Watsons, MW* 327; *Sand, MW* 391, 393, 416, 425, 427; *NA* 61, 167, 173, 194, 200; *S&S* 28, 75, 91, 194, 286, 293, 312, 317, 318; *P&P* 44, 162, 215, 249, 250, 258, 268, 292, 310, 333, 335; *MP* 28, 188, 205, 233, 302, 385, 389–390, 391, 392, 426, 447, 455; *E* 184, 303, 355, 458, 469; *P* 13, 64) was essential to the running of any household that aspired to at least the middle class. The greater the number of servants in a home (*NA* 166, 184; *S&S* 233; *P&P* 160; *E* 207; *P* 219), and the more of life's disagreeable tasks they performed, the greater the display to the world that this was the abode of prosperous and comfortable people. In the largest homes, servants did everything that required real work. They plucked the chickens, cooked the food, cleaned the plates,

---

*The naming of the first planet to be discovered in modern times presented scientists with the vexing question of how to go about naming such an important object. Names considered included Georgius Sidus ("George Star," Herschel's own invention, a nod to his patron George III), Neptune de George III, Neptune de Grand-Bretagne, and Herschelium. Uranus would not be agreed upon as the planet's new name for years to come.

swept the floors and the cobwebs built in corners, cared for the children, and washed the clothes, the carpets, the dresses, the dirty linen, and the stairs. They carried messages and packages, held the reins of horses, kept the accounts, did the shopping, and lugged chamberpots full of nighttime human waste out to "Jericho," the garden outhouse. In return, they received housing, food, and sometimes clothing and other perquisites.

This system was viewed with suspicion and discomfort from both sides. Employers carped about the poor quality of available servants, the high wages they demanded, and the difficulty of getting them to stay at one house for more than a year or two. In addition, though they did not like to dwell on this disquieting fact, they lost almost all privacy in a house full of servants (*MP* 451). Servants stood behind the chairs at dinner in order to bring food and clear plates and thus heard all the dinner conversation. They dressed their masters and mistresses in the morning and just before dinner, hearing gossip of all kinds as they did so. They also chatted with servants in other households, especially when those servants traveled from one household to another in attendance on dinner guests. Many an employer must have wondered what was being said about him in the kitchen as he played whist in the drawing room. John Trusler, writing in 1786, advised his peers never to trust a servant the way one would trust a family member. "To expect attachment from a servant is idle," he cautioned, "and betrays an ignorance of the world. Servants will now and then affect it, in order to gain the confidence of their employers; but if we suppose them in our interest, it is because we do not know them." Moreover, servants were lazy. Parson James Woodforde, on an occasion when a friend and the friend's servant both spent the night, grumbled peevishly that "Mr. Jeanes's Servant Lad G. England seems fonder of Kitchen Fire than any Work."

Jonathan Swift's *Directions to Servants* (1731) considerably predates the period under consideration, but the work performed by servants did not change radically between 1731 and, say, 1811. Nor did the expectations of employers. Swift's satirical "advice" to servants on how to cheat their masters and subvert the morals of the household may not have been meant literally, but it does offer a window into the causes of employer dissatisfaction. He mockingly urges servants not to come except when called specifically by name, to hide the bad behavior of their fellows (except when they have some grudge against the offender), to make excuses for taking too long on an errand, and to ask often for raises in pay. Those who have authority to spend money, he says, should spend money freely, without bargaining for the best price. "When you have done a fault," Swift suggests, "be always pert and insolent, and behave yourself as if you were the injured person." Servants are cautioned never to perform any task outside their strict area of specialization:

For example, if the groom be drunk or absent, and the butler be ordered to shut the stable door, the answer is ready, An please your honour, I don't understand horses; if a corner of the hanging wants a single nail to fasten it, and the footman be directed to tack it up, he may say, he doth not understand that sort of work, but his honour may send for the upholsterer.

From Swift's indirect complaints, we can see that servants wrote their names in candle smoke on their ceilings, used the employers' knives at the servants' table, gossiped, left the front door open, drank too much, forgot the names of callers, and used the same pot to "boil milk, heat porridge, hold small beer, or in case of necessity serve for a jordan [chamberpot]" but never washed it "for fear of taking off the tin."

Servants, in turn, felt constantly shortchanged. They had to work long hours, beginning work in some cases before dawn and ending, on nights when the employers attended late parties, well after midnight. They, too, had little privacy and little free time, and employers always seemed to be fussing about how that free time was spent. Seldom were they allowed to have romantic relationships, and even friendships could be difficult to maintain. The work, in many cases, was physically demanding and apparently endless, with only low wages to show for the drudgery. Books purporting to help them in their work were written from the employers' perspective and advised meek obedience and resignation. Eliza Haywood's *A New Present for a Servant-Maid* (1771) warned dissatisfied maids about yearning for greener pastures:

> as there is no perfect happiness in this world, even in the highest stations, much less ought you to expct to find every thing exactly to your mind, but resolve to make every thing so much as possible. Remember the miseries of those who are continually roaming from house to house, oftener out of place and in, without character, without money, without friends or support, in case of sickness, or any other exigence; all which, those who have lived any time in a family, have a right to demand.

The keys to succeeding in one's post, she wrote, were cleanliness, a positive attitude, industry, and an unwillingness to dawdle when sent on errands.

Yet there was no alternative. The servants needed the work, and the employers needed their servants. Besides, not every servant–employer relationship was contentious. Austen deeply appreciated the services of James, a servant her family employed while vacationing in Lyme. In September 1804, she wrote,

> James is the delight of our lives; he is quite an Uncle Toby's annuity to us.—My Mother's shoes were never so well blacked before, and our plate never looked so clean. He waits extremely well, is attentive, handy, quick, & quiet, and in short has a great many more than all the cardinal virtues.

Nor was the approval all on the employer's side. When Jane's aunt Mrs. Leigh-Perrot was falsely accused of shoplifting and held in jail for months, a former servant wrote to her husband offering his support and recalling the couple's kindness to him:

> I shall never forget yours and my mistresses great goodness to me when I was taken with the small pox in your sarvice. You sent me very careful to mothers, and paid a nurse and my doctor, and my board for a long time as I was bad, and when I was too bad with biles all over my head so as I could not go to sarvice for a many weeks you maintained me. The famaly as I lives with be a going thro' Bath into Devonshire and we stops two days at the Inn and there I heard of the bad trick as those bad shopkeepers has sarved my mistress and I took the libarty of going to your house to enquire how you both do and the housekeeper said she sent a pasel to you every week and if I had anything to say she could send a letter. I hope Honored Sir you will forgive my taking such a libarty to write but I wish anybody could tell me how to do you and mistress any good. I would travel night and day to serve you both.

This may have been self-serving loyalty, as John Trusler would assert, but it must have touched the Leigh-Perrots anyway.

Servants were simultaneously a necessity and a luxury. At least one servant was necessary for any measure of comfort (*P* 152–153, 154, 197), and only the poor would avoid hiring a maid of all work (*S&S* 277)—a girl who scrubbed, lit the kitchen fire, and did whatever else the lady of the house needed. The best example of this hardworking creature is the Bateses' Patty, who tends to the fireplace (*E* 326), cooks (*E* 173), answers the door and announces visitors (*E* 452), and can be sent on errands as necessary (*E* 296). Such a servant was so essential that in some boarding-houses in Bath, tenants would not be accepted unless they brought at least one servant to lighten the burden on the landlord's staff.

Magistrate Patrick Colquhoun estimated in 1796 that there were 240,000 families in London, with 100,000 of those employing an average of two servants. Most of the 200,000 servants in his calculations would have been women, for although large households tended to employ roughly equal numbers of men and women, the families that could afford to keep only one or two servants hired women. This was because women would work for lower wages and because women, on the whole, expected to do more work. Also, menservants were principally for show and for taking care of luxury goods such as wine cellars, hunting dogs, and carriages, exactly the sorts of possessions that one-servant households could not afford. Estimates between 1777 and 1806 put the number of menservants in England and Wales at about 100,000 to 110,000 and the number of maidservants at about 800,000, meaning that approximately one of every ten people was in service and that perhaps seven of every eight servants was a woman.

The fact that women did most of the essential domestic labor affected the structure of taxes. A tax on employing servants was first introduced in 1777 by Lord North, who set the rate at one guinea per male servant, with female servants exempt from taxation. Bachelors paid double, while families with children paid less. In 1785 Prime Minister Pitt raised the tax, creating a sliding scale based on the number of male servants employed and charging a base rate of between £1 5s. and £3 for each male servant, with the tax still doubled for bachelors. Female servants were now taxed as well, but at a lower rate, ranging from 2s. 6d. to 10s. depending on the number of women employed.

Male Servants

If we assume the existence of a large household, such as, perhaps, the one at Mansfield Park or at Pemberley, we can safely assume that there would be a substantial number of both upper and lower menservants (*Evelyn*, *MW* 183; *Watsons*, *MW* 319; *NA* 44, 46; *S&S* 26, 353; *P&P* 212; *MP* 223; *E* 20). François Alexandre Frédéric, duc de la Rochefoucauld-Liancourt, who visited England in 1784, claimed that he met English peers with "thirty or forty men-servants." In 1771, the duke of Bedford had forty-two male servants at his London home, and in 1784, Lord Stormont had seventeen.

Upper menservants* wore ordinary clothes rather than livery and were generally paid higher wages. At the top of the hierarchy—and there was a hierarchy, both within and between households, based not only on job title and pay but also on family background and the status of one's employer (*Cass*, *MW* 44; *P* 4)—was the steward. He could be a land steward (*Cath*, *MW* 195; *NA* 139; *S&S* 259; *P&P* 81, 199; *MP* 34, 36, 82, 191, 411–412), who served as the manager of his employer's estate, settling disputes, dealing with tenants, keeping accounts, and managing the acres that were not rented out but farmed directly by the employer. Or he could be a house steward, the supreme authority within the household and the chief purchaser and budgeter. Stewards were found only on large estates and might have underlings called bailiffs (*MP* 58, 191; *E* 104), who purchased seed and livestock, supervised plowmen, and might wait at table (but without donning livery). On smaller estates the functions of the steward were performed either by the employer himself, by a combined land steward-house steward, or by a bailiff. A land or house steward might make from 30 to 50 guineas a year, while a bailiff would make somewhat less. The Austens had a bailiff, John Bond, who may have been the model for Mr. Knightley's steward William Larkins.

---

*Upper servants of both sexes were usually referred to by their surnames, and occasionally an honorific such as "Mrs." would be added (*LS*, *MW* 284; *Sand*, *MW* 389; *P&P* 306, 317; *MP* 251, 277, 344; *E* 458). Lower servants were referred to by first name (*LS*, *MW* 283; *NA* 103; *S&S* 153; *P&P* 344; *E* 228, 236, 237), although one encounters the occasional hybrid form, such as a real-life maid of all work who was called "Mrs. Becky."

In especially large households, there might be a clerk of the stables, who advised his employer on travel routes, supervised the feeding and doctoring of horses, and oversaw the care of carriages and stables. There might also be a clerk of the kitchen, who disbursed funds to tradesmen after the expenses were authorized by the steward, but these were increasingly rare offices. So, too, was that of the "man cook," a male chef, preferably from France. Samuel and Sarah Adams, who wrote *The Complete Servant* (1825), explained that such a cook was

> generally a foreigner, or if an Englishman, possesses a peculiar tact in manufacturing many fashionable foreign delicacies, or of introducing certain seasonings and flavorings in his dishes, which render them more inviting to the palate of his employer, than those produced by the simply healthful modes of modern English Cooks.

This servant could well be the highest-paid member of the household. He could make anywhere from 30 to 90 guineas depending on the level of his skill, a sum that put his services out of the range of all but the richest

The Physicians Friend, 1815. A doctor thanks the French man-cook for making such tasty dishes, whose rich ingredients make people sick and thus generate business for the physician. The English kitchen maids look on in disgust. Courtesy of the Lewis Walpole Library, Yale University. 815.0.2.

employers.* The employment of a man cook conferred a great deal of status on the employer, and contemporaries who could not afford such magnificence took every chance they got to satirize such needless extravagance. In an 1815 print, the French cook is described as "The Physician's Friend," feeding English lords on decadent French sauces that are sure to injure their health. Even the Adamses, who felt obliged to note the existence of such a creature as a man cook, pointed out somewhat sourly that "the art of Cookery, or *gourmanderie*, is reduced to a regular science in France, where an egg may be cooked half a hundred ways" and only grudgingly conceded that such creativity might be necessary for those who "give frequent entertainments."

Large estates might also have a confectioner, who specialized in pastries, and a baker, who specialized in bread. At Stoneleigh, a mansion owned by a relative of Mrs. Austen's, there was, according to Mrs. Austen, a "man servant . . . called the Baker, he does nothing but brew and bake." Most wealthy men had a valet (*P* 4), who helped them to dress and took care of their clothes; such a man might make anywhere from 18 to 30 guineas a year.

The butler (*Cass, MW* 44; *P&P* 301; *E* 204, 211; *P* 142; and *MP's* "Baddeley"—273, 324–325) took care of the estate's wine, beer, glassware, and plate. When new wine was purchased in large casks, it was his job to bottle it and then to serve it with dinner. He took on the duties of the valet in households where there was none and, in any case, supervised the setting out of the breakfast things. According to the Adamses, a footman would carry the tea urn, and the butler would carry the "eatables" and possibly wait on the table during the meal. After seeing that all the breakfast dishes were removed and cleaned, the butler would take his own breakfast with the housekeeper, returning to the public part of the house to answer the door, "receive cards, deliver messages, &c." He carried in the luncheon tray and served wine if called for, kept the cellar keys, and paid the bills for wine, beer, and spirits if there was no steward to do this. At dinner he released the requisite articles of plate from their locked chest, carried in the first dish, and served wine throughout the meal. Afterward, he took his own dinner, then carried in the tea tray (*MP* 180), though he did not actually make the tea; he was also in charge of serving supper if it was wanted. He was in charge of "Slippers, dressing gown, [and] night candles" (*NA* 187), again according to the Adamses. His wages ranged, in 1825, from £50 to £80 in large households, or from £30 to £50 in smaller ones. Swift's remarks concerning butlers reveal that the fears or complaints of employers regarding butlers concerned cleanliness, promptitude, and probity. He accused butlers of poor hygiene ("Take special care that your bottles be not musty before you fill them, in order to which,

*The Adamses noted that the duke of York was reputed to pay his "French Cook" £500 a year.

blow strongly into the mouth of every bottle, and then if you smell nothing but your own breath, immediately fill it"), laziness ("Give no person any liquor till he has called for it thrice at least"), and peculation—an easy charge given that butlers had a number of perquisites in addition to their wages. They were traditionally entitled to unused candle ends, used playing cards, and, if they served as valet as well, their master's cast-off clothes. All these bits and pieces could be sold and used to pay for the butler's own clothes and laundering, which came out of his pocket.

The gardener (*Sand*, *MW* 380; *S&S* 303; *P&P* 251; *MP* 91, 104, 105; *E* 359) had responsibility for the grounds of the estate. He supervised the growing of flowers and vegetables, the maintenance of the orchard and hothouses, the construction of paths, and the mowing and rolling of lawns. He was often Scottish and usually occupied a cottage somewhere on the estate, separate from the main house. This extraordinary degree of privacy must have been prized and compensated somewhat for his lower salary than the butler's—anywhere from £10 to 20 guineas. Parson Woodforde's gardener, Will Coleman, earned "a shilling a Day and his Board for 2 Days in a Week," but he had to find his own lodgings.

Below the gardener were a host of lower servants, distinguished from the upper servants by their livery. This livery (*Cath*, *MW* 214; *Watsons*, *MW* 322; *P&P* 260, 351; *P* 22, 106) was a uniform, constructed along the lines of fashionable men's clothing but executed in special colors, often colors that were chosen from the employer's coat of arms, and heavily trimmed with "lace," that is, metallic braid. (Examples of livery can be seen in many illustrations in this book, including *Loo in the Kitchin* [Cards] or *Advantages of Wearing Muslin Dresses!* [Dishes].) Though servants often aspired to reach the ranks of the upper servants, who did not have to wear livery, they prized good livery and prided themselves on the cost of the trimmings. Servants contemplating taking a new post would often include the magnificence of the livery in their calculations.

Liveried servants included the coachman (*Sand*, *MW* 364, 386; *MP* 69, 189, 222, 251, 375; *E* 126, 128, 195), who cleaned the carriage, harnessed the horses, and drove the carriage; undercoachmen, who assisted the coachman and drove additional carriages; the gamekeeper (*MP* 114), who looked after the wild game on the estate, helped with bird shooting, and guarded against poachers; and the porter (*S&S* 165), who lived in a lodge at the gate of a country estate or sat at the door of a town house and controlled access to the front door. Coachmen made about 15 guineas a year, porters about the same.

Grooms (*Sand*, *MW* 394; *S&S* 58, 67; *MP* 99, 118, 237; *P* 104) and footmen (*NA* 184; *MP* 87, 180, 202) bore somewhat the same relationship to each other that gardeners did to butlers. One was an outdoor helper, the other primarily an indoor helper. Both were liveried servants. The groom helped with the horses and accompanied his employers when they rode out on horseback (*S&S* 86). The footman answered the door (*Sand, MW* 406; *NA* 89, 102; *S&S* 161), announced visitors (*E&E, MW* 31) and led them into the public rooms (*Cath, MW* 218, 220; *NA* 102–103; *P&P* 335), ran errands (*S&S* 353; *P&P* 276; *MP* 57; *E* 295), carried packages and messages (*S&S* 165; *P&P* 30), and waited at table (*Visit, MW* 52; *S&S* 355). In smaller households, the positions of groom, footman, and butler might be collected in one post, with the same servant bottling wine, waiting at table, opening the door, and accompanying riders and carriage passengers (*P&P* 211–212). Postilions (*L&F, MW* 85; *NA* 156), similar to grooms in their connection with horses, rode one or more horses harnessed to a carriage and

Etching by Rowlandson, 1790, detail. A groom holds a horse for a lady preparing to ride. Courtesy of the Lewis Walpole Library, Yale University. 790.6.27.1.

helped to steer; they also assisted their employers when it was time to stop for a meal or an overnight stay. Grooms made about 12 to 15 guineas a year, footmen perhaps a little more, postilions a little less.

Eliza Haywood warned maidservants about footmen, who were "pert and saucy." They were generally idle, for their job consisted in large part of standing around and waiting for the doorbell to ring or for an errand to be ordered. They also had a wider experience of the world than many servants, as they accompanied their employers to visits, dinners, and plays. Therefore, they were especially inclined to flirt with the female servants and to try to impress them with the things they had done and seen. When this ploy was attempted, however, Haywood advised her readers to "behave with an extreme civility mixed with seriousness, but never be too free."

Large estates might also have a host of craftsmen. They might devote their services exclusively to the estate or divide their time between private and public commissions. They included carpenters (*MP* 127, 130, 141–142, 184, 191) and blacksmiths. Huntsmen and whippers-in helped with the care of dogs and the conduct of foxhunts and hare hunts.

Such servants tended to be fairly well paid, unlike the footboys, who were the most junior of the male servants. These footboys were essentially servants in training and might actually receive no wages at all, or at most 4 or 5 guineas a year. They ran errands for the other servants or, in a few cases, waited on ladies dressed in gorgeous livery. They might be as young as eight or nine years old.

Female Servants

Female servants, unlike lower male servants, did not wear livery. They instead wore a simpler and often darker-colored version of fashionable women's wear, so indistinguishable from the clothes of their employers that critics complained they could not tell maid and mistress apart by their clothing. The chief female servant in a large household was the housekeeper (*NA* 158, 211; *S&S* 64, 292; *P&P* 40, 246, 248, 249, 251, 301, 317, 331; *MP* 85, 91, 104, 105–106, 180, 254, 267; *E* 84, 89, 204, 391, 469), who was immediately subordinate to the house steward, if there were one, and who served as his replacement if there were not. She bought and distributed provisions for the household, kept accounts, and sometimes hired other servants on her employer's behalf. Her equivalent in rank, and sometimes even her superior, was the lady's maid (*Watsons, MW* 350, 360; *Sand, MW* 421; *NA* 164; *S&S* 206; *P&P* 353; *MP* 202, 254, 283, 377, 450; *E* 211) to the lady of the house, who dressed the mistress (*MP* 277), took care of her clothes (*MP* 254), styled her hair (*E* 134), and waited on her throughout the day. (Ladies' maids may be seen in the illustrations *Progress of the Toilet.—The Stays* and *Progress of the Toilet.—Dress Completed* [both in the article on Clothing] and Hairdressing [Hair].) The housekeeper's immediate subordinate was the cook (*Sand, MW* 382, 414; *NA* 183; *P&P* 65; *MP* 31, 111, 215–216; *E* 105), who had the same duties (but not the same prestige) as a man cook. It was to her advantage if she had "lived under a man cook," that is, if she had served in a household as the assistant to a male chef. She could also earn higher pay if she were a "professed cook," in other words a cook who knew how to make complex dishes and sauces. A woman who could not do such things was generally described as a "good plain cook."

In smaller households, two or even three of these offices might be combined, with a single servant acting as housekeeper and lady's maid or as housekeeper and cook. Longbourn's "Hill" appears to occupy such a post, serving, it seems (though Austen is frustratingly vague about the specific duties of her upper servants) as both housekeeper and lady's maid to Mrs. Bennet (*P&P* 301, 306), while another maid helps the Bennet daughters to dress and do their hair. Netherfield's "Nicholls," likewise, may be a cook or a cook-housekeeper (*P&P* 55). Hartfield's "Serle" and Donwell Abbey's "Hodges" may fill this combined post as well (*E* 172, 211, 355). Mrs. Elton's "Wright" appears, like Hill, to fill the post of housekeeper-lady's maid or cook-lady's maid, as she does Mrs. Elton's hair and also trades recipes with other housekeepers (*E* 324, 458).

A lady's maid or housekeeper might earn about 10 to 20 guineas a year in the late eighteenth century, while a cook's salary varied widely based on her skills, ranging from as little as £7 to as much as £20. A cook who doubled as housekeeper could earn £25. In addition, cooks and ladies' maids had perquisites that added substantially to their income. Cooks, for example, got to keep all the used fat from the kitchen and sell it—a benefit that often led employers to accuse their cooks of using too much butter when cooking, simply to augment the amount of drippings left in the pan. Ladies' maids often got their mistresses' cast-off clothing, which they could either wear or sell to secondhand clothes dealers.

Below these upper female servants were various other maids (*Lesley, MW* 113; *Col Let, MW* 159; *Cath, MW* 213, 217, 236; *Watsons, MW* 315; *Sand, MW* 370; *NA* 20, 172, 232; *S&S* 26, 260, 353; *MP* 14, 379, 383, 385, 387, 444; *P* 129). The larger the household, the more their duties were divided. The smaller the household, the more likely they were to combine two or more job descriptions, until, in the very smallest establishments, all duties were united in the maid of all work. A chambermaid (*NA* 172; *P&P* 241) made the beds, swept the bedroom floors, dusted, lit the bedroom fireplaces and cleaned them, and used a bed warmer—a large brass pans with a hinged lid and a long handle, into which hot coals could be placed—to warm the chilly bedclothes before her employer retired for the night. A housemaid (*Sand, MW* 401, 414; *NA* 194, 203; *S&S* 180; *P&P* 41, 317; *MP* 87, 105–106, 270, 322; *E* 9) performed similar tasks for the entire house, cleaning stairs, fire grates and irons, hearths, carpets, furniture, locks and door knockers, mirrors, and knickknacks. She might also do some sewing (*MP* 130, 141). The duties and titles of housemaids and chambermaids were often interchangeable, and both earned in the neighborhood of £9 or £10 a year.

Eliza Haywood, in *A New Present for a Servant-Maid* (1771), described the duties of a housemaid at length. The maid was to rise early, clean the stove and fire irons, light the kitchen fire, and clean the hearth. She was then supposed to proceed to the other parts of the house to wipe the locks with an oily rag and then polish them with powdered limestone. After sweeping the carpets (*MP* 440), windows, and floors "without leaving any [dust] sluttishly in corners," she should dust the picture frames, wainscot, china knickknacks, stucco work, and furniture. Next she would head to the stairs to sweep them, "throwing on the upper stairs a little wet sand, which will bring down the dust, without flying about." The next tasks were dusting the ceilings and washing the newly swept stairs. All this was to be done before her employer's family awoke, and once they were up and about,

> she should set open the windows of the bed-chambers, and uncover the beds to sweeten and air them; which will be a great help against bugs and fleas. In making the beds, she ought to begin with that first aired, taking off the several things singly, and laying them on two chairs, without letting them touch the floor. She should shake the beds well every day, and if there be a matrass, let her turn it at least once a week. The cleaning of the head of the bed, the vallances and curtains, with a brush or whisk, is not to be omitted;

nor sweeping clean all behind and under the bedsteads. . . . By thus keeping a constant method, her business will be a pleasure instead of a fatigue.

The rest of the day was occupied in scouring the floorboards; mopping; cleaning tea-boards, silver plate, and china dishes; and cleaning and waxing the furniture. In a home without male servants, or where the male servants were otherwise occupied, the housemaid would also tackle some of the tasks normally assigned to footmen, such as answering the door (*L&F, MW* 79, 80; *Evelyn, MW* 181; *MP* 399), announcing visitors' names and showing them into the proper rooms (*L&F, MW* 80, 84; *Cath, MW* 213–214; *S&S* 173, 232; *MP* 298; *E* 452), accompanying female travelers (*NA* 224; *MP* 8, 9, 410; *E* 285, 362), serving dinner (*Visit, MW* 52, 53; *Watsons, MW* 344, 346, 347, 359; *Sand, MW* 389; *MP* 407; *E* 218, 290), and carrying messages (*Col Let, MW* 159; *S&S* 222, 311; *P&P* 31, 34; *E* 374; *P* 176). In many households, housemaids and chambermaids were expected to sew and mend as well (*P&P* 292; *MP* 141).

Ranking below the housemaids and chambermaids were kitchen maids, who assisted the cook, cleaned the kitchen (*E* 173), and scrubbed the dishes (*MP* 413, 439); the laundry maids, who sweated in the laundry shed over washtubs heated by brick ovens; and dairy maids, who milked the cows and made cheese and butter. Nursery maids (see the illustration *Matrimonial-Harmonics* [Music]) took care of small children. A laundry maid earned about £7 to 10 guineas in the late eighteenth century, and a dairy maid about 5 to 6 guineas. A maid of all work, who did many of the tasks assigned to the other types of maids, usually earned somewhere between 7 and 8 guineas a year, though sometimes the amount fell outside this range.

Servants specializing exclusively in dairying, or laundry, or cleaning bedchambers were found only in larger homes. Smaller establishments such as the Austens' home at Steventon, Parson Woodforde's, William Gilpin's, and those of the other minor gentry, were likely to have about three to five servants (*S&S* 12, 26, 260, 277)—two to five women (*Cath, MW* 218; *Watsons, MW* 341) and the rest men, with the possible exception of a boy kept at little expense to run messages and do light chores. In such households, there might be a designated cook, housekeeper, or lady's maid, but the likely division was simply between "upper" (*Watsons, MW* 336; *E* 27; *P* 45) and "lower" servants, with the lower servants receiving lower wages and doing the majority of the less pleasant and less skilled work. One of the menservants might be an "outdoor" man—that is, a farm helper rather than a domestic servant, though he might wait at table or run errands when necessary.

Hiring

Servants could be hired (*P&P* 68) either through an agent or through personal recommendation. The professional sources of hired help included statute fairs, where servants out of work lined up for inspection and interrogation by prospective employers, and employment agencies (*E* 300–301) that ranged in scope from side businesses run by publicans or chandlers to large-scale, highly professional London organizations. The large agencies, which might send one candidate a day to the employer's home for inspection, thrived mostly in large towns and cities. Servants and employers also advertised in the newspapers. Servants listed any special qualifications they might have, while employers listed salary and benefits. In the countryside, one tended to find servants through the recommendations of family and friends (*S&S* 260; *E* 284), who might know that a relative of one of their own servants wanted work or that a servant of their own wanted to change households for some reason.

In the case of a servant who was personally unknown to the employer, it was important to ask for references, known as a "character," from the previous employer or employers. One could also seek out additional sources of information; when Emma tries to think of an excuse for going to Mr. Elton's house, she raises and dismisses the possibility of using inquiring about the reputation of a specific servant as a pretext to talk to the housekeeper (*E* 84). One of the perpetual scourges of the employer was the manufacture of counterfeit characters by London forgers who specialized in this branch of the trade. The risk taken by the servant was that the household would turn out to be something other than what she expected. She might be asked suddenly to do work that she was unfamiliar with or that she considered unnecessarily onerous, and if she broke her contract, she could be jailed. Or she might become the sexual prey of her employer or his sons. Eliza Haywood warned darkly, "There are some houses which appear well by day, that it would be little safe for a modest maid to sleep in at night," and advised serving girls to check carefully on the reputation of potential employers before agreeing to a contract.

Another option was to hire a relative, as Parson Woodforde and many others did. He hired his unmarried niece Nancy as his housekeeper at £10 a year, expecting her to do a good deal of household work but treating her more as a relative than a servant and often buying her presents. The term of service for domestics was traditionally a year (*MP* 385), renewable when the term was up and breakable with sufficient notice by either master or servant, but this limitation would not apply in the case of relatives who were also servants.

Sometimes servants looking for work would hear of an opening or take a chance on there being one and simply show up at the employer's door and ask for a job. In 1784 such a servant came to Parson Woodforde's door while he was out hunting. "By the Account that Nancy gave me," he wrote in his diary, "don't think she will do—she being rather high and her late Wages 8 Pounds per Annum—Her Friends live at Foxley a place I by no means approve of." Another woman "came to offer" in 1791, and

Woodforde said that if chose to hire her, she would hear from him within a week, but in his diary he confided, "I did not like her Appearance being of a bold Masculine Cast." A local boy, thirteen-year-old John Sucker, met with better luck at Woodforde's, probably because a good recommendation had preceded him. His father brought him over for inspection, and Woodforde wrote that

> after some talk with his Father I agreed to take him then being well recommended before by Mr. and Mrs. Bodham and Mr. Smith. I gave the Boy, by way of earnest Mony 0.1.0. I am to give him per Annum for Wages 1.1.0. A Coat and Waistcoat and Hat when wanted, to allow him something for being washed out and mended—And his Friends to find him in Stockings and Shoes &c.

The best servants were supposedly the children of one's own tenants, who had a long history of deference toward the employer and strong motives for doing a good job. One could also acquire a servant from a workhouse or charity school, and this was always an inexpensive option, but such servants were not necessarily very skilled. The worst servants, according to popular opinion, were those from London. Against these servants the prejudice was so strong that some of them would leave London just long enough to hop a wagon back into town so that they could appear to have recently arrived from the country.

Conditions of Service

Wages were generally higher in London than in the countryside, but a servant's wages were only part of his total income. Until the latter half of the eighteenth century, the giving of vails had been a universal practice. Vails were tips distributed to the staff upon departing a household after a visit. The amount of the vails depended on how long the stay had been, the degree to which one wanted to ingratiate oneself with the servants, and the quality of the service experienced and, to a much lesser extent, the financial resources of the tipper. Inadequate vails were punished by the servants on return visits by slow and surly service. At the time of a guest's departure, the relevant members of the staff would line up and wait to be paid, a practice that many guests and employers found humiliating. As a result of their embarrassment, they overcame serious opposition from their servants and gradually abolished the practice, raising their servants' wages to compensate for the lost tips.

The practice of vails had not completely disappeared by Austen's time, however. Parson Woodforde often gave vails when visiting other people's houses, even when he stayed only for dinner. He usually gave a shilling but occasionally gave more. Even when vails had vanished, servants expected or at least appreciated tips in other circumstances—for example, when delivering a package or a message. The kinds of services rewarded with tips made it especially common for footmen to be the servants receiving them, a perk that added to the prestige of the job. Livery servants such as footmen also received a portion of their clothes for free. They were generally issued a frock coat, breeches, boots, and sometimes stockings and were usually responsible for buying their own shirts, cravats, wigs, and dress shoes. Employers were very specific about whether the livery was a gift or a loan; when Parson Woodforde gave his footman Briton a new suit of livery in 1785, he told the man "that I gave neither to him, but only to wear them during his Service with me." When new livery was bought, however, the servant often got to keep the old outfit.

Maids, too, received augmentations to their salaries. They were often entitled to tea and sugar as part of their wages, and ads for maids often specified how many times a day they would receive free tea (*Evelyn, MW* 189). Some employers gave an additional sum of money in lieu of tea and let the servants buy their own.

Servants might also receive board wages, a sum of money in lieu of meals, usually provided when the family was traveling with the servant in tow or when the family was living elsewhere and large dinners were therefore not routinely provided. In the last quarter of the eighteenth century, board wages ranged from about 5s. to 10s. 6d. a week. Employers liked the system because it supposedly reduced waste and theft of provisions but suspected that their servants were then idling too much in the public houses where they got their meals.

Upper servants got used goods as perquisites of their posts, and these they could use or sell as they saw fit. The butler was usually entitled to the stubs of candles and old bottles. The cook got bones and chunks of fat in addition to the buttery drippings. The coachman got the old carriage parts after they were replaced, and the gamekeeper got to keep the guns and dogs of the poachers he arrested. Valets and ladies' maids got cast-off clothes, and at card parties, the footman or butler who supplied the cards was paid "card money" for each deck. Huntsmen were paid by all the gentlemen in the hunting party every time a quarry was killed. Porters got bribes to let visitors in to see important people, and housekeepers and gardeners got tips for showing tourists around their employer's house and grounds. Stewards, who kept the books, made large purchases, and superintended leases, were in the best position to fatten their own purses. All upper servants who did any of the household purchases expected kickbacks and/or "Christmas boxes" of goodies from the shops they patronized. Some savvy shop owners even threw parties for upper servants to attract and keep their business.

Events of importance within the employer's family could also have benefits for the servants. When a death occurred in the employer's family (but not in the servant's own family), mourning clothes were distributed, and this sort of gift reduced wear and tear on the servant's own wardrobe. Bequests to faithful servants might also have been made by the deceased. When the employer celebrated, whether at a wedding or for some patriotic occasion, the servants were likely to come in for special treats such as food, drink, or the right to throw a little party of their own at a discreet distance. Some employers let their servants invite other servants over for social occasions, and when people traveled to each other's houses for dinner or long visits, they brought servants with them who then had a chance to gossip, play cards, and make new friends (see the illustration *Loo in the Kitchin* [Cards]).

These were among the reasons that many people considered service a comfortable occupation. Another of its advantages was the amount and quality of the food, which tended to be superior to that consumed by soldiers, sailors, and many artisans and laborers. At a time of steeply rising food costs, servants ate plenty of bread, reasonable quantities of meat (*Sand, MW* 393), and generous amounts of beer or ale, with other kinds of liquor on special occasions (*P&P* 307). Servants in smaller households ate, in most cases, exactly what their owners ate. In very small establishments, such as the alehouse owned by Francis Place's father, they might even eat with the family. In larger households, the servants ate at a separate table in the kitchen, sometimes seated hierarchically according to their job titles. In still larger households, there was the "first table" for the employers and their guests, a "second table" for the upper servants (this table being usually laid in the housekeeper's room—*E* 204), and a "third table" for the lower servants. In such cases, the second table ate exactly the same food as the employers, while the third table got simpler food prepared especially for them, supplemented with leftovers from the first table. This system led to complaints from some employers that the footmen serving in the dining room cleared away the platters too quickly in the hope of securing more dainties for themselves.

Another advantage of service was that, in households with kind masters, there was often a great deal of care taken to provide a reasonable standard of living for the servants. Upper servants often got rooms to themselves, and valets and ladies' maids might have very good rooms adjacent to the employers' bedrooms. Medical professionals were often brought in to diagnose sick servants, who were sometimes worried over as much as a family member would have been. Hester Thrale Piozzi wrote of a recovering coachman, "Jacob's sore throat and fever has been a great addition to my agony, but he will live, poor fellow, I thank God." Some employers paid to have their servants taught to read and write, and while this was almost certainly for their own convenience, it obviously benefited the servants as well. Footmen and grooms got to do a good deal of traveling and might go on hunts; though they were not permitted to do any actual hunting themselves, it was an exciting change of pace. Aged servants were sometimes given pensions

(*S&S* 11) or allowed to live rent-free or at reduced rent in cottages on the estate.

The disadvantages of service, however, were many. There was the loss of caste, a serious issue for people who had been raised "above" service but were driven to it by financial necessity. Middle-class employers often felt obligated to emphasize the small social difference between themselves and their servants by being especially rude. The beating of servants was common, and a maidservant unfortunate to become pregnant was certain to be fired for bringing moral corruption into the household, even if the source of the moral corruption was the employer who molested her. Servants also had to wait a long time to get married, as their wages were so small that it was hard to save enough money to start a business or amass a dowry.

Nobody's Song, 1807. Sexual harassment was often a problem for female servants, who had little privacy and little means of resisting advances by their employers. Courtesy of the Lewis Walpole Library, Yale University. 807.3.28.1.

Terminating Employment

When things went wrong, either the master or the servant could choose to end the contract (*P&P* 68), though it was legally a bit harder for servants to do so. Common reasons for leaving a post voluntarily were taking another post in a more desirable household or at better wages, personal conflict with a member of the family or staff, desire to open a business of one's own such as an alehouse, or, in the case of female servants, marriage. Employers fired servants for a host of reasons, including pregnancy, drunkenness, and insolence. Parson Woodforde dismissed a new cook because she knew "nothing of her business. . . . I believe her to be a goodnatured Girl but very ignorant." He fired his manservant Will Coleman for getting drunk and behaving "most impudently," his maid Nanny Golding for "being subject to bad fits," and another maid, Molly, for being "with Child, more than half gone." He noted in 1784 that the local squire had fired a gardener for taking produce from the estate garden and selling it at market for his own profit. *See also* Carriages and Coaches; Housework; Hunting.

Severus

After young Fanny Price's arrival at Mansfield Park, her cousins are repeatedly shocked by the deficiency of her Portsmouth education. As evidence, they cite a long list of things that they have been taught that Fanny has not, including "the Roman emperors as low as Severus" (*MP* 18). "Low" refers not to the character of Severus but to his position on a list of Roman emperors. The speaker does not clarify which Severus is meant—L. Septimius Severus, who ruled the Roman Empire from 193 to 211, or Severus Alexander, who ruled from 222 to 235—but either one would have been about halfway down a list stretching from Augustus Caesar to Constantine.

L. Septimius Severus was one of three rival candidates for emperor, all of whom, in a now-familiar pattern, were backed by their armies. Severus invaded Rome, reformed the Praetorian Guard, carried on several military campaigns, began a protective wall along the German frontier, and instituted several changes in the military, most notably increasing the importance of non-Italian soldiers, raising pay, and permitting troops on active service to marry. He weakened the Senate, restructured the court system, partitioned some of the larger provinces, and accumulated surpluses on money and grain. Under his rule, the courts institutionalized a system of punishments based on the status of the offender, with stricter penalties being imposed on the poorer classes.

M. Aurelius Severus Alexander was the designated successor of the emperor Elagabalus; when Elagabalus tried to rescind his favor, the army assassinated him and installed Severus Alexander on the throne. The real ruler of Rome during Severus' reign was his mother, Julia Mamaea; she strengthened the importance and prestige of the Senate as a counterweight to the power of the army and tried to avoid frontier wars. At last, however, Severus had to go to war against the Alamanni, a formidable German tribe, and his mother accompanied him. Mutinous troops crippled the campaign, and assassins killed both Severus and Julia Mamaea in 235.

Sewing

Needlework (*NA* 240; *P&P* 47, 104–105; *MP* 19, 296; *E* 9) was one of the essential skills for a woman and, unlike the knowledge of French or the ability to play the harp, it was considered equally essential for women of the working class, the gentry, and the nobility. The specific set of skills varied somewhat by class, with wealthier women spending a greater percentage of their time on strictly ornamental sewing, such as embroidery, than on the construction of their own garments. However, even these women would have known how to do what was called "plain sewing," for all but the richest would have done some alterations (*MP* 381; *E* 237) for themselves and sewn simple clothing for the poor (*MP* 71). Nor were advanced skills solely confined to the gentry and nobility, for many of the fine, delicate embroidered or beaded gowns worn by rich women were actually sewn by professional working-class seamstresses. Jane and Cassandra Austen, for example, are known to have made alterations to their clothing, but the original manufacture was in the hands of others. However, Edward Austen's wife, Elizabeth, made shirts (*MP* 236, 385) for her husband, and Mrs. Austen was a source of embarrassment to Jane and Cassandra for her willingness to do plain sewing (*NA* 240; *MP* 390) before company, when only tiny, ladylike, decorative projects would have been preferable.

Jane was perfectly capable of both types of "work" (*Cath*, *MW* 197; *NA* 204, 241; *S&S* 181; *P&P* 104, 335; *MP* 18, 71, 125, 126, 147, 168, 220, 336–337, 360, 390; *P* 83). Like most little girls, she probably began by making samplers (*NA* 107), mottoes and alphabets embroidered onto plain fabric as a way of practicing different types of stitches and later, as a way of demonstrating precision and prowess. Items that she sewed or embroidered still survive and show her to have been adept at the small, even stitches for which seamstresses strove. Plain sewing—seams (*MP* 166), hems (*E* 388), mending, and so on—was done in the mornings, before and sometimes during morning visits. This sort of sewing required few tools: a small, sharp pair of scissors (*S&S* 120, 360); pins (*P* 99), pincushions (*P* 155), and "pin-poppets" (lidded containers that concealed a small pinchusion); and tape measures, often marked in increments called "nails," each unit equal to 2¼". A spool for thread (*NA* 60; *MP* 236; *P* 155) might be in the barbell shape common today, or it might be a spindle concealed inside a carved miniature barrel, from which the thread was extracted through a tiny hole in the side. Needles were sometimes kept in small hinged boxes with angled tops, the front lower than the back. Inside the box were compartments for keeping paper packets of needles. Needles (*NA* 60, 241; *MP* 236) might alternatively be kept in a needle book (*S&S* 254), a tiny "book" with fabric "pages" through which the needles could be inserted. Some of these were very simple, while others were bound in expensive materials such as silver filigree. Still other needle cases were tubes of ivory or filigree, often quite elaborately carved.

Sewing tools could be kept in any of a number of containers. One popular type was the etui, a tiny, decorative holder for small implements such as scissors, miniature knives (*S&S* 120), bodkins, and "ear spoons"—the Georgian equivalent of the Q-Tip. Etuis could be hung from a chatelaine, a jeweled pendant that hung from the waist. One example from about 1780 is cone-shaped, with diminutive enameled pictures of a woman gathering flowers, an urn filled with more flowers, birds, and a playful dog. Another from about the same time is shaped like a fish and is jointed so that the tail and body can curve in different directions. The case opens at the fish's neck, ex-

Miss GOODCHILDS first SAMPLER.
231
Published 12 Nov. 1793 by Rob.t Sayer & C.o Fleet Street London.

Miss Goodchilds first Sampler, 1793. Little girls began embroidering at a very young age. This child has sewing tools in her lap and a workbag on the floor. Courtesy of the Lewis Walpole Library, Yale University. 793.11.12.1.

posing a tiny knife, scissors, and ear spoon.* For more extensive collections of sewing supplies, it was necessary to have a sewing bag (*MW* 444–445; *S&S* 120; *E* 168), basket (*E* 471), or box (*MP* 153). A common type was the "housewife" or "huswife" (*S&S* 275; *E* 157), a piece of fabric with pockets for sewing tools that could be rolled up or folded and sometimes placed in a separate cloth bag. Beautiful sewing boxes were made of wood, decorated at times with rolled gilt-edged paper, with painted or inked designs, or with inlay. They could of course contain a hodgepodge of tools from different sources, but many women owned matching sets of wooden, ivory, tortoiseshell, or metal tools.

Midway between useful and decorative sewing was patchwork quilting, which used up fabric scraps and was thus a frugal as well as an aesthetic activity. A quilt made by Jane, Cassandra, Mrs. Austen, and perhaps Martha Lloyd in spring 1811 still exists at Chawton Cottage. Sometimes less practical, but no doubt equally enjoyable, were the making and decoration of small, elegant presents for friends and family. An Austen niece made slippers for a male relative, for example, and Jane herself made a bag and housewife at age sixteen for her future sister-in-law Mary Lloyd.

These little projects took far less time than large-scale embroidery, which might be white-on-white or colored (*S&S* 160) and serve either as a border decoration on clothing or table linen or as a piece of art in its own right, looking from a distance like a painting (*S&S* 160). Embroidery used many of the same tools as plain sewing, but it had some special tools of its own. While the material being embroidered was sometimes held loosely in the hand, many women preferred to stretch it in a round or rectangular frame (*MP* 65) or hoop. Embroiderers might use a silk holder that kept spare silk thread handy in a decorative ball dangling from a bracelet. Alternatively, they might use a silk winder, a cross- or star-shaped object. The embroidery thread was wrapped around the winder between the points of the star. In some cases, the winder was roughly rectangular in shape, with undulations or points along the long sides to hold the thread. Winders were made from a variety of materials, including cardboard, lacily

*Etuis, incidentally, were also used at times by men.

carved ivory, mother-of-pearl, straw-work, steel, cut glass, ceramic, and wood.

Other needle crafts included carpet work, rug making, tatting, and netting, all of which—except for tatting (lace-making)—are mentioned in Austen's works. Carpet work (*S&S* 258, 303; *MP* 179; *E* 85) was simply embroidery with either silk or wool on a sturdy backing of canvas rather than the lightweight linens and cottons used for other work. It had its origins in Renaissance attempts to imitate the rich colors and dense ornamentation of Turkish carpets and was used primarily for upholstery rather than as floor carpeting. Rugs (*S&S* 181), like carpet work, are not necessarily the floor coverings they sound like. They can instead be blankets or coverlets, knitted of wool or worsted. Mrs. Austen was fond of knitting (*P* 155; *E* 86, 156, 454) rugs and gloves; it was useful work that must have appealed to a pragmatic mother of eight children.

Tatting makes no appearance in Austen's works, though its end product—lace—is frequently mentioned (*MW* 389; *P&P* 13; *E* 292, 329; *P* 156), leading one to believe that few women of Austen's acquaintance bothered to make their own lace. This impression is borne out by the number of shops that sold lace panels and trims and by contemporary diaries, which often record the purchase, rather than the manufacture, of lace. Austen is not generally specific about the kind or pattern of lace, or even where it is located on the clothing, although she does make one reference to "Mechlin" (*NA* 238), a high-quality lace made in Mechlin, Belgium.

Unlike tatting, the activity of netting (*NA* 201, *P&P* 39) is mentioned often. This craft was exactly what it sounds like—the making of nets—and, unlike most other needle crafts, it was often pursued by men. Jane's brother Frank and her nephews Edward and George Knight were all fond of it. Though it was not unknown for men to knit or embroider for pleasure, netting had an atmosphere of utility that made it especially acceptable to men (*P* 99). After all, the same process used to make the fine meshes that adorn purses (*P&P* 39), pincushions, and dresses was used to make fishing and fowling nets and the nets that protected fruit trees from the depredations of hungry birds. Still, like most needle crafts, it was primarily performed by women. Parson Woodforde's niece and housekeeper Nancy Woodforde was apparently quite good at it, for in 1787 he recorded in his diary that Mrs. Custance, the squire's wife, "stayed with us till 3 o'clock, learning of Nancy to make diamond-edge-netting."

Netting (*NA* 40) required several specialized tools, the most important of which were the needles, the meshes, and the clamp, box (*NA* 176; *MP* 153), or stirrup. The needles (*P* 99), unlike sewing embroidery needles, were very slightly open at the end of the eye and had an eye at each end. They came in various sizes depending on the fineness of the net to be woven. This "needle" was really more like a shuttle, as the thread, cord, or rope being used to make the net was wound around it lengthwise and

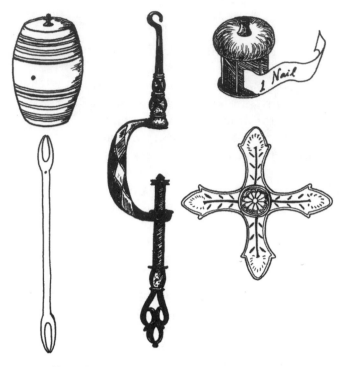

Needlework tools. Clockwise from center: steel netting clamp, early nineteenth century (about 5" tall); measuring tape, late eighteenth or early nineteenth century, about 1½" tall; nineteenth-century sandalwood silk winder, about 2¼" in diameter; netting needle, about 6" long; turned wooden thread case, c. 1800.

gradually unwound as the net took shape. The meshes (or "gauges") were thin sticks with rounded ends, rather like overly narrow tongue depressors. They were used to hold loops of thread in place. The last tool held the original loop of the net firmly anchored to a table or the floor. This could be accomplished with a clamp, which attached itself to some heavy object and caught the end of the net on a hook; with a stirrup, in which the netmaker placed his foot, using his or her own body to keep the thread taut; or with a special netting-box, distinguished from an ordinary sewing box by lead weighting to keep it stable and an interior roller with a ratchet to anchor the foundation loop. *See also* Hobbies; Housework.

Shoes

From the 1780s to the 1810s, the general trend in footwear was toward simplicity. Men's shoes (*E* 10), which had for decades been decorated with often elaborate and expensive buckles, were increasingly given long tongues and ribbon ties (*NA* 172). In 1784, Parson James Woodforde was impressed that an acquaintance, Mr. Micklethwaite, "had in his Shoes a Pair of Silver Buckles which cost between 7 and 8 Pounds" and that "Miles Branthwaite had a pair that cost 5 guineas." Twenty years later, such expenditure on shoe buckles would be very rare. The heels on men's shoes, which had risen quite high in the mid-eighteenth century, dropped lower, and colors grew more uniformly sedate, restricted in almost all cases to black or dark brown. When a man was in mourning, he always wore black shoes, but this was hardly different from his normal daily practice.

Boots (*Watsons, MW* 327) of all kinds became popular for men, partly in imitation of military uniforms and partly as an outgrowth of sporting activities in the countryside. The former influence spawned Hessian boots, which had angled tops and reached to just below the knee, and boots with metal fittings. The latter influence made top boots one of the most com-

Shoes and boots. Clockwise from top left: Striped cotton half-boot (1812–1820) with rosette near toe; top boot with white turn-down flap (c. 1810–1820s); Hessian boot with tassel (c. 1800); leather slipper with silk ribbon bow (1810); patten; tan kid half-boot with toe rosette (1815–1820).

mon footwear styles for men, so common, in fact, that cartoons of John Bull usually showed him wearing them. Top boots were tall boots, sometimes ridiculously tight, with tall tops that folded over and made a wide flap all the way around the top of the boot. They were pulled on with U-shaped straps, and these straps were such a characteristic feature of the boots that some were made with two pairs of straps—one for actual use, and one to hang outside the boot for show. Men also occasionally wore half boots, boots that rose a little above the ankle. The illustration Monstrosities of 1799 (Clothing) shows an exaggerated version of the Hessian boot, and the illustrations *A Meeting at Margate* and *A Shrewed Guess* (both in the Clothing article), as well as *The Breakfast* (Hunting) all have examples of top boots.

Women's shoes, like men's, grew generally flatter as time went on. Earlier in the eighteenth century, most women's shoes were high-heeled and made of fabric (*Scraps, MW* 176), but by the 1790s, leather was increasingly common, and heels were lower. From the 1790s through the 1810s, a variety of heel styles enjoyed popularity, often at the same time. There were wide wedge heels, narrow Italian heels, and slippers (*Scraps, MW* 176) with the faintest hint of a heel or no heels at all. Toe shapes, like heel sizes, were not uniform. Toes might be pointed or rounded, though rarely square.

Buckled shoes, as in the case of men, lost ground rapidly. The ornate buckles of former decades had come to seem out of place in an era devoted to classical simplicity. Accordingly, women adopted slippers without fasteners, faux-Greek sandals with ribbon straps, and shoes with tongues and ribbon laces. Colors (*S&S* 249) varied, with far more choice than was available to men. While black shoes (*NA* 26) were standard, women showed a willingness to wear shoes in pale colors (*Scraps, MW* 176), often chosen to match a fan, pelisse, gloves, or gown border. Colored shoes, however, were not worn all the time and were considered something of a luxury. Mr. Parker is astounded to see colored shoes in a store in *Sanditon* (*Sand, MW* 383), and Mrs. Austen was dismayed when her daughter-in-law Mary, James Austen's wife, bought a pair of colored shoes in 1811. The author of *The Mirror of the Graces* (1811) explained the proper use of color, beginning by explaining that the foot should be "arrayed soberly."

> Except on certain brilliant occasions, its shoe should be confined to grave and clean-looking colours; of the first, black, greys and browns; of the last, white, nankeen, pale blue, green, &c. according the colour of the dress and the time of day. I should suppose it almost useless to say, that (except in a carriage) the dark colours ought to be preferred in a morning. . . . The other delicate colours I have mentioned above (I repeat, except in a carriage) are confined to evening dresses. Red Morocco, scarlet, and those very vivid hues cannot be worn with any propriety until winter, when the colour of the mantle or pelisse may sanction its fulness.

The same author also mentions a type of footwear lately adopted by women that makes repeated appearances in Austen's works: the nankin or nankeen boot.

Women did not adopt the tall boots worn by men, but at some point in the first years of the new century, perhaps around 1804, they began adopting ankle-high lace-up half boots (*Watsons, MW* 347) made of leather or heavy-duty cotton (see the illustration *A Fashionable Belle* [Clothing]). These are the shoes suggested by Lord Osborne to Emma Watson, whose family is so poor it can just barely muster an appearance of gentility:

> "Have you been walking this morning?" "No, my Lord. We thought it too dirty." "You should wear half-boots. . . . Nothing sets off a neat ankle more than a half-boot; nankin galoshed with black looks very well.—Do not you like Half-boots? "Yes—but unless they are so stout as to injure their beauty, they are not fit for Country walking."—"Ladies should ride in dirty weather. . . . A woman never looks better than on horseback.—" (*Watsons, MW* 345)

R. W. Chapman, basing his estimate on information from one of Jane's great-nieces, dates the composition of *The Watsons* to 1804—in other words, just as half boots were coming into style. Lord Osborne, who reveals his social clumsiness and obliviousness to any lifestyle but his own on several occasions, does so again here. His main gaffe is in recommending any new shoe to a woman who undoubtedly cannot afford to buy a pair whenever she likes, let alone the latest fashion, which would place her in middle of a sartorial arms race she could not hope to win; he then compounds that by suggesting that she ride, when she is equally unable to buy a horse. He concludes the error two pages later by offering to give Emma the name of his sister's shoemaker (*Watsons, MW* 347), which is equally ludicrous. Women of limited means bought their shoes ready-made from shoe "warehouses" (a synonym for "stores," used to imply wide selection). Some women, for fun, embroidered and made their own, or added ribbon straps to the ankles and rosettes of ribbon or silk at the toes (*P&P* 88). Only a woman of comfortable means would still have had her shoes custom-made by a shoemaker (*MP* 361).

Half boots were designed for morning wear and especially for walking outdoors. Their increasing adoption by women as walking shoes is reflected in their recurrence in three of the later novels, *Emma* (88–89), *Persuasion* (174–175), and *Sanditon* (383). In the example from *Sanditon*, they are again made of "nankin," or nankeen, which was a sturdy yellow-brown or buff cotton fabric named for Nanking, China. Lord Osborne, in his recommendation of nankin boots, suggests not unreasonably that they be "galoshed with black," that is, partially covered with black leather.

Not all footwear was appropriate for all purposes. Even women who adopted half boots for walking or morning wear would have set these aside and put on slippers or heeled shoes for evening (*E* 127). Men preferred boots for almost every purpose, especially for hunting, traveling, and riding (*NA* 210), but they had to wear buckled shoes at court. Similarly, they adopted shoes and stockings for evening wear (*Cath, MW* 218). At Bath, boots were actually forbidden at assemblies.

Yet a woman would have been mad to wear a fine pair of slippers on a country walk or in wet weather (*S&S* 306; *P&P* 156; *E* 156, 322). Women employed various devices to protect their shoes when they had to brave the dirt, as, for example, when they were going to a ball and had to get from the house to the carriage and from the carriage to the ballroom. They might wear matching toepieces that covered the pointed toe of a shoe and looked very much like the shoe itself, fastening these decorative coverings with a strap in the back. Alternatively, they might wear overshoes called clogs (*MW* 452; *NA* 19), removing these in a cloakroom when they arrived at the ball.

Women walking around a muddy town on errands or walking along country roads might adopt pattens (*MW* 452; *NA* 184). The patten was a shoe sole with a strap over the arch of the foot that tied it on and with a metal ring on the bottom that raised the wearer's shoe an inch or two off the ground. (The laundress in the illustration *How Are You Off for Soap* [Housework] wears pattens, though they are somewhat difficult to see.) Pattens were considered rustic and awkward, but in some cases they were necessary. Bath (*P* 135), for example, could be particularly dirty during its winter season, and Betsy Sheridan, writing in 1789, proclaimed, "We ladies here trot about in pattens, a privilege granted nowhere else to genteel women." Outside Bath, pattens were generally associated with women who were relatively poor, unfashionable, and countrified.

When attempts to preserve shoes from damage failed, the shoes were more likely to be repaired than discarded. Austen refers to having some pairs of worn-out shoes "capped & heelpeiced" (*Scraps, MW* 176). This probably means that both the uppers and the lowers were replaced, which would be in keeping with the humorous tone of the piece in which the reference occurs.

Two important innovations were made in this period, although one was more of a reintroduction than a new invention. The true innovation was patent leather, also known at this time as "japanned" leather (after the black lacquer items of Japan). It was introduced in the early 1790s and soon came into widespread use. The not-so-original innovation was the reintroduction, after a lapse of nearly 200 years, of right and left shoes; since about 1600, shoes had been made as "straights," with no distinction between left and right. *See also* Clothing; Stockings.

Shops

Customers shopped (*P&P* 152; *E* 234) at establishments ranging from tiny village shops to London "warehouses" (*P&P* 288) that seemed enormous by the standards of the time but would be dwarfed by modern department stores and bulk-grocery warehouses. The smallest and humblest of all shops was the village chandler's shop, which took its name from the fact that the proprietor sold wax or tallow candles, but most chandler's shops offered an assortment of staples such as soap, butter, bacon, and tea as well. Small towns might have chandler's shops (*NA* 212; *MP* 58) and a handful of specialty shops (*S&S* 199; *P&P* 72; *MP* 403; *P* 221) such as a stationer's (*S&S* 199), which sold writing paper, ink, sealing wax, and the like, or an all-inclusive clothing shop that sold fabric for dresses, gloves, ribbons, lace, and hats. Ford's in Highbury (*E* 199–201, 235–237) is such a store. Larger towns would divide clothing sales (*NA* 20) among shops devoted to a particular article. Linen-drapers (*E* 178) sold linen and cotton fabrics by the yard, while woolen-drapers (*E* 178) sold wool cloth, haberdashers (*E* 178) sold small articles like ribbons and tapes, and milliners (*Cath, MW* 201; *Watsons, MW* 322; *P&P* 28, 219) sold women's hats, caps, and bonnets. Mercers sold silk.

The large towns would, in addition to these shopkeepers in the clothing trades, have dealers in china, wine, tobacco, furniture (*Scraps, MW* 176–177), books (*S&S* 92), prints (*S&S* 92; *P* 169), and sheet music (*S&S* 92). Then

Wedgwood & Byerly, 1809. Wedgwood's showroom in St. James' Square. Courtesy of the Lewis Walpole Library, Yale University. 809.2.0.1.

there were the food sellers: grocers (*Col Let*, *MW* 158), who sold sauces, spices, dried fruit, and imported ingredients; butchers (*S&S* 197; *MP* 379) selling meat and sometimes specialist poulterers (*MP* 212–213) selling poultry; bakers selling bread, and pastry-cooks selling pies, jellies, ices, and the "biscuits and buns" (*MP* 413) that Fanny Price sends her brothers out to buy. Parson Woodforde, on his trips to Norwich, recorded purchases at "Bakers," where he bought smelling salts, a comb, netting cord for his niece Nancy, a whip, "a Habit brush for Nancy with a looking Glass at the back of it," and a pair of riding gloves. At Mr. Priest's shop, at various times, he bought medicine, rum, and wine. From "one Studwell China Man in the Market Place," he bought basins, tumblers, beer glasses, and a teapot. At Beale's, a fishmonger, he had a running account that he paid periodically. He also made purchases from a bookseller, a silk mercer, an ironmonger, a timber merchant, a hatter, a brazier (who sold brass goods), a tailor, a tobacconist, and an upholsterer (who sold wallpaper as well as fabric for furniture). "Graham's Shop" supplied him with stockings, and his barber supplied him with wigs. A "Cabinet Maker on Hog Hill Norwich" sold him furniture, and Cook's Glass Shop sold him some cut-glass saltcellars. Clearly, Norwich had a wide variety of shops, and these were not without competition, for on at least one occasion he mentions switching from one supplier to another in the same town.

Very Slippy-Weather, James Gillray, 1808. A print shop's bow window. Courtesy of the Lewis Walpole Library, Yale University. 808.2.10.6.

Cities noted for the excellence of their shops, such as Bath (*NA* 25, 29, 217; *P* 141) and London (*S&S* 164, 182; *P&P* 152; *E* 435), had the largest shops with the widest selection of goods. Wherever the rich congregated, one could find the best luxury goods—carriages, musical instruments (*E* 214–215, 241), porcelain dishes, hunting rifles (*P* 239), and expensive jewelry (*S&S* 220–222, 226). Where the rich merely visited temporarily, there were innumerable "toy" shops that sold not children's playthings but souvenirs and small objects such as penknives, pincushions, china knickknacks, "spars" (crystalline fragments—*NA* 116), pocketbooks, purses (*NA* 116), buckles, combs, and needle cases.

Many stores extended credit to their customers, and this flexibility helped to sustain the chandlers' shops, which thus earned the business of small farmers whose earnings were largely seasonal. They might also take goods in trade; the farmer's wife might bring in eggs, for example, and take a little bacon, sugar, or tea with the credit she earned. (Sometimes the chandler *was* the farmer's wife, running a small shop part-time in order to increase her income.) The more fashionable shops also extended credit to prominent clients, with sometimes disastrous results for those who racked up huge debts with tailors, wine merchants, butchers, and such (*P&P* 294; *P* 9). Parson Woodforde, who was good about paying his debts, was only billed once a year by his butcher and paid his other suppliers either on the spot or after buying on credit for a few months.

Spectacles

Eyeglasses in one form or another had been around for centuries, but it was only in the eighteenth century that significant advances were made in keeping the eyeglasses in place. Until the early eighteenth century, spectacles (*E* 158) consisted of two round lenses attached by a springy nosepiece, and the tension in the nosepiece was supposed to keep the spectacles precariously perched on the bridge of the nose. The innovation was the

A Touch at the Times, 1805. Chandlers' shops like this one sold a variety of goods, not just candles. Courtesy of the Lewis Walpole Library, Yale University. 805.3.25.2.

addition of temple- or sidepieces to shift the burden from the nose to the ears. The idea of involving the ears was not new; more primitive spectacles had made use of cords that wrapped around the ears, but rigid sidepieces were altogether novel.

However, the sidepieces did not usually look like the ones with which we are now familiar—thin, straight bars with a curved end designed to fit snugly behind the ear. Instead, on some pairs the bar ended in a round loop that sat behind the ear and was visible above it. Other examples had "turnpin" temples—sidepieces with one section hinged to the lens frame and another section nearer the ear that could swivel to facilitate folding the glasses when they were not in use. The back sections did not drop behind the ear as we might expect but extended straight back and sometimes even met behind the head.

Variety could be found not only in the method of suspending the eyeglasses but in their lenses and the materials of which the frames were made. Lenses, which had historically been designed for farsighted readers only, were increasingly available for the nearsighted. Bifocals, too, were sold, as were glasses with tinted lenses, which were believed by some to be easier

Jack, Hove Down—With a Grog Blossom Fever, W. Elmes, 1811. This physician wears turnpin-temple spectacles. Courtesy of the Lewis Walpole Library, Yale University. 811.8.12.1.

on the eyes. The shape of the lenses was also changing. At the turn of the nineteenth century, the traditional large, round lenses were being challenged by smaller lenses and by oval and rectangular forms, patented by Dudley Adams in 1797. Oval lenses certainly predated Adams' patent, but rectangular lenses would not become popular until just after Austen's death.

Other types of eyeglasses were also in use. The old pince-nez, which perched on the nose without the aid of temple-pieces, remained popular. The fashionable might instead sport a "prospect glass"—rather like an upside-down pair of pince-nez with a handle. The Y-shaped contrivance could be held up to the eyes as needed. Alternatively, a dandy might use a quizzing glass, a single lens on a handle that was to be the ancestor of the monocle. (The monocle itself, a single lens without a handle that was held in place between the cheekbone and the eyebrow ridge, developed around 1806.) Quizzing glasses and their cousins were popular accessories, and not just for those who had trouble with their vision. The anonymous author of the conduct book *The Mirror of Graces* (1811) complained, "Some ladies, to whom nature has given a good sight and lovely orbs to look through, must needs pretend a kind of half-blindness, and they go peeping about through an eye-glass, dangling at the end of a long gold chain, hanging at their necks." Contemporary prints also reveal the popularity of single and double lenses of all kinds.

Some of these aids to vision were elaborately decorated and made of expensive materials. Silver spectacles tended to be of good quality, while cheaper pairs were made from steel or iron. Parson James Woodforde, in his diary entry of September 19, 1786, speaks of "a Pair of Spectacles with a very handsome Tortoise-shell Case and Silver mounted—they were formerly the Treasurers I believe." Tortoiseshell and leather were also used for the lens frames. A cheap pair of pince-nez could be bought for one shilling in 1773; a pair of fairly average temple spectacles cost 3s. 6d. in 1804. Whether the spectacles were cheap or expensive, however, the onus was on the customer to make sure that they functioned properly. There were no elaborate eye exams, no studying charts of letters through care-

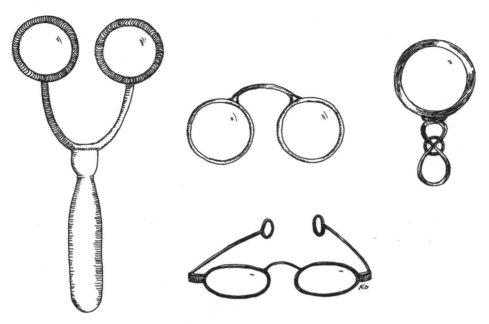

Four types of eighteenth-century eyeglasses. Clockwise from left: a double-lensed, single-handled prospect glass; old-fashioned spectacles with a spring as nosepiece; a single-lensed quizzing glass; spectacles with hinged sidepieces.

fully calibrated sets of lenses. Instead, the customer simply picked up one pair of glasses after another, trying them on until he found one that seemed to improve his vision to the correct degree.

The real questions for the reader of Austen are: What kind of spectacles is Frank Churchill fixing in *Emma*, and what is wrong with them in the first place? I was able to determine the answers, at least in part, with the invaluable assistance of Neil Handley, curator of the museum collection of the College of Opticians. The two most important clues lie in Mrs. Weston's mock criticism of Frank's progress on Mrs. Bates' spectacles and in the part of the spectacles that is blamed for the trouble.

When she enters the Bateses' drawing room, Mrs. Weston chides Frank, saying, "What! . . . have you not finished it yet? you would not earn a very good livelihood as a working-silversmith at this rate" (*E* 240). The implication, then, is that we are dealing with a pair of silver spectacles—in other words, a pair on the higher end of the spectrum of quality. This in itself is rather surprising, as we are familiar by this point in the novel with the Bateses' poverty. However, it is a genteel sort of poverty. Mrs. Bates has come down in the world, but she is still a gentlewoman, and she therefore wears a gentlewoman's spectacles.

As for the part that has gone wrong, this is said to be a "rivet" (*E* 236, 238, 242). The fullest description of the problem is given by Miss Bates, who says that Frank is fastening the rivet of my mother's old spectacles. . . . For my mother had no use of her spectacles—could not put them on. And, by the bye, every body ought to have two pair of spectacles. . . . At one time Patty came to say she thought the kitchen chimney wanted sweeping. Oh! said I, Patty do not come with your bad news to me. Here is the rivet of your mistress's spectacles out." (*E* 236)

This identifies Mrs. Bates' spectacles, with a good deal of probability, as temple spectacles, and furthermore as temple spectacles of the turnpin variety. Rivets were found on various types of temple spectacles at the points where the temple-pieces join the lens frame. According to Mr. Handley, these rivets might be left exposed on iron-framed spectacles but were unlikely to have protruded enough on a fine silver pair to have come loose. However, on turnpin temples, there was also a rivet attaching each temple-piece to its folding extension. These rivets quite frequently came loose; as evidence, Mr. Handley cites the large number of surviving examples of these spectacles that are missing one or both extensions. It is therefore not certain, but quite likely, that Mrs. Bates' spectacles are silver with turnpin temples and that the turnpin rivet is the one that has fallen out. The absence of one of the extensions would indeed make it impossible to wear the spectacles comfortably, as they would rest on only one ear.

Spleen

The use of the word "spleen" to mean anger (*MP* 120) or ill-humor (*E* 40) is a legacy of classical and medieval medicine. Early doctors had an imperfect understanding of anatomy, an almost mystical view of physiology, and relatively few diagnostic techniques at their disposal. They tended to rely on the output of bodily fluids for assessing a case, and the archetypal medieval and Renaissance image of the physician is not a caduceus or a stethoscope but a bearded man holding a flask of the patient's urine. They blamed sickness on blockages that prevented the passage of fluids and energy from one organ to another or on surfeits of heat or cold, blood or bile that needed to be diminished in order to restore health.

Each organ had its properties and was associated with certain of the prime qualities (hot, cold, dry, wet) and with one or more of the four humors (blood, yellow bile, black bile, and phlegm). Traces of these theories can still be found in English usage today. "Choleric" means inclined to anger, and "choler" is another word for bile, the humor associated with anger. (The disease cholera also takes its name from the word for bile.) Black bile, a fictitious substance, was associated with people of somber, pessimistic outlook—hence the word "melancholy," which comes from the words for "black" and "bile." A sanguine person is one with a cheerful temperament; a medieval physician would have given the credit for the attitude to a surplus of blood, hence the term "sanguine," which comes from the word for blood. We still use the word "phlegmatic" to describe a person who is extraordinarily calm, and this derives from the medieval belief that such a characteristic was the result of a surplus of phlegm.

Though the physicians of Austen's day had largely discarded the theory of the humors, the language had not been purged of allusions to it. Spleen, therefore, was a mood first and foremost and a bodily organ only as an afterthought.

Stockings

Stockings (*S&S* 306; *P&P* 32; *E* 294; *P* 122) were worn by both men and women throughout Austen's lifetime. Increasingly machine-knitted on stocking frames, they could be made of cotton, silk, or worsted; Jane reported buying "ten pair of worsted stockings" in October 1800, but these were almost certainly intended as gifts for the poor, as worsted stockings were generally cheaper and coarser than silk and cotton. Personally, she preferred silk stockings (*S&S* 274) and bought three pairs in London in April 1811 "for a little less than 12./S. a pʳ." This appears to have been a relatively good price; Lord and Lady Middleton paid 18s. 6d. a pair in Nottingham in 1799. Cotton stockings were generally of quite good quality; Jane's niece Fanny Knight, who was rich enough to buy any stockings she wanted, bought both silk and cotton stockings in 1813 at prices of 12s. and 4s. 3d. a pair, respectively.

Men tended to wear extremely plain stockings (*NA* 169). They favored white, sometimes with vertical ribs or the appearance of ribs. Vertically or horizontally striped or zigzagged stockings were not unknown, especially in the 1790s, but the flamboyant styles of the earlier eighteenth century were being replaced by simpler styles and more muted colors, and men's stockings reflected this trend. Parson James Woodforde recorded buying a variety of types of stockings, but all of them sound fairly plain—"brown thread Stockings to wear under boots &c." for 6s. in 1793; "white worsted Gauze" at 1s. 10d., also in 1793; "Castle-Cary Stockings," for which the material was not specified, at 5s. a pair, in 1794; and black silk at 16s. a pair, by far the most expensive, in 1793. He also owned silk-blend stockings at 8s. 6d. a pair, somewhat cheaper black silk stockings that he bought for as little as 12s. a pair, ribbed stockings, "ash-coloured welch stockings," white lambswool stockings for gout, and semiwaterproof stockings made with untreated wool for early-morning hunting. In general, thicker stockings were worn for riding or hunting and fine ones for evening parties and dinners; Woodforde's variety of stockings represents the variety of activities that required different modes of dress.

Women's stockings also tended to be simple, if for no other reason than that so little of the stocking was ever seen. Long skirts kept all concealed except the ankle, and it was therefore the ankle that received some form of decoration. This was usually a "clock," a triangular patch of embroidery or lace covering the ankle. It was widest at the base of the foot, tapering as it rose along the outside of the leg; the height of the decoration varied from pair to pair. The anonymous author of *The Mirror of the Graces* (1811) objected to brightly colored clocks:

> [W]e totally disapprove, at all times, of the much ornamented stocking.
>
> The open-wove clock and instep, instead of displaying fine proportion, confuse the contour; and may produce an impression of gaiety; but exclude that of beauty, whose rays always strike singly. But if the clock be a coloured or a gold one, as I have sometimes seen, how glaring is the exhibition! how coarse the association of ideas it produces in the fancy! Instead of a woman of refined manners and polished habits, your imagination reverts to the gross and repelling females of Portsmouth-point, or Plymouth-dock; or at least to the hired opera-dancer, whose business it is to make her foot and ancle the principal object which characterizes her charms. . . .
>
> . . . . the finest rounded ancles are most effectually shown by wearing a silk stocking *without any clock*. The eye then slides easily over the unbroken line, and takes in all its beauties. But when the ancle is rather large, or square, then a pretty unobtrusive net clock, of the same colour as the stocking, will be a useful division, and induce the beholder to believe the perfect symmetry of its parts.

Most women, no doubt to this author's great satisfaction, confined themselves to white or black stockings, more commonly white, with discreet clocks of white, pink, blue, or green, or no clocks at all. Clocks on black stockings were always black. At the turn of the century, there was a brief vogue for pink stockings, which made women look even more naked under the thin, almost transparent muslin dresses then in fashion. A writer in 1803 sneered, "The only sign of modesty in the present dress of the ladies is the pink dye in their stockings, which makes their legs appear to blush for the total absence of petticoats."

Stockings were held up by garters (*E* 86), thin strips of ribbon or embroidered cloth, that tied above the knee. Men also wore gaiters (*E* 287), an entirely different garment, which were designed to protect stockings from damage when walking or riding. These gaiters were cylindrical pieces that were wrapped around the lower leg and buttoned from knee to ankle. Some boots had short gaiters built into them; the boot went on up to the knee, and then the gaiter buttoned up over the knee to keep the boot from slipping down and wrinkling. *See also* Clothing; Shoes.

Swearing

The eighteenth century in England was characterized by the majority's avoidance of excess in religion. This fact, coupled with the legacy of earthiness inherited from the Restoration, made swearing a fairly commonplace activity. Nevertheless, at the end of the century, the first faint stirrings of Victorian morality can be seen. The decreasing vigor of some traditional religious dissenting groups was countered by the rise of Methodism and, toward the end of Austen's life, the first flowering of the Evangelical movement.

The Evangelicals in particular were offended by foul language. A letter to the *Evangelical Magazine* in 1807 reported a naval officer's view of the subject:

> [A]n officer cannot live at sea without swearing; not one of my men would mind a word without an oath; it is common sea-language. If we were not to swear, the rascals would take us for lubbers, stare in our faces, and leave us to do our commands ourselves.

Austen's brother Francis, himself both an Evangelical and a naval officer, was a captain given to flogging, yet he defied the conventional wisdom by never swearing aboard ship or tolerating the use of obscene language in his presence. His was an unusual case, for sailors, it was widely acknowledged, were the worst offenders of all (*MP* 402).

Swearing, for most of the eighteenth century, was widespread in all walks of life. Admittedly, not all of the oaths used were ones we would recognize today as being swearwords. Some simply sound silly and antiquated: odds bob, odds fish, zounds, by Gad, pish. Yet they were quite common, so much so that the rustic character Bob Acres in Sheridan's *The Rivals* invents a fashionable new method of swearing, in which he adds a contextually appropriate phrase to "odds," as in "Odds whips and wheels!" when discussing travel woes or "Odds blushes and blooms" when describing a lady's healthy complexion. The ubiquity of "odds," "zounds" or "oons," "fish" or "pish," and "gad" in eighteenth-century oaths stems from the religious origins of these words. "Odds" and "gad" were both corruptions of "God"; the fish (of which "pish" is another corruption) is a Christian symbol; and "zounds" (pronounced "zoons," not "zownds") is a contraction of "God's wounds"—a reference to the Crucifixion of Christ.

In addition to these rather quaint oaths, there were stronger terms that would seem more familiar to a modern ear. They rarely, however, appeared to the *eye*; when printed, they suffered the same fate as the names of prominent peers in satirical prints. All letters but the first, or sometimes the first and last, were excised, in a kind of letter-ectomy that left the word recognizable to its acquaintances but greatly diminished. Tobias Smollett's 1748 novel *Roderick Random*, therefore, has its numerous minor swearwords left intact, but its God and Christ have been surgically reduced to G—d and Ch—st. Even this nod to decency, however, came to seem inadequate as the century drew to a close. Laurence Sterne's novel *Tristram Shandy*, written in the 1760s, replaces the name of the devil with "deuce" (*Lesley*, *MW*

138)* and omits most of the letters of the few serious oaths, while even Smollett mellowed, lessening both the quantity and ferocity of his swearing in later novels and even introducing a discourse against swearing in *Humphry Clinker* (1771). Sermons and pamphlets denouncing foul language had their effect, and by the 1780s, poet James Fordyce could lecture his readers,

> It chills my blood to hear the blest Supreme
> Rudely appeal'd to on each trifling theme.
> Maintain your ranks, vulgarity despise:
> To swear is neither brave, polite, nor wise.

Leigh Hunt, a few years younger than Jane Austen, recalled in an 1850 autobiography that his mother instilled in him

> such a horror, or rather such an intense idea of even violent words, and of the commonest trivial oath, that being led one day, perhaps by the very excess of it, to snatch a "fearful joy" in its utterance, it gave me so much remorse that for some time afterwards I could not receive a bit of praise, or a pat of encouragement on the head, without thinking to myself, "Ah! they little suspect that I am the boy who said, 'd—n it!' "

He never swore again.

Nevertheless, the moral revolution associated with the Victorians had not yet taken full hold of the nation. Uproar occasioned by the French Revolution, the Napoleonic Wars, the decadence of the prince regent's circle, and the near-transparency of women's fashions made the whole world seem as if it was being destroyed and remade over the course of a few years. In the grand scheme of things, a "damme" (*F&E, MW* 11) here and there did not seem like a cardinal sin. Even women adopted some freedom of language, with "God," "Lord" (and its milder cousin, "Lud"), "Pish," and other mild oaths finding their way into the mouths of genteel ladies (*S&S* 124, 153, 176). The stronger oaths were reserved for men and for working women. Austen no doubt heard some of these words— she could, after all, even as a spinster, remark coolly in a letter on meeting a prominent man's mistress, so she was not entirely sheltered—but these words belonged principally to the masculine world, and, as such, she shuns them. There is very little swearing in the novels, or even in the wilder Juvenilia, reflecting Austen's gender, her status as a rector's daughter, and very likely her own sense of morality. *See also* Etiquette; Religion.

Sweep

The sweep (*Cath, MW* 197; *Watsons, MW* 322; *S&S* 374; *MP* 291; *E* 116, 127, 332, 392) was a circular or semicircular driveway at the front of a

---

*The name of the Devil was euphemized in other ways; see, for example, the reference to "the black gentleman" in *E* 304.

house. It was designed to accommodate horses and carriages, neither of which were particularly fond of backing up. In a sweep, the horses, having deposited their cargo of passengers at the front door, could continue on in the same direction, completing the circle or half-circle and heading along the path toward the stables.

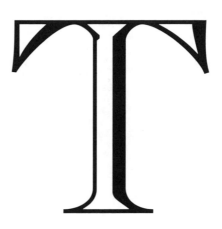

Taxes

Austen makes few mentions of taxes in her work, which is somewhat surprising, given her interest in money and the number of taxes imposed during her lifetime. Some of these were relative constants, such as the land tax. Others were new impositions designed to pay for England's wars against France.

One of the oldest taxes was the land tax (*S&S* 266), first imposed in 1690 at a rate of three shillings to the pound, or 15 percent. Parson James Woodforde, who farmed a glebe—land associated with his rectory—paid £12 per year in land taxes in the 1780s and 1790s. The rate fluctuated from time to time, rising to four shillings in the pound during the Seven Years' War, for example, and falling again to three shillings thereafter. Another long-standing tax was the salt tax, which was in effect from 1643 to 1825 and which was high enough to discourage herring fishermen from salting their catch.

The hiring of servants was first taxed in 1777 by Lord North, who initially taxed only male servants. The rationale behind this was that female servants were a necessity, as they did the principal work of the house, but that male servants were a luxury. It was true that male servants were seen as evidence of affluence; unlike female servants, they wore expensive costumes called livery, and they tended to be associated with the care of luxury items such as carriages, horses, and imported wines. The tax was graduated, but not according to the employer's income. Instead, it was graduated according to the size of his family; a married man paid a guinea per servant, while families with children paid less, and bachelors paid double. Again, the rationale was luxury. Large families had a logical need for more servants, but for a bachelor to keep a manservant was a sign that he had plenty of extra money.

In 1785, the tax on servants was expanded by Prime Minister Pitt. The flat rate of one guinea per manservant was changed to a sliding scale, beginning at £1 5s. for the first male servant and increasing per servant up to £3 apiece, according to the number of male servants kept. A tax on maidservants was also introduced, but again, as they were considered necessities, they were taxed at a lower rate. The scale, which, like that for menservants, was based on the number of servants employed, ranged from 2s. 6d. to 10s. The 1785 tax continued the practice of double-charging bachelors, a practice noted by Parson Woodforde in his diary entry for April 27, 1786:

> To Jno Pegg for ¾ of Years Servants Tax for Males and being a Batchelor, double p^d 1.17.6. To Ditto—for Female Servants Tax also for ¾ Year and being a Batchelor double p^d 0.15.0. To Ditto ½ Years Horse Tax p^d 0.10.0.

I pay for 1 Male Servant 2 Female Servants and for 2 Horses. For every Male Servant per Annum 2.10.0. For every Female Servant per Annum 0.10.0. For every Horse, for riding per Annum 0.10.0.

As Woodforde's entry notes, there was also a tax on saddle and carriage horses, determined again by the number of horses owned.

These taxes, without any additions, would have been resented, but a host of other items were taxed as well. There was a tax on windows (*MP* 85), on candles, and on carriages. Brewers paid excise fees on the beer they made and a tax on the hops they used in its production. Spirits were taxed at 5s. 4d. a gallon in the 1780s, a rate that rose to 12s. 2¾d. in 1813. Tea was taxed at a rate of 119 percent until 1784, when the Tea Act cut the tax to a paltry 12 percent. Cosmetics were taxed from 1786 on a sliding scale based on retail price; beauty products selling for less than 8d., for example, had a penny tax, while those selling for more than 5s.

The Sad and Dark Effects of the Taxes of 1784, 1784. The taxes on various goods considered to be luxuries have taken their toll in this town. The tax on horses has caused the carter to replace his horses with an ass and an ox. The woman at right is using lye for her laundry instead of soap, which was taxed, and the owners of the house have boarded up most of their windows to save on the window tax. Courtesy of the Lewis Walpole Library, Yale University. 784.6.0.1.

were taxed an extra shilling. Hair powder was taxed from 1786 to 1800; this tax was replaced from 1795 to 1869 by an annual license (one guinea in 1795) to powder one's hair. Soap, too, was taxed, from 1712 to 1853. Paper, playing cards, silver, newspaper advertisements, and the newspapers themselves were all taxed.

In addition, property owners were paying a variety of more substantial taxes. They had to pay "poor rates" to care for the impoverished members of their parish, and they also had to pay fees to maintain the parish's roads. Most hated of all was the income tax, introduced in 1799 to meet the mounting costs of the French wars. The tax was 10 percent and applied only to those making £200 or more per year, but it was so thoroughly loathed that when it was abolished, in 1816, the tax records were burned.

Tea

It's no accident that Austen mentions tea (*Watsons, MW* 326; *Sand, MW* 416; *S&S* 198; *P&P* 217, 299, 344, 346; *MP* 108, 324, 381; *E* 21, 22, 124, 255, 310, 323, 329, 344, 347, 434) more than any other beverage. The only drink to rival it in popularity during the eighteenth century was beer, and beer was drunk in contexts that were at least one degree removed from Austen's genteel female world. Tea, however, was at the heart of the gentry's social life, providing occupation for the hands, a subject for discussion, and a means, even in the way it was bought and prepared, of maintaining class distinctions. It became a part of the ritual and pace of the day and reached from the royal family all the way down to the humblest laborers.

Sources vary as to the exact amount that was consumed. Peter Clark claims that in 1800 Britons consumed 23 million pounds of tea and that consumption rose slowly but steadily thereafter; Hoh-cheung Mui and Lorna Mui state that the annual retained imports averaged 16 million pounds from 1799 to 1801. In any case, it would be hard to calculate the exact amounts involved, because so much of the tea that came into the country was smuggled and thus avoided tabulation. Richard Twining, of the famous tea-selling family, commented in his *Observations on the Tea & Window Act and on the Tea Trade* (1785) that "the smuggler has become so formidable a rival [to the East India Company], that, upon the most moderate computation, they shared the Tea-trade equally between them; and according to some calculations, the smuggler had two thirds of it." Smugglers, who were paid in tea, were depicted as carrying the leaves into the country strapped around their midriffs and thighs, packed into the panniers of ladies' skirts, and stuffed in bundles under hats. Even quite respectable people bought smuggled tea; the comfort-loving diarist Parson Woodforde certainly did so. The reduction of the tea tax from 119 per-

Rigging out a Smuggler, Thomas Rowlandson, 1810. This woman is packing not only China tea but perfume and cognac under her clothes. Her helpers sit on boxes of Souchong and Congou teas. Courtesy of the Lewis Walpole Library, Yale University. 810.9.25.1.

cent to 12.5 percent in 1784 may have diminished the trade somewhat—official consumption jumped from 5 million pounds in 1784 to 11 million in 1785—but Richard Twining was still disturbed by the problem a year after the tax cut, and tea remained one of the two most-smuggled items in the 1820s (the other was foreign liquor).

Another aspect of tea consumption that the official statistics do not reflect is the way tea made its way down the social scale. One fairly obvious measure of income, as reflected in tea drinking, is that the rich drank the better-quality and thus more expensive teas, while the less affluent purchased cheaper varieties. This comes as no surprise to modern readers, who understand perfectly well the difference between Lipton's, purchased pre-bagged in cartons at the grocery store, and a fancy, exotic variety of tea purchased by the pound in a coffee shop. Each caters to a different audience. Nor is it surprising that the rich drank more tea than the poor. The comfortably wealthy Edward Austen's household at Godmersham consumed 48 pounds of tea year, according to Jane's estimate, but their tea bill was dwarfed by the earl of Stamford's, who in the 1790s ordered 85 to 95 pounds a year from Twining's. This, too, makes perfect sense to us: if you have more money, you can buy more tea. What does come as a surprise to modern readers is the *reuse* of tea. Used cars, used clothing, used books, used CDs we understand, but secondhand tea is quite another matter. Yet, in Austen's time, tea was a valuable enough commodity to be brewed as many as three times. In well-off households, the members of the family would drink the first brew. Then the leaves would pass to the servants, to be enjoyed a second time. Finally, a servant entitled to this perquisite (usually the cook or housekeeper) would sell the twice-used leaves to the poor and pocket the money. Even within a single social episode, the tea might be steeped several times; Susannah Blamire's poem "Stoklewath; or, the Cumbrian Village," written around 1776, describes women talking over tea:

Cup after cup sends steaming circles round,
And oft the weak tea's in the full pot drowned;
It matters not, for while their news they tell
The mind's content, and all things move on well.

For these women at least, the quality of the tea was less important than the ritual of drinking it.

Opinions varied as to whether the poor should be drinking tea at all. Even thirdhand tea caused some reformers to recoil in horror at beggars' insistence on drinking it. Wholesome, traditional beer, they chided, was being forsaken for mere fashionable tea. The poor were aping their betters and wasting money on a frivolous luxury. As early as the mid-eighteenth century, a witness claimed that in Nottingham "almost every Seamer, Sizer and Winder will have her Tea in a morning . . . and even a common Washer woman thinks she has not had a proper Breakfast without Tea and hot buttered White Bread!" Jamaican sugar planter Edward Long, delighted by this turn of events, exulted that sugar was "so generally in use, and chiefly by the assistance of tea, that even the poor wretches living in almshouses will not be without it." By 1773, Richard Price was asserting that the "lower ranks of the people are altered in every respect for the worse, while tea, wheaten bread and other delicacies are necessaries which were formerly unknown to them." Frederick Eden, in the 1790s, bemoaned the change as bad for laborers' health, but by that time tea had been accepted as one of the necessities of life; in some parishes the very definition of poverty was the inability to buy tea and sugar. Roy Porter gives an example of one Oxfordshire laborer, near the turn of the century, who spent £2 10s., or about 12.5 percent of his total annual income of £31 8s., on tea and sugar. Clergyman David Davies regretted the state of affairs but did not condemn the poor for their love of tea. After all, he wrote in *The Case of the Labourers in Husbandry* (1795), more wholesome beverages were too expensive:

Were it true that poor people could everywhere procure so excellent an article as milk, there would be then just reason to reproach them for giving preference to the miserable infusion of which they are so fond. But it is not so. Wherever the poor can get milk, do they not gladly use it? And where they cannot get it, would they not gladly exchange their tea for it?. . .

Still you exclaim, Tea is a luxury. If you mean fine hyson tea, sweetened with refined sugar, and softened with cream, I readily admit it to be so. But this is not the tea of the poor. Spring water, just coloured with a few leaves of the lowest-priced tea, and sweetened with the brownest sugar . . . , is the luxury for which you reproach them.

Ironically, tea was wholesome in its own way: it forced workers to boil their often contaminated water, thus sparing them many parasitic and bacterial illnesses.

Davies might have added adulteration to his list of the deficiencies of "the tea of the poor." Dust, twigs, sloe leaves, blackberry leaves, and "smouch" were all mixed into genuine tea by unscrupulous shopkeepers. Smouch was made by drying and baking ash tree leaves, then crushing them, steeping them in copperas and sheep's dung; Richard Twining estimated that the production of smouch in one small nine-mile area amounted to 20 tons annually. Nor were shopkeepers alone to blame. The Chinese, from whom all the tea of Austen's time was purchased, knew that people expected the best green teas to have a bluish cast, and they sometimes added Prussian blue and gypsum to their teas before shipping. There was a general perception among the tea-buying public that green teas were easier to adulterate, and over time, perhaps because of this perception, preference shifted to black teas.

Several types of both green and black teas were available in the late eighteenth and early nineteenth centuries. The black teas (which were distinguished from the green teas by being dried longer) included bohea, souchong, congo (or congou), and pekoe. Of these, bohea was the cheapest, and when duties were reduced and prices fell, it was scorned. Even the unfashionable word "bohea" was avoided by tradesmen, who began mixing it with low-quality congou and selling it as "congou kind." An anonymous 1773 poem, "Morning," expressed disdain for bohea, even before the 1784 tax cut:

> Gratefully mild, the fragrant hyson tea
>   Best pleases me, exotic teas among;
> With strong distaste I shun the harsh bohea,
>   Whose grating roughness much offends the tongue.

Pekoe was the best of the black teas, but it was not popular on its own. Rather, it was mixed with other black teas to produce tasty blends. The cheapest green tea was singlo, and other green teas (*Sand, MW* 418) included hyson, caper, Twankey, gunpowder, and bloom. Like the black teas, these were often combined in special blends. Gunpowder, for example, a high-quality tea with a rolled leaf, had too intense a flavor for many, and it was often mixed with hyson. The singlo variety bloom green, conversely, was thought to be too weak on its own and was typically mixed with other varieties of singlo. There were also some intermediate teas, dried for longer than the green teas but less than the black; these included Bing and Imperial.

Within each kind of tea—bohea, gunpowder, and so on—there were nine different grades of quality recognized by the tea-trade. A well-supplied tea dealer, then, might have as many choices as a fancy coffeehouse today. While a small village shop would have few choices on hand, a large city grocer might carry six, seven, or even nine different types of hyson, plus other varieties and a whole host of blends. In 1791, London's Brewster and Gillman carried nine grades of congou, ranging in price from 3s. 3d. to 5s. per pound; nine grades of singlo from 3s. 3d. to 9s. 6d.; and twelve types of hyson, costing from 5s. 3d. to 9s. 6d. This was a fairly typical price range. Other examples from the 1790s show prices per pound falling mostly between three and ten shillings.

Unlike many commodities, tea was never sold in the outdoor public markets. By law, it had to be sold in "entered places" such as grocers' shops or the Twinings tea shop in the Strand. China, glass, wine, and brandy merchants also sometimes sold tea. In the smaller towns and villages, a chandler's shop—which dealt in a variety of wares, including bacon and candles—might be the place where locals purchased their tea and sugar. (However, when they lived at Steventon, the Austens sent to Twinings in London for their tea.) Shops that dealt in tea needed to pay an annual fee of 5s. 6d. to be licensed by the government, so there is some record of the kinds and numbers of places that retailed tea. In the tax year 1783–1784, for example, London had about 3,000 licensed tea dealers, the larger towns of England and Wales about 7,000 more, and the small towns and villages an additional 24,000. The total number of tea dealers in 1783 was 32,754, a figure that rose to 48,263 by 1787 and to 56,248 by 1801. Of course, there may have been many more individuals selling smuggled tea without paying the license fee.

Once purchased, tea was kept in a locked chest or closet, partly to prevent pilfering and partly to monitor the supply for fear of running out. It was drunk both at breakfast (*NA* 175) and at the close of the afternoon; the idea of "tea" as a distinct meal was yet to evolve, but already the ceremony of drinking tea and perhaps eating a little something was fully entrenched as a way of ending the afternoon and beginning the evening (*Watsons, MW* 354; *NA* 118; *S&S* 99, 106, 166; *P&P* 68, 160, 166; *MP* 104, 177, 180, 227; *E* 8, 209, 210, 311, 382–383). Tea was "brought in" or "handed round" at a specified interval after the beginning of dinner, typically about three hours, which allowed plenty of time for a leisurely meal and either a walk or some after-dinner conversation (*Sand, MW* 390–391). The Edwardses, in *The Watsons*, drink their tea at 7:00 P.M. (*MW* 326); the Watsons appear to drink it at about the same time, as they are sitting at tea when a guest calls on his way "home to an 8 o'clock dinner" (*MW* 355). Tea might also be enjoyed at evening social events (*Watsons, MW* 332; *NA* 21, 23, 25; *P* 189) such as parties, dances, and concerts; at a "fete" at Kingston Hall in 1791, the hostess, Frances Bankes, served orgeat (a barley or almond-based drink), lemonade, two types of negus, and tea. Though tea was usually drunk indoors, the great public gardens at Ranelagh and Vauxhall had given people a taste for taking their tea outside as well. Accordingly, people who could afford to indulge in landscaping often added little buildings to their gardens in which they could serve tea and partake of the surrounding scenery (*E* 27). By the 1810s, tearooms had sprung up in resort towns to free travelers from the necessity of preparing the beverage in their lodgings; like a good circulating library and a sizable ballroom, the tearoom became an indispensable attraction for a tourist town.

When tea was made at home, servants (*MP* 180) would bring in the "tea things" so often mentioned by Austen (*Watsons, MW* 326, 355; *MP* 335, 379, 383). These included cups (*MP* 439), which for much of the eighteenth century had no handles—hence the expression "a dish of tea," which became a vulgarism by the end of Austen's life (*Watsons, MW* 326; *MP* 379). Saucers (*MP* 439) and spoons were also provided; when a drinker had finished, he or she was supposed to place the spoon in or across the cup to signal that no more tea was desired. On occasion, the spoons themselves were numbered, so that the hostess could return the appropriate cup to each guest after refilling it. Lumps of sugar were retrieved from a bowl with a small set of tongs, and, in any household that could afford it, milk or cream would be offered as well. The hostess brewed the tea herself (*Watsons, MW* 319; *S&S* 98, 163; *P&P* 341; *MP* 219, 335, 344), either in a teapot or in an urn (*MP* 344), a large metal container shaped rather like a Greek vase. The water inside the urn was kept hot either by a charcoal fire in the base or by inserting a red-hot cylindrical piece of metal. While lovely ceramic teapots figure in many engravings and oil paintings of the era, the urn was for many people of Austen's time the definitive symbol of tea. *See also* Beverages; Coffee.

Teeth

It was understood that care of the teeth was important, and people aspired to have good teeth (*Lesley, MW* 119; *MP* 44) and good breath. How to accomplish this goal was somewhat trickier, for there was no suitable way yet of straightening teeth (*P* 34), and the proper method of cleaning them was a matter of much discussion. Various sorts of tooth powders were sold in apothecaries' shops, each apothecary mixing his own particular variety. Greenough's, near St. Sepulchre's in London, sold one-shilling Greenough's Tinctures, one of which supposedly cured toothache and the other of which promised that it "perfectly cures the scurvy in the gums, fastens and preserves the teeth, renders them white and beautiful, prevents their decaying and keeps such as are decayed from becoming worse." Some bought these premixed powders, but others chose to make their own at home. Books such as *The Toilet of Flora* (1775) explained how to make various kinds of dentrifices, including tooth powders, tooth liquids, toothbrushes made of licorice roots and marshmallow roots, and "A Coral Stick for the Teeth" in which tooth powder was mixed with gum tragacanth to make sticks that were then rubbed against the teeth. Some of the preparations in this book would have done far more harm than good:

A Receipt to clean the Teeth and Gums, and make the Flesh grow close to the Root of the Enamel.

Take an ounce of Myrrh in fine powder, two spoonfuls of the best white Honey, and a little green Sage in fine powder; mix them well together, and rub the teeth and gums with a little of this Balsam every night and morning.

Ditto, to strengthen the Gums and fasten loose Teeth.

Dissolve an ounce of Myrrh as much as possible in half a pint of Red Wine and the same quantity of Oil of Almonds: Wash the mouth with this fluid every morning.

This is also an excellent remedy against worms in the Teeth.

Other tools used to clean the teeth included a piece of wood bitten and softened to separate the fibers and egg-sized sponges dyed red and infused with "Essential Oil of Cinnamon, Cloves, Lavender, &c." (The poor, lacking adequate access to oil of cinnamon, simply rubbed their teeth with soot.) *The Toilet of Flora* also gives instructions for making different types of tooth powders, one of which sounds exceedingly abrasive:

Take Pumice-Stone and scuttle-fish-Bone, of each half an ounce; Tartar of Vitriol and Mastich, of each half a drachm; Oil of Rhodium four drops; mix all into a fine powder. An approved dentrifice.

This, the anonymous author promises, will rid the user of tartar, which he or she calls "false enamel"—no doubt it eliminated some of the real enamel as well.

This was part of the problem with eighteenth- and early-nineteenth-century dentistry. Practitioners and patients had a tendency to do far too much or far too little to the teeth, often with truly disgusting results. Thomas Berdmore, the first man to be appointed dentist to the royal family and author of an important 1768 treatise on dental and periodontal disease, recorded the case of a twenty-three-year-old bank employee whose teeth "gave him constant pain":

I found them perfectly buried in Tartar, by which each set was united in one continuous piece, without any distinction, to show the interstices of the teeth, or their figure or size. The stony crust projected a great way over the gums on the inner side, as well as on the outer, and pressed I upon them so hard as to have given rise to the pain he complained of. Its thickness at the upper surface was not less than half an inch.

At the other extreme, Berdmore discovered that some tooth powders could wear away the enamel of the teeth in as little as an hour. He applied the scientific spirit of the age to dentistry, using a microscope to study the parts of the teeth, researching the action of different acids on the teeth, and advocating the sensible use of tooth powders.

He also understood that sugar played a role in tooth decay, something that not all of his contemporaries knew. The causes of tooth decay were still extremely mysterious. Some still thought that caries was caused by tiny worms within the teeth, hence the reference to worms in one of the mouthwash recipes above. John Hunter, a celebrated surgeon and author of two important texts on dentistry, *The Natural History of the Human Teeth* (1771) and *A Practical Treatise on the Diseases of the Teeth* (1778), understood tooth decay only in part. He did a superb job of explaining the structures of the mouth, particularly the role of the muscles in chewing and the appearance of periodontal disease. He named the incisors, cuspids, and bicuspids and argued against the existing practice of pulling baby teeth to allow the adult teeth to erupt. He recognized the importance of eating fruits and vegetables, theorizing that their acids helped to prevent the buildup of plaque. However, he was still convinced that tooth decay was a form of scurvy rather than a separate condition, that it sometimes began inside the tooth, and that it could not be spread from one tooth to another.

Hunter's suggestions for treatment ranged from excellent to cruel and life-threatening. He suggested an early form of gingivectomy for advanced periodontal disease, which is laudable, and he also understood the need to completely destroy the diseased pulp of the tooth before attempting to fill it. However, his methods of accomplishing this make one feel a painful sympathy for the toothache sufferers of long ago. His preferred method was to remove the tooth, boil it to kill all its living tissue, and reimplant it in the mouth. If this were rejected, he suggested cauterizing the nerve of the tooth with acid. He touches lightly on the subject of fillings, leaving dental historians to surmise that he saw few examples of the procedure and recommends lead as a filling material, which of course would have poisoned the patient. His most pernicious theory was that a tooth could be safely removed from one person and implanted into the mouth of another. He based his belief both on the successful reimplantation of teeth within the *same* person's mouth and also on a bizarre experiment he performed in which he transplanted a still-growing human tooth into a rooster's comb. Hunter's sterling surgical reputation assisted him in promoting the transplantation of teeth, and in the late eighteenth century there was a vogue for replacing pulled teeth with those of poor children hired to sacrifice some of their own. Hunter, in an especially ghastly image, suggests having several such children handy, so that if the first tooth pulled does not fit, another child can be subjected to the procedure. The newly implanted tooth was tied to its neighbors until it had set firmly in place.

Aside from the ethical issues, which are substantial, Hunter's procedure was deeply flawed. In the first place, transplantation, though occasionally successful, usually lasted only a few months before the foreign tooth had to be removed. In the second place, diseases—most notably syphilis—were passed from one individual to another along with the teeth. It was the fear of disease, more than concern for the children, that killed the practice of transplantation sometime in the nineteenth century.

Another reason to abandon transplantation was the gradual improvement in making dentures, known as porcelain or "mineral" teeth. By 1782, wax was being used to take impressions of the mouth for use in making artificial teeth, which were then sculpted from bone or ivory. However, it was not until years later that dentists mentioned using a tray to hold the wax, so it is quite possible that the early models warped as they were removed, making the plaster of paris models less accurate. Significant advances were made, however, in the materials used for artificial teeth. In the late 1780s, Nicolas Dubois de Chémant invented a process for making porcelain dentures, and these were introduced to England shortly thereafter.

Dentistry was still emerging as a serious medical practice. No specialized training was required to set up shop, and the treatment afforded by most dentists tended to be limited to pulling offending teeth. A few notable practitioners performed more advanced surgical techniques, performed reimplantations and transplantations, or made fillings of gold or metal alloys. These people tended to refer to themselves as "dentists," a term derived in the 1750s from French that sounded more sophisticated than "tooth-drawer." The tooth-drawer was the more common practitioner, and all he required was a pair of forceps or, if he were especially well equipped, a dental key, a tool that looked rather like a large house key with a claw at one end. The tooth-drawer used this key to grab the tooth, twist, and wrench it out with one enormous pull (*Sand, MW* 388). Parson James Woodforde described the process in October 1785:

> The Tooth-Ach so very bad all night and the same this Morn' that I sent for John Reeves the Farrier who lives at the Hart and often draws Teeth for People, to draw one for me. He returned with my Man about 11 o'clock this Morning and he pulled it out for me the first Pull, but it was a monstrous Crash and more so, it being one of the Eye Teeth, it had but one Fang but that was very long. I gave Johnny Reeves for drawing it 0.2.6. A great pain in the Jaw Bone continued all Day and Night but nothing so bad as the Tooth Ach.

As Woodforde's diary entry points out, the local tooth-drawer was as likely as not to be a farrier or blacksmith; he rarely knew anything more advanced about dentistry than how to grab and pull. Dentists, who provided a range of other treatments, were not required to study their craft, but many signed up for short training courses or even apprenticeships of several years. They needed to be able to scrape off tartar, lance abscesses, kill infections in teeth, and fill cavities. The fact that Harriet Smith goes to London to visit a dentist (*E* 451, 463), rather than resorting to a local tooth-drawer, means that she is probably interested in preserving the tooth, or perhaps in diagnosing the cause of her pain. She might have visited someone like James Spence, a protégé of Hunter's who eventually be-

The LONDON DENTIST.

The London Dentist, 1784. Courtesy of the Lewis Walpole Library, Yale University. 784.0.76.

came dentist to George III. The actor Samuel Foote visited his shop in hopes of ending a toothache and found it to be neat and clean, with a painted hand in the window, lace-cuffed, holding a tooth, and with pulled teeth exhibited around the room "as white and polished as ivory, the only wonder was how they came to lose their destined homes and how they were found where I saw them." The difference between the tidy, professional Spence and Woodforde's farrier is no doubt why Harriet Smith chose to go to London. Many people, terrified of having a tooth drawn (*Sand, MW* 387), dreaded going to the dentist at all (*Cath, MW* 208–209). Jane wrote pityingly of her nieces in 1813; they, too, had gone to London to see a dentist, and Lizzy had had hers "filed & lamented over," while Marianne had two of hers extracted to the accompaniment of "two sharp hasty Screams."

Tenant

A tenant could be a tenant in the modern sense of the word—one who rents a house or an apartment from the owner (*MP* 295; *P* 17, 19, 125, 162, 188). A tenant (*Cath, MW* 195; *P&P* 81, 249; *MP* 404; *E* 23; *P* 36) could also be a tenant farmer, one who did not own his own farm but merely farmed land belonging to a much wealthier property owner. In the latter case, a variety of arrangements were made for rent (*J&A, MW* 21) but usually involved the provision of money or produce, or a combination of the two, in exchange for the right to farm the specified piece of land.

There was no particular shame in renting land at a time when a great deal of land was concentrated in the hands of a comparatively small number of families. In the 1790s, an estimated three-quarters of the arable land in England was farmed not by the actual owner but by tenants of one sort or another. Even fairly substantial property holders might rent land if they wanted to farm a plot contiguous with their own acreage. Lady Russell, for example, is described as being a tenant of Sir Walter's (*P* 11). However, one's status was enhanced by actually owning a certain amount of land outright.

Theater

Theatergoing (*NA* 25, 26, 34, 70, 92–93; *P&P* 152; *P* 180) was a popular pastime for rich and poor alike. Prices at the Drury Lane theater ranged from 6s. for a box to 1s. for the highest gallery, half that for patrons who came in after the end of the third act of the five-act main presentation. The typical theater (*MP* 169) had a pit (*MP* 124) section with long undivided benches on the floor and rows upon rows of private boxes (*NA* 35, 92–93, 95; *MP* 124; *P* 223) built up along the walls. Until the 1760s, patrons could pay a fee of 10s. to sit on the stage itself at both Drury Lane and Covent Garden, but the practice was abolished and customers sent to their proper places. Cheaper tickets could be had in a balcony or "gallery" section (*MP* 124), and this was where the common people, the footmen, and the prostitutes sat. Some prostitutes also ensconced themselves in the minute upper boxes, but the more spacious lower boxes were reserved for the well-bred and prosperous members of society.

Footmen had attended for free during most of the eighteenth century. They had been sent by their masters to hold seats for them in the pit, for seats (except for boxes, hence the term "box office") could not be reserved in advance. Their masters could arrive fashionably late and displace their servants, who migrated up to the upper gallery or balcony area. In the second half of the eighteenth century, however, this practice was abolished, and footmen had to pay for their seats or convince their employers to do so. Periodic attempts to raise prices usually failed; one such attempt at Covent Garden in 1809 resulted in riots.

The principal London theaters, the only ones that possessed royal patents for producing spoken-English plays, were Drury Lane (*S&S* 330) and Covent Garden (*L&F, MW* 109). These were the largest theaters in the kingdom, seating 3,600 and 3,000, respectively, by the 1790s and even more after being rebuilt in the wake of fires in 1809 and 1808. Large stages allowed for monumental scenery but caused a loss of intimacy that was regretted by patrons who could recall the smaller, older incarnations of these theaters. Austen attended performances at Covent Garden in April 1811, September 1813, and March 1814 and, though she was sometimes critical of the actors' performances, appears to have had no quarrel with the design of the theater itself.

These two theaters were usually open from September to June for their principal season. During the summer months, London's stars often toured the provinces in their most heralded roles, hoping to make a little extra

The Yorkshireman in London . . ., 1806, detail. The stage at Covent Garden. Courtesy of the Lewis Walpole Library, Yale University. 806.11.8.1.1.

money. Operas were performed at the King's Theatre, Haymarket, and at George Colman's Little Theatre (*P&P* 319); the latter of these was permitted to perform spoken dramas during the summer months when Drury Lane and Covent Garden were closed, and in the winter it staged operas.

In season, plays were performed every night except Sundays. The theaters also closed for a few religious holidays, such as Ash Wednesday and the week leading up to Easter. During Lent, the Wednesday and Friday plays were replaced by oratorios. All theaters closed in the event of a royal death.

Plays were advertised in advance in the newspapers, announcing the titles of the principal play and afterpiece, the names of the starring actors, ticket prices, times of performance, and (where relevant) the composer of the music. Performances typically began at 6:00 P.M., and the doors opened an hour earlier. People planning to sit in the pit or galleries lined up well in advance of 5:00, however, in order to get the best possible seats. On occasion, when interest was high at the opening of a new play, for example, doors might open especially early—as much as two or three hours beforehand.

Once safely inside, people could buy oranges to eat and programs to read from the "book women" who walked about with their paper-lined fruit baskets. About half an hour before the curtain rose, the orchestra would play for half an hour or so, and a warning bell would sound to advise people to take their seats. Theater orchestras were quite substantial in size, consisting of as many as thirty musicians and various functionaries such as music copyists, keyboard tuners, and a chorus master. The orchestra was conducted either by the music director from the harpsichord or pianoforte or, if he were not present, by the lead violinist.

When the music concluded, the curtain (*MP* 123, 141, 195) would be gathered along ropes that ran vertically at various points along its length. The gathering pulled it into festoons that remained visible at the top of the stage (*MP* 167). An actor came out and recited a verse prologue to the mainpiece—the principal play of the evening. A typical night at the theater, with the exception of oratorio nights, contained the main play or opera and a lighter, shorter afterpiece (*MP* 124), sometimes called the farce; less commonly, three afterpieces would be performed instead of a mainpiece and an afterpiece. Interspersed between these pieces were dances and songs (*MP* 124).

The behavior of the audiences was generally fairly rowdy. The low gallery prices ensured that a broad cross-section of society was admitted, and not even the gentry were entirely silent during the play. They talked among themselves or looked in the other boxes for friends or celebrities rather than paying strict attention to the play. Of course, some theatergoers were more disruptive than others. At a play in 1779, Fanny Burney observed a madman, Tom Willet, who knew the people she was with. Willet, seated in the pit, began grimacing and commenting loudly on the play,

> commending, disapproving or adding at his pleasure: but though this was diverting enough to *us*, the Players by no means approved of it; and in the 2d Act, one of the Women, who had to say "A servant should be Deaf and Dumb," upon his adding aloud "Ay, and blind too!" said to her fellow Comedian "That man puts me out so, I don't know how to go on." And then this fellow Comedian, coming forward, said "Upon my word, Sir, if you talk so I can't recollect one word of my part!"

As this episode indicates, the actors sometimes broke character to chastise particularly annoying members of the audience, and this disruption onstage does not seem to have been upsetting or unexpected to the audience at large. They were perfectly capable of restoring their suspension of disbelief as soon as the play resumed, though they respected actors who could continue to concentrate in the midst of distractions.

Scenery (*MP* 141, 164, 191) was expensive and often reused from play to play. Some of the scenery was painted on backcloths that could be raised or lowered quickly. Other pieces were painted on flats and wings that were set in grooves and slid back and forth by ropes. Costumes were not always historically accurate; in fact, before the turn of the century, they were almost never so. There was an increasing interest in making the costumes fit the play, however, largely as a result of the activism of the actor John Philip Kemble (1757–1823), who managed Covent Garden from 1803 to

1817. Lighting was by means of candles, some of which were set in front of the stage and could be lowered below it to darken the scene, and some of which were placed on sidepieces or in chandeliers; these, too, could be moved in order to dim or raise the level of light, but the stage could not be made entirely dark.

London's minor theaters had to restrict themselves to forms other than traditional drama and comedy. Instead, they staged puppet shows, equestrian performances, exhibitions of wild animals, pantomimes, burlettas, and musical performances, none of which came under the terms of the 1737 Licensing Act limiting the patented theaters to two. One of these theaters was the Lyceum, which Austen attended in 1811; normally the Lyceum was restricted to quasi-theatrical entertainments such as hot-air balloon displays and animal acts, but during this period it housed the Drury Lane company while Drury Lane was being rebuilt after the fire. She went to the Lyceum again in 1813.

In the provinces, traveling troupes of actors (*L&F, MW* 107; *Cath, MW* 240) staged performances for a few days or weeks, moving on when the audiences thinned to a different town. Some provincial towns, dissatisfied with this peripatetic entertainment, built their own theaters. The theaters went up first in resort towns, where the families of invalids come to drink the spa waters hungered for a way to spend their extra time and money. Eventually, there were theaters in York, Canterbury, Bristol, Bath, Cheltenham, Tunbridge Wells, and Norwich. Austen is known to have visited the Theatre Royal in Southampton in 1807 and the Orchard Street theater in Bath in 1799. It is not known whether she ever attended the new Bath theater in Beaufort Square, which had better traffic access, but it was typical of many provincial theaters. Decked out at a cost of £20,000 and opened in 1805, it had crimson and gold décor, cast-iron pillars, expensive chandeliers, and three exits—this last an important factor when one was part of an impatient crowd eager to depart after the show.

Provincial theater tickets tended to be cheaper than those in London. At the Norwich theater, Parson James Woodforde paid 12s. for four box seats in 1784, and much less, only a shilling, for two box seats in 1794; perhaps he saw the latter show at half price. At Drury Lane in 1795, however, he paid 7s. for only two tickets, and he does not specify that these were box seats. In fact, they would have been seats in the pit, which went for 3s. 6d. each at the time.

Plays

There is evidence, both within her writings and in her letters, that Austen was exposed to a large number of plays (*NA* 79, 92, 217; *P&P* 154; *MP* 130, 167, 338; *E* 276; *P* 223). She read them, she saw them performed, and at times she even acted in them at home. It is not always possible, however, to tell in which way she familiarized herself with individual plays.

Most of her references are to the works of Shakespeare. In her writings she refers to *Macbeth* (*L&F*, *MW* 108; *MP* 131), *Henry IV* (*Hist Eng*, *MW* 139), *Henry VIII* (*MP* 336–338), *Julius Caesar* (*MP* 126–127), *Hamlet* (*MP* 130), and *Othello* (*MP* 131). The *History of England* contains a reference to Shakespeare's portrayal of Catherine of Valois in *Henry V* (*Hist Eng*, *MW* 139). Henry Crawford's interest in playing either Shylock or Richard III (both cruel characters, as David Selwyn has noted) alludes to both *The Merchant of Venice* and *Richard III* (*MP* 123). Austen had a special interest in *The Merchant of Venice*, for in 1814 Edmund Kean made his debut as Shylock, electrifying theater audiences with his revolutionary acting style. Austen saw him in this role only a month after his debut, and while she was unimpressed with most of the cast, she found his individual performance outstanding. She does not name *Midsummer Night's Dream*, but Emma quotes from it, noting that a Hartfield edition of Shakespeare would have a long annotation to the line, "The course of true love never did run smooth" (*E* 75). David Selwyn observes a number of nods to Shakespeare, or at least thematic similarities to his work, in Austen's novels. He likens the wilderness at Sotherton to the wood in *Midsummer Night's Dream*, Marianne Dashwood to Ophelia, and the overall plot of *Mansfield Park* to the theme of filial fidelity in *King Lear*.

Playwrights other than Shakespeare whose works are alluded to include Nicholas Rowe, who wrote *Jane Shore* (*Hist Eng*, *MW* 140); George Colman the Younger, who wrote *The Heir at Law* (*MP* 131); Susanna Centlivre, author of *The Gamester* (*MP* 131); Richard Cumberland, whose *Wheel of Fortune* (*MP* 131) features a misanthropist named Penruddock, a son who (like Tom Bertram) is jeopardized by his gambling, and a lawyer named Timothy Weasel; John Home, author of *Douglas*, the play in which the phrase, "My name was Norval" (*MP* 126–127) appears; and Richard Brinsley Sheridan, manager of Drury Lane and author of *The Critic* (*Hist Eng*, *MW* 147), *The Rivals* (*MP* 131), and *School for Scandal* (*MP* 131). At a private theatrical performance at Godmersham in 1808, in fact, Austen played Mrs. Candour in *School for Scandal*. Her juvenile fragment *The Visit* alludes to the line, "The more free, the more welcome" (*MW* 50), from James Townley's *High Life Below Stairs*, a play that was performed in amateur theatricals at Steventon.

Finally, she gives Tom Bertram a singularly tactless joke that turns on the title of the afterpiece *My Grandmother* by Prince Hoare. When the death of Lord Ravenshaw's grandmother ends the amateur theatricals at Ecclesford, he says, "Lovers' Vows were at an end, and Lord and Lady Ravenshaw were left to act My Grandmother by themselves" (*MP* 123). One wonders if Austen had in mind, as well as the title of the play, its previous association with death; it was one of three Hoare works being performed at a royal command performance at the Little Theatre in the Haymarket on the night of February 1, 1794. Michael Kelly, whose mem-

Lovers Vows. Left to right: Amelia, Anhalt, the Baron, Agatha, Frederick. Courtesy of the Lewis Walpole Library, Yale University.

oirs record many details of theatrical performances at the time, recalled what happened:

> The crowd was so great that at the opening of the doors, in going down the steps which led to the pit, three or four persons slipped and fell and several others were hurried over them; sixteen persons were trampled to death and upwards of twenty were taken up with broken limbs.
>
> The news of this fatal accident was, very judiciously, kept from their Majesties until after the performance was over, when they evinced the deepest sorrow and regret at the event.

Austen's most sustained theatrical reference, however, is to *Lovers' Vows*, Elizabeth Inchbald's adaptation of *Das Kind der Liebe* (*The Love Child*) by the German playwright August von Kotzebue. The play is about Agatha Friburg (*MP* 132, 135, 137), who has been seduced, impregnated, and abandoned by Baron Wildenhaim (*MP* 132), and their illegitimate son Frederick. Frederick, after robbing his father and revealing his identity, convinces the baron to marry Agatha. Meanwhile, the clergyman Anhalt (*MP* 132, 144, 358) is wooed in an inversion of gender roles by the baron's daughter Amelia (*MP* 133, 135, 137), who does not wish to marry the idiotic Count Cassel (*MP* 122, 132, 138–139, 144), her father's choice for her husband. Paula Byrne has studied the play and its casting in *Mansfield Park* and finds satisfying correspondences between the parts and the players: Tom Bertram, who can take nothing seriously, snaps up all the minor comic roles (*MP* 132, 164); the empty-headed Mr. Rushworth plays the equally brainless Count; the clergyman Anhalt is played by the future clergyman Edmund and his aggressive lover by the brazen Mary Crawford. Fanny Price is drafted for the role of Cottager's Wife (*MP* 134, 135, 146), a role considered appropriate at Ecclesford only for the governess, and which Fanny, ever shy, feels unable and unwilling to play. Henry Crawford takes the hero's part, and Maria Bertram gets to play his mother, a role that involves, according to the stage directions, repeated embraces of her "son." At one point, they embrace (*MP*,

LV 483); on the next page she leans her head on his chest (484); a few pages later, there is another embrace (488), and then she "presses him to her breast" (489). At the play's end, he "throws himself on his knees by the other side of his mother—She clasps him in her arms" (536). The play, like *Mansfield Park*, is concerned with the plight of a woman who loves but is denied the right to speak her feelings by convention and the right of parents to arrange their children's marriages despite lack of love.

Inchbald toned down the play a good deal from the original German, and her play was extremely popular. However, not all people found it tasteful. German drama was often described as encouraging young people to indulge in fits of emotion and hasty elopements. An *Ode to the German Drama* (1799) captured its reputation:

> Daughter of Night, chaotic Queen!
>   Thou fruitful source of modern lays,
> Whose subtle plots and tedious scene
>   The monarch spurn, the robber raise—
> Bound in thy necromantic spell,
> The audience taste the joys of hell;
> And Britain's sons indignant groan
> With pangs unfelt before at crimes before unknown.
>
> When first, to make the nation stare,
>   Folly her painted mask displayed,
> Schiller sublimely mad was there,
>   And Kotz'bue lent his mighty aid—
> Gigantic pair! their lofty soul,
> Disdaining reason's weak control,
> On changeful Britain sped the blow,
> Who, thoughtless of her own, embraced fictitious woe.

Furthermore, the themes of illegitimate birth, seduction, and assertive female courtship of this particular play were offensive to some, making it the perfect play to test the morals and character of the Mansfield group. Despite the fact that they know its subject matter to be questionable, and despite the fact that they all know, to a greater or lesser extent, that Sir Thomas would disapprove of their actions, they all, except for Fanny, become seduced by the idea of performing it just as surely as Agatha is seduced by the baron. Austen sticks closely to the text of the play, referring to its stage sets of "cottages and ale-houses" (*MP* 143; *MP*, *LV* 481), to the love scene between Anhalt and Amelia (*MP* 168, 358; *MP*, *LV* 504–505), and to Frederick's imprisonment (*MP* 135; *MP*, *LV* 513–514).

In all, Austen refers to more than forty plays, and it must be assumed that she saw and read far more than this number. We know with certainty that she saw Hannah Cowley's *The Belle's Stratagem*, a play that resembles *Pride and Prejudice* in its use of false impressions and the search of five country sisters for husbands. She also saw Isaac Bickerstaffe's *The Hyp-ocrite*, an adaptation of Molière's *Tartuffe*; Garrick and Colman's *The Clandestine Marriage*; Charles Dibdin's *The Farmer's Wife*; and Thomas Arne's opera *Artaxerxes*. Notably, the first theater performance on record as having been attended by her was *The Birthday*, Thomas Dibdin's adaptation of a play by Kotzebue, whose heroine, Emma Bertram, has an invalid father and feels unable to marry as a result. Musical pieces and farces that she saw included *Bluebeard*, *The Beehive*, *Don Juan*, Charles Coffey's *The Devil to Pay*, Thomas Dibdin's and Michael Kelly's *Of Age Tomorrow*, and Samuel Beazley's *The Boarding House: or Five Hours at Brighton*.

Actors and Acting

Actors of Austen's time operated with a stock catalogue of theatrical gestures and postures that conveyed, more iconically than realistically, the emotions they were supposed to be portraying. They declaimed in tones that would sound stilted today, and many adopted a "ranting" (*MP* 123, 164, 394) style of delivery, shouting in a manner that was supposed to sound grand but bore little resemblance to actual human speech. Comic characters were delineated less by their mannerism than by their outlandish dress (*MP* 179–180), which signaled to the audience that they were to be laughed at.

A revolution began in the late eighteenth century with the somewhat more natural style of Charles Macklin and David Garrick. It continued at the end of the period with Edmund Kean's portrayal of Shylock. Nonetheless, Austen, who had been an enthusiastic patron of the theater in her younger years, gradually became disenchanted with the performances she saw. Too many male actors relied on old tricks she had seen before; too many celebrated young women were nothing more than pretty faces and, occasionally, pretty voices. While she often refers to specific actors in her letters, she mentions only two in her works: the "*Lewis & Quick*" of *Love & Freindship* (*MW* 109). William Thomas Lewis (1748–1811), known as "Gentleman" Lewis for his refined voice and style, acted for thirty-five years at Covent Garden in a wide variety of comedies. John Quick, who often acted with him, was another comedian best known for playing bumpkins.

Nonetheless, there were many famous thespians on the stage in her day, and she saw most of them at one time or another. She lived during the dawn of modern theater criticism, and in an age without movies, the escapades of stage actors were discussed with great interest. Players like Sarah Siddons, John Philip Kemble, and Dorothea Jordan, all of whom she saw onstage, were the first great show-business celebrities. Other popular actors included Richard Yates, the comedian who originated the role of Oliver Surface in *School for Scandal*, and his wife, Mary Ann Yates, a leading tragic actress in Garrick's company. Their last name is shared by the enthusiastic amateur actor Mr. Yates in *Mansfield Park*, and Henry and

Mary Crawford share their last name with Ann and Thomas (Billy) Crawford, a married pair of actors. Theater managers (*L&F, MW* 107–108; *MP* 123), too, enjoyed fame, as their control over the great London playhouses controlled what thousands of theatergoers saw.

At the same time, actors (*L&F, MW* 107–108) enjoyed a poor personal reputation. Actresses were considered little better than prostitutes, and it did not help matters that some, like Dorothea Jordan, carried on highly publicized sexual relationships with peers of the realm. The actress Elizabeth Farren was accused of having a lesbian affair with Anne Seymour Damer, and the great Mrs. Siddons herself had her name romantically linked with that of her fencing teacher. Though many women participated in amateur theatricals with their reputations untarnished, one can imagine why Sir Thomas Bertram might object to having his daughters pretend to be actresses, especially in a play considered indecorous in itself.

Attitudes toward the Theater

Sir Thomas and Edmund Bertram (*MP* 124–127) were not alone in their disapproval of amateur theatricals. Many people went a great deal further in their censure of the theater, criticizing the silly behavior of the audience and the immoral plays staged by the actors. Austen's friend Anne Lefroy, asked to play the role of Alicia in *Jane Shore*, declined on the grounds that it was inappropriate for her to appear on the stage in such a role. To soften the blow, she issued her refusal politely and in verse:

> Can I, a Wife, a Mother, tread the Stage,
> Burn with false fire & glow with mimic Rage,
> Quit of domestic peace the calm retreat,
> As mad Alicia teach my Heart to beat.

A stronger voice against the theater was that of the anonymous author of *Female Tuition: or, an Address to Mothers, on the Education of Daughters* (1784):

> The theatres, under proper management, might be a school of useful and virtuous instruction, as well as a scene of innocent recreation.
>
> Tragedy is calculated to ennoble, refine, and expand the best affections of the heart, and to render our natures susceptible and sympathetic, and to teach by example the most interesting lessons of humanity.
>
> Comedy will also familiarize the ductile minds of your daughters to what may be called the elegant and fashionable minutiae of life. . . .
>
> The object of modern writers, however, is not always either so elevated or so pure. Their aim is only to fill the house. The public taste must for this end be consulted and caressed. And that, perhaps, was never less chaste, less correct, or less delicate, than at present.
>
> So that you can hardly send your daughters too seldom, where the virtues of innocence, of modesty, of oeconomy [*sic*], and of truth, are rarely mentioned but to raise a laugh; where innuendoes the loosest and most easily

understood, are uttered with emphasis, and received with complacency; and where principles and examples of the grossest profligacy, garnished with vivacity and wit, extort universal applause from high and low.

Evangelicals, who were gaining ground toward the end of Austen's life, also disapproved of the theater and of amateur theatricals. Exposure to the wild life of the stage, the questionable morals of playwrights, the love of attention that a successful performance might feed, and the general frivolity of the stage made amateur theatrical loathsome to them. Amateur theatricals were also associated with the aristocracy (*MP* 121–123), which could afford to put up purpose-built miniature theaters, and which was assumed by most of the gentry and middle class to be debauched as a whole.

Yet Austen, despite the prim tone she adopts when discussing *Lovers' Vows* at Mansfield Park, was not one of those who flatly rejected the theater or even amateur performances of plays in private homes. We have already seen that she went to a great many plays, read others, alluded to them frequently, and was an intelligent critic of acting styles. Furthermore, amateur theatricals, popular entertainments in many genteel families, were often acted at Steventon in her youth. The Steventon barn, fitted up as a theater, hosted performances of *The Rivals*, Thomas Francklin's *Matilda*, Bickerstaffe's *The Sultan: or A Peep into the Seraglio*, Townley's *High Life Below Stairs*, Garrick's *Bon Ton: or High Life Above Stairs* and *The Chances*, Centlivre's *The Wonder: A Woman Keeps a Secret*, and Henry Fielding's *Tragedy of Tom Thumb*. Cowley's *Which Is the Man?* (*3S, MW* 65) was considered for performance but may not have been staged. *See also* Entertainment; Opera.

Time

The schedule of the gentry differed greatly from the schedule followed by working people. Farmers and fishermen, for example, were dominated by the natural world; tides and unmilked cows wait for no man. Workers also had little money to spare for expensive candles (*Col Let, MW* 156), so they regulated their day by the course of the sun. Once it set, little was done, and bedtime soon followed. However, some people could and did stay up late: the gentry, nobility, and prosperous workers such as merchants and substantial tenant farmers. Instead of rising at or before dawn, they stayed in bed a little longer and extended their day into the evening, when the glow of several, or even dozens of candles set a distinctive mood.

Austen ignores the workers' schedule and pays great attention to the nuances of the hours kept among the gentry. In a society that valued consumption and display, late hours meant more candles and therefore more wealth, which was definitely a good thing (*Col Let, MW* 157; *Watsons, MW*

346). During Austen's lifetime, there was a slow, but deliberate, movement toward later and later hours (*MP* 266), for meals particularly, with the somewhat comical result that supper was gradually being eliminated as dinner came later and later, while lunch was slowly emerging to fill the place vacated by dinner, resulting in much the same meals under different names.

Since there was this gradual inflation of hours, and since the hours kept in one household often differed markedly from those down the street or across town, it can be hard to state with certainty that people got up or ate or went to bed at such-and-such an hour. A rough picture, however, can be drawn. People of Austen's class might rise at 8:00 A.M. or so, then walk, play music, or write letters until breakfast at nine or ten (*P&P* 319; *E* 443). Departures from this pattern were typically made only for the sake of travel (*NA* 228; *P* 95) or from extreme asceticism (*S&S* 343). Men might go hunting before breakfast (*Watsons, MW* 347; *P* 37). In fashionable London, however, breakfast was served later. An 1812 letter to *The Gentleman's Magazine* from "A Constant Reader" offered a humorously exaggerated account of the late hours kept in the capital:

> I was asked by a lady at whose house the best company in town are to be seen, to partake of a public breakfast. No hour being mentioned on the card, and judging that the late London hours might naturally make breakfast-time rather later than with us in the Country, I delayed my setting out till midday. When I arrived, a servant informed me that if I wished to see the Lady of the house, he believed she was not yet stirring—"That," said I, "is impossible; for I am invited this very day to breakfast with her."—"Lord, Sir!" says the porter, "the breakfast hour is from 4 to 5." I was more astonished than ever at this distribution of time; which not suiting the craving of my appetite, I found it necessary at a neighbouring hotel to make a hearty dinner previous to my partaking of her Ladyship's splendid breakfast.

From the end of breakfast until the beginning of dinner, people took care of their daily business. Women sewed, supervised the servants' dinner preparations, and engaged in charitable work. Men wrote business letters (*S&S* 304) or supervised the care of their land, crops, horses, and dogs. Both sexes paid so-called morning visits (*Watsons, MW* 338; *MP* 298), which might take place until as late as 3:00 or 4:00, depending on when dinner was served. They might also read (*NA* 60), walk for exercise and amusement (*NA* 80, 177), or go out riding on horseback or in carriages (*NA* 45, 67).

Dinner officially ended the morning and began the afternoon. The unfashionable ate it at 3:00 P.M. (*Watsons, MW* 344), the fashionable at 6:30 (*Watsons, MW* 355; *P&P* 35), with many people setting the time somewhere in between (*Sand, MW* 411; *NA* 193, 195, 199, 214; *S&S* 74; *MP* 89, 221; *E* 188–189). (The Austens, for example, ate at three in 1798 at Steventon, but their dinner hour had crept back to 5:00 by 1808.) An

1819 letter to the *Gentleman's Magazine* gave the dinner hour as 5:00 (*Col Let*, *MW* 159) or 6:00 and asserted that this was, by then, a standard time for the meal among the gentry and nobility. Everyone ate together for a time, and then the ladies withdrew to talk among themselves in another room, while the gentlemen lingered over port and conversation in the dining room. When the gentlemen joined the ladies, tea and coffee were served (*E* 8), usually about three hours after the commencement of dinner, that is, somewhere between 6:00 and 10:00 P.M. (*Watsons*, *MW* 326, 355; *S&S* 315); this light meal officially began the "evening," though the people enjoying it had been in their evening dress since dinner. Cards (*Watsons*, *MW* 359) and conversation, possibly music or dancing as well, filled the hours after tea until people either ate supper (*Watsons*, *MW* 359) or went to bed. On nights when there was company in the house, people tended to stay up a little later.

Joseph Farington, writing in 1800, summarized the schedule of each evening in his lodging house in Bath:

> The Ladies retire about ½ past 5. // The gentlemen quit the room at ½ past Six that it may be prepared for Tea at 7. // After Tea Card parties are made. // Supper at Ten. // Retire about Eleven.

Parson Woodforde, likewise, tended to dine between 3:00 and 5:00; he considered 5:00 as late enough to be worthy of note in 1785. When he dined out, he usually returned at about 9:00. He and his niece-housekeeper Nancy rose at seven, but this appears to have been something of a struggle; they had to fine themselves sixpence for failure to rise early. For the most part, he appears to have gone to bed relatively early, around 10:00 or so, but on special occasions he stayed out very late indeed. In July 1784, he stayed at a friend's until 4:00 A.M. and did not get back home until 5:00. More typically, he went to bed at about midnight after social gatherings.

Jane Austen seems to have kept similar hours. In August 1805, she wrote to Cassandra that she had stayed out late and gotten home "considerably past eleven." Sometimes dinner parties kept her up late; at other times, it was the theater. At least we know for certain when she finished dancing in Bath; there, the assemblies shut down at 11:00, even in the middle of a dance. Not so at Tunbridge Wells, where a correspondent of the Austens' danced till 2:00 A.M. in 1787. Bedtime for most of the gentry was between 10:00 P.M. and midnight (*NA* 222; *P&P* 273; *E* 126), with exceptions made for special parties and other forms of entertainment (*S&S* 44); Fanny Price's late night at her debut ball is a good example of such an exception (*MP* 279). The ball in *The Watsons* ends earlier; it has already been going on for some time when a young guests notices that it is eleven o'clock (*Watsons*, *MW* 332).

There was one other way of measuring out the day besides the timing of meals, but it does not appear in any of Austen's novels. However, since she does make frequent reference to the navy, it is perhaps appropriate to make some mention of how time was kept aboard ship. A half-hour "hour-glass" was kept on deck and turned as it ran out. Each time the glass was turned, a bell was struck—once the first time it was struck, twice the second time, and so on, up to eight bells. At eight bells, a new watch took over, and the next time the bell was struck it would be struck only once. Most watches lasted four hours and therefore had eight bells, but the first and second dog watches lasted only two hours each and thus had only four bells before the pattern began again.

Watch	Hours*	Bells
First	20–24 hours	8
Middle	0–4 hours	8
Morning	4–8 hours	8
Forenoon	8–12 hours	8
Afternoon	12–16 hours	8
First Dog	16–18 hours	4
Second Dog	18–20 hours	4

Most days of the week were similar in their pattern, but Sunday (*MP* 401) was different. Ideally, people of all classes were supposed to throng to their parish churches for morning service, then eat and take a walk, or engage in some other innocent diversion, and return in the afternoon for evening service (*NA* 190). In practice, this was not always the case. Servants tried to absent themselves from church in order to socialize with each other; Dissenters went to their own chapels after or instead of the parish church; some of the gentry and aristocracy skipped divine service altogether, for which they were often chided by reformers who insisted that they set a good example for the lower orders. To the dismay of clerics and reformers alike, many laborers also skipped services and went instead to the local alehouse. For many people, Sunday had a holiday feel to it, and even those who went dutifully to church services felt themselves entitled to a little fun.

In many towns, this meant that after church, throngs of people took walks simultaneously in some public place (*NA* 232). This had the advantage of being conveniently close to home and also afforded people a chance to stop and chat informally with acquaintances. Austen shows her readers this traditional promenade twice: once in Bath, where the principal strolling was done in the area around the Royal Crescent (*NA* 35), and once in Portsmouth, where the gathering place is the ramparts (*MP* 408–409).

---

*Using twenty-four-hour rather than twelve-hour notation, so that "20," for example, means 8:00 P.M.

There were cycles not only to the days and weeks but also to the months and seasons of the year. Among farmers, it was the relevance of the seasons to agricultural labor that mattered. They plowed, planted, and harvested according to the time of year and sometimes, superstitiously, according to the phases of the moon. Austen's world, however, is aware of the cycles of farming but not intimately involved in it; in her novels, the seasonal change that matters is the one between London (or watering places) and the country. Though she demonstrates in *Mansfield Park* that she understands the demands of the harvest season (58), which was so critical to financial success that responsible farmers reserved the best laborers months ahead of time, and though *Emma* is a book subtly propelled by agricultural rhythms, Austen's characters are mostly moved by the fashions and customs of the winter and summer social seasons.

Winter and summer were ruled to some extent by competing migrations, but the oldest pattern and the one most people yearned to follow was the winter migration to London (*P&P* 238). Parliament opened in October or November (*MP* 199) and conducted business until the spring (*MP* 20, 202; *E* 259, 308), usually May; the members (*MP* 20) then returned to their country homes (*MP* 422) to supervise their estates, preside over the harvest, and enjoy the fall hunting season, which began September 1 (*P&P* 318; *MP* 114, 181). The families of the members of Parliament naturally trotted along in their wake, setting up London households for the winter season (*S&S* 153, 214). Since the members of Parliament included some of the most notable men in the kingdom, as well as all the peers and bishops, their arrival in the capital naturally drew acquaintances and would-be acquaintances who longed to mingle with the rich and powerful. As lodgings in the West End—the fashionable part of London—were not to be had cheaply, a London season was a luxury that women in particular craved. A house in London (*S&S* 153; *MP* 20), to which one could return year after year, was a still greater prize; Austen does not seem to have thought much of women who yearned for one, but her works are a testament to London's attraction.

Some people spent a part of the year in a watering place, either instead of, or in addition to, London. These sites featured some sort of mineral spring with supposedly healthful properties, which invalids would drink in hope of a cure. Their families, like the families of MPs, came along with them and amused themselves at balls, plays, and concerts. Each spa town had its own season; Southampton's was from July to October, Clifton's from late March to late September. Bath had two principal seasons, one from February to June, the other from September to Christmas (*MP* 202–203). It was practically deserted in the summer. Toward the end of Austen's life, seaside towns were also developing seasons of their own, often during the summer months (*Sand, MW* 389).

Titles

The English system of titles (*Sand*, *MW* 395; *MP* 47–48), if the royal family is excepted, had seven levels, not all of which conferred membership in the peerage (*L&F*, *MW* 77). Each level had its own rules for addressing the title-bearer himself, his wife, and his children. At the top of the hierarchy were dukes, and at the bottom were knights. For the purposes of clarity in the following discussion, assume that "Smith" is the last name of our fictional titled family and that "Whateverington" is the title name. (A well-known example of the difference between the two would be George Gordon, Lord Byron; Gordon is his family name and Byron the title name.) It was not unknown for the title name and the surname to be identical, but again for clarity we will assume that the two names are different.

A duke and his wife, a duchess (*H&E*, *MW* 35), were addressed as His (or Her) Grace (*H&E*, *MW* 35, 36; *Cass*, *MW* 44). Their eldest son held the next-highest family title, example, earl or marquess. Other sons were lords (e.g., Lord John Smith), and were referred to in conversation as Lord John or Lord James. John's and James' wives bore the title "Lady" along with their husbands' first names, that is, "Lady John" and "Lady James." The duke's daughter, on the other hand, would use her own first name, example, Lady Anne (*H&E*, *MW* 35) or Lady Anne Smith. As will be seen, Lord and Lady were titles that appeared at several ranks, and it can thus be difficult to tell the exact rank of many of Austen's characters.

The next highest rank was that of marquess (*NA* 139). The marquess could be referred to variously as the marquess of Whateverington, the Most Honorable the marquess of Whateverington, or simply Lord Whateverington. His wife was likewise the marchioness of Whateverington, the Most Honorable the marchioness of Whateverington, or Lady Whateverington. The titles and forms of address were exactly the same for the sons and daughters of marquesses as for the sons and daughters of dukes.

Earls occupied the next level. An earl was referred to as the earl of Whateverington, the Right Honorable the earl of Whateverington, or Lord Whateverington. His wife was a countess (*Cass*, *MW* 45; *NA* 232), referred to as the countess of Whateverington, the Right Honorable the countess of Whateverington, or Lady Whateverington. An earl's daughter had the same titles as a duke's or a marquess's—Lady Anne Smith—but the sons' titles were somewhat different. The eldest, like the eldest son of a duke or a marquess, bore the next-highest title held by the family, but a younger son would be known as the Honorable John Smith or Mr. Smith, and his wife as the Honorable Mrs. John Smith or Mrs. Smith.

The next rank was viscount (*Cass*, *MW* 45; *NA* 251). The viscount was known as the viscount Whateverington, the Right Honorable the viscount

Whateverington, or Lord Whateverington. His wife was the viscountess Whateverington, the Right Honorable the viscountess Whateverington, or Lady Whateverington (*NA* 251; *P* 148). All sons, including the eldest, bore the title "Honorable" and the family surname, as in the Honorable John Smith; in conversation, like the earl's younger son, he might be called Mr. Smith. John's wife would be the Honorable Mrs. John Smith or simply Mrs. Smith. A viscount's daughter was either the Honorable Anne Smith or Miss Smith (*P* 148).

Barons followed a similar pattern. The baron himself was the Right Honorable Lord Whateverington—never Baron Whateverington—or Lord Whateverington. His wife, if she held her title by virtue of her marriage, was the Right Honorable Lady Whateverington or Lady Whateverington. If she held the title in her own right, she could also be addressed as Baroness Whateverington. Sons and daughters of barons followed the same pattern as the sons and daughters of viscounts.

As readers have no doubt noticed, there are a great number of ranks at which someone may be referred to as "Lord" or "Lady," which can make it very difficult to determine the exact rank of the various lords (*NA* 18; *S&S* 251; *MP* 361; *P* 19–20) and ladies (*MP* 359) who appear in Austen's novels. The "Lady Dorothea" of *Love and Freindship* (*MW* 81) could with equal likelihood be the daughter of a duke, a marquess, or an earl. Mr. Dudley, "the Younger Son of a very noble Family" (*Cath, MW* 195), could be the younger son of an earl, viscount, or baron, all of whom would have been referred to in ordinary conversation as "Mr." "The Honourable John Yates" (*MP* 121), who marries Julia Bertram, belongs somewhere in the same three ranks. Lord Osborne, of *The Watsons*, could hold almost any rank.

Lady Catherine de Bourgh presents an especially interesting case. Mr. Collins describes her as "the Right Honourable Lady Catherine de Bourgh, widow of Sir Lewis de Bourgh" (*P&P* 62), and she is repeatedly referred to by others as Lady Catherine, not as Lady De Bourgh. Her rank, therefore, comes not from her husband but from her birth into a noble family, a fact confirmed by the fact that her sister is called "Lady Anne" (83, 212) rather than Lady Darcy. A peer's daughter who married a knight, baronet, or commoner was permitted to keep her rank and precedence, which appears to have happened in both these cases, but exactly what rank the two ladies retained is unclear. "Honorable" was a common addition to titles of the daughters of peers (*S&S* 224), but "Right Honorable" was reserved for earls, viscounts, barons, and their wives. Daughters were not entitled to this magnification of the honorific. It seems likely, then, that the addition of "Right" is Mr. Collins' error and merely one more example of his tendency to exaggerate Lady Catherine's importance.

Frequently, however, it simply is not important. The lords (*P* 4) and ladies, by their very titles, are identified as significantly superior in social status to Austen's heroines, and this is usually all that matters. One important detail to remember, however, is that a Lord John or Lord James, in other words any pairing of "lord" followed by the first name, will always refer to the son of a peer, not a holder of a title by inheritance. Lord Whateverington or John, Lord Whateverington, is the actual title, not a son's courtesy title.

Baron was the lowest rank of the peerage, and it is worth noting at this point that actual modes of address could vary widely depending upon the length of acquaintance between the parties and their relative social rank. An inferior, for example, would always address a duke as "Your Grace" or "Sir," while a social equal could call him "Duke," and a close friend might be able to get away with "Whateverington" (*S&S* 252). The formality with which one addressed a peer also depended greatly on the circumstances. Addresses on letters and announcements of the peer's arrival by servants were intended to be more formal than the terms and titles used in conversation. In conversation, even though an acknowledgment of the peer's title was expected at first, for the rest of the conversation, "my lord" (*Watsons*, *MW* 345) or "my lady" was usually sufficient ("sir" or ma'am" for dukes and duchesses). Among equals who were friends, particularly if they were both men, the use of the title name only was perfectly acceptable, just as among the gentry, men commonly referred to each other by surname only (*Lesley*, *MW* 117). Austen accepted that this was common practice among men, but she found it vulgar in women; only her more distasteful young women use men's surnames without an honorific (*NA* 120, 144; *E* 278, 353, 456). She also found it unpleasant when, instead of an honorific, a more casual appellation was added; thus, Mr. Price's reference to a comrade as "Old Scholey" (*MP* 380) reveals his lack of good manners.

Several rules regarding titles applied specifically to women. Women could inherit peerages and retain these titles even after marriage to a man of inferior rank, but their husbands did not acquire the corresponding male title by their marriage to a peeress. Women who held titles in their own right could not sit in the House of Lords, nor could they undertake any hereditary government posts associated with the title; these duties would be performed by their husbands. A woman who acquired a title through marriage, such as Austen's cousin Eliza, the comtesse de Feuillide, lost it again if she married again. The comtesse de Feuillide, for example, when she married Austen's brother after being widowed, became simply Mrs. Henry Austen. If a woman were married to a peer who died, her eldest son inherited the title, and she became the dowager marchioness/countess/etc. of Whateverington (*P* 148).

Titles below the Peerage

There were two ranks among the upper gentry that merited special titles, and they were very similar in their usage. Both baronets (*Col Let*, *MW*

163; *LS, MW* 296; *NA* 16, 18, 206; *MP* 3, 42, 395; *P* 4, 11, 75) and knights (*P* 11) were referred to as Sir Robert Smith (*P&P* 18; *P* 158) or Sir Robert (*E&E, MW* 30; *Visit, MW* 51; *P* 20), but never Sir Smith. One difference between them was that a baronet could add an abbreviation after his name in writing: Sir John Smith, Bart., or Sir John Smith, Bt. A more important difference between the two titles was that a baronetcy could be inherited, while a knighthood could not. The wives in both cases were referred to as Lady Smith, as the use of a first name would have made it seem as if the woman in question was a peer's daughter rather than a knight's wife. Thus, we encounter Lady Russell (*P* 11), Lady Lesley (*Lesley, MW* 116), and so on (*J&A, MW* 15; *E&E, MW* 30; *Visit, MW* 51; *Col Let, MW* 152; *P&P* 222; *P* 75). Daughters of baronets and knights bore no special titles, but their sons (*L&F, MW* 80) might add the title "Esquire" (*MP* 434) to their names, example, John Smith, Esq. (*J&A, MW* 12; *Mount, MW* 40; *Amelia, MW* 47; *Cass, MW* 49; *S&S* 246; *P&P* 336; *P* 3, 4). Esquire was a term of uncertain boundaries; in theory, it was applicable only to the sons of upper gentry, judges, military officers, and people of similar standing (such as the chief local landowner or "squire"—see *NA* 16), but in practice it could safely be adopted by almost any gentleman.

Members of the gentry, yeoman farmers, and most merchants and artisans would be known by the honorific titles still in use today in the United States, such as Mr., Mrs. (*P&P* 317), and Miss. Husbands and wives addressed each other with far more formality than is now customary, calling each other "Mr. Smith" and "Mrs. Smith" in front of others (*Lesley, MW* 133), including servants and children. It was considered disrespectful to do otherwise (*E* 272, 278). Some families were no doubt a little less formal (*E* 172), calling the patriarch "your Papa" instead of "your father," but the Austens appear to have fallen into the more formal camp. Even when we know that letters were often read aloud to friends, it sounds strange to modern ears to hear Jane writing to Cassandra of "my mother," when of course she was mother to both of them. Use of a person's first name required either long acquaintance and an invitation to advance to this level of familiarity or a family relationship, whether by blood relation, marriage, or betrothal (*S&S* 59–60; *MP* 303; *E* 324).

Unmarried sisters were distinguished by the use of first names for any younger sisters and the title and surname alone for the eldest. Thus, in a family with three unmarried girls, the eldest would be Miss Smith, the second Miss Jane Smith, and the youngest Miss Catherine Smith (*Cass, MW* 49). When the eldest married, Jane would now be referred to in public as "Miss Smith," while Catherine would have to wait until Jane married to inherit that title. Grown-up sons of the gentry were referred to as "Mr.," but young sons were called "Master" instead (*Watsons, MW* 332).

Some titles were occupational. "Doctor," which today is most usually associated with the practice of medicine or with advanced academic degrees, in Austen's time was predominantly applied to doctors of divinity, that is, to certain clergymen. Austen never uses the title "Dr." for a physician, reserving it instead for the clergy (*S&S* 218; *MP* 119). Servants were usually called either by their first names alone or by their last names alone, depending on their status within the household and on the custom of the family for whom they worked. The use of the first name alone was probably more typical, especially in households with only a handful of servants, but in large establishments, the upper servants were called by their last names. On occasion, one sees a hybrid form of address, such as the case of one eighteenth-century maid of all work, who was referred to by her employer as "Mrs. Becky." A companion or a governess would possess a status on the fringes of gentility and would be called by her last name, along with Mrs. or Miss (*P&P* 158).

Ton

"Ton" or "bon ton" (pronounced boh toh, with just a hint of an "n" on the end of each word) meant "fashion" or "the fashionable world." Using French terms was in itself a statement of fashionable knowledge, although by Austen's time "ton" had entered mainstream English usage. Interestingly, in *Mansfield Park*, a novel that explicitly pits English culture against French culture with obvious distaste for the latter, the term "ton" is used by Edmund Bertram, the archetypal defender of English virtue (*MP* 92). However, he uses it, appropriately enough, in the context of rejecting the fashionable world, when he says that a "clergyman cannot be high in state or fashion. He must not head mobs, or set the ton in dress." Roger Sales suggests that the word enters Austen's works in one other context, again with an implicit rejection of all that it stands for. He suggests that the name of the town Sanditon stands for "sandy ton," implying that "fashionable society is built on shifting sands."

Toys

Toys (*S&S* 119; *MP* 14) came in great variety, though nothing to approach the variety available during and after the Victorian period. During the eighteenth century childhood first came to be perceived in Europe as a special state, with its own cognitive patterns and peculiar innocence. As a result, parents were tempted to spend money on goods uniquely for children.

However, "toys," in Austen's time, did not always mean playthings for children, nor did "toy shops" deal exclusively in goods for the young. Just as the concept of childhood was evolving, so, too, was the concept of the toy shop, which initially meant merely a store selling small, attractive objects such as china, buckles, or combs, and only later took on its modern

The Reception of the Diplomatique and His Suite, at the Court of Pekin, 1792. Lord
Macartney brings, among other things, offerings of British toys, including, from left to
right, a bat, trap, and ball for trap-ball; a dice cup; a toy windmill; a battledore and
shuttlecock; a magic lantern for projecting scenes on a wall (next to his knee); a toy
man-of-war (behind his hand); a toy balloon (floating above him); and a toy carriage
and rocking horse, held by other members of the British delegation. Courtesy of the
Lewis Walpole Library, Yale University. 792.9.14.1.

meaning. In Austen's day, the modern sense had taken hold to a great extent, but not entirely. Fortunately, she is unambiguous in her usage; when
she says "toys," she means children's toys. These would have been made
at home or bought in toy shops, which were found chiefly in sizable towns
and sold not only English-made toys but expensive and fashionable French
toys and cheaper ones from Germany and Holland.

Boys' toys included tops, which had been popular for centuries. The
tops were started and kept spinning with whips. Boys also enjoyed two-
inch-high toy soldiers, made originally of tin and later of lead. Some toy
soldiers were made of paper or cardboard, and these were obviously flat,
but even the metal soldiers were flat, rather than fully three-dimensional.
Boys also rolled hoops, played trap-ball with specially made traps, shot toy
guns (*First Act*, *MW* 172–174), and played games with marbles.

Girls had skipping ropes and, of course, dolls. Some were jointed dolls
of wood, china, alabaster, or wax, while others were made from cloth or

paper. Some looked like miniature grown-ups, some like babies; some were ladies and gentlemen, others working people of various trades. Numerous paintings and engravings from the period show little girls holding favorite dolls. One type of doll was an early form of the dress-up paper doll—a series of costumes with a transferable head—that came with a story about the doll, named either "Henry" or "Fanny." Wealthy girls might own extremely elaborate dolls' houses made by the estate carpenter.

Many toys were enjoyed by children of both sexes. Younger children might pull the toddlers in the family around in a small wagon or a miniature carriage, while the older children flew kites (*E* 95), produced puppet shows with marionettes, and played battledore and shuttlecock. Noah's arks were popular from the first; one of the earliest London toy stores, in the modern sense, was named the Noah's Ark. Some children rode hobbyhorses, a name applied to both the stick variety and to rocking horses. Others played with music boxes, wheeled pull-toys in the shapes of animals, and yo-yos (then called "bandelures").

Some toys and games involved mental or physical challenges. One such game was bilboquet or, as Austen called it, "bilbocatch," a game of hand-eye coordination at which Jane Austen was said to excel, and which she wrote of playing in 1808 with her nephew George. This game used a ball with a small hole in it and a handle that ended in either a cup or a point; the goal was to toss the ball in the air and catch it either in the cup or on the point. James Edward Austen-Leigh wrote that Jane would "catch it on the point above an hundred times in succession, till her hand was weary."

Jigsaw puzzles in the true sense did not exist yet, but puzzle maps were common (*MP* 18) for teaching geography. Other educational toys included alphabet blocks, alphabet cards, and the alphabet tiles used by Mr. Elton to send secret messages to Jane Fairfax in *Emma* (347–349). Board games, usually of the kind in which players race to be the first around a track divided by spaces, were sometimes intended to teach facts or morals; "The New Game of Human Life," created in 1790, was one of these, and was intended to encourage children to "contrast the happiness of a Virtuous & well spent life with the fatal consequences arising from Vicious & Immoral pursuits." Others were meant purely for fun. As dice were associated with the "Vicious and Immoral pursuit" of gambling, some games substituted a top for dice to determine the number of spaces moved. *See also* Cards; Children; Games.

Travel

Travel (*NA* 155–156; *MP* 375; *E* 104–106, 285; *P* 13) was improving in Austen's day. Earlier in the eighteenth century roads (*L&F*, *MW* 85; *Sand*, *MW* 426; *MW* 445; *NA* 198; *P&P* 275, 281, 282; *MP* 39, 82; *E* 83, 127) had been hazardous in the extreme, full of fatally deep potholes and bone-jarring ruts (*MP* 189), and often impassable (*Sand, MW* 363–364; 373) in the winter (*MP* 189). This was, in part, because each parish was responsible for the upkeep of the roads within its boundaries, and the task was simply too huge for many localities to manage well. Labor was hard to come by, and in parishes through which heavy London traffic passed, the road surveyors (*Watsons, MW* 349–350) could not keep up with the continual damage. The answer was the formation of turnpike trusts, whose creation peaked during the third quarter of the eighteenth century. The trusts, formed by means of a private act of Parliament (private because the drafting and passage were privately funded), built and maintained the turnpikes (*Ode, MW* 75; *L&F, MW* 97; *Watsons, MW* 321; *Sand, MW* 367; *S&S* 197; *P&P* 275) and erected toll gates (*Watsons, MW* 322). Most people, livestock, carts, wagons, and carriages were subject to a toll every time they passed a gate, though mail coaches and troops were exempt.

As soon as it was clear that turnpikes could be profitable, they snaked across the map of England like the roots of some fast-growing plant. Hundreds were built, cooperating with improvements in horse breeding and carriage design to increase the rate at which people could travel. Furthermore, turnpikes, which were naturally placed along the busiest city-to-city routes, eased the pressure on local road surveyors. Increased interest in the state of the roads also developed during the wars with France, when rapid troop movement could be of great importance. From the mid-eighteenth century, cartographers had been making road maps specifically designed for travelers, sometimes showing only one town-to-town route with distances, villages, and likely places to stop along the way (*NA* 45).

This is not to say that travel became free from all inconvenience. On the contrary, filthy inns (*E* 193, 306), stinking or snoring fellow passengers, and poor weather (*NA* 19) remained as irritating as always. Travelers packed their trunks and boxes (*L&F, MW* 89; *NA* 227; *P&P* 213–214; *MP* 444; *E* 186) and loaded them on a stagecoach, post chaise, or stage wagon, tying the luggage to the vehicle's top with rope or shoving it into the huge basket that hung off the back of the coach (*Sand, MW* 406, 407; *P&P* 216).* A few items could be kept under the coach seat (*NA* 163), in laps (*P&P* 221), in side pockets sewn into the coach lining (*NA* 235), or in a woman's reticule or a man's coat pocket. Everything else remained out of reach. The roads, even the turnpike roads, were still bumpy and rutted in places, although this situation was gradually improving. Travelers hoped that the coach wouldn't lose a wheel or, still worse, be overturned (*Sand, MW* 364; *NA* 19; *E* 126), as both kinds of accidents were fairly common. Mr. Woodhouse's fear about "the corner into Vicarage-lane" (*E* 280) is a fear of being overturned. Highwaymen haunted the

---

*Heavy baggage was sent either by water or overland by wagon (*P* 38–39).

turnpike roads, and their numbers were multiplied in the minds of fearful passengers (*NA* 19). The experience was summed up in *Country and Town*, a 1797 poem by Charles Morris:

In the country how charming our visits to make
Through ten miles of mud for formality's sake,
With the coachman in drink and the moon in a fog,
And no thought in our head but a ditch and a bog.

As Morris points out, on dark nights (*E* 128) travel was especially dangerous, for the coachman could not always see every obstacle in time to avoid it. Nighttime journeys, therefore, tended to be performed when the moon was full, and people scheduled balls and other events accordingly (*Col Let, MW* 159; *Evelyn, MW* 189; *S&S* 33).

Stops, in most coaches, were frequent. The coachman would rein in his horses at a decent-looking inn and either rest or change the horses, perhaps allowing the passengers time to get something to eat (*L&F, MW* 106). If the stop were near the intersection of two major roads, he might need to allow some passengers to disembark (a process that entailed finding and unloading their luggage) so that they could wait for a coach that ran along the intersecting route (*NA* 232, 235). When the hour grew late, a halt would be called for the night, and the passengers would stumble wearily into an inn, where they would be shown to their possibly vermin-infested beds. Once they reached their destination, they might find that they had left belongings behind in one of these inns or else in the coach itself (*NA* 235), and there would be little or no hope of retrieving their lost property.

Slower conveyances traveled at about 4 to 6 miles per hour, though higher speeds were possible in light carriages (*NA* 88). Darcy, with good carriages and excellent horses at his command, can call "fifty miles of good road" just over "half a day's journey," implying that his top speed is somewhere in the neighborhood of 8 miles per hour (*P&P* 179). General Tilney, likewise, estimates that a 20-mile trip (*NA* 212) will take him about two hours and forty-five minutes (*NA* 210), giving him an average speed of a little over 7 miles per hour. Normally, in a post chaise or similar vehicle of ordinary capabilities, a journey of about 100 miles would take two days of travel. The journey from Sotherton to Mansfield Park, then, a distance of about 10 miles (*MP* 73, 104), and not all of it good road, would take about two hours. A multiple-day journey might well take longer if it included a Sunday. Many travelers still followed the old habit of not traveling on Sunday (*P* 161), though this rule was often broken by the end of the eighteenth century.

Most of Austen's travel times are accurate. Journeys of any length take two to three days (*E&E, MW* 30; *Sand, MW* 409; *S&S* 160, 301–302, 304, 341; *P&P* 285–286; *MP* 446), which is about right for the distances involved. Some travel times, however, are intentionally wrong. For the sake of humor, for example, she has a character travel from Scotland to London in minutes or hours (*L&F*, *MW* 92), when in fact the journey took several days. On the opposite end of the spectrum, she sends Mr. Clifford from Devizes to Bath, "which is no less that nineteen miles," in a full day of travel. She then has him travel from Devizes to Overton, a distance of about 35 miles, in three days of "hard labour," where he collapses and has to spend five months recuperating. He then takes four days to travel from Overton to Basingstoke, a journey of about six miles (*Clifford*, *MW* 43–44).

All of the journeys above were assumed to take place in some sort of vehicle. A man on foot obviously traveled more slowly, and a man on horseback (*Evelyn*, *MW* 187; *S&S* 86; *P&P* 49) could travel a bit more quickly, though he would still have to stop periodically to allow his horse to rest. Gentlemen traveling on horseback, as well as ladies and mixed parties out for day rides, would take along a mounted groom or two (*S&S* 86–87) to hold the horses, see that they were fed and watered when feasible, and help anyone who needed assistance to mount or dismount. Working-class women might ride in a coach alone, and men of all ranks did so, but genteel young women were supposed to have an escort (*NA* 225, 226; *S&S* 280; *P&P* 211–212; *MP* 12, 410, 425). This might be a male relative, an older woman, or a servant.

Travel by water could be faster than travel overland, but it had its own set of woes (*Cath*, *MW* 205; *MP* 108, 125, 178, 235). England's new system of canals had generated an entrepreneurial boom that foreshadowed the turnpike craze. Each canal linked two rivers together and, like a turnpike, had to be authorized by a private act of Parliament (*MW* 449). Canals were useful for transporting cargo, but they were not fast enough to attract passenger business. Sea travel was occasionally used to get from one far-flung part of the British Isles to another or to send cargo between coastal towns (*S&S* 26), but its main passenger business was in carrying people abroad (*Amelia*, *MW* 47; *Evelyn*, *MW* 185; *E* 221, 364–365)—to the Continent for sightseeing trips, to fields of battle across the world, to tea plantations in India, and to sugar plantations in the West Indies. To reach these places, passengers faced the possibility of seasickness, enemy privateers (*MP* 180), storms (*Evelyn*, *MW* 185), and delays due to uncooperative winds (*MP* 225). A passage to America (*H&E*, *MW* 38) or the Caribbean or back could take several weeks (*MP* 32, 34, 107). Travelers to the Caribbean also confronted the peril of tropical diseases, which were so feared that soldiers posted there often deserted or injured themselves to avoid the trip.

Within England, however, travel was so much easier than it had been in the past that a new industry, the tourism industry, arose. People visited inland spas and seaside resorts (*Sand*, *MW* 374), which competed with each other to provide the best amenities and touted the health benefits of their waters and air. Nor were such trips only for the wealthy. Middle class people also visited such places, and one or two were close enough to London to be frequented by a broad cross-section of society, omitting only the very upper and very lower ends. People visiting a new town such as Bath or Tunbridge Wells laid out a few shillings for souvenirs, such as a pincushion painted with the legend, "A Gift from Bath." The gift-shop trinkets of today thus have a very long pedigree indeed.

People also took day trips to visit sites of interest nearby. Old churches (*P* 131), the graves of famous people, and heights from which a good stretch of countryside could be seen were all popular destinations, as were public gardens and that marvelous novelty, the factory. Parson James Woodforde, entertaining guests in June 1790, took them to "Bunns Rural Gardens and the Iron-Foundery" to see the wonders of nature and of technology in a single day.

A growing belief in the uplifting powers of nature also drew people to sites of scenic beauty within Britain, such as mountains and the northern Lake District (*P&P* 154, 238–240). Hester Lynch Piozzi wrote about the "*Rage for the Lakes*" in 1789, when tourists in search of the picturesque crowded along the shores of Windermere, Derwentwater, and Ullswater. They packed into sightseeing boats, listened to tour operators fire a cannon to demonstrate the mountain echoes, and frequently, like many modern tourists, stayed only long enough to be able to say they had seen the lakes. One spectator heard a gentleman on Windermere gush,

> "Good God! how delightful!—how charming!—I could live here for ever!— Row on, row on, row on, row on"; and after passing one hour of exclamations upon the Lake, and half an hour at Ambleside, he ordered his horses into his phaeton, and flew off to take (I doubt not) an equally *flying* view of Derwent water.

Educated visitors searched the landscape for resemblance to the works of Claude, Poussin, and Rosa. Windermere was thought to evoke the works of Claude, in the words of novelist Ann Radcliffe, because of its "Diffusiveness, stately beauty, and, at the upper end, magnificence." Tourists considered Ullswater more appropriate to be depicted by Poussin, though some reversed their judgment, awarding Ullswater to Claude and Windermere to Poussin. Almost everyone agreed that only Rosa could have done justice to Derwentwater. Guides for travelers written from a picturesque point of view advised visitors where to stand and what to look for so that they could make the most of their journey.

Another popular tourist activity was visiting stately homes (*MP* 95–96). These were not old mansions preserved as museums but homes, old or new, that were still inhabited by their owners. No one knows who first strode up to the door of some great family, knocked, and asked to be shown around, or how he convinced the servant to take him around the house. No doubt it involved a monetary bribe, preserved in the habit of giving tips to the servants who conducted the tours, but, whatever the origin, the pastime grew extremely popular. People were admitted to a house, provided they looked genteel, and led from room to room by a servant, usually the housekeeper, who illuminated the history of each object and painting. Novelist Fanny Burney, after touring the duke of Dorset's home in 1779, wrote enthusiastically about the paintings and furniture. One of the state bedrooms, she wrote,

> was magnificence itself!—it was fitted up for King William;—the Bed-Curtains, Tester, Quilt, and Valens, were all of the richest Gold flowers worked upon a silver Ground,—its value, even in those Days, was £7000!—The Table, a superb Cabinet, Frame of the looking Glass, and all the Ornaments, and I believe, all the Furniture in the Room, were of solid massive silver, curiously embossed!—Nothing could be more splendid.

Sometimes, the visit to a house would be combined with a look at the gardens, although in many cases it was the gardens that were the main attraction. Wealthy landowners spent small fortunes remaking their grounds in the latest style, and a passion for gardening, for nature, and for fashionable improvement drew many visitors into wildernesses and walks, parks and paths. Some gardens, in fact, were so popular that their owners were forced to ban all tourist traffic (*S&S* 62).

Within cities and towns, travel presented a different set of problems. Here the streets (*NA* 91; *P&P* 72; *E* 162; *P* 107, 115, 179) could be narrow and dirty, and wash water or even the contents of chamberpots could be flung out of upper windows by servants. Many of the bigger towns invested in better drains, street lighting, and wide pavements (*NA* 87) to ameliorate the condition of the streets, hiring street sweepers (often children) to brush the filth from the crossings, but in bad weather, even the sidewalks could be dirty (*NA* 82; *E* 179, 195). A thick pall of coal smoke hung over many towns, particularly early in the morning when servants in almost every home were busy lighting the day's first fires. In London, the fog could be so thick that people ran into each other in the streets, pinballing their way to their destinations.

Those who could afford to do so took sedan chairs or carriages through London's streets, but traveling this way could create its own set of problems. London's layout, except in the newly constructed, spacious streets of the West End, was still based on fairly narrow streets, and traffic jams formed frequently. Other cities sometimes had similar problems. The crowds on foot (*NA* 44) were so thick that a servant sometimes had to walk ahead to clear the way, and in some parts of town, carriages met and passed in such numbers that the passengers might be stuck in one place for a long while or make such slow progress that it would have been faster to walk. *See also* Carriages and Coaches; Chair; Inns.

Tunbridge Ware

An interest in traveling the late Hanoverian era led to the development of a new industry: the manufacture of souvenirs. People vacationing in resort towns would come home with pincushions, needle cases, or snuffboxes that had "A Gift from Bath" or a similar message painted on them. One of the sites that developed a booming business in such trinkets was the spa of Tunbridge Wells, located conveniently close to London.

Not all of these items were made of wood. There were thimble holders and pincushions of ivory; buckles, brooches, and bracelets of steel; pencil cases, snuffboxes, candle snuffers, scissors, needle cases, corkscrews, and buttons of silver; and even a few items made of gold. At first these souvenirs were actually made in Tunbridge; later, they were made primarily in Birmingham and shipped to Tunbridge for sale. The most famous, characteristic, and genuinely local souvenirs were the "Tunbridge ware" (E 338)—turned and inlaid wood items. There were work boxes, desks, tea caddies, chess boards, and cribbage boards of Tunbridge ware. Sewing boxes, tea caddies, and other small boxes were very common.

The inlaid designs were created with a variety of different woods; sometimes they were dyed in red, green, or black, but the more characteristic method was to finish each wood in as close to its natural color as possible. Holly, broom, laburnum, plum, oak, walnut, yew, chestnut, furze, acacia, lilac, laurel, birch, sycamore, pear, and cherry woods were all used. Barberry yielded a yellow wood, and downed oak branches attacked by a kind of fungus furnished a natural green. Holly soaked in the local spa water turned gray. As the trade expanded, nonlocal woods such as satinwood, mahogany, and ebony were introduced, offering a wider range of colors.

Numerous different patterns for the inlay were used. The Vandyke was a pattern of long triangles and was often used. Another extremely common pattern was a plane of intersecting cubs that appeared to be three-dimensional. Borders on Tunbridge items might be made up of inlaid squares, diamonds, triangles, or stars, or of painted designs of various kinds.

Ult.

It was customary in letters and other documents of the time to use certain abbreviations that are less common today. One of these is "ult." (*E* 440), short for the Latin word *ultimo* (last), and referring to the previous month. A letter written in February, for example, referring to "the 2nd ult.," would be referring to January 2. A related abbreviation was "inst.," for *instant*, also from the Latin, and referring to the current calendar month. "the 2nd inst.," in the sample letter given above, would refer to February 2.

Umbrellas and Parasols

In Austen's lifetime, umbrellas and parasols were not entirely new, but they were very nearly so. Both came into fashion for the first time in the latter half of the eighteenth century, overcoming skeptics who thought them silly, effeminate, or awkward. Both were initially imported from overseas; for most of the eighteenth century, France and Italy made the best ones, and those made in England were rather shoddy, but once the English embraced the concept, they began to innovate, and soon there were patents for folding umbrellas, collapsible pocket umbrellas, and umbrellas that opened automatically.

The terms parasol and umbrella were sometimes used interchangeably, but Austen uses them in the modern sense. The parasol, for her, is a shade against the sun, while the umbrella offers protection from the rain. In an 1801 letter, she describes a walk up Sion Hill, near Bath, with a Mrs. Chamberlayne: "we posted along under a fine hot sun, *she* without any parasol or shade to her hat, stopping for nothing." Here the parasol is clearly meant to be a sunshade; in the novels and fragments, the term is either indeterminate (*Sand, MW* 374, 381; *P&P* 238) or used in the context of protection from the sun (*P&P* 352). Her umbrellas, in contrast, are usually explicitly introduced in the context of rain or the chance of rain (*Col Let, MW* 159; *NA* 82–83; *MP* 205; *P* 177).

The parasols of Austen's youth, in the 1770s to 1790s, were often "staff" parasols (a later term). The typical staff parasol was mounted near the top of a long stick, almost as tall as the woman herself. The staff might be topped with a knob or a token hook and may have been meant to echo the pastorally inspired "shepherdess" fashions with their hitched-up back skirts. By 1799, many parasols had become smaller, with shorter sticks and shades mounted on "marquise" hinges so that they could fold parallel to the sticks (see the illustration *Monstrosities of 1799* [Clothing]). These round, rather shallow parasols often had sticks of turned wood—that is, they were shaped on a lathe, like a fancy chair leg—and shades of green silk. Around 1807, the turned sticks were replaced by plain ones, and the marquise hinges and plain, shallow shades went out of fashion around 1810. At about this time, a new shape became fashionable—the "pagoda" shape, in which the parasol had a wide bottom that rose steeply, swept in horizontally, and then pointed up again in the center with the help of an internal spring. From 1800 to 1810, it was common to find parasols that were fringed at the edge, and colors other than green eventually became popular. Around 1816, turned sticks again came into favor, and some of the more elaborate examples from this period had turned ivory sticks intricately carved with Chinese motifs.

Men did not carry parasols, but both men and women eventually made use of umbrellas (*E* 12, 178, 321; *P* 127). They were introduced to the country by philanthropist Jonas Hanway, who carried a pocket-sized, folding, foreign-made model with a carved ebony handle, a green silk outside and a gray satin lining. His enthusiasm for the new device led it to be nicknamed a "Hanway," but the moniker didn't stick, and by Austen's life-

The Battle of Umbrellas, Collings and Thomas, 1784. The newly fashionable umbrella as a source of pain, confusion, and embarrassment. Courtesy of the Lewis Walpole Library, Yale University. 784.9.1.2.

time, the name "umbrella"—from the Latin word for "shade"—had become standard.

At first people felt awkward about using umbrellas. After all, carrying one meant that the user was at the mercy of the weather. In other words, he was walking rather than riding in a coach. Genteel men were also somewhat unaccustomed to having their hands occupied as they walked. Furthermore, the early umbrellas were difficult to use, hard to open, and subject to damage by strong winds. No one seemed to know, at first, how to walk down a street filled with open umbrellas. Popular prints depict the social unease: did one lift one's umbrella so that it cleared those of other passersby? how did one cope with the impediment to vision? how could one avoid poking one's neighbor with the tip? It was all very confusing.

However, the usefulness of an umbrella in the wet English climate was too obvious to be resisted for long. London footman John Macdonald, who had been mocked in the 1770s for his Frenchified habit of carrying an umbrella, reported in 1790 that umbrella-making "is become a great trade in London and a very useful branch of business." In 1810 the *Universal Magazine* noted that people of all classes carried umbrellas. Even children and servants were equipped for wet weather. Fashionable men, who still refused to carry parasols, could sometimes be observed using an umbrella as a sunshade.

In the last decade of Austen's life, umbrellas might be found with wood or metal sticks and decorative wooden, ivory, or antler handles. The ribs, which ran along the inside of the cover, were usually of whalebone or cane,

Umbrellas and parasols.

with brass tips that stuck out beyond the cover; the cover itself was of waxed cloth—silk in the better models, cotton in the others, with green, blue, red, and brown the dominant colors. The stretchers, which spread the cover outward away from the stick, were usually of steel.

Under-hung

The OED defines "under-hung" (*P* 141) as having a projecting lower jaw. Characteristically, it is the appearance-conscious Sir Walter Elliot who uses the term.

Valley of Tempé

The humor of this reference relies on the passion for classical references in the art and literature of Austen's day. It also draws, perhaps, on Austen's frequent use of geographical inaccuracy to exemplify ignorance or absurdity. The reference occurs in a scene that is clearly set in the British Isles, in the fictional village of Crankhumdunberry; a lovely garden there has "a verdant lawn enamelled with a variety of variegated flowers & watered by a purling Stream, brought from the Valley of Tempé by a passage under ground" (*F&E, MW* 5). This would be a remarkable feat of engineering, as the Valley of Tempé is located in Thessaly, between Mt. Olympus and Mt. Ossa, and was the mythological site of a famous battle between Apollo and the Python.

Visiting

There were two principal kinds of visits: the long visit and the morning call. Long visits were paid to friends or family who lived far away (*Evelyn, MW* 190; *Cath, MW* 197; *NA* 224; *S&S* 231; *P&P* 63, 146, 317; *MP* 28; *E* 435; *P* 128). They entailed a certain amount of expense for coach fare and a great deal of trouble in packing and preparing. Therefore, these visits tended to last several days or even several weeks. As a child, Austen saw her parents host guests in this way—usually at the Christmas holidays, when Mr. Austen's pupils had gone home to see their own parents. As an adult, Jane paid such visits herself, traveling to London to stay with her brother Henry, to Kent to visit her brother Edward, and to Ibthorpe to visit the Lloyd family. The length of such visits tended to be linked to the closeness of the relationship between guest and host and also to the host's ability to cater to the needs of another person for an extended period of time; in her Juvenilia, Austen includes an instance of a deliberately exaggerated stay of "five or six months" (*Scraps, MW* 171–172); a stay of such duration would not even have been suggested by Austen's wealthy brother Edward, let alone the characters whom Austen describes.

The other kind of visit (*F&E, MW* 6; *Watsons, MW* 337; *S&S* 168; *P&P* 5, 147; *MP* 62; *E* 53, 184; *P* 39–40, 47, 149, 162, 165) was the polite social call, paid in the "morning" (*S&S* 74; *MP* 39; *E* 17–18, 46, 455; *P* 87, 212, 215). Morning was understood in the contemporary sense of "everything between breakfast and dinner," a span of time that could last from 9:00 or 10:00 A.M. until 6:00 or 6:30 (*LS, MW* 303; *MP* 298), depending on how late the visited family ate dinner. Out-of-sync dinner hours sometimes caused confusion and hurt feelings, as one person who tended to eat late might accidentally call in the middle of dinner at a house that took its meal earlier in the day. Most visitors, however, could safely call between 12:00 and 3:00 (*Watsons, MW* 338), which they usually did, as it was generally considered incumbent on the visitor to choose a reasonable time, especially if the visitor's superior rank made it impossible to refuse an untimely visit (*Col Let, MW* 158–159).

A visitor rang the bell or used the knocker at the front door and waited for someone—usually a servant (*MP* 399)—to open it. She would identify herself to the servant and be asked to wait while the servant determined whether or not the visited party was "at home" (*LS, MW* 303; *E* 452). The servant, of course, already knew whether the visited party was in the house, but being *at home* was different from being in the house. Being at home meant being willing and ready to receive visitors of any kind, specifically, the visitor who waited at the door. The servant could deny that his master or mistress was at home (*J&A, MW* 15; *NA* 91; *S&S* 294) for a host of reasons, including genuine absence (*NA* 89), illness, disinclination to receive guests, and personal animus against the visitor in question. If told that the visited party was not at home, the visitor left her card (*NA* 89, 91; *S&S* 169, 177, 230, 287; *P* 138, 149) as evidence that she had stopped by; she could then expect to receive a return visit, assuming she and the resident of the house were on good terms. Sometimes people left their cards not only to show that they had visited but to announce their presence in town, for example, upon arriving in Bath, London, or another place where people took lodgings for extended stays (*S&S* 168, 170). A call where only a card was left (*S&S* 216; *P* 215) could, with due politeness, be repaid with only a card in exchange. A card, however, that was left by a complete stranger required no acknowledgment (*P* 138).

The visiting card was a piece of cardstock, often the approximate size of a business card, but sometimes larger or more nearly square. The Lewis Walpole Library has a collection of visiting cards from the period, the smallest of which is about 2½" by 1¾" and the largest of which is 4¾" by just over 3". The back of each card is plain or has a simple repeated design. On the front, often surrounded by a decorative border, is the name of the visitor in ink that may be black, green, or blue. Many of the cards of different ladies have identical borders, implying that printers had a selection of standard borders from which customers could choose. The borders are mostly neoclassical in design; one for "Lady Archer" has an acanthus-leaf border, while one for "Lady Catherine Stanhope" has a classical swag.

If the visitor were admitted, she was shown by the servant (*P* 142) into a parlor (*Col Let, MW* 151; *Cath, MW* 214; *E* 190) or drawing room (*Sand, MW* 394), and the servant, in many households, announced her name (*Watsons, MW* 338). In this room, the lady or ladies of the house would already be sitting, perhaps "working" (i.e., sewing) or taking some sort of refreshment. If the latter, they would offer food and drink to the

Calling cards. Courtesy of the Lewis Walpole Library, Yale University.

guest. Sometimes, even if they were not eating, they would invite the guest to stay and take some sort of refreshment with them (*Sand, MW* 390–391); this might be accepted or declined, as the visitor might have other visits to pay before heading home for her own dinner. Fifteen minutes was the absolute minimum duration for politeness (*Scraps, MW* 172; *S&S* 229; *P&P* 147; *E* 185–187, 199). To leave more quickly would be tantamount to a snub unless all parties were very good friends and the visit was for a very specific purpose.

Often a visit was mandatory or nearly so. Those who expected to be absent for a long time would usually pay farewell visits before departing (*P&P* 145). People returning home after a long absence could likewise expect to be visited by their friends (*E&E, MW* 31; *P&P* 332–333; *MP* 192). Similarly, when a woman married, it was incumbent upon her nearby friends and relatives to pay a call on her at her new home as soon as she had returned from her honeymoon (*S&S* 213, 216; *E* 9, 17–18; *P* 251). If she were moving into a new neighborhood, her husband's friends and acquaintances would be expected to call upon her also (*E* 271, 280, 290). She would then have to return these visits; virtually all visits required a reciprocal visit (*P&P* 9, 21, 147, 266; *E* 185, 305; *P* 48, 53, 168), so that once one started visiting at a particular house, it was hard to stop. Unlike the paper exchanges in which cards were left back and forth, a visit in which the parties met face-to-face required a similarly personal visit in response.

Sometimes, in order to avoid all the formalities associated with paying a visit, or perhaps merely to display that one had plenty of servants on staff, a servant was sent instead. This was never done in place of a required social call, but only in cases where there was a specific purpose in mind. For example, a person of genteel rank would not bother to walk to his neighbor's house to deliver a gift of produce from his garden. He would send a servant with a basket instead. A host giving a large party might deliver printed invitations personally (*P&P* 86; *P* 226–227, 236), if it were convenient to do so, and might combine this delivery with a social visit, but he might equally choose to send a servant on this errand, as did the host who invited Parson James Woodforde to a ball and supper in 1788:

> Rec[eive]d. this morning by Mr. Custance's Servant Rich[ar]d. Enclosed in a Cover from Mr. and Mrs. Coke of Holkham, containing an Invitation to me and my Niece the fifth of November next to a Ball and Supper at Holkham. The Card was printed all but our Names and in these words. Mr. and Mrs. Coke desire the honour of Mr. and Miss Woodford's Company the 5th of November, at eight o'clock to a Ball and Supper, in Commemoration of the glorious Revolution of 1688. Holkham, Oct. 1788. The Favour of an Answer is desired. My Servant, Briton, paid for the same 0.0.8.

Servants, as Woodforde notes at the end of the entry, expected to be tipped for their efforts in delivering goods and invitations to prosperous households. On occasion, they would also be invited in for something to eat or drink—but in the kitchen, with the other servants, rather than in the parlor or drawing room.

Men could pay visits to women (*S&S* 99; *MP* 298; *E* 455), but the reverse was not true. The majority of visiting consisted of visits paid by women to women, although men made some morning calls, and children might be brought along as they matured in order to teach them the rudiments of the ritual (*Col Let*, *MW* 150). Some people objected to the whole idea of visits. The anonymous author of *Female Tuition; or, an Address to Mothers, on the Education of Daughters* (1784) concluded, "*Visiting*, especially as practised among the great, seldom terminates in any thing but vanity, scandal, or intrigue."

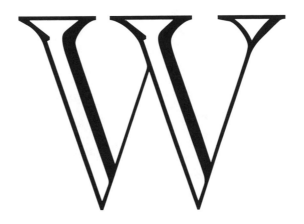

Walking

Walking (*Lesley, MW* 111; *Evelyn, MW* 190; *NA* 35, 80, 85, 103; *S&S* 41; *P&P* 157; *MP* 334; *E* 8, 18, 26, 58, 191, 195, 196, 294, 333, 344, 356, 362; *P* 39–40, 41, 60, 84, 132, 168–169, 227) was a necessity for the working class (*E* 29, 31), who had few transportation options and walked on many occasions to get to market and to visit friends. Even among the gentry, who might not own a coach or might not have it at their disposal because the horses were being used for other purposes, walking was likewise necessary for making morning visits (*Sand, MW* 406; *S&S* 40, 343; *P&P* 28, 293; *E* 456, 457). Mr. Weston walks to Hartfield, for example, because his wife has already gone over in their carriage, and the distance is short (*E* 302). Those who lived in town, gentry or not, might walk for the purposes of running errands (*NA* 114; *P&P* 28; *MP* 205; *E* 293–295), whether for the pleasure of walking, for lack of a carriage, or because calling for the carriage was too time-consuming.

For many, walking was an avocation, a way of spending time between breakfast and dinner (*Sand, MW* 384; *E* 209), of seeing interesting landscape (*S&S* 40–41, 88, 343), and of keeping one's figure in a time when beef and butter constituted a large part of the evening meal. Physical exercise of some sort was also considered necessary for good health (*MP* 322, 409; *E* 296), and walking had the advantage of being as inexpensive as possible. The anonymous author of *The Mirror of the Graces* wrote in 1811 that, to be beautiful, a woman must exercise outdoors and recommended the "morning, about two or three hours after sun-rise," as "the most salubrious time for a vigorous walk." A number of Austen's characters take her advice and walk in the morning, either just before or just after breakfast (*S&S* 83; *P&P* 32–36; *E* 293; *P* 102, 104).

Jane Austen herself was an avid walker and had great respect for anyone who could keep up with her. In 1801, she was impressed with the stout walking pace of her companion, a Mrs. Chamberlayne:

> in climbing a hill Mrs Chamberlayne is very capital; I could with difficulty keep pace with her—yet would not flinch for the World.—on plain ground I was quite her equal—and so we posted away under a fine hot sun, She without any parasol or any shade to her hat, stopping for nothing, & crossing the Church Yard at Weston with as much expedition as if we were afraid of being buried alive.—After seeing what she is equal to, I cannot help feeling a regard for her.

Many of Austen's most admirable characters, such as Elizabeth Bennet (*P&P* 36) and Anne Elliot (*P* 174, 176), are likewise enthusiastic walkers (*Sand, MW* 416; *NA* 174; *P&P* 257); many of her less admirable characters, such as Mary Musgrove (*P* 83), are not (*Col Let*, *MW* 159; *P&P* 365).*

Walking was also customary after morning church services on Sundays (*MP* 401), when whole families would stroll around the streets together. In Bath the Royal Crescent was a favorite spot for this activity (*NA* 35, 68, 97, 100–102), while Portsmouth had its ramparts (*MP* 408) and Lyme its Cobb (*P* 108). Some towns, such as Dawlish, had a specially built promenade for afternoon walks, such as the fictional "Terrace" at Sanditon (*Sand*, *MW* 395). In seaside resorts and spas, walking was a way of getting outside the limits of the town and finding attractive views (*P* 183). Sidmouth, in 1810, was said to have "very pleasant" walks. Southampton, too, had some lovely routes nearby; when Jane Austen lived there in the first decade of the nineteenth century, she often walked to Chiswell, a little less than two miles from town.

At country estates that had their own gardens, walks could be taken along level gravel paths. In parks (*P&P* 253–254; *MP* 15), which were more extensive, the ground was often more rolling, and the landscapes, if one walked far enough, were usually more varied. Walks in gardens (*F&E*, *MW* 5; *J&A*, *MW* 18; *Cath*, *MW* 230; *NA* 179, 240; *P&P* 156, 182, 195, 301, 351, 352–353; *MP* 322; *E* 196) afforded a certain measure of privacy that was not available in a house full of servants, and it is not surprising that Austen uses the intimacy and privacy of garden strolls for dramatic purposes. Many of her characters become engaged while walking in gardens or in the countryside; Elizabeth and Darcy come to an understanding while walking, as do Anne and Captain Wentworth, Henry Tilney and Catherine Morland, and Emma and Mr. Knightley. Charlotte Lucas contrives to be walking in order to be proposed to by Mr. Collins, an awkward, false arrangement that perfectly mirrors their marriage (*P&P* 121). Paintings, porcelain figurines, and popular prints, too, showed garden walks as occasions for conversation, flirtation, and informal socializing.

On long walks outdoors, young women were expected to take a companion (*NA* 114–115; *P&P* 36), male or female, to guard against a host of real and imagined dangers. Any outdoor walk also required the adoption of special clothing. Men were expected to wear hats out of doors (*NA* 177), while women wore bonnets (*NA* 177) that protected them to some extent from the sun. Walks in dirty town streets or on wet rural roads required the use of pattens, overshoes with a wide metal ring on each sole that slightly raised the walker's feet above the ground. On cooler days, a woman might wear a pelisse (a long coat—see *LS*, *MW* 276) or a spencer (a short, high-waisted coat). When Elizabeth Bennet goes "up stairs to get ready" for a long walk (*P&P* 375), she is probably finding her bonnet and perhaps one of these two types of outer garment.

*The system is not infallible, however; Mr. Collins (*P&P* 71) and Lady Denham (*Sand*, *MW* 390) are also good walkers. While formidable characters, they cannot really be said to be admirable.

However, not every day was suitable for an outdoor walk. When it was raining, or when recent rain had left the ground especially wet and muddy, walking was simply out of the question for those who wished to preserve their expensive clothing (*Watsons, MW* 345; *NA* 84, 85; *S&S* 40–41, 88; *P&P* 36, 88). It was also impossible to take long walks at night. Therefore, those who wished for exercise at such times walked indoors, walking up and down long galleries or round and round in drawing rooms after dinner (*Lesley, MW* 127; *NA* 33, 71, 134, 147; *P&P* 56).

Men had special duties when they walked with women. In town, it was their responsibility to keep the women from walking in puddles and filth (*E* 195) and to steer them toward the clearest and driest parts of the pavement. On long walks, men were expected to lend an arm to anyone who became tired (*NA* 87; *MP* 94; *P* 90, 169). (Good friends of either sex might also walk arm in arm—see *NA* 37; *P* 142.) Men were also expected to help women over stiles (*P&P* 32; *P* 86, 89, 109)—steps that allowed walkers to cross over fences without having to open and close a gate. They certainly were not expected to march on ahead without bothering to see whether they were leaving their female companions behind, as does the boorish Mr. Price (*MP* 403).

West Indies

The casual reader of Austen's works, and certainly the public that knows her novels primarily through movie versions, may wonder what on earth Jane Austen has to do with the West Indies at all. Her books and their settings are so thoroughly English and confined moreover to a few counties within England, that it seems bizarre to traipse so far afield. Why not talk about her relationship to Russia, too? Or Japan? Yet the careful reader finds numerous references to the West Indies (*MP* 197, 236), references that would have meant a great deal more to Austen's audience than they do to most readers today. In short, the West Indies meant sugar, profit (*Sand, MW* 392), danger, slavery, and war, and everyone in England knew it.

In capital letters, boldface, and italics, the West Indies meant sugar, a commodity that had meant relatively little to the English in 1700. By 1800, however, it was a dietary staple, consumed not only in confections but also—indeed, principally—in tea. Tea with sugar, an eccentric delicacy at the beginning of the eighteenth century, was by its close considered so essential that in 1792 the inability to buy it constituted the definition of poverty in some parishes. In 1700, the average Briton consumed four pounds of sugar per year; a hundred years later, that figure had more than quadrupled, to eighteen pounds.

Almost all of Europe's sugar (e.g., in the 1780s, almost 90 percent) came from the Caribbean, and adaptations to European dependence on West Indian sugar had been made on both sides of the Atlantic. In Britain, the "West India Interest" in Parliament, composed of planters residing in Britain, investors in sugar plantations, sugar processors, slave traders, and their allies, made certain that favorable legislation remained intact and that Parliament was duly apprised of all the difficulties and expenses entailed in the production of sugar. British magnates, attracted by occasional, but spectacular returns, of 10 percent a year, almost double what they could make in more conservative investments, funneled enormous sums into the island colonies. It took approximately £30,000 to set up a medium-sized plantation, and with such sums involved, it is not surprising that Britons soon had more money invested in the West Indies than in any other overseas region.

The British also made sizable commitments of manpower. Although whites were consistently vastly outnumbered by blacks in the islands, a steady stream of ambitious men continued to flow toward the colonies. Not all worked as planters; in fact, very few of the white settlers owned large estates. The rest were managers and foremen on the estates, lawyers, doctors, ministers, sailors, soldiers, merchants, clerks, and craftsmen. The sailors in particular were of value to the nation as a whole. Their experience on large merchant vessels was utilized when they were impressed into naval service during war; though the navy also drew heavily on sailors in the coastal coal trade and the East India trade, sailors in the West India trade constituted perhaps an eighth of all men afloat and were thus an important element of national defense.

In the Caribbean, planters grew sugar to the near-exclusion of every other crop, focusing so exclusively on the profitable commodity that they had to import almost everything else: shoes, clothes, timber, livestock, and food. British islands tended to plant sugar more exclusively than French islands; by 1770, for example, sugar and its by-products constituted 93 percent of the exports of Barbados (*Cath*, *MW* 205), and this was a typical figure. The cycle of the year—agricultural, naval, mercantile—revolved around the weather and the sugar crop. As sugar was labor-intensive to plant, harvest, and process, and as white labor was not plentiful or cheap enough to fill the need, a ravenous demand for slaves required its own set of adjustments. This need for African slaves would make itself felt in the politics of the islands, the rise of the Evangelical movement in England, and even in the novels of Jane Austen.

The typical late-eighteenth-century sugar estate, according to Jamaican planter Bryan Edwards, was about 900 acres, of which about 300 would be planted with sugarcane, with the remaining 600 devoted to fallow fields, pasturage for livestock, and timberland for the enormous amounts of wood needed to fuel the sugar refining fires. On some estates, additional crops such as tobacco, coffee, cocoa, or ginger might be grown in smaller quantities. Amid these fields stood the house of the planter or his steward, the houses of other whites who lived on the plantation, the ramshackle dwellings of slaves, the slaves' gardens, livestock pens, mills for cane grinding, and factory buildings for boiling and barreling the sugar. The mills were run by water power whenever a suitable stream was present and by wind or muscle power if no running water was nearby; steam power was still a rarity in the islands.

There were two seasons in the West Indies: the wet season (also known as "the sickly season" because during these months disease-bearing parasites bred rapidly in the damp lowlands) from May or June through December or January, and the dry season. Cane cultivation followed these seasons, and different tasks were assigned to each. During the wet season, slaves wielding hoes dug large square holes, about five or six inches deep and five feet on a side, and set cane tops in them to propagate, filling in the holes over time with mold, soil, and the animal dung that was the eighteenth century's principal fertilizer. Slaves, mostly women, carried the dung into the fields in baskets, since the cane holes prevented the approach of carts. For a few weeks, until the canes filled in the fields, the slaves pulled weeds and thinned, separated, and redistributed the new canes. Meanwhile, new holes were being dug and new cane tops planted and fertilized, so that when harvest came, not all the cane would become ripe at once.

Beginning in about January, the canes planted eighteen months before were ready for harvest. The planting season was hard, but harvest was backbreaking, often lethal work, made all the more urgent by cane's tendency to spoil in the fields if it was not cut at exactly the right time or to ferment if it was not milled within twenty-four hours of the harvest. The slaves moved through the fields at top speed with sharp machetes, cutting the canes and removing the leaves, then chopping the cane into sections about a meter long and fashioning them into thick, heavy bundles to be carted or carried to the mills. Every part of the cane served a purpose. What was not boiled and refined became *megasse*, or cane trash, and was used as fuel. Even the stubble left in the ground after harvest was not useless. It regrew into new canes in a process called ratooning; this regrowth was less sweet than new cane, but it was much less labor-intensive to grow and took less time to ripen, and fields might be rationed for as long as twenty years.

At the mill, the cane was ground between rollers, yielding a juice that was piped to the boiling-house. Slaves worked furiously to stoke the boiling-house fires with wood and *megasse* as the juice passed to smaller and smaller copper pans, over hotter and hotter fires that raised the already hot Caribbean air temperature to 120°F. Some slaves were assigned to add lime to the boiling liquid as a catalyst; others skimmed off dross; still others became expert in knowing when the sugar syrup was ready, testing the extract by stretching it between finger and thumb. The syrup was poured into hogsheads or troughs with perforated bottoms, where it cooled and crystallized, while the surplus liquid—molasses—dripped out the holes and was collected and returned to the boiling-house. The sugar that remained in the barrels, called *muscovado* (from the Portuguese for "less finished") sugar, was shipped to Europe for further refining; planters coveted land with beach access, so that the barrels could simply be rolled downhill to the waiting ships.

This was often the end of the line for the English colonial refining process, but some planters took the next step of making "clayed" sugar. They packed the *muscovado* into cone-shaped clay molds and drained away even more moisture. Once the sugar had been packed and shipped, the leftovers were used to make two types of liquor: *garapa* or *grappe,* a cheap, caustic beverage made of the fermented skimmings of the boiling-house; and rum, made from fermented molasses. The former was drunk by the poor and by slaves, the latter by rich colonists and by the Americans and Europeans to whom it was exported.

The stereotypical West Indian magnate of Austen's day was an absentee planter, living the good life in England and educating his children at the best English schools (*Sand* 387), or, less commonly, a resident planter who sent his spoiled and wealthy children back to England for their schooling. The "Miss Lambe" of *Sanditon* is a characteristic literary creation, as motherless West Indian schoolgirls show up with some regularity in the novels and plays of the time and seem to have been a standard "type," along with the indolent, sexually available West Indian wife and the callous, bullying West Indian husband. In practice, it actually was customary to send the scions of wealthy island families back to England to school, so much so that a *History of Jamaica* (1774) complained,

> It has long been the custom for every father here, who has acquired a little property, to send his children, of whatever complexion, to Britain, for education. They go like a bale of dry goods, consigned to some factor, who places them at the school where he himself was bred, or any other that his inclination leads him to prefer. The father, in the meanwhile, sends remittance upon remittance, or directs a liberal allowance, that his son may learn the art of squandering from his very infancy; and, not infrequently, to gratify a little pride of heart, that little master may appear the redoubted heir to an affluent fortune.

The author of the history despised the practice, which he said taught the children only to waste money and "to renounce their native place, their parents, and friends." Meanwhile, their labor was lost to their homeland, and they learned little at school that could help them to make a living in the colonies.

Though the problem seemed an epidemic to the author of the *History*, in truth, there were fewer such planters and planters' offspring as time went on. The wealthy families tended to buy up the holdings of failed planters, yielding larger, richer plantations. The island of Nevis had 100 plantations in 1719, fewer than 36 in 1819, two years after Austen's death. In 1775, Jamaica, the largest British sugar producer at that time, had 19,000 white residents, 193,000 slaves, 40,000 tons per year of sugar exports, and only 775 plantations. It bucked the trend of consolidation, but, even so, the number of estates had risen to only 859 by 1806. The Sir Thomases of England may have cut a large figure, but there were relatively few of them, and the stereotype tended to obscure the fact that many people made indirect fortunes from the West Indies. Some of these lived in the West Indian colonies, but many had never set foot on a Caribbean island, or visited only in passing.

Among the latter were many of the sugar refiners, who set up shop primarily in London or Bristol. Later in the eighteenth century, Liverpool and Glasgow began refining sugar as well. Restrictive laws penalized planters who exported clayed sugar, leaving greater profit for domestic refiners, who reheated the *muscovado*; added clarifying agents such as egg whites, vinegar, or cattle blood; skimmed and reboiled the remainder; and cooled and crystallized the now-white sugar. (France was less strict about allowing planters to export clayed sugar, with the result that French islands produced more molasses, which they sold to American rum distillers; Parliament's 1764 attempt to eliminate this trade was one of the many causes of the Revolutionary War.) Huge fortunes were made in the domestic sugar trade; planter John Pinney came home from the islands in 1783 with £70,000, went into the sugar business, and died in 1818 with £340,000. His type, perhaps, is the model for Mrs. Elton's father in *Emma*:

> a Bristol—merchant, of course, he must be called; but, as the whole of the profits of his mercantile life appeared as very moderate, it was not unfair to guess the dignity of his line of trade had been very moderate also. (*E* 183)

Mrs. Elton's revered brother-in-law Mr. Suckling also appears to be a Bristol nouveau riche and is perhaps another sugar baron. It is possible that both these gentlemen dealt in slaves rather than, or in addition to, sugar; it would explain Austen's reticence about the source of their wealth. However, if she had wanted to make them slavers and to identify their line of trade unquestionably in her readers' minds, she would have placed their home in Liverpool, which was by her day the world's largest slave-trade port. In any case, sugar-trading and slave-trading were only one degree removed from each other, as no plantation of any size operated without slaves. Mrs. Elton herself seems to confirm that her brother-in-law is involved in either one or the other when she takes a perceived "fling at the slave-trade" as an insult to Mr. Suckling and insists that he "was always rather a friend to the abolition" (*E* 300).

Others made their fortunes off West Indian sugar, too, besides the 180 refiners in London and the twenty in Bristol. There were chocolatiers, manufacturers of import goods for the islands, and weavers whose cheap cotton goods went to Africa to purchase new shiploads of slaves. There were agents and attorneys who handled the affairs of planters, receiving a commission of about 6 percent. (It may be in this capacity that Mrs. Price offers her ten-year-old son William to Sir Thomas, wondering if "there was any chance of his being useful to Sir Thomas in the concerns of his West Indian property" [*MP* 5].) Of course, there were the captains and crews of the slave ships, who plied their way across the ocean on a three-legged journey, carrying trade goods to Africa, slaves from Africa to the West Indies, and West Indian sugar and rum back to Europe. When Sir Thomas returns unexpectedly early to Mansfield Park, he does so by sailing straight to Liverpool "in a private vessel" (*MP* 178), perhaps an innocent merchantman filled with *muscovado*—or perhaps a slave ship on the third leg of the triangular trade.

Still another category of ambitious man made his fortune not through trade with the West Indies, but by the defense of that region. Eighteenth- and early-nineteenth-century Britain was an aggressively and exuberantly commercial realm, delighted with anything that promised personal gain. During the wars with France at the turn of the nineteenth century, soldiers and sailors willing to brave the hazards of West Indian service could profit handsomely from success. Captain Josias Rogers of the frigate *Quebec* had made a tidy sum and bought a country estate after the Revolutionary War, but he lost half his money when his banker failed. To his worried friends, he quipped, "Cheer up, I'll go to sea and get more," and he did, capturing ten prizes worth an estimated £10,000 in the first five weeks of 1794. Lieutenant General Sir Charles Grey and Vice Admiral Sir John Jervis, who led the 1793–1794 campaign in the West Indies and conquered several islands, demanded to be reimbursed not only for the ammunition and enemy ships they had captured but also for the value of the French estates, towns, and even entire islands that they had conquered. Their planned extortion of huge sums from St. Lucia and Martinique, in combination with their illegal establishment of their own prize court to adjudicate the awards and their overeager seizure of neutral American ships, galled even a generally sympathetic British public and delayed the granting of peerages to both men, but Jervis still cleared over £11,000 from the expedition, and Grey made over £26,000. Captain Robert Otway, an especially fortunate sailor, took 200 prizes worth £50,000 in just six years. For the military men who served in the West Indies, like Jane Austen's own brother Francis, there was always the hope that a captured shipment of French sugar would yield a huge payoff.

However, the West Indies were synonymous with risk as well as with sugar and wealth. Weather, war, and disease were constant threats to both personal profit and national defense. The summer hurricane season interrupted commercial shipping and paralyzed Caribbean fleets in their ports. Reinforcements and fleets of conquest were often delayed until the preferred sailing month of September, which allowed them to arrive in November after the worst periods of storm and epidemic had passed.

War with France, almost a constant during Jane Austen's lifetime, interrupted sugar shipments to Europe and shipments of essential goods to the islands. In part, this was the result of blockades and the harrying of enemy commerce; in part, it was a result of actual conquest of islands or ports. Both French and British islands tended to be sparsely defended and sporadically reinforced, which made their riches all the more tempting to military planners. As a result, colonies passed back and forth between French and British hands throughout the French Revolutionary and Napoleonic Wars. In 1793–1794, for example, the Grey-Jervis expedition cut a stunning swath through the Caribbean, taking Martinique, St. Lucia, Guadeloupe, and Port-au-Prince, but many of these victories dissipated the following year when the French sent an opposing force across the Atlantic. If we choose to focus on the reversals of ownership of just one island, St. Lucia was conquered by the British in 1762, returned to the French in 1763, retaken in 1778 and ceded back to France in 1783, retaken in 1794, seized by the French in 1795, conquered by the British again in 1796, returned to France in 1802, taken yet again by the British when hostilities resumed in 1803, and yielded permanently to British control in 1814.

In these conflicts, the British had the advantage of generally superior naval forces and more numerous Caribbean naval bases, while the French had another sort of weapon: emancipation. The egalitarian designs of the Republic appealed to slaves and to free blacks, and French agents worked hard to stimulate revolutionary impulses on British and British-occupied islands. Defense of the West Indies was a constant distraction, draining men and money away from the fight against Napoleon in Europe, but the government could not bring itself to abandon its Caribbean possessions; too much money was at stake. In fact, British leaders stated that they feared more to see an enemy force of 10,000 to 15,000 men off Jamaica than in Ireland or even England itself.

Conquest by France was an abhorrent thought to English planters, but the interruption of trade could be a mixed blessing. True, it made life uncomfortable on the islands, but many planters lived in Britain, and, true, it made one's revenue stream fairly erratic, but there were compensations as the scarcity of supply drove up the price of sugar. The years 1791 to 1815, coinciding with most of Austen's adult life, saw record high prices for sugar on the London market. (Unfortunately for the planters, the English began to tire of this vulnerability in the system, and Asian sources of cane were found, while beet sugar, which could be cultivated in Europe, became an alternate source of sweetening; after Austen's death, West Indian sugar prices and profits would plummet.) In times of peace, with stores of previously unshippable sugar flooding the market, prices would drop precipitously.

The West Indian trade, therefore, was always a risky business, especially for the men who traveled there to conduct business. Sea travel was always associated with a certain level of danger from storms, shipboard fires, and disease; in wartime there was the additional concern that the ship might be captured by the enemy. Once in the islands, planters and their employees faced slave rebellions, deadly tropical diseases, and the omnipresent threat of invasion. This last was no idle worry, for while invading armies left the precious sugar fields intact, they were becoming increasingly brutal to the conquered aristocracy. French and British alike slaughtered captives, including, in some cases, patients in military hospitals and at least one colonial governor. Residents and troops were shot, hanged, deported, guillotined, robbed, and terrorized. No wonder that, in *Mansfield Park*, when Sir Thomas is abroad in Antigua (*MP* 107, 177, 251), or in transit across the Atlantic, Edmund is so galled by the staging of theatrical festivities, or Mrs. Norris is so convinced that news of Sir Thomas' death will reach them any day. Travel anywhere outside England was perilous in wartime, travel to the West Indies especially so (*MP* 34).

None of the dangers of the islands terrified Europeans more than disease. Illness decimated armies and navies, slaughtered newly arrived slaves, ravaged port towns, and casually ended the lives of thousands who hoped to repair their shattered fortunes with sugar wealth. In 1794, as part of their spectacular expedition of conquest, Grey and Jervis left Martinique for Port-au-Prince with 518 men. Of these, 120 had to be left at Jamaica because they were too sick to fight, and another 108 died and were buried at sea. In the expedition as a whole, casualty rates were similarly daunting. Disease and battle reduced their army of 9,750 (on February 1, 1794) to barely more than 3,000 ten months later. In the years 1793 to 1801, Michael Duffy has estimated that between 64,250 and 69,250 troops were killed in the Caribbean, either by French enemies or by microbial ones, and panicked contemporary estimates ran still higher. Statistics like these led old soldiers to call the West Indies "the grave of the British army." Wave after wave of troops would be sent to the region, only to fall victim to one disease or another as soon as "the sickly season" arrived.

On the ships across the Atlantic, sailors and soldiers fell victim to scurvy, a debilitating illness caused by vitamin C deficiency, and to typhus, a louse-borne disease characterized by high fever, rash, muscle pain, headache, cough, and delirium. In the tropical heat, the lice died, and typhus abated, but it was replaced by equally deadly sicknesses. Crowded military camps with their poor hygiene bred enteric (typhoid) fever and dysentery, spread by direct contamination of food and water, or indirect contamination by the swarms of flies that buzzed from cesspit to mess and back again. Another danger that lurked in the camp was the *Aedes aegypti* mosquito,

The Torrid Zone. Or, Blessings of Jamaica, A. J., 1803. The British view of the Caribbean colonies is iconically summed up. A panting and rum-soaked angel gazes down upon a series of indolent figures, beneath whose feet lurk hellish creatures and symbols of death. The central and most fearsome figure is the personification of Yellow Fever as a flaming skeleton holding an hourglass. Courtesy of the Lewis Walpole Library, Yale University. 803.10.1.3+.

which bred in the water barrels and cisterns from which the men drank. The result was yellow fever, so called because one of its symptoms was jaundice; another of its common symptoms gave it the hideous nickname "black vomit." Breeding not in drinking water but in the marshes, *Anopheles* mosquitoes carried malaria, which attacked the red blood cells and caused fever, chills, weakness, and headache, among other symptoms. It could either linger as a debilitating chronic condition or kill suddenly by damaging the lungs, kidneys, and brain. In some cases, an apparently well man would sink rapidly into fever, convulsions, coma, and death.

The effect on the troops of such fatalities was demoralizing. There was a perpetual shortage of men willing to serve as officers in such conditions, and the rank and file deserted in droves—or attempted to do so—when told where they were bound. The army had to resort to drastic expedients, such as armed patrols around troops preparing to embark, substantial rewards for the apprehension of deserters, and even placing the embarkation points on islands to prevent flight. Some men, it appears, were so terrified of the West Indies that they mutilated themselves; there is circumstantial evidence that some of them, somehow, induced leg sores that statutorially barred them from service overseas.

Those who could not escape and who managed to survive the really deadly diseases, were still subject to a host of commonplace discomforts. Britons were not used to tropical heat, and soldiers laboring heavily in thick wool coats in the Caribbean midday sun were, unsurprisingly, stricken by a host of heat-related disorders from heatstroke to rashes. Miserable and frightened, they resorted to huge quantities of cheap rum, patent medicines, and a devout avoidance of the military hospitals, which they viewed as death traps.

The Austen family had many reasons to be familiar with the diseases of the West Indies, but one of these was more poignant than the rest. Jane's only sister, Cassandra, was engaged to a young clergyman named Tom Fowle, a former pupil of their father's. Fowle was dependent on his cousin Lord Craven for future preferment within the church and had hopes of a valuable living in Shropshire that was within Craven's gift. Although he already had a small rectory—also a gift from his cousin—Fowle chose to abide by his patron's wishes and serve as chaplain with Lord Craven's regiment in the West Indies. In February 1797, he was stricken by yellow fever and buried at sea.

If the numbers of European deaths in the West Indies were impressive, the numbers of African deaths were staggering. Britain, by far the leading transporter of slaves, exported an estimated 576,967 Africans between 1771 and 1790, most of whom ended up somewhere in the West Indies. In the first three years of "seasoning," or exposure to the lethal potpourri of Caribbean diseases, 15 to 20 percent of the slaves died. Hard work, poor diet, and illness kept fertility low, and for two centuries of West Indian slavery, from about 1600 to 1800, deaths outpaced births. A steady supply of new slaves was therefore required. Each pound of sugar sent to Europe had required twenty pounds of raw cane to produce; each mid-sized plantation of 900 acres required about 250 slaves to make it run. Each slave worked a sixteen- to eighteen-hour day during harvest, and the mills and boiling houses ran day and night. The appetite of the plantations for slaves was even more ravenous than the appetite of Britons for their sugar at teatime. Every time the "tea things" are produced in Jane Austen's works, and every time Sir Thomas worries about his Antigua holdings in *Mansfield Park* (*MP* 24, 30), the labor of slaves is in the background.

A newly arrived slave was generally put into the care of a "Creole negro"—a native-born or assimilated and "seasoned" slave, who served as a kind of mentor, teaching the new arrival his duties and enough English to get by. The mentoring duty was eagerly sought, for the host got, according to Sir William Young, who toured the Windward Islands in

1791–1792, "a knife, a calabash to eat from, and an iron boiling pot for each" guest slave. More significantly, the host got the benefit of the guest's labor in the host's personal garden plot.

Once the slave survived his initial battles with disease, depression, and displacement, he was put to work in one of several "gangs." The sugar gangs, who worked the hardest and had the least liberty, labored in the fields, digging holes, planting cane, dunging, harvesting, milling, and boiling. They were supervised by whip-wielding slave drivers who were themselves usually slaves. Discipline was harsh; John Gabriel Stedman, writing of slavery in Surinam in the 1770s, described how the plantation overseer would bring forth slaves before their owner for punishment:

[H]aving made his bows at several yards distance, [the overseer] with the most profound respect informs his Greatness what work was done the day before; what negroes deserted, died, fell sick, recovered, were bought or born; and, above all things, which of them neglected their work, affected sickness, or had been drunk or absent; the prisoners are generally present, being secured by the negro-drivers, and instantly tied up to the beams of the piazza, or a tree, without so much as being heard in their own defence; when the flogging begins, with men, women, or children, without exception.

Robert Renny, in his 1807 *History of Jamaica*, estimated that about a third of the adult male and female slaves were part of these sugar gangs. The gangs, bearing their tools and their breakfast, were summoned to the fields before sunrise by the blowing of a conch-shell horn and worked until 8:00 or 9:00 A.M., "when they sit down in the shade to breakfast, which has been in the meantime prepared by a certain number of women, whose sole employment is to cook. This meal consists of boiled yams, eddoes, ocra, calalue, and plantains, or as many of these vegetables as can be easily procured; and the whole when seasoned with salt, and cayenne pepper, is a very agreeable and wholesome breakfast." Work resumed until noon, when there was a two-hour lunch break, and continued until sunset. Renny thought that the typical workday, except in harvesttime, was about ten hours.

The second gang, as described by Renny, was "composed of young boys and girls, pregnant females, and convalescents, who are chiefly employed in weeding the canes, and other light work," and the third was made up of "young children, attended by a careful old woman, who are employed in collecting green-meat for the pigs and sheep, or in weeding the garden." A favored few were given more specialized and skilled tasks; these were trained as domestic servants, carpenters, coopers, masons, bricklayers, spinners, weavers, merchants, cooks, bakers, tailors, hairdressers, entertainers, silversmiths, and cigar makers. Many of these skilled slaves lived not on plantations but in the larger towns, where they often had lighter workloads and more personal freedom than plantation slaves. The chief difference between their labor was that between "ganging"—in which all slaves worked the same hours at the same task—and "tasking," in which the slave had a set amount of labor to complete each day, setting his own pace. As the years passed, more and more island industries and crops shifted from ganged to tasked labor, chiefly because tasked slaves lived longer.

After their work hours were over, slaves returned to their quarters, usually tiny two-room straw and mud huts thatched with grass, cane, or palmetto. Beds and other furniture were not provided, so slaves slept on the ground. Similarly, little food was provided by the masters; slaves were expected to tend small garden plots and raise livestock to feed themselves, though on islands where sugar land was at a premium, the masters might forgo this requirement and import corn and beans for their slaves. The slave diet was monotonous and protein-poor: rice, corn, bean, or millet gruels; root vegetables such as yams and potatoes; greens; fruit; and the occasional bit of pork, chicken, salt beef, or salt fish. Laws required masters to clothe their slaves once a year, but there was a great deal of latitude in how they satisfied this condition. Some handed over actual clothing, while others simply provided bolts of cloth and insisted that the slaves sew their own clothes. In practice, the slaves were nearly naked as they worked in the fields, and shoes, even for slaves who lived in towns, were almost unheard of. The predominant sentiment was that slaves should provide for their own food, clothing, and housing, with as little assistance from the white planters as possible.

Each island was its own miniature nation, and each passed its own laws concerning the treatment of slaves. Jamaica, for example, passed a "Consolidated Slave law" in 1784, regulating punishment, food, clothing, and length of workdays for slaves, and prohibiting the separation of slave families by sale. Further legislation in 1787 mandated the provision of garden plots, the conversion of slaves to Christianity, and the 5:00 A.M. to 7:00 P.M. workday with its half-hour breakfast and two-hour lunch. It also banned the practice of discarding slaves when they became too old or sick to work but simultaneously banned certain types of slave gatherings and imposed a sentence of death or life at hard labor for a slave who struck a white person. The problem with slave laws on all the islands was that they were hard to enforce. For example, a law on Barbados forbade punishments of more than thirty-nine lashes. One planter, whose behavior was reported to the abolitionist William Wilberforce, evaded the law by simply applying thirty-nine lashes, then thirty-nine more, then thirty-nine more, until an entire night had passed in flogging one African girl.

Another hardship of the slave's life and one that was much satirized in prints and popular literature was the sexual predation of masters and their overseers. The West Indian schoolgirl of *Sanditon* is the result of such a coupling; as Elaine Jordan points out, her name, "Miss Lambe" (*Sand,*

MW 421), is meant to evoke images of lambs' wool—that is, curly hair. The will of one Duncan Campbell, dated August 19, 1811, gives ample proof of the liberties that masters allowed themselves. He left bequests as follows:

> [U]nto each of my quadroon reputed daughters Mary Ann Campbell and Christiana Campbell £100, unto my reputed quadroon son Duncan Campbell £200 and each of my three reputed mulatto daughters by Esther, belonging to Retrieve Estate Old Works, named Susanna Campbell, Jane Campbell and Ann Campbell £100, and unto my reputed mulatto son William Campbell by the same mother £300; and the last named 4 mulatto children I will shall be immediately manumised.

English audiences were morbidly fascinated by the idea of sex with black women. Londoners flocked to see the "Hottentot Venus," an African woman exhibited "as if naked," first while she was alive, and then even after her death. An 1808 print entitled *Johnny Newcome in Love in the West Indies* shows, in its first panel, a fragile-looking white man in a red coat and tall hat becoming smitten by an enormous black woman, easily three times his mass, with pendulous, torpedo-shaped breasts. He wins her affection and makes her "Queen of the Harem"; that he has his pick of his slaves is made evident by the four other women, two light-skinned and two dark, watching his courtship of his new love. In the penultimate panel, he bids farewell to his large family as he prepares to return to England for a visit, and in the last panel, nine of his biracial offspring are exhibited so that the viewer can peruse their features and their names, typical of the classical and quasi-classical monikers that masters chose for their property: "Cuffy Cato Newcome," "Caesar Cudjoe Newcome," "Aristides Juba Newcome," and so forth. The tone of the print is satirical—look at the silly white man "going native"—but also prurient, peeking lasciviously at the open, available, fleshy, physically powerful but legally helpless black woman.

Images such as this one had once dominated the English view of slavery, but during Jane Austen's lifetime, a revolution in public attitudes took place. A procession of enlightened thinkers from both the Anglican and the Dissenting churches declared themselves in favor of abolition: writer Samuel Johnson, Methodist founder John Wesley, economist Adam Smith, activists Thomas Clarkson and Granville Sharp, parliamentarian and Evangelical William Wilberforce, Austen's favorite poet William Cowper, and potter Josiah Wedgwood, whose medallion of a kneeling slave, with the legend, "Am I not a man and a brother?" became the movement's defining image, a powerful counterweight to Johnny Newcome and his mulatto children.

A much-lauded court ruling in the 1770s was widely (though erroneously) perceived as outlawing slavery in Britain itself, but the slave trade

The Abolition of the Slave Trade, Isaac Cruikshank, 1792. Toward the end of the eighteenth century popular attitudes shifted against slavery, or at least the British trade in slaves. Abolishing slavery altogether was a trickier proposition, as it endangered the profitability of the British sugar colonies. Courtesy of the Lewis Walpole Library, Yale University. 792.4.10.3.

(*MP* 198) continued unabated in the colonies. In response, Quakers presented the first antislavery petition to Parliament in 1783. On May 22, 1787, Granville Sharp and some like-minded colleagues founded the Society for the Abolition of the Slave Trade, better known as the Abolition Committee. Petitioning campaigns garnered increasing enthusiasm throughout the 1780s; one 1788 drive resulted in two-thirds of Manchester's men affirming their abolitionist sympathies. Over 100 towns in all sent petitions to Parliament in favor of ending the slave trade. Another campaign in 1792 resulted in 500 petitions, and Parliament acted to end the trade in four years, only to go back on its word.

The abolitionists refused to give up. "We are all guilty," Wilberforce told the Commons in 1789, and many Britons agreed with him. Some, like the writer Anna Maria Barbauld, began boycotting sugar because of the obvious link between sugar and slavery; Cowper, drawing the same connection, subtitled his abolitionist poem "The Negro's Complaint" "A Subject for Conversation at the Tea-table." If one is to judge from a contemporary print, however, many tea-drinkers were unenthusiastic about a boycott of their favorite luxury. The print shows John Bull and his snaggle-toothed wife enjoying a sugarless cup of tea, Bull exulting, "O delicious! delicious!" while his wife exhorts her bevy of reluctant and resentful daughters to

> Taste it! you can't think how nice it is without Sugar;—and then consider how much Work you'll save the poor Blackeemoors by leaving off the use of it!—and above all remember how much expence it will save your poor Papa!

Boycotts of rum were organized as well, though these, like the sugar boycotts, were mocked. Visits to morally threatened areas were another abolitionist tactic. Thomas Clarkson, whose many admirers included Jane Austen, visited the cities most deeply involved in the slave trade, among them Liverpool and Bristol, receiving death threats and in one case barely avoiding an assassination attempt.

He was not the only abolitionist to be publicly targeted. The unmarried Wilberforce was accused of having a black wife—in other words, of being a kind of Johnny Newcome, in thrall to the mysterious and dangerous sexuality of black women, and therefore unreasonable and vaguely un-English. Yet Wilberforce refused to be silenced. Year after year he proposed abolition in Parliament, only to be voted down, until finally the measure passed in 1807. Effective as of January 1, 1808, it abolished only the trade in slaves, not the ownership of them. A stronger law in 1811 upped the penalty for violations from a fine to transportation for as many as fourteen years. Full emancipation would not be granted until 1833.

One reason that abolition and emancipation took as long as they did to enact was that slave rebellions, a relatively frequent occurrence in the Caribbean, terrified Europeans and convinced them that freeing the slaves would be tantamount to a death sentence for the islands' heavily outnumbered whites. In Jamaica, for example, in 1791, according to Bryan Edwards, there were 30,000 whites and 250,000 blacks. Edwards cited similarly disproportionate numbers for other British islands, including Barbados (16,167/62,115), Dominica (1,236/14,967), and Sir Thomas' Antigua (2,590/37,808). Though slaves more commonly fought back against their masters by means of theft, sabotage, or suicide, rebellions (or plots of rebellion) occurred with some regularity. During Austen's lifetime, there were nearly twenty major uprisings involving hundreds of slaves, with a few (Dominica, 1785–1790; Grenada, 1795; Martinique, 1789–1792; St. Lucia, 1795–1796; St. Vincent, 1795–1796) that involved thousands. Jamaica, with its semi-independent community of escaped slaves, had the most rebellions in the eighteenth century, involving the most participants, with the most damage to property. The most widespread rebellions occurred in 1795, when the French used the promise of immediate emancipation to spur slaves in British-held islands to violence.

Mansfield Park, which is of all the Austen's novels the one most directly connected with West India trade, is presumed to be set in the years

1808 and 1809, when the abolition of the slave trade was a subject of great interest. Roger Sales points out that in these years, Antigua was deeply affected by France's efforts to cut England off from its colonies and from trade with the Continent and that the extension of Sir Thomas' visit to Antigua (*MP* 38) may be connected with the necessity of confronting—as all the planters were forced to do—the end of legal slave importation. The drying up of the slave trade meant that planters had to take better care of the ones already on site, and laws and customs changed accordingly, becoming somewhat more humane. (Warren Roberts, however, sets Sir Thomas' trip in 1805 to 1807, a similarly turbulent time, when rebellions were rife throughout the West Indies and sugar prices dropped alarmingly, causing the bankruptcy of the Antiguan government in 1805 and the failure of a great many sugar estates in the succeeding two years.)

The Austen family, like many gentry families, had many ties of family and acquaintanceship to the West Indies (in addition to Cassandra's unfortunate fiancé Tom Fowle). Several Austen cousins, including the Hampsons, the Walters, and the Leigh-Perrots, had West Indian investments (*P* 210, 251), as did Austen friends the Holders, the Beckfords, and the Wildmans. One of George Austen's college friends, James Langston Nibbs, owned an Antigua plantation (of which George Austen was a trustee), and, like Sir Thomas, took his spendthrift son James with him to Antigua to knock some sense into him (*MP* 32, 51). Like Johnny Newcome and Duncan Campbell, James Nibbs the elder had availed himself of his female slaves; one wonders if Sir Thomas did likewise. Nibbs' story ends tragically, however; both his white son, James Nibbs the younger, and his slave son, Christopher Nibbs, died in Antigua.

The Austens had ties to the West Indies by marriage as well. Jane's aunt Leigh-Perrot was Barbadian by birth, and Jane's brother James married the daughter of a Dominican planter. The youngest Austen, Charles, married first one daughter and then the other of the attorney-general of Bermuda.

Charles, like his older brother Francis and, for that matter, like William Price (*MP* 236), Frederick Wentworth (*P* 65), and Admiral Croft (*P* 70), entered the Caribbean on naval service. Francis sailed there in company with Nelson shortly before the Battle of Trafalgar, returning in 1806 to distinguish himself in the Battle of San Domingo as flag-captain of the *Canopus*. Charles, after being promoted to commander in 1804, spent six and a half years on the American side of the Atlantic, some of it as an enforcer of the ban on slave trading. Both brothers were to return to the West Indies after Jane's death—Charles in 1826 to continue his work against slavery, Francis in 1844, at the age of seventy-one, as commander in chief of the North American and West India Station. Because of her brothers, other relatives, friends, and in-laws; because of the national interest in the West Indies, sugar wealth, and tropical perils; and because of her sympathy with the abolitionist movement and its heroes, Jane Austen was acutely aware of conditions in the Caribbean.

Widow

The widow (*H&E, MW* 36; *Mount, MW* 41; *Cass, MW* 46; *LS, MW* 247; *E* 163; *P* 11) was often an object of charity in Austen's time, for women could make far less money than men and, in the case of gentry widows, were not permitted to work at all without loss of caste (*E* 275–276). Even the impoverished invalid Mrs. Smith (*P* 152–153) works not for her own keep but in order to offer charity to others. Widowhood almost always meant a loss of income, as the oldest son inherited the bulk of a family's estate. The widow received a jointure (*J&A, MW* 13; *Sand, MW* 401; *S&S* 36, 226; *MP* 123)— customarily, but not always, a third of the estate—which was agreed upon at the time of the marriage. This might be ample for some women, but for others, a fraction of their previous income was simply not sufficient for their needs. The case of widows of the clergy, such as *Emma*'s Mrs. Bates (*E* 21) and Austen's own mother, was even more perilous. If the husband had not managed to save a substantial sum, or if he had no independent property of his own, his widow could be left virtually penniless. Once the husband was gone, so, too, was his "living"—the income he derived from tithes and church land—and the widow could be left with little or nothing. In Mrs. Austen's case, it took voluntary contributions from most of her sons to give her enough to live on, as her own property was quite small.

Wealthy widows (*H&E, MW* 35; *Watsons, MW* 352; *Sand, MW* 375, 400; *S&S* 36, 228; *MP* 202–203), however, were in a unique position that many of them quite relished. For the first time, they were free from the oversight of a man, be he father or husband, and they could make their own legal and financial decisions. These basic rights were denied to married women, whose legal identity was subsumed in their husbands', but widows had control over their own lives and property. No doubt many declined to remarry because they had truly loved their first husbands, but others, one suspects, knew that remarriage would deprive them of their legal freedom. Others hastened to remarry, out of love, financial necessity, or fear of conducting their own business; such motives were understood, but a certain degree of disapproval attached to a widow who remarried (*LS, MW* 299; *S&S* 47; *P* 5). Remarriage by widowers (*E* 96) was viewed far less harshly. *See also* Death.

Witch

Belief in witches (*NA* 49) was widespread in England in the seventeenth century, fed by the superstitions of prominent people (including King James

I), by popular folklore and entertainment, and by purportedly serious books on the subject. However, trials of witches were never as common in England as they were on the Continent, and by the late seventeenth century the furor had mostly died out; the last execution for witchcraft in England took place in Exeter in 1685, whereas the last execution in Germany took place in 1775, and the last execution in Poland happened as late as 1793. The English in the Enlightenment were far more skeptical of belief in witches than their forebears had been, which is not to say that they were not superstitious. They engaged in all sorts of quasi-magical practices designed to thwart bad luck and attract good. But they were beginning to turn their spirit of scientific inquiry toward their own practices, questioning the purposes and origins of such behavior. Numerous letters to the popular *Gentleman's Magazine* from Austen's lifetime are inquiries to fellow readers along the lines of, "The people in the village of——do this odd, traditional thing on Easter, or at the full moon, or the day after Christmas; can anyone tell me where this comes from?" In other words, the English were turning an anthropological eye on their own customs.

They no longer attributed bad luck or disease to witchcraft, and if isolated instances of belief in witches could be found, such theories would be ridiculed by the educated. In one letter to the *Gentleman's Magazine*, for example, an unfortunate duck was believed by a maidservant to be a witch. She tortured the duck to death in an oven, hoping to exorcise its evil, but the reaction of her neighbors was not to thank her for ridding them of a witch but to chastise her so severely for her cruelty that, at the time the letter was written, she was believed to be near death from fits brought on by guilt and fear. The servant's story does serve as a reminder that isolated belief in witches still persisted. Methodist leader John Wesley, for example, was one of those who thought that witchcraft was real, but such believers were remnants of an older time, and they did not dominate the intellectual world in which Austen moved.

Wolsey

Cardinal Thomas Wolsey (c. 1475–1530) was a favorite of Henry VIII. The eloquent son of a butcher, he became a trusted counselor and rose, in 1515, to lord chancellor, a position he was to hold for fourteen years. The principal architect of Henry's divorce from his first wife, Catherine of Aragon, he failed to secure permission for the divorce from Rome and was supplanted in his post by Sir Thomas More and in Henry's trust by the more effective Thomas Cromwell. Wolsey's fall thereafter was swift. His arrogance and greed had earned him many enemies at court, and his life did not long outlast his king's favor. Ousted from his post in 1529, he was summoned to be tried for high treason in 1530, and he died at Leicester Abbey on his way to answer the charges.

Writing

Elegant handwriting (*S&S* 328; *P&P* 47, 116; *E* 297–298, 305) was prized in Austen's day, not only by the gentry and nobility but by the mercantile class as well. It was taught (*NA* 14) by tutors or specialized writing masters (*E* 297), by books that provided model styles of penmanship to copy, and at boarding schools; Charles Austen, the youngest of Jane's siblings, studied it at the Portsmouth Naval Academy, where he showed "industry" and "improvement" in his writing

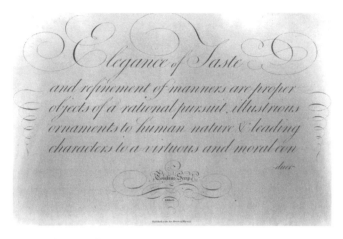

A sample page from Thomas Tomkins' handwriting manual, *The Beauties of Writing Exemplified* (1808). Library of Congress.

from 1792 to 1794. In earlier ages, he might have been learning how to ornament every line of his writing with elaborate, fanciful flourishes; in the late years of the eighteenth century, however, he would have learned a more practical, streamlined handwriting, so as to become, in the words of one handwriting book's title, a "Useful Penman." For the most part, English handwriting was clear and legible, with few Baroque flourishes, though some handwriting models emphasize the difference between thin and thick strokes so much that the writing becomes hard to read. The "coarse and modern characters" (*NA* 172) read by Catherine Morland are probably discernible as modern because they lack complex flourishes of an antique "hand."

In order to write (*NA* 105; *P&P* 238, 304; *MP* 59, 64, 73, 296–297, 362) a letter, a bill of lading, a letter of credit, or any other document, the writer needed several supplies (*MP* 16, 307; *P* 229): pen, ink, paper, a tool for blotting, a penknife, and wax or wafers. Pens were usually made of goose quills, and they were shaped and mended with small penknives. The penknife could also be used in some instances to scrape mistakes off the paper. The ink was typically an iron-gall ink, composed of ground and steeped gall nuts (also called "oak apples") and copperas (hydrated ferrous sulfate, also known as "green vitriol"). Gum arabic was added to make the ink smoother, and water to make it thinner. Additional ingredients might be added to intensify the blackness of the ink.

Some people made their own ink at home, but it could also be bought from itinerant ink sellers or from apothecaries. Once purchased, the ink needed to be stored carefully to prevent it from drying out or growing moldy. It could be kept in its original bottle or transferred to an inkwell or inkstand. Inkwells might be made of stone, lead, or ceramic and were typ-

Inkwells and quill pens.

ically squat and heavy-bottomed to minimize the chance of spills. Inkstands had an inkwell plus other features, such as holes in which to prop quills.

Once a document was written, it frequently needed to be blotted (*P&P* 48) to remove excess ink. There were two ways to do this. One was by placing a sheet of absorbent paper, called blotting paper, over the inked page; this method grew increasingly popular after 1800. Another method was to use a sander, a container looking much like a salt shaker but with a convex lid, filled sometimes with chalk but more commonly with sand. The sand was shaken onto the page, where it wicked excess ink upward, increasing the surface area and speeding drying. The sand was then poured back from the page into the sander to be used again. Some writing sets also had a pounce container; pounce was a gum resin that decreased the absorbency of writing paper.

Paper (*P&P* 382; *E* 76) was made primarily from cotton or linen rags, frequently by hand. The rags were dusted, sorted by quality to be made into either good or coarse brown paper, washed, chopped up, and laid in piles to rot. The mass of fermented cotton was then washed and pounded, sometimes by large hammers driven by a waterwheel, sometimes by a machine called a "Hollander" that had a huge bladed roller. Mixed in tubs with warm water, the fibrous mass, called stock or stuff, waited for a papermaker to dip his mold, a rectangular screen in a wooden frame with an insert called a deckle. In a "laid" mold, fine wires ran perpendicular to a few heavier wires, and there might also be a piece of wire twisted into a design identifying the type or size of paper and the manufacturer. In a "wove" mold, fine wires were woven together to create a fabriclike network of perpendicular lines; here, too, there might be a wire design identifying the paper. As the stock settled in the mold, the wire created thinner areas that show up in handmade paper as fine lines and as a watermark that is easily visible when the paper is held up to the light. The papermaker shook the fibers in the mold to interlock them, then handed it to an assistant, who turned the wet sheet of paper onto felt. Felt and paper were alternated until a large stack—usually 144 sheets—had been assembled, and then the entire stack was placed into a press and squeezed until it was merely damp. This job took about six men to accomplish; then the sheets of paper were removed from the felt by another assistant and pressed again. Small groups of pages were then draped over ropes to dry further, after which paper intended for writing (*S&S* 287, 328, 372; *P&P* 309; *MP* 16, 415; *P* 241) would be dipped in a material called size* to keep it from absorbing too much ink. Sized paper would be dried again and then polished. Really fine writing paper would also be "hot pressed" (*P&P* 116), pressed between glazed boards and hot sheets of metal to smooth the surface. Finally, the paper was stacked in quires (24 sheets) and reams (240), folded in half like a greeting card, and wrapped for sale, in gray paper with the mill's label on it.

Paper was sometimes treated in other ways. Chlorine, discovered in 1774, was being used for whitening paper by the early 1790s. China clay was added in some cases to whiten paper or to increase its weight. From the 1770s, lined paper was produced, and manufacturers began making embossed paper in 1796.

Demand for all types of paper was steadily increasing, as literacy improved and newspapers became more popular. By 1800, Britain's 400 paper mills could no longer find enough cotton and linen rags at home and were importing about £200,000 worth of rags every year from other countries. Consumers were urged to save their rags to conserve this valuable resource. Desperate attempts were made to find another source of paper pulp, and experiments were made with various plants, straw, and wood. However, though wood had been suggested by the French as a possible source of paper pulp as early as 1719, it was not in wide use during Austen's lifetime.

Inventors also tried to find improved ways of turning the pulp or stuff into paper. The invention of the steam engine had inspired many creative thinkers to devise ways of applying its power, and it was only a matter of time before steam was harnessed for making paper. A steam engine was first employed at a paper mill in about 1786, and in 1803 a paper-making machine was invented. Vast improvements in productivity followed. A papermaker and his staff could create about 50 to 60 pounds of paper a day; a machine could make as much as 1,000 pounds, although the paper still needed to be hung up to dry in the old-fashioned way, on ropes.[†] John Dickinson of Hertfordshire invented a woven-wire cylinder that continuously rotated through a vat of stuff, but the most significant development in the industry during Austen's lifetime was the invention, in 1810, of the Fourdrinier machine.

Developed by two brothers, Henry and Sealy Fourdrinier, who owned a stationery firm in London, the machine used a wove-patterned belt, rather than a cylinder, to distribute the stuff. It created long rolls of unwatermarked paper and quickly became standard equipment in any mill large enough to afford its steep price. Commercial use of the Fourdrinier

---

*Typically made of starch or gelatin.
†This problem would not be solved until 1820, when Thomas Bonsor Crompton patented a heat-drying machine.

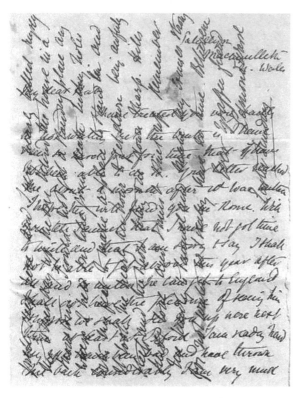

"Crossed" letter. Courtesy of Eunice and Ron Shanahan.

machine began in 1812, and its appearance, like that of many new machines designed to replace human labor, was greeted by riots.

Because paper was sold already folded in half, it became customary to write letters (*H&E, MW* 34; *L&F, MW* 76–109; *Col Let, MW* 164; *Sand, MW* 385, 394; *NA* 27, 139, 201, 203, 235, 250; *S&S* 63, 173, 202, 259; *P&P* 47–48, 51, 61, 177, 281, 292, 295, 296, 346, 361–363; *MP* 50, 107, 108, 114, 232, 425, 437; *E* 51, 96, 119, 379; *P* 50, 148–149, 162) as if the folded paper were a little, four-page book (*P&P* 383). The writer began on the first page, then opened the sheet and continued to write on pages 2 and 3, and might possibly write a little on page 4 as well, though an important blank space was left on this page. If the writer had more to say and wished to save the cost of posting a second sheet of paper (*MP* 429), she might turn her paper 90 degrees and "cross" her writing, making a new series of lines at right angles to the first, and intersecting her original lines to make a kind of woven or checkerboard pattern (*E* 157). Once all of the space had been used twice, the lack of additional room ended the letter, whether the writer wanted to conclude or not (*S&S* 278). The letter was finished with a formulaic compliment or statement of humility, such as, "I am, very sincerely, your must humble servant, Kirstin Olsen." Since almost all letters ended in a similar fashion (*P&P* 325), Austen frequently omits the compliments and writes "&c." (*F&E, MW* 28), but real correspondents in her time did not sign their letters, "Your's, &c." or "I am, &c." (*S&S* 278; *P&P* 149). They wrote out the whole phrase.

When the letter was finished, it was folded with the blank space on the fourth page on the outside (*NA* 14; *P&P* 63, 205; *MP* 435; *E* 266, 453). The address, or "direction" (*NA* 216, 228; *S&S* 134; *P&P* 273), was written here, and, if the letter was being sent through the post, it was stamped or franked in the same area. On the other side, the letter was sealed (*P* 236) either with wax or with a wafer. Wax was melted on the outside of the letter, over the fold, and might be stamped as it cooled with a signet ring or stamp to identify the sender and inhibit tampering; it is this sort of "seal" that John Dashwood seeks to buy for his wife in *Sense and Sensibility* (222). Sealing wax was usually red, although black wax was customary in mourning. It was melted either in a spoonlike melter that was held over a lamp or by directly melting the end of the wax stick and dripping the wax onto the paper. The latter method was messier and less thorough; it could take several rounds of melting to get enough wax in the right place.

Wafers, on the other hand, went underneath the fold. They were made of flour, water, gum, possibly gelatin, and some type of coloring—red for everyday and black for mourning, though some were made in light blue, and Austen herself, in 1799, mentions receiving a letter sealed with a yellow one. Wafers were moistened and applied to the underside of one flap and the top of the other; they were sold in boxes that each had a sample wafer glued to the outside. Inkstands sometimes contained a special compartment to hold wafers.

Austen sometimes refers to envelopes (*P&P* 116), though these are not the premanufactured, pregummed envelopes of today. The envelope was merely another sheet of paper, wrapped and folded around the letter and sealed, as an ordinary letter would be, with either wax or a wafer. Few people would pay the extra postage to receive a blank sheet of paper, so an envelope in this sense was generally reserved for messages carried by servants from one house to another. When a letter was sent through the post, the "envelope" was simply the name given to the outer portion of the letter when folded, the portion that was addressed and sealed.

With all the equipment that writing required, it was easiest to do it sitting down at a comfortable desk or table (*P&P* 305). However, there were writing sets for travelers, with small quantities of the requisite supplies packed in a compact box or an angled tabletop writing "desk" (*NA* 155). Portable writing desks provided both a writing surface and storage for supplies.

Rules of etiquette governed the sending and receiving of letters. Anxious parents, for example, forbade their daughters to engage in correspondence with men other than relatives, husbands, or fiancés (*NA* 250; *S&S* 80, 134, 172). The sending of letters might also be governed by class; novelist Fanny Burney, who had served in the royal household, had to get permission from Queen Charlotte before embarking on a correspondence with one of the princesses. The reading of letters, too, was subject to the rules of politeness; if one received a letter while in company, it could not be read silently before the others unless the recipient was invited to do so (*Watsons, MW* 338). Finally, letters might or might not be intended to be read aloud, and it was usually the recipient who had the final say over what might be shown to others (*Sand, MW* 386; *P* 204). *See also* Pen; Pencil; Post.

Z

Zephyr

Like most of the classical allusions of the Juvenilia, the reference to "the Eastern Zephyr" (*L&F*, *MW* 98) is not meant to be taken seriously. While it is possible that Austen means "Zephyr" purely in the sense of a generic wind or breeze, it is more likely that she is having a little fun at her character's expense. The Austen family, who served as the main audience for the Juvenilia, was extremely well read and would have spotted the speaker's mistake at once. Zephyr is not the east wind in Greek mythology; the east wind was Eurus. Zephyr was the west wind. What seems to most readers now, if they notice it at all, to be a trifling substitution of one minor mythological character for another would have been, to the Austens, an example of laughable ignorance.

Timeline

Year	The Austens	Political/Military	Religious/Cultural	Medical, Technological, Scientific
1731	George Austen born			
1739	Cassandra Leigh born			
1743				Astronomer Edmond Halley (b. 1656) dies
1747	George Austen receives the Tonbridge Fellowship at St. John's, Oxford			
1749				Benjamin Franklin discovers that lightning is a form of electricity
1753	George Austen becomes a deacon at St. John's College, Oxford			
1756				Carbon dioxide discovered
1760	George Austen, Jane's father, takes orders	George III inherits the throne		
1761	November: George Austen acquires the Steventon living from Thomas Knight (the elder), but continues to reside at Oxford			Kaspar Faber establishes a pencil manufacturing facility in Germany
				Surveyors George Dixon and Charles Mason travel to the Cape of Good Hope to observe the transit of Venus and to extensively survey the area
1763				Surveyors George Dixon and Charles Mason survey the Pennsylvania-Maryland border (the Mason-Dixon line)

Year	Austen Family	Historical & Social Events	Literature & Arts	Science & Technology
1764	April 26: George Austen marries Cassandra Leigh in Bath's Walcot Church. Late April: George Austen takes up his duties as rector of Steventon	Franking Act withdraws the franking privilege from some	Horace Walpole publishes *The Castle of Otranto*	
1765	Mr. and Mrs. Austen's first child, James Austen, born	Act permits towns to set up their own Penny Posts; postage for shorter distances reduced; Penny Post weight restricted to four ounces. HMS *Victory* is launched	James Fordyce, *Sermons to Young Women*	John Harrison wins prize for clock accurate enough to be used in calculating longitude at sea
1766	The Austens' second child, George, is born; handicapped in some way, he will live out his life in the care of another family		John Spilsbury, London engraver and mapmaker, makes first English wooden puzzle map of Europe (*MP* 18)	Joseph Priestley discovers the law of inverse squares, which states that the attraction or repulsion between two electric charges is inversely proportional to the square of the distances between them
1767				Joseph Priestley, *History and Present State of Electricity*
1768	Edward Austen (later Edward Knight) born	Bath acquires the first royally patented theater in the provinces. Sheffield plate begins appearing in shops		Captain James Cook's first voyage begins
1769		August 15: Napoleon Bonaparte born		James Watt patents his steam engine. Richard Arkwright patents his "water frame," a machine-driven spinning process

Year	The Austens	Political/Military	Religious/Cultural	Medical, Technological, Scientific
1770		Act of Parliament imposes six-month imprisonment for nighttime poaching		Bedlam stops its popular practice of admitting tourists to gape at, and make fun of, the mentally ill
1771	Henry Austen born; the Austens move from Deane to the rectory at Steventon		The New (or Upper) Rooms open in Bath	Surgeon John Hunter publishes *The Natural History of the Human Teeth*
1772	Cassandra Austen born			Cook's second voyage begins
1773	A relative, Francis Austen, buys the living of Deane for George Austen	London's Penny Post established		
1774	Francis (Frank) Austen born			Chlorine discovered
				Parliament orders regulation of private madhouses
1775	December 16: Jane born at Steventon		Banks are forbidden to issue notes with a face value of less than £1	Birmingham's Lunar Society, famous scientific and engineering club, founded
			Bath's Royal Crescent is completed	
1776		American Declaration of Independence	David Garrick retires as the manager of the Drury Lane theater, London; the new managers are Richard Brinsley Sheridan and his father-in-law, Thomas Linley, a Bath music teacher	Cook's third voyage begins
			Adam Smith publishes *The Wealth of Nations*	

1777

George Austen's sister, Philadelphia Hancock, and her daughter, Eliza Hancock, travel to Paris, where they are received at Versailles

Lord North imposes a tax on the hiring of male servants

John Howard, *The State of the Prisons in England and Wales*

The Trent and Mersey canal opens

1778

The French seize the Caribbean colony of Dominica

December: The British successfully defend St. Lucia against French attack

The King's Theatre, Haymarket, London's Italian opera house, is sold to Richard Brinsley Sheridan, manager of the Drury Lane theater, and Thomas Harris, manager of Covent Garden; the theater is remodeled during this year at a cost of £4,000

Two famous horse races are founded. The St. Leger stakes, first run in 1776, acquires its new name from one of its organizers, General Anthony St. Leger. The other, the Oaks at Epsom, named for an inn owned by the twelfth earl of Derby, is planned in this year and first run in 1779

Fanny Burney, *Evelina*

Jean-Jacques Rousseau dies

Marylebone Gardens closes

Spode opens a London showroom

John Hunter publishes *A Practical Treatise on the Diseases of the Teeth*

Water closet patented by Joseph Bramah

Year	The Austens	Political/Military	Religious/Cultural	Medical, Technological, Scientific
1779	June: Charles Austen born	Summer: The French seize St. Vincent and Grenada from the British	Goethe's *Sorrows of Young Werther* is translated into English London's first Sunday newspaper, the *British Gazette and Sunday Monitor*, begins publication	Astronomer William Herschel completes a survey of all stars visible (at that time) down to the fourth magnitude The basic principles of photosynthesis are discovered Samuel Crompton invents successful spinning machine, known as a "mule"
1780	July: James matriculates at St. John's College, Oxford	Postmasters lose their monopoly on renting post-horses June 1–2: Gordon Riots: London mobs attack the Catholic district of Moorfields, Newgate Prison, and the Bank of England; troops defend the bank and the adjacent church of St. Christopher-le-Stocks June 9: Anti-Catholic mob burns the Catholic chapel in Bath	The Epsom Derby is first run; a contest for three-year-old racehorses, it is unusually short (only a mile, expanded to a mile and a half in 1784)	England's first steel writing pens produced
1781	George Austen's niece Eliza Hancock marries the comte de Feuillide	Franking Act February: The British take Dutch colonies of Sint Eustatius, Saba, Sint Maarten, Saint-Barthélemy May: The French conquer the British colony of Tobago	Peter Beckford, *Thoughts on Hunting in a Series of Familiar Letters to a Friend*	Manchester Literary and Philosophical Society, noted scientific club, founded March 13: Astronomer William Herschel discovers the planet Uranus, at first believing it to be a comet

Year	Austen's Life	Historical Events	Theatre and Culture	Science
1782		November: The French seize the Dutch colonies conquered by the British in February	The King's Theatre, Haymarket, is gutted and given a new stage and auditorium at a cost of between £8,000 and £10,000 Fanny Burney publishes *Cecilia*	Argand lamp invented Josiah Wedgwood invents a pyrometer for measuring kiln temperature
1783	Jane, Cassandra, and their cousin Jane Cooper at Mrs. Cawley's school in Oxford; after the school moves to Southampton, an epidemic breaks out, with Jane's life jeopardized; Jane's aunt Mrs. Cooper brings home her own daughter Jane and, in nursing her, catches the illness and dies	January: The French seize Saint Kitts, Montserrat, Nevis Britain captures Grenada from the French Treaty of Paris ends American Revolutionary War Hangings moved from Tyburn to Newgate	The Kings' Theatre, Haymarket, declares bankruptcy Prince regent's first visit to Brighton	Antoine Lavoisier uses a guinea pig to prove that animals breathe in oxygen and breathe out carbon dioxide Joseph and Etienne Montgolfier launch the first unmanned balloon
1784	Jane and Cassandra return home from school after the epidemic	Tea and Window Act reduces the total excise and duty on tea from 119 percent of its value to 12 percent August 2: John Palmer's first mail coach leaves Bristol on its way to London	Duties on tea are reduced to 12.5 percent	John Richardson, *The Philosophical Principles of the Science of Brewing* Balloon ascent in London James Watt defines the unit of horsepower
1785	Jane begins attending the Abbey School in Reading, which she will attend until 1787	Taxes on keeping servants increase; employing maidservants is taxed for the first time	William Wilberforce joins the Evangelical movement Sunday School Union established	J. P. Blanchard and John Jeffries cross the English Channel in a balloon

Year	The Austens	Political/Military	Religious/Cultural	Medical, Technological, Scientific
1786	Edward Austen departs on the Grand Tour for two years Eliza de Feuillide visits England April: Francis leaves for the Portsmouth naval academy	Mail coaches exempted from toll charges December: The Prince of Wales secretly marries Maria Fitzherbert, a twice-widowed Catholic Cosmetics and hair powder are taxed		
1787	Eliza de Feuillide visits England and sets up a house in London	Transportation of convicted felons to Australia begins	1787: Royal Proclamation against Vice, followed by crackdowns on alehouses, etc.	
1788	Eliza de Feuillide visits England again Henry goes to Oxford Jane makes her first known visit to Kent December 23: Frank leaves the Portsmouth Naval Academy and signs on board the *Perseverance* (*J&A, MW* 12; *Harley, MW* 40) as a Volunteer	George III suffers a bout of madness that lasts for several months, precipitating the first Regency crisis	*London Times* established Proclamation Society established to help enforce king's proclamation against vice from the previous year Hannah More, *Thoughts on the Importance of the Manners of the Great*	William Bligh's voyage to Tahiti to export breadfruit to the West Indies; mutiny on the *Bounty* James Smith founds Linnaean Society, Britain's oldest natural history organization
1789	February 9: Frank sails from Spithead for India	George III recovers from his long bout of madness	Society for the Encouragement of Good Servants founded	William Herschel discovers a sixth moon of Saturn, Enceladus

Year				
	September 3: Frank arrives in Madras December: Frank, already aboard ship as a Volunteer, becomes a midshipman	French National Assembly established July 14: storming of the Bastille August 4: France's National Assembly abolishes aristocratic and clerical privileges November: All French church property is seized by the state	George III's first visit to Weymouth stimulates new interest in sea-bathing June 17: The King's Theatre, Haymarket, London's Italian opera house, burns down; its soprano Nancy Storace, the best comic soprano of the day, moves to Drury Lane, where her brother Stephen is a composer	Antoine Lavoisier, *An Elementary Treatise on Chemistry*
1790	James becomes a curate	June 19: Hereditary titles abolished in France November: Edmund Burke, *Reflections on the Revolution in France*		
1791	The comte de Feuillide joins the royalist insurgency against the French Revolution July: Charles leaves for the Portsmouth naval academy Summer: Edward travels to the Lake District with the Knights November: Francis follows his commanding officer, Commodore Cornwallis, from the *Perseverance* to the *Minerva* (38) December: Edward marries Elizabeth Bridges	Thomas Paine, *The Rights of Man* June: French royal family caught trying to leave the country. July 14: Joseph Priestley's house attacked because of his support for the French Revolution September: Emma (Lyon) Hart, one day to become paramour of Admiral Nelson, marries Sir William Hamilton	First public handicap race for more than two horses is the Oatlands Stakes at Ascot The new King's Theatre, Haymarket, is rebuilt; it will remain London's principal Italian opera house until the 1840s The Prince of Wales is forced to retire from active sponsorship in horse races after rumors of race-fixing June 4: The Drury Lane theater in London is condemned as unsafe, torn down, and	

Year	The Austens	Political/Military	Religious/Cultural	Medical, Technological, Scientific
			closed for almost three seasons	
1792	Francis becomes a lieutenant	Increasing violence in Paris makes the English apprehensive; a mob storms the Tuileries	Particular Baptist Missionary Society, first British society to convert the "heathen," founded	
	March: James marries Ann Mathew, daughter of General Mathew, owner of neighboring house of Laverstoke	Mary Wollstonecraft, *Vindication of the Rights of Woman*	January 14: London's Pantheon opera house burns down	
	August: Jane writes (or at least dedicates) *Catharine, or the Bower*	June: riot in London; the duke of Richmond fortifies the Tower and the bank		
	December 11: Jane's cousin Jane Cooper marries Lieutenant Thomas Williams (from Steventon, as both her parents are dead)	August: in Paris, executions of aristocrats and other "traitors" begin; Louis XVI is deposed		
		August 13: French royal family imprisoned		
		September: Maximilien Robespierre's Jacobins seize control of the French government		
		September 21: French monarchy abolished		
1793	Henry enlists in the Oxfordshire militia	Habeas corpus suspended, reinstated; a period of harsh crackdown on political dissent begins, in response to the French Revolution		France adopts the metric system
	According to Brian Southam, Jane composes *Lady Susan* in about this period			

	November 13: Frank returns to England, having taken passage in an East India Company ship; arrives Steventon November 14	Local Penny Posts open in Edinburgh, Manchester, Bristol, Birmingham January 21: Louis XVI executed February 1: France declares war on Britain May: Britain, led by Prime Minister Pitt, declares war on France August 23: France institutes military conscription October 16: Marie Antoinette executed	March 12: The rebuilt Drury Lane theater opens for oratorios; the full opening is on April 21
1794	Edward's adoptive father, Thomas Knight, dies; Edward inherits the Knight family properties of Godmersham and Chawton Jane and Cassandra visit Edward at Rowling February 22: The comte de Feuillide is guillotined March: Francis returns home from the East Indies and is posted into the *Lark* (16), which Roberts says is a thinly disguised version of William Price's *Thrush* (*MP* 299, 372, 380, 384)	Suspension of habeas corpus and acts limiting freedom of the press June 1: "The Glorious First of June," the first major naval engagement between the French and English in the wars resulting from the French Revolution; the English fleet's limited victory is greeted in England with wild enthusiasm July: Robespierre falls Britain invades Guadeloupe, Martinique, St. Lucia, Port-au-Prince; the French retake Guadeloupe, guillotine more than 1,200 planters	1794 to 1796: Erasmus Darwin publishes *Zoonomia*, early zoological text

Year	The Austens	Political/Military	Religious/Cultural	Medical, Technological, Scientific
1795	September 14: Charles joins the crew of the *Daedalus*	Habeas corpus suspended	London Missionary Society (LMS), interdenominational missionary society, established	
	According to some, begins first version of *Elinor and Marianne*, epistolary precursor of *S&S*	An act is passed limiting the formation of "combinations" (early labor unions)	Thomas Paine, *Age of Reason*	
	According to Austen family tradition, Jane composes *Lady Susan* at about this time	Franking Act lowers the maximum weight on franked letters to one ounce, limits their number to fifteen received and ten sent per day, and mandates that the user of the frank be within twenty miles of the sending or delivery point of the letters		
	May: James' first wife, Ann, dies; their two-year-old daughter Anna goes to live with Jane and Cassandra at Steventon			
	May to November: Lieutenant Francis Austen serves on four different ships in a failed search for a post as first lieutenant	The Prince of Wales, £630,000 in debt, agrees to marry his cousin, Caroline of Brunswick, in a deal with Parliament		
		January: anti-government rally at St. George's Fields, London November: Admiral James Gambier, a patron of Francis', becomes First Naval Lord		
1796	Jane and Henry visit Edward at Rowling		Matthew Lewis publishes *The Monk*	Joseph Priestley, *Considerations on the Doctrine of Phlogiston*
	January 8: Cassandra's fiancé Tom Fowle sails for the West Indies		Act of Parliament authorizes some bishoprics to raise curates' salaries to £75 per annum	

			Nicolas Dubois de Chémant, *A Dissertation on Artificial Teeth*
September: Frank is assigned to the frigate *Triton* (32)			
October: Jane begins *First Impressions* (forerunner of *P&P*), according to Cassandra			
1797	Henry promoted to captain	Matthew Boulton and James Watt begin producing copper pennies and twopences for the government, a departure from the traditional reliance on gold and silver coinage	Wilberforce's *Practical View of Christianity*, influential Evangelical text
	January: James marries Mary Lloyd	Serious naval mutinies at Spithead and the Nore	Thomas Malthus, *Essay on the Principle of Population*
	February: Cassandra's fiancé Tom Fowle dies of yellow fever and is buried at sea	February: The British invade Trinidad	
	May: News of Tom's death reaches Cassandra, who puts on full widow's weeds		
	August: Jane completes *First Impressions*, according to Cassandra; begins or revises *Elinor and Marianne*, epistolary first version of *S&S*		
	November 1: *First Impressions* offered to Cadell, Ann Radcliffe's publisher; rejected		
	November: Jane visits Bath with Cassandra and their mother		
	December: Henry marries Eliza, comtesse de Feuillide, at the Church of St. Marylebone		
	December: Charles is appointed a lieutenant in the *Scorpion*		

Year	The Austens	Political/Military	Religious/Cultural	Medical, Technological, Scientific
1798	Jane begins *Catherine* (later *NA*) Mr. Austen gives James his curacy of Deane, worth £50; stops taking pupils; gives up his carriage Edward's adoptive mother, Mrs. Knight, retires on an income of £2,000 a year and leaves Godmersham to Edward and his wife, Elizabeth February: Frank moves from the *Seahorse* to the *London* (98), as first lieutenant August: Lady Williams (former Jane Cooper) dies in carriage accident December: Jane reports that Frank is made a commander (posted into the sloop *Petrel* [16]); Charles is posted into the *Tamar*	Rome falls to Napoleon August: Nelson victorious in the Battle of the Nile	August Kotzebue's *Lovers' Vows*, adapted by Elizabeth Inchbald, debuts at London's Covent Garden; over the next decade it will also be performed at Drury Lane and at the Theatre Royal, Bath William Wordsworth and Samuel Taylor Coleridge publish *Lyrical Ballads*, sparking the Romantic movement in literature	Paper-making machine invented by Nicholas-Louis Robert (France); patented 1799 Astronomer Caroline Herschel revises John Flamsteed's star catalog
1799	Jane finishes *NA*, though she will revise it later Francis cruises in the Mediterranean Jane visits Ibthorpe and, with Mrs. Austen, possibly Mr. Austen, Edward and Elizabeth, and two of their children, visits Bath as well	Income tax introduced An act against combinations is passed; the London Corresponding Society and certain other groups critical of the government are banned October: Jacobins overthrown by Napoleon	Religious Tract Society established April 12: Society for Missions to Africa and the East (better known as the Church Missionary Society or CMS) established	

First effective production of wood-pulp paper, which will not become popular for many more years

Humphry Davy, *Researches, Chemical and Philosophical; Chiefly Concerning Nitrous Oxide . . . and Its Respiration*

The electric battery is invented by Alessandro Volta

Combination Act makes it a crime to unite for higher wages or better working conditions

August: Mrs. Leigh-Perrot accused of shoplifting in Bath

Charles serves near Algeciras as lieutenant on the *Endymion* (*MP* 380)

March: Francis, in *Peterel* (16), takes on, in his words, "a ship, brig (*La Ligurienne*), and xebecque, belonging to the French Republic; two of which, the ship and xebecque, I drove on shore, and, after a running action of about one hour and a half, . . . the third struck her colours"

March: Mrs. Leigh-Perrot acquitted in her trial for shoplifting

Summer: Francis with Sir Sydney's Smith's squadron off Alexandria

October: Francis promoted to post rank for the victory over *La Ligurienne*, becomes flag-captain to Admiral James Gambier in the *Neptune* (98)

November: Mr. and Mrs. Austen's decision to move to Bath is reported suddenly to Jane, who reportedly faints upon hearing the news

1800

Year	The Austens	Political/Military	Religious/Cultural	Medical, Technological, Scientific
1801	Henry Austen leaves the Oxfordshire militia May: Mr. and Mrs. Austen, Jane, and Cassandra move to Bath, settling at 4 Sydney Place	January 1: Political union of Britain and Ireland; some naval promotions are made as a result, but neither of Austen's brothers benefits. London postal prices raised; "Penny Post" becomes "Twopenny Post" Habeas corpus reinstated Royal Military College founded	John Overton, *The True Churchmen Ascertained*, which claims that only Evangelicals are true to the spirit of the English Reformation	The first asteroid discovery is made by Italian Giuseppe Piazzi (1746–1826) There are 2,191 steam engines in Great Britain
1802	At peace, Francis goes on half-pay The Austens visit Dawlish and possibly Teignmouth Jane accepts, then rejects, a proposal of marriage from Harris Bigg-Withers	Peace of Amiens The Marines become the Royal Marines, and uniforms are redesigned; in an effort to reduce the numbers of marines during the peace, many are discharged, especially those who are old, short, or foreign-born	Society for the Suppressing of Vice founded	
1803	At outbreak of war, Francis organizes "Sea Fencibles" The Austens visit Lyme Jane sells *Susan* (later *NA*) to Crosby for £10	War renewed with France Royal Navy adopts Sir Home Popham's Telegraphic Signals or Marine Vocabulary, devised in 1800, making it possible to signal commonly used words or phrases with a single flag Act of Parliament imposes death penalty for poachers who use guns in resisting arrest	Spode begins using the bat printing process Thomas Sheraton, *The Cabinet Directory*	Joseph Fox, dental surgeon at Guy's Hospital, publishes *Natural History of the Teeth*

1804

Charles promoted from lieutenant to commander; posted to America to interrupt trade between the United States and France, to search for British deserters on American ships, and to prevent traffic in slaves between the United States and the British West Indies

The Austens visit Lyme again with Henry and Eliza; Henry, Eliza, and Cassandra go on to Weymouth

The Austens move from 4 Sydney Place, Bath, to the cheaper and less fashionable Green Park Buildings

February: Francis meets his future first wife, Mary Gibson, in Ramsgate

May: Francis Austen appointed to the *Leopard* (50) as flag-captain to Rear Admiral Thomas Louis, begins duty on blockade of Napoleon's Boulogne fleet

October: Charles given command of the sloop *Indian*

November: A planned French invasion of England fails to materialize

May 18: Napoleon named emperor of the French

December: Napoleon crowned emperor in the presence of Pope Pius VII

British and Foreign Bible Society established

Philosopher Immanuel Kant (b. 1724) dies

Thomas Sheraton begins publishing *The Cabinet-Maker, Upholsterer and General Artist's Encyclopedia*, which will remain incomplete at his death in 1806

Chemist Joseph Priestley (b. 1733) dies

Richard Trevithick builds the world's first steam railway locomotive

Year	The Austens	Political/Military	Religious/Cultural	Medical, Technological, Scientific
1805	This year is the date found on the fair copy of *Lady Susan* Jane visits Godmersham and Goodnestone (home of Elizabeth Austen's mother) January: Mr. Austen dies April: Francis Austen in Mediterranean with Nelson's fleet April: Mrs. Lloyd dies; her daughter Martha Lloyd moves in with the Austen women May 11–June 4: Francis Austen sails 3,200 miles to the West Indies with Nelson's fleet June 15: Nelson's fleet starts back from the West Indies July 17: Nelson's fleet reaches Gibraltar August 30: Jane writes to Cassandra from Edward's house in Kent, obliquely mentioning troop movements intended to stop a French invasion September: Francis, with Nelson's fleet, blockades Cadiz October: Francis' ship *Canopus* (*MP* 378) sent back to Gibraltar with others to resupply; while he is gone, the French fleet comes out of	Russia allies with England against Napoleon May: Napoleon crowns himself king of Italy August: Austria joins the Anglo-Russian alliance Late August–early September: Napoleon appears ready to invade England	Ranelagh closes	

Cadiz, and he misses the Battle of Trafalgar (*Sand*, *MW* 380; *P* 21–22)

According to Roberts, Sir Thomas's fictional trip to Antigua (*MP*) begins in this year, as French blockades cause sugar prices to fall (Southam places William's promotion in 1813)

1806   This is the "year six" of *P* 63

Jane visits Warwick Castle, which had previously been described by William Gilpin in his tours in search of the "picturesque"

February 6: Francis Austen in battle of St. Domingo (*P* 26)

June: The Austen women move away from Bath for good, heading first for the resort town of Clifton

July: Francis marries Mary Gibson; the Austen women leave Bath and, after several months' visiting around the country, will move in, at the end of 1806, with Frank and Mary

July: Mrs. Austen's relative Mary Leigh of Stoneleigh dies; Stoneleigh goes to Reverend Thomas Leigh; as Mrs. Austen,

Minimum age to pass for lieutenant in the navy reduced from twenty to nineteen

February 6: In naval battle of St. Domingo, French squadron defeated by superior British force (*P* 26)

November 21: Napoleon orders Continental ports not to admit British ships

English fashion magazine *Belle Assemblée* begins publication

Year	The Austens	Political/Military	Religious/Cultural	Medical, Technological, Scientific
	Jane and Cassandra are visiting Thomas Leigh at Adlestrop Rectory at the time of his inheritance, they travel to Stoneleigh, staying until at least August; after leaving Stoneleigh, they travel to Hamstall Ridware to visit Mrs. Austen's nephew Edward Cooper Fall: The Austen women and Martha Lloyd move in with Francis and Mary Austen			
1807	Frank, Mary, Mrs. Austen, Jane, and Cassandra move into a house in Castle Square, Southampton Charles marries seventeen-year-old Fanny Palmer, daughter of the ex-attorney general of Bermuda According to Roberts, Sir Thomas returns from his fictional trip to Antigua in *MP* March: Francis posted to the *St. Albans* (64), where he will spend three and a half years accompanying merchant convoys to St. Helena, the Cape, and China	February 23: slave trade abolished March 6: five-day court-martial of Sir Home Popham begins	Thomas Hope, *Household Furniture and Interior Decoration*, popularizes classical-style furniture	

1808	Jane at Manydown for Twelfth Night, plays Mrs. Candour in amateur production of *The School for Scandal*	Legal battle between earl of Essex and his half brother Reverend William Capel results in decision that foxhunters must ask permission to follow fox across others' land and pay any damages	First English patent for steel writing pens.
	June: Jane visits Godmersham with James and his wife, Mary	Covent Garden theater burns and begins rebuilding	
	October 10: Elizabeth (Bridges) Austen dies after the birth of her eleventh child		
1809	Jane visits Godmersham	The *Quarterly Review* is first published	First cylinder-style paper machine, making paper in long rolls
	April: Jane writes to Crosby to inquire about their nonpublication of *Susan*; they offer to sell it back to her for the £10 they paid her in 1803, but apparently have no intention of publishing it themselves	London Society for Promoting Christianity among the Jews founded	
	April 2: The Austen women and Martha Lloyd spend their last night as residents of Southampton, though remodeling on Chawton Cottage will need to take place before they can move in	English fashion magazine *Repository of Arts, Literature, Manufactures, Fasion and Politics*, popularly known as Ackermann's Repository, begins publication	
	July: The Austen women and Martha Lloyd move to Chawton Cottage	Hannah More, *Coelebs in Search of a Wife*; Jane did not like the name of the hero or the theology of the author; "I do not like the Evangelicals," she commented	
		Drury Lane theater burns and begins rebuilding	
1810	September: Francis resigns his command of the *St. Albans* in the hope of spending more time at home		

Year	The Austens	Political/Military	Religious/Cultural	Medical, Technological, Scientific
	September: Charles takes command of the *Cleopatra* (*MP* 380)			
	December: Francis joins the *Caledonia* (120) as flag-captain to Admiral Gambier			
1811	February: Jane begins *MP*	Troops deployed to suppress Luddite activity in the midlands and north		
	April: Jane in London correcting *S&S* proofs and visiting Henry and Eliza at 64 Sloane St.	A new law makes slave trading a felony, increases penalty from a fine to transportation for up to fourteen years		
	July: Francis moves from the *Caledonia* (120) to the *Elephant* (74—see *MP* 380), where he will remain until May 1814	February 6: The Prince of Wales is sworn in as regent for the ailing George III		
	August: Charles returns home from 6½ years on the North American station with his wife and two children			
	October 31: publication of *S&S* announced in *Morning Chronicle*; the novel is published at Austen's own expense by T. Egerton			
	Earle Harwood, a possible model for *MP*'s Mr. Price, dies			
	November: Charles posted into the *Namur* as flag-captain to Admiral Sir Thomas Williams			

	Austen's Life	Historical Events	Literary Events	Science and Technology
1812	Edward Austen, honoring his adoptive parents, takes the surname "Knight"	Troops deployed to suppress Luddite activity in the midlands and north	Crabbe's *Tales* are published	Fourdrinier paper-making machine goes into production in England
	Jane interrupts work on *MP* to revise *P&P*, sells the copyright to *P&P* for £110	Napoleon retreats from Moscow		
	August: Francis, in the *Elephant*, sent to cruise off the Azores	August–December: British navy suffers humiliating defeats in battles with American ships in War of 1812		
	December 28: Francis, in the *Elephant*, takes a Boston privateer, the *Swordfish* (12)	Prince regent's powers are expanded		
1813	Jane visits Godmersham	East India Company loses its monopoly status; control of territory in India is transferred from the company to the crown		
	First and second editions of *P&P* published; second edition of *S&S*	Wellington's army gains control of most of Spain		
	Henry Austen becomes receiver-general of Oxfordshire	May: Severe deflation will cut wholesale prices by a third between now and December 1815		
	January 28: *P&P* is advertised in the *Morning Chronicle* for 18s.			
	April 25: Eliza (de Feuillide) Austen dies			
	June or shortly after: *MP* finished			
	November: Jane visits Elizabeth Bridges Austen's younger sister, Harriot Bridges Moore, and her husband, Reverend George Moore of Wrotham			

Year	The Austens	Political/Military	Religious/Cultural	Medical, Technological, Scientific
1814	*P* set in this year (*P* 8).	April 6: Napoleon abdicates; end of "The Long War" follows (*P* 17, 233)		Paper by astronomer William Herschel notes that large clusters of stars are more common in the plane of the Milky Way
	January 21: Jane begins writing *E*			First steam-driven newspaper press goes into operation
	April 8: news of Napoleon's abdication reaches Chawton	June 8: Admiralty announces new, higher peacetime pay scale		
	May: *MP* published by Egerton			
	May: Francis returns to England from duty in the Baltic			
	Autumn: first edition of *MP* sells out			
	September: Charles' wife, Fanny, dies in childbirth			
1815	March 29: Jane finishes writing *E*	Wars with France end; national debt at £860 million	Henry Ryder becomes first Evangelical bishop	Apothecaries' Act
	August: Jane begins writing *P*	Financial troubles lead to multiple bank collapses		
	October: Henry seriously ill, attended by Court physician Matthew Baillie; Jane nurses him through his illness	March: hostilities end in War of 1812		
	November 13: Jane, through Baillie connection, visits prince regent's Carlton House library by special invitation	March 1: Napoleon lands at Cannes with an army of 1,500 after escaping from Elba in February		
	December 21–23: publication of *E* announced in *Morning Chronicle*, but title page dated 1816	March 21: Admiralty suspends its demobilization efforts		
		June 18: Napoleon defeated at Waterloo (*Sand, MW* 380)		

Year		
1816	Strand Bridge, begun in 1811, renamed Waterloo Bridge by Act of Parliament	Second edition of *MP* (like *E*, printed not by Egerton but by John Murray)
		1,250 of the 2,000 printed copies of *E* are sold
		February: Charles' ship *Phoenix* (36), near Smyrna fighting piracy, is run aground by a pilot during a hurricane; a court-martial will clear Charles, but the incident will follow him throughout his career; it will take him ten years to get another ship
		March 16: Henry bankrupted
		May: Jane and Cassandra visit Cheltenham
		July 18: Jane completes *P*
1817	Bad harvest, high wheat prices	A third edition of *P&P* is published by Egerton
		Jane buys back the rights to the unpublished *Susan* from Crosby (RWC says 1816)
		January: Jane Austen begins writing *Sand*
		March: Austen abandons *Sand* due to ill health
		May: Jane travels to Winchester to be attended by Mr. Lyford, a medical man who it is hoped can help her

Year	The Austens	Political/Military	Religious/Cultural	Medical, Technological, Scientific
	July 18: Jane dies in Winchester			
	July 24: Jane is buried in Winchester Cathedral			
1818	*NA* and *P* published			
1819	James Austen dies			
1820	Charles Austen given a Coast Guard command	George III dies; the prince regent becomes George IV		
	August: Charles marries his late wife's older sister, Harriet			
1822				Astronomer William Herschel (b. 1738) dies
1823	July: Mary Austen, wife of Francis, dies			
1826	Charles Austen posted again to the West Indies, commanding the frigate *Aurora* (44)			
	Steventon Rectory torn down			
1827	Mrs. Austen dies			
	The Austens' handicapped second son, George, dies			
1828	Francis Austen marries Martha Lloyd, his second wife		Parliament repeals the Test and Corporation Acts, granting political rights to Dissenters	
	Charles Austen becomes flag-captain to Admiral Colpoys on the West Indies Station			

Year		
1829	Charles becomes flag-captain to Admiral Sir Edward Colpoys aboard the *Winchester* (52)	Emancipation Act grants political rights to Catholics; Jews still banned
1830	Charles invalided home after a fall from a mast Frank is made a rear admiral	
1833	Second edition of *E* printed	Slavery outlawed in all British dominions
1838	Charles becomes captain of the *Bellerophon* (80) June: Frank is made a vice admiral	
1840		Uniform postage rates introduced for the whole nation Franking abolished
1844	Francis Austen becomes commander of the North America and West Indies Station	
1845	Cassandra Austen dies Francis is given command of the North American and West Indies station	
1846	Charles becomes a rear admiral	
1848	Francis superseded as head of the American Station by Thomas Cochrane, a vice admiral and the earl of Dundonald Francis is made a full admiral	

Year	The Austens	Political/Military	Religious/Cultural	Medical, Technological, Scientific
1850	Henry Austen dies			
	January: Charles Austen becomes commander of the East Indies and China Station			
1852	Edward (Austen) Knight dies			
	April: Charles leads the British capture of Rangoon			
	October 7: Charles Austen dies			
1859			Vauxhall closes	
1863	Francis reaches the navy's highest rank, admiral of the fleet			
1865	August 10: Francis Austen dies; his daughter Fanny destroys many letters, including those from Jane			
1871	The first few pieces from the Juvenilia are published			
1872	Addition to Jane's memorial in Winchester Cathedral notes that she was "known to many by her writings"			

Bibliography

BEHAVIOR

Doddridge, P. *The Friendly Instructor; or, A Companion for Young Ladies and Gentlemen.* London: W. Baynes, 1807.

Gomme, George Laurence, ed. *The Gentleman's Magazine Library—Vol. 1: Manners and Customs.* 1883. Reprint. Detroit: Singing Tree Press, 1968.

Gregory, John. *A Father's Legacy to His Daughters.* 1773. Reprint. Boston: Joseph Bumstead, 1804.

Holmes, Richard. *Redcoat: The British Soldier in the Age of Horse and Musket.* New York: W. W. Norton and Company, 2001.

The Mirror of the Graces. 1811. Reprint. Mendocino, CA: R. L. Shep, 1997.

Montagu, Ashley. *The Anatomy of Swearing.* New York: Macmillan, 1967.

Southam, Brian. *Jane Austen and the Navy.* London: Hambledon and London, 2000.

BUSINESS, WORK, AND FINANCE

Adams, Samuel, and Sarah Adams. *The Complete Servant.* 1825. Reprint. Lewes, East Sussex: Southover Press, 1989.

Clark, Peter. *The English Alehouse: A Social History 1200–1830.* London: Longman, 1983.

Ellis, William. *The Country Housewife's Family Companion.* 1750. Reprint. Totnes, Devon: Prospect Books, 2000.

Fitzmaurice, Ronald Myles. *British Banks and Banking: A Pictorial History.* Truro, Cornwall: D. Bradford Barton, 1975.

Fussell, G. E., and K. R. Fussell. *The English Countryman: His Life and Work from Tudor Times to the Victorian Age.* 1955. Reprint. London: Orbis, 1981.

Haywood, Eliza. *A New Present for a Servant-Maid*. London: G. Pearch, 1771.

Hecht, J. Jean. *The Domestic Servant in Eighteenth-Century England*. 1956. Reprint. London: Routledge & Kegan Paul, 1980.

Hembry, Phyllis. *The English Spa 1560–1815: A Social History*. London: Athlone Press, 1990.

Hixson, William F. *Triumph of the Bankers: Money and Banking in the Eighteenth and Nineteenth Centuries*. Westport, CT: Praeger, 1993.

Kowaleski-Wallace, Elizabeth. *Consuming Subjects: Women, Shopping, and Business in the Eighteenth Century*. New York: Columbia University Press, 1997.

Langford, Paul. *A Polite and Commercial People: England 1727–1783*. 1989. Reprint. Oxford: Oxford University Press, 1992.

Langton, John, and R. J. Morris, eds. *Atlas of Industrializing Britain 1780–1914*. London: Methuen, 1986.

Monckton, H. A. *A History of the English Public House*. London: Bodley Head, 1969.

Mui, Hoh-Cheung, and Lorna H. Mui. *Shops and Shopkeeping in Eighteenth-Century England*. Montreal: McGill-Queen's University Press, 1989.

Plumb, J. H. *England in the Eighteenth Century*. 1950. Reprint. London: Penguin Books, 1990.

Porter, Roy. *English Society in the Eighteenth Century*. 1982. Reprint. New York: Penguin Books, 1990.

Richardson, A. E., and H. Donaldson Eberlein. *The English Inn, Past and Present: A Review of Its History and Social Life*. London: B. T. Batsford, 1925.

Seebohm, M. E. *The Evolution of the English Farm*. 1927. Reprint. London: George Allen & Unwin, 1952.

Sutherland, C.H.V. *English Coinage 600–1900*. London: B. T. Batsford, 1973.

Swift, Jonathan. *Directions to Servants*. 1731. Reprint. New York: Pantheon, 1964.

Virgin, Peter. *The Church in an Age of Negligence: Ecclesiastical Structure and Problems of Church Reform 1700–1840*. Cambridge: James Clarke & Co., 1989.

Woodforde, James. *Passages from the Five Volumes of the Diary of a Country Parson 1758–1802*, selected and edited by John Beresford. New York: Oxford University Press, 1935.

CLOTHING AND ACCESSORIES

Armstrong, Nancy. *A Collector's History of Fans*. New York: Clarkson N. Potter, 1974.

Black, J. Anderson. *A History of Jewelry*. New York: Park Lane, 1981.

Bruton, Eric. *Clocks and Watches 1400–1900*. London: Arthur Barker, 1967.

Buck, Anne. *Dress in Eighteenth-Century England*. New York: Holmes & Meier, 1979.

Bury, Shirley. *Jewellery 1789–1910: The International Era. Volume 1, 1789–1861*. Woodbridge, Suffolk: Antique Collectors' Club, 1991.

Byrde, Penelope. *Jane Austen Fashion: Fashion and Needlework in the Works of Jane Austen*. Ludlow: Excellent Press, 1999.

Corson, Richard. *Fashions in Eyeglasses*. London: Peter Owen, 1980.

———. *Fashions in Hair: The First Five Thousand Years*. 1965. Reprint with revised supplement. London: Peter Owen, 1984.

Crawford, Morris de Camp. *The Heritage of Cotton*. New York: Fairchild, 1948.

Crawford, T. S. *A History of the Umbrella*. Newton Abbot, Devon: David & Charles, 1970.

Cumming, Valerie. *Gloves*. New York: Drama Book Publishers, 1982.

Cunnington, C. Willett. *English Women's Clothing in the Nineteenth Century*. 1937. Reprint. New York: Dover, 1990.

Cunnington, C. Willett, and Phillis Cunnington. *The History of Underclothes*. 1951. Reprint. New York: Dover, 1992.

Cunnington, Phillis, and Catherine Lucas. *Costume for Births, Marriages and Deaths*. London: Adam and Charles Black, 1972.

Davidson, D. C., and R. J. S. MacGregor. *Spectacles, Lorgnettes and Monocles*. Princes Risborough, England: Shire, 2002.

De Marly, Diana. *Fashion for Men: An Illustrated History*. 1985. Reprint. London: B. T. Batsford, 1989.

Farrell, Jeremy. *Socks and Stockings*. London: B. T. Batsford, 1992.

———. *Umbrellas and Parasols*. London: B. T. Batsford, 1985.

Foster, Vanda. *Bags and Purses*. New York: Drama Book Publishers, 1982.

———. *A Visual History of Costume: The Nineteenth Century*. 1984. Reprint. London: B. T. Batsford, 1986.

Hart, Avril. *Ties*. New York: Costume and Fashion Press, 1998.

Hart, Avril, and Emma Taylor. *Fans*. New York: Costume and Fashion Press, 1998.

Mackrell, Alice. *Shawls, Stoles and Scarves*. London: B. T. Batsford, 1986.

The Mirror of the Graces. London: B. Crosby, 1811. Reprint. Mendocino, CA: R. L. Shep, 1997.

Pratt, Lucy, and Linda Woolley. *Shoes*. London: V&A Publications, 1999.

Ribeiro, Aileen. *The Art of Dress: Fashion in England and France 1750 to 1820*. New Haven, CT: Yale University Press, 1995.

Ribeiro, Aileen. *A Visual History of Costume: The Eighteenth Century*. 1983. Reprint. London: B. T. Batsford, 1986.

Swann, June. *Shoes*. New York: Drama Book Publishers, 1982.

Taylor, Lou. *Mourning Dress: A Costume and Social History*. London: George Allen and Unwin, 1983.

The Toilet of Flora; or, a Collection of the Most Simple and Approved Methods of Preparing Baths . . . . London: J. Murray, 1775.

Wilcox, Claire. *Bags*. London: V&A Publications, 1999.

Williams, Neville. *Powder and Paint: A History of the Englishwoman's Toilet*. London: Longmans, Green and Co., 1957.

EDUCATION AND INTELLECTUAL LIFE

A Compendious Geographical and Historical Grammar: Exhibiting a Brief Survey of the Terraqueous Globe. London: W. Peacock, 1795.

Andrews, Malcolm. *The Search for the Picturesque: Landscape Aesthetics and Tourism in Britain, 1760–1800*. Stanford, CA: Stanford University Press, 1989.

Barker, Hannah. *Newspapers, Politics and English Society 1695–1855*. Harlow, Essex: Pearson, 2000.

———. *Newspapers, Politics, and Public Opinion in Late Eighteenth-Century England*. Oxford: Clarendon Press, 1998.

Black, Jeremy. *The English Press in the Eighteenth Century*. London: Croom Helm, 1987.

Crone, G. R. *Maps and Their Makers*. 4th ed. London: Hutchinson University Library, 1968.

Gilpin, William. *Observations on the Coasts of Hampshire, Sussex, and Kent, Relative Chiefly to Picturesque Beauty: Made in the Summer of the Year 1774*. London: T. Cadell and W. Davies, 1804.

———. *Observations on the Western Parts of England*. Richmond, Surrey: Richmond Publishing Co., 1973.

———. *Observations, Relative Chiefly to Picturesque Beauty, Made in the Year 1776, on Several Parts of Great Britain; Particularly the High-Lands of Scotland*. London: R. Blamire, 1789.

Jordan, Elaine. "Jane Austen Goes to the Seaside: Sanditon, English Identity and the 'West Indian' Schoolgirl." *The Postcolonial Jane Austen*, edited by Youme Park and Rajeswari Sunder Rajan. London: Routledge, 2000.

Lister, Raymond. *How to Identify Old Maps and Globes*. Hamden, CT: Archon, 1965.

Mayhew, Robert J. *Enlightenment Geography*. New York: St. Martin's, 2000.

Price, Uvedale. *An Essay on the Picturesque, as Compared with the Sublime and the Beautiful; and, on the Use of Studying Pictures, for the Purpose of Improving Real Landscape*. London: J. Robson, 1796.

Thrower, Norman J. W. *Maps and Man*. Englewood Cliffs, NJ: Prentice-Hall, 1972.

Tooley, R. V. *Maps and Map-Makers*. 1949. Reprint. New York: Dorset Press, 1990.

ENTERTAINMENT

Altick, Richard D. *The Shows of London*. Cambridge, MA: Belknap, 1978.

Bayne-Powell, Rosamond. *The English Child in the Eighteenth Century*. New York: E. P. Dutton, 1939.

Beaufort, James. *Hoyle's Games Improved*. London: S. Bladon, 1775.

Beckford, Peter. *Thoughts on Hunting in a Series of Familiar Letters to a Friend*. London: Methuen & Co., 1951 8th ed. (1st ed. 1899; orig. pub. 1781).

Brander, Michael. *Hunting and Shooting from Earliest Times to the Present Day*. London: Weidenfeld and Nelson, 1971.

Brinsmead, Edgar. *The History of the Pianoforte*. 1879. Reprint. Detroit: Singing Tree Press, 1969.

Byrde, Penelope. *Jane Austen Fashion: Fashion and Needlework in the Works of Jane Austen*. Ludlow: Excellent Press, 1999.

Byrne, Paula. *Jane Austen and the Theatre*. London: Hambledon and London, 2002.

Castle, Terry. *Masquerade and Civilization: The Carnivalesque in Eighteenth-Century English Culture and Fiction*. Stanford, CA: Stanford University Press, 1986.

Chalmers, Patrick. *The History of Hunting*. Philadelphia: J. B. Lippincott, 1936.

Colley, Linda. *Britons: Forging the Nation 1707–1837*. New Haven, CT: Yale University Press, 1992.

Dawson, Lawrence H., ed. *The Complete Hoyle's Games*. 1950. Reprint. Ware, Hertfordshire: Wordsworth, 1994.

Female Tuition; or, an Address to Mothers, on the Education of Daughters. London: J. Murray, 1784.

Fiske, Roger. *English Theatre Music in the Eighteenth Century*. London: Oxford University Press, 1973.

Girdham, Jane. *English Opera in Late Eighteenth-Century London: Stephen Storace at Drury Lane*. Oxford: Clarendon Press, 1997.

Harding, Rosamond E. M. *The Piano-Forte*. 2nd ed. Old Woking, Surrey: Gresham Books, 1978.

Hare, Arnold, ed. *Theatre Royal Bath: A Calendar of Performances at the Orchard Street Theatre 1750–1805*. Bath: Kingsmead Press, 1977.

Hembry, Phyllis. *The English Spa 1560–1815: A Social History*. London: Athlone Press, 1990.

Hoyle's Games: Containing the Rules for Playing Fashionable Games. Philadelphia: Henry F. Anners, 1859.

Hoyle's Games Improved: Being Practical Treatises on the Following Fashionable Games . . . London: W. Wood, 1782.

Keller, Kate Van Winkle, and Genevieve Shimer. *The Playford Ball: 103 Early Country Dances 1651–1820*. Chicago: A Cappella Books, 1990.

Langford, Paul. *A Polite and Commercial People: England 1727–1783*. 1989. Reprint. Oxford: Oxford University Press, 1992.

Le Beau Monde, September 1807, p. 94.

Longrigg, Roger. *The English Squire and His Sport*. London: Michael Joseph, 1977.

———. *The History of Horse Racing*. New York: Stein and Day, 1972.

Manning-Sanders, Ruth. *The English Circus*. London: Werner Laurie, 1952.

The Netting Book. Seabrook, NH: Tower Press, 1981.

Parlett, David. *The Oxford Guide to Card Games*. Oxford: Oxford University Press, 1990.

Piggott, Patrick. *The Innocent Diversion: A Study of Music in the Life and Writings of Jane Austen*. London: Douglas Cleverdon, 1979.

Playford, John. *The English Dancing Master*. 1651. Reprint. London: Dance Books, 1984.

Porter, Roy. *English Society in the Eighteenth Century*. 1982. Reprint. New York: Penguin Books, 1990.

Price, Curtis, Judith Milhous, and Robert D. Hume. *Italian Opera in Late Eighteenth-Century London, Vol I: The King's Theatre, Haymarket 1778–1791*. Oxford: Clarendon Press, 1995.

Rensch, Roslyn. *The Harp: Its History, Technique, and Repertoire*. New York: Praeger, 1969.

———. *Harps and Harpists*. London: Duckworth, 1989.

Richardson, Philip J. S. *The Social Dances of the Nineteenth Century in England*. London: Herbert Jenkins, 1960.

Selwyn, David. *Jane Austen and Leisure*. London: Hambledon Press, 1999.

Sharp, Cecil J. *The Country Dance Book, Part II*. 3rd ed. London: Novello and Company, 1927.

Sharp, Cecil J., and George Butterworth. *The Country Dance Book, Part III*. 2nd ed. London: Novello and Company, 1927.

————. *The Country Dance Book, Part IV.* 3rd ed. London: Novello and Company, 1927.

Sharp, Cecil J., and Maud Karpeles. *The Country Dance Book, Part V.* London: Novello and Company, 1918.

Taunton, Nerylla. *Antique Needlework Tools and Embroideries.* Woodbridge, Suffolk: Antique Collectors' Club, 1997.

Thompson, Allison, "The Felicities of Rapid Motion: Jane Austen in the Ballroom." *Persuasions Online* 21, no. 1.

Vamplew, Wray. *The Turf.* London: Allen Lane, 1976.

Walton, John K. *The English Seaside Resort: A Social History 1750–1914.* New York: St. Martin's, 1983.

Woodfield, Ian. *Opera and Drama in Eighteenth-Century London: The King's Theatre, Garrick and the Business of Performance.* Cambridge: Cambridge University Press, 2001.

Woodforde, James. *Passages from the Five Volumes of the Diary of a Country Parson 1758–1802,* selected and edited by John Beresford. New York: Oxford University Press, 1935.

FOOD AND DRINK

Accum, Frederick. *A Treatise on Adulterations of Food.* 1820. Reprint. N.p.: Mallinckrodt Collection of Food Classics, 1966.

Ashley, William. *The Bread of Our Forefathers: An Inquiry in Economic History.* Oxford: Clarendon Press, 1928.

Black, Maggie, and Deirdre Le Faye. *The Jane Austen Cookbook.* Chicago: Chicago Review Press, 1995.

Bradley, Richard. *The Country Housewife and Lady's Director in the Management of a House, and the Delights and Profits of a Farm.* London: 1736. Reprint. London: Prospect Books, 1980.

Briggs, Richard. *The English Art of Cookery.* Dublin: P. Byrne, 1798.

Burnett, John. *Plenty and Want: A Social History of Diet in England from 1815 to the Present Day.* Rev. ed. London: Scolar Press, 1979.

Carter, Susannah. *The Frugal Housewife, or Complete Woman Cook.* London: E. Newbery, 1795.

Charsley, Simon R. *Wedding Cakes and Cultural History.* London: Routledge, 1992.

Cheke, Val. *The Story of Cheese-Making in Britain.* London: Routledge & Kegan Paul, 1959.

Clark, Peter. *The English Alehouse: A Social History 1200–1830.* London: Longman, 1983.

Collingwood, Francis. *The Universal Cook, and City and Country Housekeeper.* 3rd ed. London: C. Whittingham, 1801.

Ellis, William. *The Country Housewife's Family Companion.* 1750. Reprint. Totnes, Devon: Prospect Books, 2000.

Farley, John. *The London Art of Cookery.* 1783. Reprint. Lewes, East Sussex: Southover Press, 1988.

The French Family Cook: Being a Complete System of French Cookery. London: J. Bell, 1793.

Glasse, Hannah. *The Art of Cookery Made Plain and Easy.* 1796 rev. ed. Reprint. Schenectady, NY: U.S. Historical Research Service, 1994.

Grossman, Anne Chotzinoff, and Lisa Grossman Thomas. *Lobscouse and Spotted Dog.* New York: W. W. Norton and Company, 1997.

Hackwood, Frederick W. *Inns, Ales, and Drinking Customs of Old England.* Reprint. London: Bracken Books, 1985.

Harrison, Sarah. *The House-keeper's Pocket-book; And Compleat Family Cook.* London: R. Ware, 1748.

Hartley, Dorothy. *Food in England.* 1954. Reprint. London: Little, Brown and Company, 1999.

Hunter, Alexander (using pseudonym Ignotus). *Culina Famulatrix Medicinae.* York: T. Wilson, 1805.

Lane, Maggie. *Jane Austen and Food.* London: Hambledon Press, 1995.

Latham, Jean. *A Taste of the Past.* London: Adam and Charles Black, 1975.

Mennell, Stephen. *All Manners of Food: Eating and Taste in England and France from the Middle Ages to the Present.* 1985. Reprint. Urbana: University of Illinois Press, 1996.

Millington, Charles. *The Housekeeper's Domestic Library; or, New Universal Family Instructor.* London: M. Jones, 1805.

Monckton, H. A. *A History of the English Public House.* London: Bodley Head, 1969.

Pendergrast, Mark. *Uncommon Grounds: The History of Coffee and How It Transformed the World.* New York: Basic Books, 1999.

Pettigrew, Jane. *A Social History of Tea.* London: National Trust, 2001.

Raffald, Elizabeth. *The Experienced English Housekeeper.* 1769. Reprint. Lewes, East Sussex: Southover Press, 1997.

Roberts, Jonathan. *The Origins of Fruit and Vegetables.* New York: Universe Publishing, 2001.

Rundell, Maria. *A New System of Domestic Cookery.* 1816. Reprint. New York: Vantage Press, 1977.

Simpson, Helen. *The London Ritz Book of Afternoon Tea: The Art and Pleasures of Taking Tea.* New York: Arbor House, 1986.

Wilson, C. Anne. *Food and Drink in Britain from the Stone Age to the 19th Century.* 1973. Reprint. London: Constable, 1991.

Woodforde, James. *Passages from the Five Volumes of the Diary of a Country Parson 1758–1802,* selected and edited by John Beresford. New York: Oxford University Press, 1935.

HISTORY AND THE STATE

Carpenter, S. C. *Church and People, 1789–1889: A History of the Church of England from William Wilberforce to "Lux Mundi."* 1933. Reprint. London: SPCK, 1937.

Cary, M., and H. H. Scullard. *A History of Rome Down to the Reign of Constantine.* 3rd ed. 1975. Reprint. New York: St. Martin's, 1979.

Clark, Peter. *The English Alehouse: A Social History 1200–1830.* London: Longman, 1983.

A Compendious Geographical and Historical Grammar: Exhibiting a Brief Survey of the Terraqueous Globe. London: W. Peacock, 1795.

Emsley, Clive. *Britain and the French Revolution.* Harlow, England: Longman, 2000.

Langford, Paul. *A Polite and Commercial People: England 1727–1783.* 1989. Reprint. Oxford: Oxford University Press, 1992.

Mattingly, Garrett. *Catherine of Aragon.* 1941. Reprint. New York: Quality Paperback Books, 1990.

Newman, Gerald, ed. *Britain in the Hanoverian Age 1714–1837.* New York: Garland, 1997.

Porter, Roy. *English Society in the Eighteenth Century.* 1982. Reprint. New York: Penguin Books, 1990.

Pringle, Patrick. *Hue and Cry: The Story of Henry and John Fielding and Their Bow Street Runners.* New York: William Morrow, 1955.

Reed, Michael. *The Age of Exuberance: 1550–1700.* London: Routledge & Kegan Paul, 1986.

Roberts, Warren. *Jane Austen and the French Revolution.* New York: St. Martin's Press, 1979.

Sales, Roger. *Jane Austen and Representations of Regency England.* London: Routledge, 1994.

Turner, E. S. *The Court of St. James's.* New York: Ballantine, 1959.

Woodcock, Thomas, and John Martin Robinson. *The Oxford Guide to Heraldry.* Oxford: Oxford University Press, 1988.

THE HOUSEHOLD

Adams, Samuel, and Sarah Adams. *The Complete Servant.* 1825. Reprint. Lewes, East Sussex, England: Southover Press, 1989.

Banfield, Edwin. *Antique Barometers: An Illustrated Survey.* Long Ashton, Bristol: Wayland Publications, 1977.

———. *The Italian Influence on English Barometers from 1780.* Trowbridge, Wiltshire: Baros Books, 1993.

Bell, Geoffrey Howard, and E. F. Bell. *Old English Barometers.* Winchester: Warren & Son, 1952.

Bruton, Eric. *Clocks and Watches 1400–1900.* London: Arthur Barker, 1967.

Buehr, Walter. *The Story of Locks.* New York: Charles Scribner's Sons, 1953.

Byrde, Penelope. *Jane Austen Fashion: Fashion and Needlework in the Works of Jane Austen.* Ludlow: Excellent Press, 1999.

Clark, Garth. *The Book of Cups.* New York: Abbeville Press, 1990.

Clark, Peter. *The English Alehouse: A Social History 1200–1830.* London: Longman, 1983.

Copeland, Robert. *Spode's Willow Pattern and Other Designs after the Chinese.* 3rd ed. Bath: Studio Vista, 1999.

Crone, G. R. *Maps and Their Makers.* 4th ed. London: Hutchinson University Library, 1968.

Crowley, John E. *The Invention of Comfort: Sensibilities and Design in Early Modern Britain and Early America.* Baltimore, MD: Johns Hopkins University Press, 2001.

Dawson, Aileen. *Masterpieces of Wedgwood in the British Museum.* London: British Museum Publications, 1984.

Eras, Vincent J. M. *Locks and Keys Throughout the Ages.* Amsterdam: H. H. Fronczek, 1957.

Girouard, Mark. *Life in the English Country House: A Social and Architectural History.* New Haven, CT: Yale University Press, 1978.

Goldberg, Benjamin. *The Mirror and Man.* Charlottesville: University Press of Virginia, 1985.

Goodison, Nicholas. *English Barometers 1680–1860.* London: Cassell, 1969.

Greysmith, Brenda. *Wallpaper.* London: Studio Vista, 1976.

Hadfield, Miles. *A History of British Gardening.* London: Spring Books, 1969. (Originally published as *Gardening in Britain*, 1960, Hutchinson & Co.)

Haywood, Eliza. *A New Present for a Servant-Maid.* London: G. Pearch, 1771.

Hecht, J. Jean. *The Domestic Servant in Eighteenth-Century England.* 1956. Reprint. London: Routledge & Kegan Paul, 1980.

Hembry, Phyllis. *The English Spa 1560–1815: A Social History.* London: Athlone Press, 1990.

Hill, Bridget. *Servants: English Domestics in the Eighteenth Century.* Oxford: Clarendon Press, 1996.

Hoskins, Lesley, ed. *The Papered Wall: History, Pattern, Technique.* New York: Harry N. Abrams, 1994.

Hunt, John Dixon. *Gardens and the Picturesque: Studies in the History of Landscape Architecture.* Cambridge, MA: MIT Press, 1992.

Hunt, John Dixon, and Peter Willis, eds. *The Genius of the Place: The English Landscape Garden 1620–1820.* New York: Harper and Row, 1975.

Kowaleski-Wallace, Elizabeth. *Consuming Subjects: Women, Shopping, and Business in the Eighteenth Century.* New York: Columbia University Press, 1997.

Latham, Jean. *A Taste of the Past.* London: Adam and Charles Black, 1975.

Lister, Raymond. *How to Identify Old Maps and Globes.* Hamden, CT: Archon, 1965.

Meikleham, Robert (using pseudonym Walter Bernan). *On the History and Art of Warming and Ventilating Rooms and Buildings.* London: George Bell, 1845.

Meister, Peter Wilhelm, and Horst Reber. *European Porcelain of the 18th Century*, translated by Ewald Osers. Ithaca, NY: Cornell University Press, 1983.

Musgrave, Clifford. *Regency Furniture 1800 to 1830.* 1961. Reprint. London: Faber and Faber, 1970.

Pettigrew, Jane. *A Social History of Tea.* London: National Trust, 2001.

Price, Percival. *Bells and Man.* Oxford: Oxford University Press, 1983.

Quest-Ritson, Charles. *The English Garden: A Social History.* London: Viking, 2001.

Roberts, Hugh D. *Downhearth to Bar Grate.* Bath: Dawson & Goodall, 1981.

Swift, Jonathan. *Directions to Servants.* 1745. Reprint. New York: Pantheon, 1964.

Taunton, Nerylla. *Antique Needlework Tools and Embroideries.* Woodbridge, Suffolk: Antique Collectors' Club, 1997.

Thoday, A. G. *Barometers.* London: Her Majesty's Stationery Office, 1978.

Thrower, Norman J. W. *Maps and Man.* Englewood Cliffs, NJ: Prentice-Hall, 1972.

Tooley, R. V. *Maps and Map-Makers.* 1949. Reprint. New York: Dorset Press, 1990.

Watkin, David. *The English Vision: The Picturesque in Architecture, Landscape and Garden Design*. London: John Murray, 1982.

Wilkinson, Vega. *Spode-Copeland-Spode: The Works and Its People 1770–1970*. Woodbridge, Suffolk: Antique Collectors' Club, 2002.

Woodforde, James. *Passages from the Five Volumes of the Diary of a Country Parson 1758–1802*, selected and edited by John Beresford. New York: Oxford University Press, 1935.

Wright, Lawrence. *Home Fires Burning: The History of Domestic Heating and Cooking*. London: Routledge and Kegan Paul, 1964.

Young, Hilary, ed. *The Genius of Wedgwood*. London: Victoria and Albert Museum, 1995.

Younghusband, Ethel. *Mansions, Men and Tunbridge Ware*. Slough: Windsor Press, 1949.

JANE AUSTEN

Austen-Leigh, William, and Richard Arthur Austen-Leigh. *Jane Austen: Her Life and Letters*. New York: Russell and Russell, 1965.

Cecil, David. *A Portrait of Jane Austen*. London: Constable, 1978.

Halperin, John. *The Life of Jane Austen*. Baltimore, MD: Johns Hopkins University Press, 1984.

Hodge, Jane Aiken. *The Double Life of Jane Austen*. London: Hodder and Stoughton, 1972.

Le Faye, Deirdre, ed. *Jane Austen's Letters*. 3rd ed. Oxford: Oxford University Press, 1995.

MILITARY LIFE

Baynham, Henry. *From the Lower Deck: The Old Navy 1780–1840*. London: Hutchinson and Co., 1969.

Blake, Nicholas, and Richard Lawrence. *The Illustrated Companion to Nelson's Navy*. Mechanicsburg, PA: Stackpole Books, 2000.

Chandler, David, ed. *The Oxford Illustrated History of the British Army*. Oxford: Oxford University Press, 1994.

Cochrane, Thomas, Earl of Dundonald. *The Autobiography of a Seaman*. 2nd ed. London: Richard Bentley, 1861.

Duffy, Michael. *Soldiers, Sugar, and Seapower: The British Expeditions to the West Indies and the War against Revolutionary France*. Oxford: Clarendon Press, 1987.

Haythornthwaite, Philip, and Charles Hamilton Smith. *Wellington's Army: The Uniforms of the British Soldier, 1812–1815*. London: Greenhill Books, 2002.

Haythornthwaite, Philip, and William Younghusband. *Nelson's Navy*. London: Osprey, 1993.

Holmes, Richard. *Redcoat: The British Soldier in the Age of Horse and Musket*. New York: W.W. Norton & Company, 2001.

Houlding, J. A. *Fit for Service: The Training of the British Army, 1715–1795*. 1981. Reprint. Oxford: Clarendon Press, 2000.

Hubback, J.H., and Edith C. Hubback. *Jane Austen's Sailor Brothers*. 1906. Reprint. Westport, CT: Meckler Publishing, 1986.

Kemp, Peter, ed. *The Oxford Companion to Ships and the Sea*. 1976. Reprint. Oxford: Oxford University Press, 1994.

Lavery, Brian. *Nelson's Navy: The Ships, Men and Organisation 1793–1815*. London: Conway Maritime Press, 1989.

McGuane, James P. *Heart of Oak: A Sailor's Life in Nelson's Navy*. New York: W.W. Norton & Company, 2002.

Roberts, Warren. *Jane Austen and the French Revolution*. New York: St. Martin's Press, 1979.

Rogers, H.C.B. *The British Army of the Eighteenth Century*. London: George Allen and Unwin, 1977.

Southam, Brian. *Jane Austen and the Navy*. London: Hambledon and London, 2000.

Tuchman, Barbara. *The First Salute: A View of the American Revolution*. New York: Alfred A. Knopf, 1988.

PEOPLE

Bayne-Powell, Rosamond. *The English Child in the Eighteenth Century*. New York: E.P. Dutton, 1939.

Bernier, François. *Travels in the Mogul Empire A.D. 1656–1668*, translated by Irving Brock and Archibald Constable. Delhi: S. Chand & Co., 1968.

Charsley, Simon R. *Wedding Cakes and Cultural History*. London: Routledge, 1992.

Endelman, Todd M. *The Jews of Britain, 1656 to 2000*. Berkeley: University of California Press, 2002.

———. *The Jews of Georgian England 1714–1830: Tradition and Change in a Liberal Society*. Philadelphia: Jewish Publication Society of America, 1979.

Eraly, Abraham. *The Mughal Throne: The Saga of India's Great Emperors*. London: Weidenfeld & Nicolson, 2003.

Gisborne, Thomas. *An Enquiry into the Duties of the Female Sex*. 7th ed. London: Cadell, 1806.

Gregory, John. *A Father's Legacy to His Daughters*. 1773. Reprint. Boston: Joseph Bumstead, 1804.

Johnson, Samuel. *The Letters of Samuel Johnson,* edited by Bruce Redford. Princeton, NJ: Princeton University Press, 1992.

Kittredge, George Lyman. *Witchcraft in Old and New England*. 1929. Reprint. New York: Russell & Russell, 1956.

Notestein, Wallace. *A History of Witchcraft in England from 1558 to 1718*. 1911. Reprint. New York: Russell & Russell, 1965.

Olsen, Kirstin. *Chronology of Women's History*. Westport, CT: Greenwood Press, 1994.

Opie, Iona, and Peter Opie. *The Oxford Dictionary of Nursery Rhymes*. 1951. Reprint. Oxford: Oxford University Press, 1995.

Sales, Roger. *Jane Austen and Representations of Regency England*. London: Routledge, 1994.

Sidky, H. *Witchcraft, Lycanthropy, Drugs, and Disease: An Anthropological Study of the European Witch-Hunts*. New York: Peter Lang, 1997.

Srivastava, Ashirbadi Lal. *The Mughal Empire (1526–1803 A.D.).* 3rd rev. ed. Agra: Shiva Lal Agarwala & Co., 1959.

Stone, Lawrence. *Road to Divorce.* 1990. Reprint. Oxford: Oxford University Press, 1995.

Taylor, Lou. *Mourning Dress: A Costume and Social History.* London: George Allen and Unwin, 1983.

Vesey-Fitzgerald, Brian. *Gypsies of Britain: An Introduction to Their History.* 1944. Reprint. Newton Abbot, Devon: David & Charles, 1973.

Woodcock, Thomas, and John Martin Robinson. *The Oxford Guide to Heraldry.* Oxford: Oxford University Press, 1988.

PLANTS AND ANIMALS

Plumb, J. H. *England in the Eighteenth Century.* 1950. Reprint. London: Penguin Books, 1990.

Porter, Roy. *English Society in the Eighteenth Century.* 1982. Reprint. New York: Penguin Books, 1990.

READING AND WRITING

Barker, Hannah. *Newspapers, Politics and English Society 1695–1855.* Harlow, Essex: Pearson, 2000.

———. *Newspapers, Politics, and Public Opinion in Late Eighteenth-Century England.* Oxford: Clarendon Press, 1998.

Black, Jeremy. *The English Press in the Eighteenth Century.* London: Croom Helm, 1987.

Browne, Christopher. *Getting the Message: The Story of the British Post Office.* Stroud, Gloucestershire: Alan Sutton, 1993.

Crocker, Alan. *Paper Mills of the Tillingbourne: A History of Papermaking in a Surrey Valley 1704 to 1875.* Oxshott, Surrey: Tabard Private Press, 1988.

Ellis, Kenneth. *The Post Office in the Eighteenth Century: A Study in Administrative History.* London: Oxford University Press, 1958.

Hemmeon, J. C. *The History of the British Post Office.* Cambridge: Harvard University Press, 1912.

James, Alan. *The Post.* London: B. T. Batsford, 1970.

Joyce, Herbert. *The History of the Post Office from Its Establishment down to 1836.* London: Richard Bentley & Son, 1893.

Kelly, Thomas. *Early Public Libraries.* London: Library Association, 1966.

Lewis, Matthew. *The Monk.* 1796. Reprint. Oxford: Oxford University Press, 1998.

Nickell, Joe. *Pen, Ink, & Evidence.* Lexington: University Press of Kentucky, 1990.

Radcliffe, Ann. *The Mysteries of Udolpho.* 1794. Reprint. Oxford: Oxford University Press, 1983.

Shorter, A. H. *Paper Making in the British Isles.* Newton Abbot, Devon: David & Charles, 1971.

Tomkins, Thomas. *The Beauties of Writing Exemplified.* London: Published for the Author, Foster Lane, 1808.

Whalley, Joyce Irene. *English Handwriting 1540–1853*. London: Her Majesty's Stationery Office, 1969.

———. *Writing Implements and Accessories*. Newton Abbot, Devon: David & Charles, 1975.

RELIGION

Albers, Jan. " 'Papist Traitors' and 'Presbyterian Rogues': Religious Identities in Eighteenth-Century Lancashire." *The Church of England, c. 1689–c. 1833*, edited by John Walson. Colin Haydon, and Stephen Taylor. Cambridge: Cambridge University Press, 1993.

Barrie-Curien, Viviane. "The Clergy in the Diocese of London in the Eighteenth Century." *The Church of England, c. 1689–c. 1833*, edited by John Walsh, Colin Haydon, and Stephen Taylor. Cambridge: Cambridge University Press, 1993.

Burns, R. Arthur. "Diocesan Reform in the Church of England." *The Church of England, c. 1689–c. 1833*, edited by John Walsh, Colin Haydon, and Stephen Taylor. Cambridge: Cambridge University Press, 1993.

Carpenter, S.C. *Church and People, 1789–1889: A History of the Church of England from William Wilberforce to "Lux Mundi."* London: Society for Promoting Christian Knowledge, 1933. Reprint. London: SPCK, 1937.

Collins, Irene. *Jane Austen and the Clergy*. London: Hambledon Press, 1993.

Ditchfield, G.M. "Ecclesiastical Policy under Lord North." *The Church of England, c. 1689–c. 1833*, edited by John Walsh, Colin Haydon, and Stephen Taylor. Cambridge: Cambridge University Press, 1993.

Elbourne, Elizabeth. "The Foundation of the Church Missionary Society: the Anglican Missionary Impulse." *The Church of England, c. 1689–c. 1833*, edited by John Walsh, Colin Haydon, and Stephen Taylor. Cambridge: Cambridge University Press, 1993.

Fitzpatrick, Martin. "Latitudinarianism at the Parting of the Ways: A Suggestion." *The Church of England c. 1689–c. 1833*, edited by John Walsh, Colin Haydon, and Stephen Taylor. Cambridge: Cambridge University Press, 1993.

Gibson, William. *The Church of England 1688–1832: Unity and Accord*. London: Routledge, 2001.

Gregory, Jeremy. "The Eighteenth-Century Reformation: The Pastoral Task of Anglican Clergy after 1689." *The Church of England, c. 1689–c. 1833*, edited by John Walsh, Colin Haydon, and Stephen Taylor. Cambridge: Cambridge University Press, 1993.

Gregory, John. *A Father's Legacy to His Daughters*. 1773. Reprint. Boston: Joseph Bumstead, 1804.

Nockles, Peter. "Church Parties in the Pre-Tractarian Church of England 1750–1833: The 'Orthodox'—Some Problems of Definition and Identity." *The Church of England, c. 1689–c. 1833*, edited by John Walsh, Colin Haydon, and Stephen Taylor. Cambridge: Cambridge University Press, 1993.

Price, Percival. *Bells and Man*. Oxford: Oxford University Press, 1983.

Reed, Michael. *The Age of Exuberance: 1550–1700*. London: Routledge & Kegan Paul, 1986.

Smith, Mark. "The Reception of Richard Podmore: Anglicanism in Saddleworth 1700–1830." *The Church of England, c. 1689–c. 1833*, edited by John Walsh, Colin Haydon, and Stephen Taylor. Cambridge: Cambridge University Press, 1993.

Virgin, Peter. *The Church in an Age of Negligence: Ecclesiastical Structure and Problems of Church Reform 1700–1840*. Cambridge: James Clarke & Co., 1989.

Vonier, Anscar. *The Angels*. New York: Macmillan, 1928.

Walsh, John, and Stephen Taylor. "The Church and Anglicanism in the 'Long' 18th Century." *The Church of England, c. 1689–c. 1833*, edited by John Walsh, Colin Haydon, and Stephen Taylor. Cambridge: Cambridge University Press, 1993.

Woodforde, James. *Passages from the Five Volumes of the Diary of a Country Parson 1758–1802*, selected and edited by John Beresford. New York: Oxford University Press, 1935.

RIDING AND HUNTING

Beckford, Peter. *Thoughts on Hunting in a Series of Familiar Letters to a Friend.* 8th ed. (1st ed. 1899; orig. pub. 1781). London: Methuen & Co., 1951.

Brander, Michael. *Hunting and Shooting from Earliest Times to the Present Day.* London: Weidenfeld and Nelson, 1971.

Chalmers, Patrick. *The History of Hunting*. Philadelphia: J. B. Lippincott, 1936.

Landry, Donna. "Learning to Ride at Mansfield Park." *The Postcolonial Jane Austen*, edited by You-me Park and Rajeswari Sunder Rajan. London: Routledge, 2000.

Longrigg, Roger. *The English Squire and His Sport.* London: Michael Joseph, 1977.

———. *The History of Horse Racing.* New York: Stein and Day, 1972.

Vamplew, Wray. *The Turf.* London: Allen Lane, 1976.

Woodforde, James. *Passages from the Five Volumes of the Diary of a Country Parson 1758–1802*, selected and edited by John Beresford. New York: Oxford University Press, 1935.

SCIENCE, MEDICINE, AND TECHNOLOGY

Accum, Frederick. *A Treatise on Adulterations of Food.* 1820. Reprint. N.p.: Mallinckrodt Collection of Food Classics, 1966.

Bader, Ted. "Mr. Woodhouse Is Not a Hypochondriac." *Persuasions Online* 21, no. 2 (Summer 2000). http://www.jasna.org/po103/bader.html.

Banfield, Edwin. *Antique Barometers: An Illustrated Survey.* Long Ashton, Bristol: Wayland Publications, 1977.

———. *The Italian Influence on English Barometers from 1780.* Trowbridge, Wiltshire: Baros Books, 1993.

Bell, Geoffrey Howard, and E. F. Bell. *Old English Barometers.* Winchester: Warren & Son, 1952.

Brock, William H. *The Norton History of Chemistry.* New York: W. W. Norton, 1993.

Corson, Richard. *Fashions in Eyeglasses.* London: Peter Owen, 1980.

Davidson, D. C., and R.J.S. MacGregor. *Spectacles, Lorgnettes and Monocles.* Princes Risborough, England: Shire, 2002.

Duffy, Michael. *Soldiers, Sugar, and Seapower: The British Expeditions to the West Indies and the War Against Revolutionary France.* Oxford: Clarendon Press, 1987.

Goodison, Nicholas. *English Barometers 1680–1860.* London: Cassell, 1969.

Guerini, Vincenzo. *A History of Dentistry from the Most Ancient Times until the End of the Eighteenth Century.* 1909. Reprint. Amsterdam: Liberac, 1967.

Langford, Paul. *A Polite and Commercial People: England 1727–1783.* 1989. Reprint. Oxford: Oxford University Press, 1992.

Lindsay, Lilian. *A Short History of Dentistry.* London: John Bale, Sons and Danielsson, 1933.

North, John. *The Norton History of Astronomy and Cosmology.* New York: W. W. Norton & Company, 1994.

Porter, Roy. *English Society in the Eighteenth Century.* 1982. Reprint. New York: Penguin Books, 1990.

Prinz, Hermann. *Dental Chronology.* Philadelphia: Lea & Febiger, 1945.

Ring, Malvin E. *Dentistry: An Illustrated History.* New York: Harry N. Abrams, 1986.

Thoday, A. G. *Barometers.* London: Her Majesty's Stationery Office, 1978.

Walton, John K. *The English Seaside Resort: A Social History 1750–1914.* New York: St. Martin's Press, 1983.

Williams, Guy. *The Age of Agony: The Art of Healing, 1700–1800.* 1975. Reprint. Chicago: Academy Chicago Publishers, 1996.

Wiltshire, John. *Jane Austen and the Body.* Cambridge: Cambridge University Press, 1992.

Wynbrandt, James. *The Excruciating History of Dentistry.* New York: St. Martin's Press, 1998.

TIME AND PLACE

Augier, F. R., and Shirley C. Gordon. *Sources of West Indian History.* 1962. Reprint. Trinidad: Longman Caribbean, 1970.

Barker, Felix, and Peter Jackson. *The History of London in Maps.* New York: Cross River Press, 1992.

Duffy, Michael. *Soldiers, Sugar, and Seapower: The British Expeditions to the West Indies and the War against Revolutionary France.* Oxford: Clarendon Press, 1987.

Egan, Patrick. *Walks through Bath.* Bath: Meyler and Son, 1818.

Edwards, Anne-Marie. *In the Steps of Jane Austen.* 2nd ed. Ashurst, Southampton: Arcady Books, 1985.

Fawcett, Trevor, comp. *Voices of Eighteenth-Century Bath.* Bath: Ruton, 1995.

Gerzina, Gretchen. *Black London: Life before Emancipation.* New Brunswick, NJ: Rutgers University Press, 1995.

Gomme, George Laurence, ed. *The Gentleman's Magazine Library—Vol. 1: Manners and Customs.* 1883. Reprint. Detroit: Singing Tree Press, 1968.

Halperin, John. *The Life of Jane Austen.* Baltimore, MD: Johns Hopkins University Press, 1984.

Hembry, Phyllis. *The English Spa 1560–1815: A Social History*. London: Athlone Press, 1990.

Hodge, Jane Aiken. *The Double Life of Jane Austen*. London: Hodder and Stoughton, 1972.

Hyde, Ralph. *The A to Z of Georgian London*. Lympne Castle, Kent: Harry Margary, 1981.

Jordan, Elaine. "Jane Austen Goes to the Seaside: Sanditon, English Identity and the 'West Indian' Schoolgirl." *The Postcolonial Jane Austen*, edited by Youme Park and Rajeswari Sunder Rajan. London: Routledge, 2000.

Lane, Maggie. *Jane Austen's England*. New York: St. Martin's Press, 1986.

Lasdun, Susan. *The English Park: Royal, Private and Public*. New York: Vendome, 1992.

Porter, Roy. *English Society in the Eighteenth Century*. 1982. Reprint. New York: Penguin Books, 1990.

———. *London: A Social History*. Cambridge, MA: Harvard University Press, 1995.

Rogozinski, Jan. *A Brief History of the Caribbean: From the Arawak and the Carib to the Present*. New York: Facts on File, 1992.

Sales, Roger. *Jane Austen and Representations of Regency England*. London: Routledge, 1994.

Selwyn, David. *Jane Austen and Leisure*. London: Hambledon Press, 1999.

Walton, John K. *The English Seaside Resort: A Social History 1750–1914*. New York: St. Martin's Press, 1983.

Watson, Jack. *The West Indian Heritage: A History of the West Indies*. 2nd ed. London: John Murray, 1982.

TRANSPORTATION AND TRAVEL

Adams, Samuel, and Sarah Adams. *The Complete Servant*. 1825. Reprint. Lewes, East Sussex, England: Southover Press, 1989.

Aldcroft, Derek H., and Michael J. Freeman. *Transport in the Industrial Revolution*. Manchester: Manchester University Press, 1983.

Andrews, Malcolm. *The Search for the Picturesque: Landscape Aesthetics and Tourism in Britain, 1760–1800*. Stanford, CA: Stanford University Press, 1989.

Bayne-Powell, Rosamond. *Travellers in Eighteenth-Century England*. London: John Murray, 1951.

Borer, Mary Cathcart. *The British Hotel through the Ages*. Guildford: Lutterworth Press, 1972.

Brown, R. A. *One Hundred Horse Drawn Carriages*. Welwyn Garden City, Hertfordshire: Quartilles International Limited, 1973.

A Compendious Geographical and Historical Grammar: Exhibiting a Brief Survey of the Terraqueous Globe. London: W. Peacock, 1795.

De Quincey, Thomas. *Joan of Arc and the English Mail-Coach*. Boston: D. C. Heath & Co., 1907

Felton, William. *Treatise on Carriages*. London, 1796.

Gilpin, William. *Observations on the Coasts of Hampshire, Sussex, and Kent, Relative Chiefly to Picturesque Beauty: Made in the Summer of the Year 1774*. London: T. Cadell and W. Davies, 1804.

————. *Observations on the Western Parts of England.* Richmond, Surrey: Richmond Publishing Co., 1973.

————. *Observations, Relative Chiefly to Picturesque Beauty, Made in the Year 1776, on Several Parts of Great Britain; Particularly the High-Lands of Scotland.* London: R. Blamire, 1789.

Hecht, J. Jean. *The Domestic Servant in Eighteenth-Century England.* 1956. Reprint. London: Routledge & Kegan Paul, 1980.

Ingram, Arthur. *Horse-Drawn Vehicles Since 1760.* Poole: Blandford Press, 1977.

Reid, James. *The Evolution of Horse-Drawn Vehicles.* N.p.: Institute of British Carriage and Automobile Manufacturers, 1933.

Richardson, A. E., and H. Donaldson Eberlein. *The English Inn, Past and Present: A Review of Its History and Social Life.* London: B. T. Batsford, 1925.

Rowlandson, Thomas. *Rowlandson's Drawings for a Tour in a Post Chaise.* San Marino, CA: The Huntington Library, 1963.

Straus, Ralph. *Carriages & Coaches: Their History & Their Evolution.* London: Martin Secker, 1912.

Sumner, Philip. *Carriages to the End of the Nineteenth Century.* London: Her Majesty's Stationery Office, 1970.

Swift, Jonathan. *Directions to Servants.* 1745. Reprint. New York: Pantheon, 1964.

Thompson, John. *Horse-Drawn Carriages: A Source Book.* Fleet, Hampshire: John Thompson, 1980.

Thrupp, G. A. *The History of Coaches.* 1877. Reprint. Amsterdam: Meridian, 1969.

Vale, Edmund. *The Mail-Coach Men of the Late Eighteenth Century.* 1960. Reprint. Newton Abbot, Devon: David & Charles, 1967.

Walrond, Sallie. *Looking at Carriages.* 1980. Reprint. London: J. A. Allen, 1992.

Walton, John K. *The English Seaside Resort: A Social History 1750–1914.* New York: St. Martin's Press, 1983.

Woodforde, James. *Passages from the Five Volumes of the Diary of a Country Parson 1758–1802,* selected and edited by John Beresford. New York: Oxford University Press, 1935.

WEB SITES

These were helpful in my research and contain reliable enough information to be of use to other researchers. Listing them here does not mean that I endorse any specific product or for-profit service supplied by the hosting company or organization, nor have I received financial consideration for their inclusion.

www.botanical.com and *www.habitas.org.uk*
   Useful information about English flora and ingredients in food and medicines of the period.

http://lwlimages.library.yale.edu/walpoleweb/
   Search page for images at the Lewis Walpole Library. To search by year, enter the last three digits of the year under "Call Number Query." Items without day

or month information will be indicated by a zero and an item number, for example 799.0.14. If month and day of publication are known, these will be indicated in American rather than European order; for example, 799.3.12 would indicate a print issued on March 12, 1799.

Keyword searches return results only if the keyword is in the title of the print. This can cause difficulties, since the titles are not necessarily obvious. For example, enter "Symptoms" in this box to see how a particular format was applied to a variety of topics.

Images can be enlarged on this Web site and examined closely. They can also be seen in color and printed out. Highly recommended. Many of the illustrations in this book can be seen there in color and in greater detail.

http://users.sisna.com/justinb/rni.html
Excellent charts of the differences between naval uniforms by rank and period; depictions of admirals' flags.

www.gamesacrosstheboard.com
Game rules.

http://freepages.genealogy.rootsweb.com/~genmaps/index.html
Photographs and scans of old maps of the British Isles by country, by county, and sometimes by city. The quality of the images varies according to the methods used to create them, and each search generates pop-up advertisements, but the maps can be very helpful in getting a feel for distances, roads, and physical features.

www.geog.port.ac.uk/webmap/hantsmap/hantsmap/milne1/milne1.htm
Excellent high-resolution clickable map of Hampshire in 1791, clearly showing the towns Austen visited and resided in.

www.davidparlett.co.uk/histocs/
Rules for several historical card games.

www.pemberley.com
Good information about details from Austen's novels with extensive and reliable footnotes.

www.printsgeorge.com
A delightfully tongue-in-cheek Web site full of reproductions of maps and prints that can be ordered for reasonable prices. A CD-ROM with maps of and facsimiles of contemporary books about Jane Austen's Bath.

http://users.bathspa.ac.uk/greenwood/imagemap.html
Excellent clickable high-resolution map of London in 1827.

www.motco.com/Map/
Excellent high-resolution clickable maps of London and the London area, including maps from 1799, 1802, and 1830.

www.jasna.org
   Home page of the Jane Austen Society of North America, with a good deal of information, links to the organization's online journal, and links to other information on the Web about Jane Austen.

www.victorianweb.org/previctorian/letters/free.html and
www.home.gil.com.au/~ears/free.html
   Sites showing franked letters.

Index

Page references in **bold** type indicate main entries in the encyclopedia; pages in *italics* refer to illustrations.

Hedgerows, 5, 319
Heir at Law, The, 667
Henry, Robert, *History of England*, 579
Henry and Emma, 584
Hepplewhite, George, 301
Heraldry, **351–352**
Hereford, *535*, 546, 553
Hertfordshire, *535*, 546
High Life Below Stairs, 667, 672
Highwaymen, 133, 189, 192, 448, 508, 684–685
History, 579
Hobbies, **352–353**
Hobbyhorse, **353–354**
Holidays, **354–356**
Holyhead, 534, *535*
Honiton, *535*, 537, 553
Hornbooks, 228
Horrid Mysteries, 589
Horse Guards, 31. *See also* Army
Horse racing, 310, *361*, 361–363, 508, 739, 740, 743; and prince regent, 743
Horses, 128, 241–243, **356–363**; breeds of, 356–357; care of, 11, 30, 38, 46, 359–360; and carriages, 53, 118–120, 124–125, 128, 136, 137, 358–359; color of, 45–46, 359n; dealers in, 65; for hunting, 360, 375; taxes on, 359
Hosiers, 65, 66
Hotels, 67, 384
Hounslow, *547*, 549, 553
Housekeepers, 21, 65, 617, 620, 625, 626; relatives as, 623. *See also* Servants
Housework, 14, 229, **363–368**
Hume, David, *History of England*, 579
Hunter, John, 180, 660–661, 738
Hunter, William, 180
Hunting, 360, **368–377**, 549, 740; dogs for, 373–375; guns for, 372–373; qualifications for, 370; season for, 369–370; servants involved in, 371, 619, 625; tactics,

373, 375–377; timing of, 368–369, *369*; types of, 375–377
Huntingdon, *535*, 546
Hussars, 30
Huswifes, 630
Hymen, **377–378**
Hypocrite, The, 670

Ibthorpe, 540, *540*, 553, 748
Ice cream, 65, 258, 287; dishes for, 216
Ice houses, 286
Idler, The, 581
Illegitimacy, **381**
Inchbald, Elizabeth, 668, 669, 748
Income, **382–383**. *See also* Wages
India, 427, 599; military presence in, 36, 37; Mughal emperors of, 339–340
Inheritance, 212; and illegitimacy, 381; of jewelry, 395
Ink, 725–726
Inns, 7, 11, 35, 39, 41, 383–386, *386*; balls at, 196, 385; clubs at, 177; as post offices, 385, 561, 562; and transportation, 123, 137, 385; and wagon passengers, *132*, 133, 385; White Hart, 66, 384
Insanity, **386–388**, 738
Introductions, 246
Investments, 383, 450
Ireland, 750; sites in, mentioned by Austen, *530*, 532, 534, *535*
Irish car, 334
Isle of Wight, *540*, 541
Italian, 235, **388–389**, 515
Italian, The, 589
Italian chair, 134
Italy, sites in, mentioned by Austen, *530*, 532

Jacobins, 8, 295, 744, 748
Jaconet, 174
Jane Shore, 587, 667, 671
Japanning, 301, 353
Jellies, 77, 258, 273, 283, 286–287
Jenner, Edward, 437

About the Author

KIRSTIN OLSEN is an independent scholar and the author of several Greenwood reference works, including *All Things Shakespeare: An Encyclopedia of Shakespeare's World* (2002).